# RUSSIAN COLONIAL SOCIETY
# IN TASHKENT, 1865–1923

# RUSSIAN COLONIAL SOCIETY IN TASHKENT, 1865–1923

Jeff Sahadeo

INDIANA UNIVERSITY PRESS

*Bloomington & Indianapolis*

This book is a publication of

Indiana University Press
601 North Morton Street
Bloomington, Indiana 47404-3797 USA

www.iupress.indiana.edu

*Telephone orders* 800-842-6796
*Fax orders* 812-855-7931
*Orders by e-mail* iuporder@indiana.edu

First paperback edition 2010
© 2007 by Jeff Sahadeo
All rights reserved

♾ The paper used in this publication meets the minimum requirements of
the American National Standard for Information Sciences—Permanence
of Paper for Printed Library Materials, ANSI Z39.48-1992.

Manufactured in the United States of America

The Library of Congress cataloged the original edition as follows:

Sahadeo, Jeff, [date]
Russian colonial society in Tashkent : 1865–1923 / Jeff Sahadeo.
p.    cm.
Includes bibliographical references and index.
ISBN 978-0-253-34820-3 (cloth : alk. paper)
1. Tashkent (Uzbekistan)—History—19th century. 2. Tashkent (Uzbekistan)—
History—20th century. 3. Uzbekistan—Foreign relations—Russia. 4. Russia—Foreign
relations—Uzbekistan. 5. Imperialism. 6. Russia—Territorial expansion. I. Title.
DK949.35.S34 2007
958.7—dc2                                2006016494

ISBN 978-0-253-22279-4 (pbk.)

2   3   4   5   6      15   14   13   12   11   10

To my family,
past and present

# CONTENTS

# Acknowledgments

I owe debts of gratitude to many people and organizations that assisted me in this project's realization. Musallam Juraev and Ergash Umarov offered invaluable aid to navigate Tashkent's libraries and archives. I encountered friendliness and willingness to help at all these institutions, and particularly want to thank Erkin Abdullaev, Marhamat Sagatovna Turahojaeva, and Sharafat Fazylovna Muminjanova. I will always remember the offers of melon at the rare book room of the Alisher Navoi state library and tea at the Uzbek Central State Archive as I pored over my documents.

I benefited from an exceptional group of colleagues that included Antoinette Burton, Keith Hitchins, Adeeb Khalid, and Mark Steinberg. Above all, Diane Koenker has been a wonderful mentor, colleague, and friend. Her unfaltering enthusiasm for the project was an inspiration. The University of Illinois at Urbana-Champaign's Slavic Library, in particular reference librarians Terri Miller and Helen Sullivan, provided invaluable assistance. Dave Bielanski, Brent Maner, Michelle Moran, Andrew Nolan, Lynda Park, Joe Perry, David Prochaska, Mary Stuart, Tom Trice, and Christine Varga-Harris offered valuable comments. Heather Coleman has unfailingly provided sound advice and support. Others who have read portions of the manuscript and have given insightful commentary include Nick Breyfogle, Kathleen Brosnan, Peter Gatrell, Doug Northrop, Adele Perry, Abby Schrader, Ted Weeks, and Paul Werth. Janet Rabinowitch shepherded this project to publication, and I thank her for continued support. The anonymous reviewers for the manuscript, as well as for related journal articles, also have improved the quality of this work, and Carol Kennedy gave the manuscript a careful copyedit.

A grant from the Social Sciences and Humanities Research Council of Canada provided the main source of funding for this project. I also received financial support from the University of Illinois, the University of Tennessee, and Carleton University. I thank the History Department of the University of Tennessee, in particular John Bohstedt, for launching my academic career. Al Scott at Graphic Services at Carleton University prepared the maps for this volume. I also want to thank *Slavic Review, Canadian Slavonic Papers,* and the *Canadian Review of Studies in Nationalism* for allowing me to print material previously published in these journals.

Throughout the research and writing process, I have enjoyed the friendship and support of many wonderful individuals. Richard K. Debo's classes in Russian history at Simon Fraser University inspired me, as an undergraduate, to follow my chosen career path. Susan Brazier, Joan Debardeleben, Kerry Franchuk, Craig Smillie, John W. Strong, and others offered a wonderful environment to pursue my interests during graduate work at Carleton University. We had a wonderful circle of friends in Urbana. Russell Zanca connected me to Uzbek scholars in Tashkent. Kurt Piehler and Michael Kulikowski supported my work on the book at Tennessee, and Piotr Dutkiewicz did the same at Carleton University. I owe special thanks to those who befriended a wayward Canadian in Tashkent, including Nargiza Abraeva, Roxana Bonnell, Michael Thurman, and Jennifer Utrata. Donna Leftwich provided me a wonderful home base as I traveled between the United States and Uzbekistan.

Most importantly, my family has provided immense support. My parents, Brahm and Judie Sahadeo, have inspired me with their accomplishments and their love. My biggest regret surrounding this project is that my sister, Elizabeth, passed away before it finished. Bohumil, Vesna, and Karin Alince have given me a wonderful second family. Petra Alince has been my single greatest source of support over the years that I have worked on this book. She has helped me to keep my balance, and has always reminded me that academic and professional accomplishments come behind the people we love. Our children, Caroline and Andrew, provide the greatest example of this, and are a constant source of wonder and joy.

# Note on Transliteration

Just as this work involves the encounter between two cultures, it involves the encounter between two languages. I have wrestled with issues of transliteration for some time. I employed the standard Library of Congress system to render Russian terms, preserving the differences between Imperial and Soviet orthographies. Local Uzbek terminology created more difficulties. In the end I sought to balance my audience's likely familiarity with the Russian transliteration of Central Asian terms (and their more frequent appearance in Russian official documents) with a desire to recognize that these transliterations often vary from those of the local language. For words transliterated directly from Uzbek, I again sought to favor readability, especially given the lack of a standard transliteration system for the modern language, much less for its variety of forms in the early twentieth century. I realize that issues of transliteration often evoke heated disputes, but I hope that my decisions do not detract from the content of the text.

# RUSSIAN COLONIAL SOCIETY
# IN TASHKENT, 1865–1923

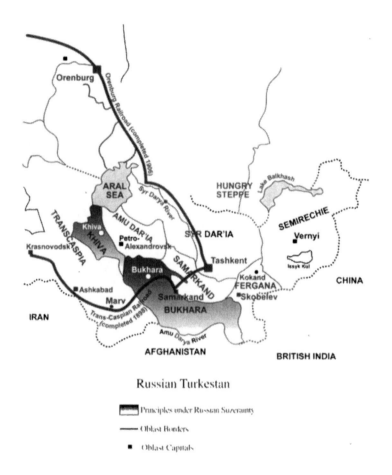

Russian Turkestan

◻ Principles under Russian Suzerainty
— Oblast Borders
■ Oblast Capitals

Figure 1. Map of Russian Turkestan.
Graphic Services, Carleton University.

# Introduction

"If I die as governor-general," read the words of K. P. fon Kaufman on a monument erected to his memory in the center of Russian Tashkent in 1910, "please bury me here, so that all may know that here is true Russian soil, where no Russian need be ashamed to lie." To create Russian soil from a desert oasis, Governor-General Kaufman had directed the transformation of a ragged military encampment on the edge of the Central Asian city of Tashkent into a European-style urban settlement, the capital of the new tsarist province of Turkestan. Administrators and settlers came by the thousands to populate this new "Russian section" after the conquest of Tashkent in 1865. Two thousand kilometers from European Russia, amid a predominantly Muslim population, and confronted with arid surroundings, these newcomers fashioned an unusual piece of Russian soil. They constructed a new urban space that reflected the influence of their environment and their position as colonizers over the inhabitants of Central Asia. Relations with the local population, successive waves of settlers, economic transformation, world war, revolution, and civil war all affected and altered the society and culture of the colonial city from 1865 to 1923, when Bolshevik commissars asserted tight control over the region.

Kaufman and leading tsarist administrators planned Russian Tashkent as a symbol of Russia's status as a powerful and advanced Western empire. The capital, it was hoped, would impress Central Asians[1] as well as observers from Europe and central Russia. Officials graduating from institutes of higher education envisioned the city as a centerpiece for their own civilizing and modernizing missions in Asia. These missions did not prevent imperial elites—top bureaucrats, officers, and merchants before 1917, and Russian workers and soldiers afterward—from turning the imbalances of colonial rule to their own benefit. Their efforts to exercise dominance as well as spread progress confronted the complexities of colonial society. Residents of postconquest Tashkent continually negotiated and challenged multiple axes of power. Central Asian notables, merchants, and labor, whose skills proved vital to the functioning of the imperial city, contested their subordinate status through a balance of accommodation and defiance. Poor Slavic settlers sought access to the fruits of colonial power, even as their presence and behavior challenged elite visions of a clear separation between modern Western colonists and backward Asians. Numerous subject groups, from Central Asian modernist thinkers to lower-class Russian women, gained strong voices in imperial Tashkent by the turn of the century. Alliances and rivalries crossed as well as enforced ethnic, national, class, gender, religious, and generational boundaries. Individuals, from Central Asian politicians to Russian Orientalists and workers, sought to navigate this complicated colonial society in their own quest for power and privilege.

Challenges from subordinate groups eroded imperial administrators' confidence and abilities to present themselves as agents of power and progress in Tashkent, even as the growing city was realizing their dreams of creating an "Asian St. Petersburg." By the turn of the century, top officials and Russian liberal intellectuals struggled to reconcile evolving ideas of "civilization," including democratic government and social justice, with the reality of empire. Central policies, which increasingly saw Turkestan as a reservoir for raw materials and a dumping ground for unwanted migrants, strained relations between the imperial center, or metropole, and periphery. Even as war and revolution swept away tsarist elites in favor of the workers of the Tashkent soviet, however, visions of imperial power and civilization endured. Russian skilled workers asserted their own claim as agents of European progress and denied equality to their Central Asian counterparts in their new, ostensibly socialist regime. Military force, flowing from the soldiers' barracks on the outskirts of the city, continued as the ultimate arbiter of relations.

This study exposes the intricacies of imperial rule in Tashkent from the Russian conquest to the early soviet period. Using material from local, national, and state archives and periodicals, it explores power and resistance, violence and weakness, and interconnections and interdependencies in colonial society. Empire generated multiple strategies of accumulation, accommodation, and alliances. I examine how imperial Tashkent developed and prospered for decades after the conquest, but also how tensions spread across the city in the late nineteenth and early twentieth centuries. Divisions, murders, and destruction in Tashkent and its immediate surroundings compelled leading Bolshevik officials to impose strict controls on the political and economic life of the region. Yet even at the height of the violence, linkages among individuals and constituencies in Tashkent existed alongside the inequalities and dividing lines of empire.

From its local perspective, this study of Russian colonial rule in Tashkent seeks to contribute to wider debates on the nature of imperial power in Russia and Europe in the late nineteenth century. Tashkent Russian administrators were builders of an expanding empire at a time of crisis and change, both in imperial Russia and in the imperial world.[2] They consciously sought to use their position not only to fix Russia as a modern European empire, but also to define relations between core and periphery, elite and mass, Russian and non-Russian in the late imperial era. Multiple subordinate groups not only challenged imperial power but also offered their own visions of modern imperial societies. I argue that a study of Kaufman's "Russian soil" and colonial Tashkent can help us to understand the links between power, empire, and modernity on the one hand and race, class, gender, and nation on the other. Intricate local relationships altered visions and practices of imperial rule, offering unexpected opportunities and dangers for local actors and reverberating from Tashkent to the heart of empire.

Recent studies on empire in Russia, a rapidly expanding field but still one in its infancy, have underscored the importance placed on imperial ventures by tsarist-era elites. Mark Bassin has maintained that 1830s Russian nationalists' "imperial visions" lauded the Asian periphery as a place where Russia could discover its "messianic destiny."[3] Seymour Becker has argued that the educated public in the 1840s–1850s envisaged Central Asia as a region where Russia could assert its status as an advanced Western imperial state. Russia's long history as a multiethnic empire would allow it to bridge the gap between Europe and Asia and peacefully spread enlightenment and progress.[4] Prospects of new, rich agricultural lands, trade opportunities, and the chance to challenge the British empire in the "Great Game," or, as the Russians called it, the "Tournament of Shadows," for control of the region drew the attention of elites in the metropole to Central Asia as a place to explore Russia's future.

Daniel Brower's recent study of Russian Turkestan examines tsarist administrators' efforts to use the province as a testing ground for modern ideas of administration in the era of the Great Reforms.[5] Brower cogently details tensions between "liberal" visions of rule, which sought to extend citizenship and "civilization" to the local population, and more conservative viewpoints that saw Central Asians as inexorably alien and respectful only of brute force. Yet Brower's focus on policy making overlooks the complicated dynamic between policy and practice. The complexities of colonial society produced many of the contradictions and tensions among administrators that determined, in Brower's words, the "fate" of Russian Turkestan. My approach presents a more nuanced evaluation than the "flawed and failed" imperial undertaking presented by Brower.[6] Empire offered prospects as well as risks to both Russians and Central Asians, and the violence of 1916–21 should not completely obscure Tashkent's and Turkestan's transformation under imperial rule.

Soviet leaders, in Tashkent and in central Russia, continued to envision Turkestan as a launching pad for European power and progress in Asia. Soviet Russians, in the words of Douglas Northrop, sought to use the region as a "kind of civilizational laboratory, a place for thousands of Russian men and women to work out who they were."[7] Yet Russians could never create controlled conditions on the ground under which to carry out their experiments, and as a result this quest complicated, instead of guided, Russian efforts to discover national, imperial, and, later, socialist identities.

Given the polyglot nature of the tsarist and early soviet states, where Russians constituted a minority of the population, there have been remarkably few studies of everyday interactions and relationships between ethnic groups on the edges or in the center of empire.[8] The existing literature on empire has focused on Russian administrators, or specific factions, such as clergy or liberal intellectuals.[9] Among recent studies of Central Asia, this work engages Adeeb Khalid's study on modernist Central Asian intellectuals, the Jadids. This work extends Khalid's view that the encounter between the Russian empire and local peoples "profoundly reshaped local understandings" of culture and religion to the realms of society, economics, and politics in Tashkent, examining the colonizer as well as the colonized.[10] This idea of a transformative colonial encounter expands existing literature that finds complicated dynamics between accommodation and violence, between common interests and otherness, on the Russian borderlands.[11] Russians and Central Asians alike found their power, status, and identities constantly shifting during the period of colonial rule. I agree with Virginia Martin, whose study of the Kazakh steppe nomads concludes that "the realities of empire were constructed on the everyday level," and I argue further that these realities restructured conceptions of race, class, and nation as well as empire.[12]

Russian intellectuals in Tashkent, though many had served in tsarist ventures from Poland to the Caucasus, more often compared themselves to the British in India or the French in Algeria than to Russians in other areas of their own empire. These engineers, geographers, scientists, and other functionaries, many of whom chose Turkestan as a permanent posting, along with growing numbers of educated businessmen and writers, considered the region unique among tsarist possessions, given, among other factors, the distance to the metropole and the character of the local population, seen as completely isolated from modern "civilization." These factors, along with the difficult steppe and desert terrain lying between them and European Russia, led Tashkent Russians not to see their imperial region as geographically contiguous with the rest of the empire. Like their British and French counterparts, Russian intellectuals saw their task as using European concepts of progress to restore distant former cradles of civilization to glory; the first private newspaper in Tashkent, *Okraina*, said, "Fate has brought Russians to develop a European culture and civilization."[13] Application of these concepts to Central Asia would affirm the still-contested notion that Russia was a modern European state. Success through peaceful means, these Tashkent Russians argued, would establish Russian superiority to Great Britain, whose violent methods had provoked the Indian rebellion of 1857.

I argue that discourse and practices of imperial rule at the local level identify Russia as a modern European empire. This conclusion remains contentious among historians of imperial Russia and unproven to many specialists in postcolonial studies. Robert Geraci has argued that history and geography have made it "impossible for Russia to shake off the Eastern aspects of its identity."[14] Nathaniel Knight contends that Russia defies the Occident/Orient divide posed by the foundational text in postcolonial studies, Edward Said's *Orientalism*.[15] Both maintain that Said, who never mentions Russia in his works, cannot be seamlessly applied to the tsarist empire, much less the Soviet Union. Russians as a people straddled East and West, with a long history of contact across poorly established borders. My study, however, supports Adeeb Khalid's criticism of Knight's view. Elite Russian arguments of a special understanding, tolerance, and compassion toward Eastern peoples were intellectual devices designed to convince the British and other Europeans of Russia's superior potential as civilizers.[16] Russian intellectuals drank from a common well of European thought on the issue of the "Orient." This study will seek to demonstrate that practices of rule in Tashkent, flowing from global imperial knowledge as well as the intricacies of colonial societies, reflected Russia as European, even as Russians fought to overcome feelings of marginality as compared to the powers of Great Britain and France.

This work addresses and seeks to contribute to important concepts and debates in the broader field of colonial studies. Postconquest Tashkent, with its separate Russian enclave, resembled colonial cities built by Europeans worldwide, from Casablanca to New Delhi. Through its architecture and its military character, Russian Tashkent served, as did these other cities, as "theaters of colonial domination."[17] Ann Laura Stoler, David Prochaska, and Dane Kennedy have discussed in their respective studies of Dutch, French, and British colonial communities how domination coexisted with multiple social and cultural connections in "plural societies."[18] My study examines this type of society through a deep source base that incorporates archival and published information, from newspapers to novels, in the languages of both the rulers and the ruled. I pay greater attention than the abovementioned authors to subordinate groups in colonial society, seeking their own voices wherever possible. Multifaceted viewpoints of the colonial "contact zone" introduce nuance into more strident views in colonial studies that present simple dichotomies of power and resistance.[19] One important but underexamined constituency to emerge in this study is "poor whites." David Arnold has signaled this group's importance in British India, but mainly as a subject of concern for imperial elites.[20] In Tashkent, "poor whites" also played key roles in transforming relations between colonizer and colonized. This study's focus on the local level, all the while examining crucial, constantly shifting connections with outside Russian and Asian worlds, intertwines concepts of imperialism and colonialism, often arbitrarily separated in colonial studies. Theorists Ania Loomba and Robert Young see the former as flowing from the metropole, representing the ideology as well as the economic and military strength that enables expansion, and the latter as the exercise of power, and the realities of rule, on the periphery.[21] Relations between the center and the margins emerge in this study as a complicated, and contested, two-way communication, even as leaders in St. Petersburg or Moscow and Tashkent realize their mutual interests in exploiting Central Asian lands and labor. Finally, Russian elites' efforts to model their rule on, even as they portrayed themselves as superior to, other European empires provide a fascinating example of the extent and limits of the "exportability" of dominant British and French models of empire across the imperial world.

At the same time, this work will examine Tashkent as a unique configuration, one influenced by the particular character of its population, as well as the policies applied to it. Local stories provide some of the richest accounts of the complexity of empire. Central Asian business success, most visible in the numbers of stores owned by local merchants on the main shopping street of Russian Tashkent, led author A. I. Dobrosmyslov to warn in 1912 that "soon, we Russians, due to our laziness and absence of entrepreneurship, will be in full dependence on the local Jews and Muslims."[22] I will argue that frequent references to Central Asian business superiority served particular rhetorical purposes; nonetheless, they reflected a dynamism in local society encouraged by the conquest. Yet ultimate political power consistently escaped Central Asians. An alliance between Russian workers and Austro-Hungarian prisoners of war thwarted efforts to establish a democratic state following the 1917 revolutions. Russian women as well played highly visible roles in local society, demonstrating and rioting from 1916 to 1919, claiming power as colonizers even as they sought to upset class and gender hierarchies. Tashkent Russian workers launched their bid for power before the October revolution in St. Petersburg, with the goal of maintaining their power as colonizers over Central Asians.

Power is a guiding concept in this study. I follow Michel Foucault, who argues that power is multifaceted, operating on several levels, down to micro-relations in society. In defining power widely, however, Foucault also argues that it works as "capillary action," flowing from the modern state. In Tashkent, the source of real power lay outside the heart of the city, in the military garrison where thousands of soldiers maintained a constant presence. Yet I see power flowing from other sources as well. Adeeb Khalid has applied to Central Asian elite struggles Pierre Bourdieu's model of "cultural capital," where discursive strategies to make sense of the world in themselves constitute a form of power.[23] As we will see, Russian administrators and intellectuals, and later activist women and workers, strove to build cultural capital through their visual and rhetorical representations of city, community, and civilization. Central Asians' economic prosperity, and their knowledge of the local environment, allowed a degree of power and independence from the imperial state that inverted colonial hierarchies.

Power met a complex dynamic of accommodation and resistance. I argue that crucial to an understanding of the exercise of colonial power is, in the words of Ronald Robinson, a "collaborative mechanism."[24] Whereas Robinson used the term principally to reflect the relationship between core and periphery, I apply it within colonial society. I use the term "mediator" instead of "collaborator" to designate Central Asian elites who considered themselves simultaneously responsible to their own population and to Russian overseers. In their desire for personal status and advancement, these mediators operated, in the words of Edward Lazzerini, in an "ambiguous world of cooperation and resistance."[25] Other subordinate groups, including lower-class Russians and Central Asians, employed what James Scott called "weapons of the weak"—foot dragging, evasion, and nonparticipation in elite schemes of power—before, and along with, open resistance.[26] Subordinate groups who offered resistance claimed that they were the rightful recipients of colonial privilege. Russian workers and lower-class women argued that the color of their skin entitled them to a share of the spoils of colonialism; Central Asians maintained that the "civilizing mission" and, later, socialist ideology should favor them.

Russian elites, imperial and soviet, made strong efforts to present Tashkent as a model of "civilization." Yet civilization (*tsivilizatsiia*) was a charged term in the colonial city. It was equated, along with "culture" (*kul'tura*) and "progress," (*progress'*) firmly with Europe. I argue that we can equate these terms with contemporary understandings of modernity. Modernity contains concepts of order, urbanism, rationality, education, knowledge, technology, and science that were apparent in the discourse of Russian intellectuals in Tashkent. Laura Engelstein has argued that attaining modernity, firmly associated with Europe, was an important goal of intellectuals in central Russia in the late nineteenth century.[27] This study links the quest for modernity simultaneously to empire and Russia. According to Michael Adas, concepts designated "modern" were done so in the specific belief that the non-Western populations would be unable to match European accomplishments in these fields.[28] Tashkent Russians sought to apply modern concepts to their own city and society to assert power and prove their Europeanness. Some intellectuals claimed that they could use the urban landscape of Tashkent to serve as a vanguard for modernist elements in Russia, with its legacy of stultifying tsarist rule. As well, their efforts would inspire the imperial world, still recovering from the savagery of the 1857 Indian rebellion.

European modernity as the creation of order from chaos, however, produced tensions in colonial Tashkent. As Zygmont Bauman has argued, the modern obsession with separation, classification, and hierarchies led to shock when mixing and ambiguities occurred.[29] In the Russian city, anxieties over prostitution demonstrated this fixation. Further, subordinate groups seized upon growing arguments at the turn of the century that absolute political, legal, and social equality were essential concepts of a modern state. Enforcing this discourse were growing feelings in Europe as well as Asia that empire symbolized Western exploitation, not Western civilization. Observers across the imperial world noted the paradox between the "civilizing mission" and the depth of imperial domination and colonial inequality.[30] Such tensions, I will argue, were particularly acute for Tashkent Russians. Failure in the mission might confirm the belief that Russians themselves did not possess the attributes of "civilization" and were a "weak link" in the spread of European modernity to the rest of the world. I contend as well that Russian intellectuals in Tashkent, as did many elsewhere in Europe, began themselves to question the value of certain concepts that linked empire and modernity, in particular European capitalism, which they saw as "polluting" to the national spirit.[31]

In the end, imperial and soviet elites' desire for power trumped the need to spread modern civilization in imperial Tashkent. Violence and military force regulated disputes along social, ethnic, and gender lines. Political authority remained in the hands of small circles of Europeans, ruling with the assistance of select groups of Central Asian mediators. Yet, as I will demonstrate, links and interconnections in Tashkent subverted as well as supported these narrow structures of power. Multiple lines of domination and subordination provided opportunities and risks for individuals across colonial society.[32]

The book consists of a prologue and eight chapters, divided at times thematically, though maintaining an overall chronological progression. The prologue examines preconquest Asian Tashkent and the impact of the Russian conquest in 1865. Tashkent was a major center of regional trade with a highly developed social and political structure. Local notables, accustomed to external rule imposed by neighboring khanates, established strategies to limit Russian intrusion into matters of local culture and to profit from closer economic links to the north.

Efforts of Russian administrators, led by K. P. fon Kaufman, to construct and to shape the urban space of the "Russian section" of Tashkent form chapter 1. Public ceremonies displayed imperial power and offered rituals of community to the emergent Russian population. These ceremonies, I argue, also offered occasions for individuals and groups, from intellectuals serving in the administration to military veterans and Central Asian notables, to assert their own prominence in colonial society. Urban planning, architecture, and cultural institutions all emerged as cornerstones in efforts by Kaufman and his successors to portray Russian Tashkent as a symbol of European superiority and civilization.

The second chapter examines endeavors of Russian intellectuals to fix their place in Tashkent, as well as the place of the colonial city in the wider world, at once part of the Russian empire, imperial Europe, and colonized Asia. A close reading of their discourse and actions displays at once confidence and confusion in their identity and their mission. Intellectuals traversed unclear boundaries between state and society, employed by the tsarist regime but viewing an independent societal sphere as a critical component of modern progress. Russian writers mixed a belief that they could be leaders of a Russian nation and an imperial world with an acute awareness of their social, ethnic, and geographical marginality. They condemned their own colleagues in the tsarist administration, who used their position in Turkestan for personal enrichment and career advancement instead of participation in civilizing and modernizing missions.

Chapter 3 addresses the dynamics between Central Asians and Russians in Tashkent. Colonial relationships were at once multifaceted and volatile. Residents of Asian Tashkent adapted to the new colonial regime, seeking to guard their own cultural autonomy and resist, or at least reduce, the demands of their tsarist overlords. Russian administrators and writers perpetuated images of inherent Asian backwardness to justify their rule, even as they admitted local superiority in various fields, including healing and engineering. Relative ethnic peace nonetheless prevailed until 1892, when Russian soldiers and civilians killed one hundred Central Asians in a riot during a cholera epidemic. Russian policies and Central Asian reactions to the epidemic and the riot itself underscored the thin line between harmony and violence in Tashkent.

Growing diversity within the Russian community constitutes the focus of the fourth chapter. Russian elites considered increased numbers of poor Russians, characterized as drunk and dirty, as a threat to the image and the exercise of imperial rule. Contacts with Central Asians, it was feared, notably through prostitution, would blur the boundary between colonizer and colonized. Demonization of these lower classes extended to Russian railway workers, whose presence and skills, alongside other settler workers, fueled a growing economy. Schooled in the language of protest and claiming to represent a new, more progressive socialist modernity, railway worker activists challenged tsarist rule in 1905. Activists, however, isolated themselves from Central Asians and poor Russians, using the same typologies of civilization and backwardness as their imperial overlords.

Chapter 5 discusses growing tensions in Russian imperial society as the tsar announces, and then abandons, plans for progressive reform in the years following the 1905 revolution. In prominent positions in the business community and imperial administration, Russian liberals in Tashkent condemned continued tsarist resistance to democracy, representative government, and civil rights, yet struggled to reconcile this stance with their own desire to keep imperial privileges based on their status as colonizers. St. Petersburg's decision to ship hundreds of thousands of migrants to Turkestan further worsened center-periphery relations. Russians began to wonder, with the emergence of a modernist Islamic intellectual movement, if the local Central Asian population, considered to possess a superior business acumen and a more temperate view toward life, was surpassing Russia on the road to progress. Even as the economy of Tashkent expanded, conflicts along generational and ideological lines combined with those of class and race to increase tensions on both sides of the city.

Although imperial Tashkent was thousands of kilometers from the front, the First World War had a significant impact upon it. In chapter 6, numerous constituencies in colonial society, from local businessmen to minority European nationalities, used wartime exigencies to improve their wealth and status in colonial society. The arrival of thousands of refugees and prisoners of war, however, worsened a growing food crisis in a region that, before the implementation of central policies favoring cotton growth, had been self-sufficient in food supplies. Women, both Russian and Central Asian, initiated demonstrations against those, from local merchants to tsarist authorities, they deemed responsible for hardships sharpened by wartime. Efforts to stem a growing rebellion across Turkestan elevated the roles of Central Asian mediators and Slavic prisoners of war, but the growing food crisis began to polarize social and political forces in Tashkent.

Chapters 7 and 8 discuss the revolutionary era in Tashkent. Chapter 7 focuses on the worker-activists who ascended to power in 1917. Following the 1905 revolution, these Russian skilled workers had gained an elevated status in colonial society, drawn in by tsarist elites against increasingly active Central Asians and settler lower classes. Russian socialist workers spoke the language of internationalism, but denied the existence of a working class or consciousness among the local population. Along with rebellious soldiers, worker activists deprived the Central Asian majority of power in 1917. As a food crisis worsened, leaders of the Tashkent soviet imposed unequal rationing regimes and launched raids for supplies into the Asian city. Some Russian workers, however, cooperated with Central Asian farmers in a climate of crisis and hardship. Tashkent soviet leaders also expressed great hostility to the new Bolshevik government; this relationship provides the central focus of chapter 8. Workers and soldiers resisted central efforts to invite widespread Central Asian participation in a socialist regime. Central Asians sought to take advantage of new roles envisioned by their central patrons. Members of central Bolshevik commissions in Tashkent, however, wrestled with their own ambiguous views on class and race, and realized that their primary goal was to restore the cotton economy of the region to feed industry in central Russia. Famine and the Red Army killed hundreds of thousands of Central Asians and kept the region under Russian control. Continued resistance by Tashkent Russians to the center, however, as well as continued micro-relations across as well as along lines of race and class, forced the Bolsheviks to assert tight central control over the city in 1923.

# Prologue: Tashkent before the Russians and the Dynamics of Conquest

On the eve of the 1865 Russian conquest, Tashkent was a center of trade in Inner Asia. Active artisanal and manufacturing sectors profited from the city's position along routes linking neighboring khanates and extending to Russia, the Kazakh steppe, Persia, India, Afghanistan, and China. From the late 1700s, these khanates' efforts to control Tashkent engendered political turmoil. A vigorous urban culture, a tradition of independence, and a desire for continued prosperity posed formidable challenges for these would-be conquerors. Russian officers, as they marched their troops south from the Kazakh steppe, encountered a dynamic society and economy that belied many of their images of Asian stagnation and backwardness. Even as these myths persisted, in many ways enforced by the ease of the conquest, tsarist leaders actively solicited cooperation from the newly colonized population to help them navigate the complexities of urban society in one of the largest cities in Central Asia.

A wide, albeit fragmentary, group of sources exists for examining the history of pre-Russian Tashkent: a small number of written accounts from local residents, who rarely employed print as a medium, complemented by a few reports of European travelers.[1] Most histories of the city and region, however, were produced by Russian Orientalist scholars in the late nineteenth century.[2] Uzbek historians used these sources in the Soviet period primarily to formulate Tashkent's history in terms of a progressive conflict between classes, and in the later Soviet era, to describe the Russian conquest itself as progressive.[3] Examining pre-Russian Tashkent on its own terms requires filtering stereotypes that course through European and Soviet descriptions of the Asian city and continent. Employing similarities with other contemporary local and Islamic cities can offer important indications on the development of urban culture, virtually absent from primary sources of the era. Tashkent emerges as a segmented society ruled by a decentralized power structure, but bound by a common regional and Islamic culture.

## Tashkent before the Conquest

Tashkent is located in a fertile valley of the Chirchik river, a tributary of the Syr-Darya (Jaxartes) river. The valley is one of the many oasis belts in the arid grasslands, sandy deserts, and plains of Central Asia.[4] Grassy steppe lands suitable for pastoralist tribes spread to the north of the valley. The Kizil Kum desert belt stretches northwest of Tashkent, but other fertile Central Asian oases hold the renowned cities of Samarkand and Bukhara to the south and the newer urban and agricultural centers of Kokand and Fergana to the east. The western range of the Tien Shan mountains rise to the northeast, continuing eastward toward the borders of China. A continental, subtropical climate characterizes the region, bringing extreme ranges in temperature. Averages in the early twentieth century ranged from 27.9 degrees Celsius in July to 1.1 degree Celsius in January.[5] Dry, hot summers last from April to October. The climate and the fertile loess soil of the valley nonetheless provide Tashkent with a rich harvest of agricultural goods. The abundance of melons, grapes, and other fruits, as well as nuts and grain, constantly impressed visitors. Cotton also grows easily in this climate. Bountiful harvests produced inside city walls and numerous poplar trees gave Tashkent a reputation as a "garden city."[6]

Tashkent entered written historical records as a part of one of many contests over the oasis by outside powers. Chinese and Arab forces battled for control of the city, then called Chach, in the seventh century. An Arab victory implanted the seeds of Islam within the largely Turkic population, which had migrated there a century earlier and coexisted with peoples of Persian descent.[7] Tashkent, along with other cities in the region, flourished under the Persian Samanid dynasty from the ninth to eleventh century. At this point the city gained its current name, meaning "city of stone," for its strong inner and outer fortifications and its citadel built to protect its recent prosperity.

Regional trade escalated, with large fairs, gathering steppe and oasis merchants, held on the eastern edge of the city. As the population expanded, construction began on vast irrigation canals to draw water from the Chirchik river, nine kilometers away. Irrigation facilitated urban growth and allowed farmers to produce food for export.[8] The Mongol invasion, which destroyed Tashkent in 1220, only temporarily stunted the city's development.[9] Under Amir Temur and his successors, the city retained a significant degree of autonomy, and by the sixteenth century a new wave of urban construction, in particular of mosques, greatly impressed foreign travelers.[10] By the sixteenth century, the city's population was estimated at thirty thousand inhabitants.[11] Tashkent's wealth attracted the many successors that arose from the Timurid collapse, including nomadic Great Horde Kazakhs and Kalmyks, along with emergent khanates of Bukhara and Kokand. Bukharan forces gained control of Tashkent from Kazakh leaders in 1740.

A decentralized political structure in Tashkent allowed the smooth functioning of municipal affairs throughout periods of political uncertainty. Outside rulers generally did not intervene in internal municipal power structures. Local resident Nurmuhammed Alim Khan reported in 1735 that the governing of the city rested with a ten-person magistrate of local officials. These leaders had a great deal of power in relations with the nomadic Kazakh khan, who lived outside the city and whose purview was principally military.[12] As throughout the region, however, the exercise of power remained informal, with personal relationships often more important than established power structures.[13] Under Bukharan rule, multiple elites based in different parts of Tashkent competed for the emir's favor. By 1784, one of these power clusters, led by Muhammad Yunus Khoja, chased the Bukharans from Tashkent.

Economic growth continued throughout the seventeenth and eighteenth centuries. Raw materials, including coal extracted from nearby deposits, combined with highly developed secondary industries, chiefly metalworking, to fuel the city's prosperity. Local agriculture and artisanal industries, particularly clothing, wool, and leather, enhanced the reputation of Tashkent as the economic hub of Central Asia.[14] A network of long, straight streets connected the city gates to multiple bazaars. The tsarist establishment of the city of Orenburg in 1735 following conquests in the steppe opened Russian, and European, markets for the traders of Central Asia. Cotton, silk, wheat, and fruit, as well as a number of artisanally produced goods, including wool and leather, invigorated the export sector of the economy. Tashkent rulers solicited increased trade; Muhammad Yunus Khoja wrote to the Russian government in 1792 to improve economic relations, resulting in a visit from a Russian embassy four years later.[15] An early nineteenth-century wave of construction pushed the numbers of mosques from approximately 40 to 150. Russian geographers who visited Tashkent in 1800 estimated its population at forty thousand male inhabitants.[16] The lush gardens that grew within and outside city walls, however, retained the greatest allure for foreign visitors.

The development of Tashkent as a major center of trade affected the identities and social relations of the city's inhabitants. By the seventeenth century, urban residents, along with those of other settled trading areas in the region, began to refer to themselves as "Sarts," a word that is sometimes translated as "merchants" but whose origins remain obscure.[17] Each neighborhood (*mahalla*) of Tashkent developed its own economic sphere of activity. One specialized in saddles, another in satin, still another in footwear or leather production.[18] Numbering between two and three hundred, the mahallas sold their goods either on the streets or in the dozens of city bazaars; the main bazaar in central Tashkent consisted of approximately 2,400 stores. In the years preceding the conquest, fifteen to eighteen thousand camels traveled annually between central Russia and Tashkent, as the total volume of trade trebled in the 1850s alone.[19] Central Asian trade also benefited from easier connections with Great Britain, as British activity ebbed and flowed along the borders of Afghanistan. The volume of trade sparked the appearance of a number of extremely wealthy merchants. Their value, however, was difficult to calculate; one municipal leader, Mirza Ahmed, upon accumulating significant funds, formed tax-exempt religious charities and schools (*waqf*) in his mahalla to shelter his riches.[20] The growing emphasis on artisanal and manufactured goods and a growing urban population rendered the city dependent on the surrounding region for food. Urban inhabitants, nonetheless, bridged these worlds. Each mahalla controlled a section of farmland outside city borders to be divided among those residents willing to work it.[21]

The mahalla, gathering an area of roughly thirty to sixty houses often clustered around a mosque or other common public building, provided not only the central economic unit of the city, but the central political and social one as well. Janet L. Abu-Lughod has noted the phenomenon of "neighborhoods" in Islamic cities throughout Asia and Africa, as a sign of the power of local social bodies against a weaker state.[22] Neighborhood units served as ideal principles of organization for everyday relations based on the family unit and the intimacy of the mosque. Mahallas in Tashkent grouped peoples based upon a variety of criteria, including original place of origin, extended family or clan units, religious belief, or economic activity. Some mahallas contained people of minority backgrounds, such as Jews.[23] Indian traders lived separately as well, in caravanserais. Each mahalla was under the authority of elders (*aksakals*[24]). Aksakals made a variety of important decisions, from vetting potential newcomers to supervising the labor of their mahalla's residents.[25] Mahalla leaders generally worked to maintain social cohesion, and wealthier members were expected to help the less fortunate.

Each mahalla apparently chose a representative to participate in larger administrative matters in Tashkent, although the role of formal political structures remains unspecified in existing sources. By the eighteenth century, Tashkent was divided into four districts (*daha*). One senior aksakal headed each of these districts: Kokcha, Beshagach, Sebzar, and Sheikhantaur.[26] These aksakals guarded the independence of their sections, but cooperated on issues of economic regulation and legal matters.[27] Once he assumed power, Muhammad Yunus Khoja, former leader of the Sheikhantaur district, worked to gain the support and unity of other leading aksakals, with the goal of preventing future attacks on the city. The daha, however, retained separate characters and were divided by walls. Reflecting the diversity of the mahallas, each specialized in certain types of industry. Sheikhantaur, on the northeast corner, appeared to be the most involved in manufacturing, specializing in iron making, cloth weaving, and saddlery. Beshagach, meanwhile, maintained large plantations within its walls in the nineteenth century.[28] Segmentation did not isolate city-dwellers from each other or the outside world. Many urban residents were fluent in both local Turkic and Persian dialects, and did not consider language a major component of their identities. The term "Sart" worked well to describe the residents of Tashkent and neighboring cities, as its generality unified peoples of different regional, linguistic, and cultural backgrounds who mixed in these urban areas.

Political power and social influence in Tashkent evolved throughout the nineteenth century. Local observers, including cleric Muhammad Salih, have noted the ascendancy of the *khoja*s, an aristocracy whose wealth was based on either land or trade.[29] These notables appeared to have increasing political influence. Muhammad Yunus Khoja established the position of *bashi-khoja* as a second-in-command charged with ensuring the economic health of the city. Yet links between social influence, economic wealth, and political power were nebulous in nineteenth-century Central Asia.[30]

Tashkent's architecture signaled a decentralized power structure. By the mid-nineteenth century Tashkent resembled many Islamic cities in the Middle East and Central Asia. Long, straight streets had been replaced by clusters of houses, walled off by narrow lanes, that shielded the privileged private sphere from public life.[31] Only individual doors marked the way inside the separate houses behind these walls. Interiors featured a sheltered courtyard, with a garden, or at least a few trees. Space, therefore, was valued most as a private domain in the city of Tashkent.[32]

Urban architecture also displayed local religion and culture. Diverse strains of Islamic thought and practice coursed through Tashkent, although information on both the practice of the religion and the character of the religious leadership remains fragmentary.[33] Each mahalla contained its own mosque, and larger central places of worship existed in the city. Festivals and holidays were almost exclusively religious in character.[34] Religious judges (*qazis*) enforced Islamic law, and spiritual police (*reis*) walked the streets to prevent transgressions of religious custom. The established Muslim clergy, the *ulama*, apparently employed the practice of *taqlid*, whereby adherents were required to follow the messages of their religious leaders, although the extent to which laypeople subscribed to this practice is unknown. The ulama also worked to influence local politics, though again their success in such endeavors remains obscure.[35] The Hanafite Sunni branch of Islam practiced by the majority population allowed for religious toleration and diversity. Sufi *ishan*s commonly led religious services and may have been gaining increasing popularity among urban youth in the early nineteenth century. The ulama, however, dominated the educational system, operating fourteen religious colleges (*madrasa*s) and the majority of elementary schools (*maktabs*).[36]

Political turmoil sweeping through Central Asia engulfed Tashkent in the early nineteenth century. A new khanate, Kokand, challenged Kyrgyz and Qipchaq steppe tribes and the emirate of Bukhara for power. The escalating wealth of the region, spurred by increased sedentarization and continually growing trade, sparked new conflicts over territory, with Tashkent as the biggest prize.[37] In 1810, Qipchaq troops loyal to Kokand overwhelmed Tashkent's defenses, inaugurating a new period of foreign subjection for the city. Kokandian rule, however, never achieved stability. Internecine fighting among commanders and tribes led to Qipchaq and other leaders becoming more interested in extracting revenue from Tashkent's residents and forcing them to billet troops than in facilitating economic development. Several minor uprisings against Kokandian rule culminated in a major local rebellion in 1847 that drove the Qipchaq ruler, Aziz Parvonachi, from the city.[38] A resulting power vacuum attracted new contenders from various factions in Kokand.

Even as traders from Europe and Asia traversed the region in the early nineteenth century, Central Asian political and military leaders ignored strategic and technological advances of larger states and societies to the east or west. The geographic position of the region, not bordering directly on any major Eurasian state, allowed these elites, in a military sense, the "luxury of isolation."[39] Leaders of khanates had employed their knowledge of the land to defend themselves from small-scale in-

Figure 2. Sheikhantaur Madrasa ca. nineteenth century.
F. Azadaev, *Tashkent vo vtoroi polovine XIX veka:*
*Ocherki Sotsial'no-Ekonomicheskoi i Politicheskoi Istorii*
(Tashkent: Izdatel'stvo Akademii Nauk Uzbekskoi SSR, 1959), 16.

cursions by British and Russian troops probing Central Asia as part of a nineteenth-century contest for power and suasion.[40] The ability to play these imperial powers against each other lessened the need to adopt military innovations sweeping Europe and Asia. Numerous European foreign travelers discussed the military weaknesses as part of a pattern of depravity, impoverishment, and torture that stemmed from decades of internecine warfare.[41] In comparison to European soldiers of the period, Central Asians appeared undisciplined, ill-armed, and poorly led.[42] Local troops were at a great disadvantage when large numbers of Russian soldiers approached from the north in the 1860s.

## Russia and Tashkent

Russia had manifold political and economic interests in the Central Asian khanates in the early nineteenth century. Merchants from across the empire, including many Tatars, traveled to the region in rapidly increasing numbers to trade for cotton, silk, paper, and other products. Central Asian leaders levied elevated taxes and other duties on these traders and goods, and often sanctioned the raiding of caravans. Several Russian merchants were also held in Central Asian prisons. A major Russian military operation to retaliate against such practices in Khiva, led by General V. A. Perovskii, failed miserably, as hundreds of troops died in combat with local steppe tribes in 1839.[43] Yet numerous tsarist embassies continued to press Central Asian leaders for better access to markets as well as support in any potential contest with Great Britain.[44]

Extensive military activities in Central Asia began in 1863 with the activation of a long-stalled plan to close a six-hundred-mile gap between the Orenburg and Semipalatinsk fortified lines, which protected recent Russian conquests on the Kazakh steppe. Frontier commanders quickly realized their superiority over poorly trained and equipped troops from local tribes. Anxious for promotion and military glory, these commanders moved southward, justifying their operations, which came against central orders, by their need to solve the "anarchy" reigning on their "defensive" frontier.[45] Overcoming significant resistance, tsarist forces drove into Central Asia, conquering the city of Turkestan in 1863. Frontier commanders correctly anticipated that conquests would ultimately gain central approval. St. Petersburg had increased its interest in Central Asia following the Crimean War of 1854–56. D. A. Miliutin, appointed minister of war in 1861, argued that the region provided an ideal theater for a military offensive, as victories could unnerve the British and reverse the humiliation suffered in the Crimea.[46] Adding to its empire would affirm Russia's place among the great imperial powers of Europe and allow a new field to practice the "civilizing mission."[47] Finally, drastic increases in world cotton prices stemming from the United States' civil war sparked arguments that a conquered Central Asia could provide an assured supply of affordable cotton.[48] For Tsar Alexander II, who had promoted Miliutin and other advocates of a military advance toward Central Asia, glory appeared as a primary motive to approve unauthorized conquests. The tsar delighted in lavishing medals and honors on his military.[49] Yet, despite all these motives, no coherent plans for Central Asian conquest existed in the early 1860s; the foreign and finance ministries voiced strong opposition over the potential of another conflict with Great Britain and increased spending at a time when the empire had initiated profound domestic reforms.

General M. G. Cherniaev, among the most aggressive commanders in Central Asia, nonetheless saw the tsar's retroactive approval of conquests as a carte blanche for further military operations.[50] Seeking political notoriety and military fame, Cherniaev decided to mount an attack upon Tashkent in October 1864. Against direct orders from superiors, he led 1,500 troops to the gates of the city. The attack turned into a debacle, as Kokandian forces led by Alim Qul killed sixteen Russian soldiers, forcing a retreat. Cherniaev's hopes, based on talks with Tashkent merchants who had fled the city, that the local population would support his forces in a "liberation" from Kokandian rule proved unfounded. The failed attack boosted Alim Qul's prestige, but uprisings against increased taxation in the winter of 1865 demonstrated the regime's fragility.[51] Cherniaev, who retained his position despite the failed attack, used internal unrest to justify a new move against Tashkent in the summer of 1865. Tsarist troops sent out to seize control of the city's water supply killed Alim Qul in a May 9 battle. The decision of local leaders, including the leading Islamic legal scholar (qazi-kalan), to request assistance from Bukhara hastened Cherniaev's June 15 decision to attack Tashkent, despite the fact that his forces, numbering 1,951 with twelve cannons, were not significantly larger than during the last failed storming.[52]

Remaining Kokandian forces, numbering anywhere from ten to thirty thousand, mounted a stout defense along with soldiers from elsewhere in the region, though the extent of resistance from local residents remains unclear.[53] After two days of battle that killed hundreds of Central Asians and twenty-five tsarist soldiers, city aksakals arranged a surrender with General Cherniaev. Surrender terms obliged local leaders and troops to recognize tsarist control. In return, Cherniaev promised not to billet troops with the local population, to refrain from interference in religious, cultural, and legal life and norms, and not to levy any taxes on the population for at least one year.[54] This agreement remained a feature of tsarist rule over the city throughout the imperial period.

Upon hearing of the conquest, Tsar Alexander commented that it was "a glorious affair" and presented honors to Cherniaev and his leading officers, cementing official approval of another action undertaken against direct orders.[55] The relative ease of the conquest and the lack of indignation from the British quieted any opposition within the tsarist administration to the seizure.[56] Debates in St. Petersburg revolved around the city's future status. The Foreign Ministry and Orenburg governor-general N. A. Kryzhanovskii argued for the establishment of an independent city-state with a vassal relationship to Russia, seen as the cheapest option and the one least likely to invite resistance from Bukhara.[57] Cherniaev, however, who had, in the tradition of past city rulers, established a modest personal residence on the edge of town, made his case for direct rule.

The Russian general fostered a working relationship with local notables in Tashkent.[58] Wealthy merchant Seid Azim Muhammed bai proved one of Cherniaev's leading supporters. Seid Azim spoke Russian and moved comfortably within the worlds of both imperial and local business and politics. He had previously gained the favor of tsarist administrators by buying the freedom of Russian slaves in the region. Seid Azim's goals extended beyond gaining lucrative contracts or a leading position within the colonial administration. Letters to tsarist officials attest to his strong commitment to improving local education under Tashkent's new rulers.[59] Seid Azim's position nonetheless gained him significant profits. He recruited local labor to assist in the building of Cherniaev's one major project for Tashkent: a new Russian citadel.[60] Cherniaev also struck up relationships with leading administrative figures of the city, particularly qazi-kalan Ishan Khoja. The two visited frequently, and Cherniaev felt sufficiently comfortable with Ishan Khoja to leave him in charge of the city while the Russian general was absent on military campaigns.[61]

As Cherniaev established connections with local rulers, leading figures in St. Petersburg grew increasingly comfortable with adding Tashkent to the empire, as the capital of a new province of Turkestan. As the British appeared to acquiesce to Tashkent's conquest, Foreign Minister Gorchakov saw the potential value of the surrounding region as a producer of valuable raw materials, such as cotton, silk, and tobacco. Miliutin and Kryzhanovskii actively courted leading Russian business figures to begin investing in Turkestan.[62] Tsar Alexander II signed an official decree of annexation of Tashkent to Russia in 1866. Although administrative details of the annexation had yet to be decided, Tashkent became an official part of the Russian empire.

# 1.

# *Ceremonies, Construction, and Commemoration*

Residents of the new "Russian section" of Tashkent anxiously awaited the arrival of Konstantin Petrovich fon Kaufman, the first governor-general of the province of Turkestan, on November 7, 1867. Tashkent was to become the administrative center of the newly conquered lands of Central Asia. For its first residents, Kaufman's arrival signified the beginning of the transformation of Russian Tashkent from a dusty military settlement to a permanent and vital capital city. To commemorate the arrival of the governor-general, Russian merchants erected a "magnificent" arch at the eastern edge of the Russian section at the cost of one thousand rubles.[1] The arch was decorated with flaxes that surrounded a shield with the monogram of the tsar. On the appointed day, residents gathered on rooftops to watch the entrance.

Anticipation turned to surprise as messengers sent word that Kaufman had chosen to enter Tashkent not through the arch, but by way of the larger Asian city. Swords bared, a Cossack honor guard escorted the governor-general and his entourage through its winding streets and bazaars. The Russian welcoming delegation, in "bewilderment" according to a newspaper account, quickly moved to the western gate that divided their settlement from Asian Tashkent.[2] They arrived in time to present the new governor-general with the traditional offering of bread and salt. Kaufman responded with a short speech on the value of the community to Russia's mission in Central Asia. The city was illuminated that night, heralding a bright future for Russia in Tashkent.

Governor-General Kaufman and the officials and settlers who awaited him both sought to exploit the occasion of his arrival. Kaufman's decision to march through Asian Tashkent with only a small honor guard projected his might and fearlessness before a population that only two years earlier had fiercely resisted tsarist troops. His decision upset the fledgling Russian community, which hoped to impress upon the governor-general the importance of developing the "Russian section" as a center of power and European civilization before the large and rich Asian city. Both depictions sought to harness the ritual power of representation, utilizing a public event to construct a vision of imperial power and society.

Public representations of power emerged as critical elements of authority and identity in Russian Tashkent. Imperial leaders, as in central Russia, shaped ceremonial displays and public space to signal the potency and character of their rule. Privileged differentiation of selected characteristics in representation, according to Catherine Bell, can structure reality, generating hierarchical schemes within an apparent communal and historical unity.[3] Ceremonial gatherings in Tashkent infused meaning into the colonial enterprise. Governor-General Kaufman developed an urban plan and civic symbols to underline the Russian city's powerful and "civilizing" character against its Asian neighbor. I argue, however, that public ceremonies and spaces become sites of contestation as well as community. Imperial leaders and elites lacked full control over their, to use Richard Wortman's term, "scenarios."[4] Constituencies from Russian merchants and veterans to Central Asian notables sought to influence ceremonies in order to assert their own status in colonial society. Changes in the form and content of ritual public gatherings and civic symbols and spaces at once reflected and generated shifting balances of power within this new imperial city.

## Welcoming the Governor-General

Russians in Tashkent hoped that Kaufman's arrival would ease their sense of insecurity. The first two years of Russian presence following the conquest had been difficult, as the status of Tashkent had remained undetermined. General M. G. Cherniaev had left only a simple military encampment in the city following his victory, as he shifted his attention to the neighboring emirate of Bukhara in a bid for further military glory. Only in the late fall did Cherniaev return to Tashkent and consider it a potential center for Russian rule in the region. The general purchased lands from wealthy Central Asian landowners beside the citadel built by the khanate of Kokand.[5] He offered small family plots to officers and soldiers who had summoned their wives and children for the winter. Two-room clay houses rose between the citadel and the foundations for a new fortress that Cherniaev had begun to construct. The foundations of a permanent colonial settlement were laid by D. I. Romanovskii, appointed in 1866 as Cherniaev's successor to administer the tsar's newly conquered Central Asian lands. Romanovskii envisioned Tashkent as a regional administrative center of tsarist power. As large numbers of bureaucrats began to arrive, Romanovskii and other officers established a municipal committee to plan the "Russian section" of Tashkent in the summer of 1866.[6] Small buildings along a street plan designed by military architect M. N. Kolesnikov housed new government offices and the residences of leading officers and functionaries.

St. Petersburg and Moscow newspapers praised the initial development of the new district. The newspaper *Golos* reported that by fall 1867 one hundred houses had been built in Russian Tashkent. Russian traders Khludov and Pervushin were importing goods in caravans that comprised up to 16,000 camels.[7] *Russkii Invalid*, the official military newspaper, described two new state buildings, a club, and the house of the military governor, all of which stretched out from the square in the center of Kolesnikov's grid scheme. Several shops and a staff building completed the center of the Russian section, which now held a place as part of the long history of the Silk Road city of Tashkent.[8]

Correspondents and bureaucrats alternated calling the settlement the "Russian section" or the "European quarter." P. I. Pashino, who arrived in 1866 to work as a translator, noted the exotic as well as the European feel of this new enclave in Tashkent. Pashino praised the commemoration of the Ming-Uriuk gardens, the first park in Russian Tashkent.[9] Soldiers ringed the park to prevent any incursions from the local population as Russian officers, administrators, scholars, and traders celebrated. Fireworks hailed the opening of a European refuge.[10] Pashino was struck, however, by the presence of emissaries from Bukhara, at the time still engaged in battle with tsarist troops, at the celebration. Military Governor Romanovskii may have wished to impress upon the embassy Russian permanence and power.[11] Whatever the reason, the Bukharan presence set a precedent of Central Asian attendance at all major ceremonies in imperial Tashkent. Their integration allowed them to enforce their importance in the city and province even as it displayed their subject status.

The first steps in Russian Tashkent's development were not without growing pains. *Golos*, even as it hailed the new city's potential, reported that "the European quarter contains little to remind one of Europe."[12] Rumors of Tashkent as a city of progress and riches fell flat. One soldier seeking "El Dorado" reported on his bitter disappointment, as the threat of tropical diseases and scorpion bites far outweighed the minor benefits

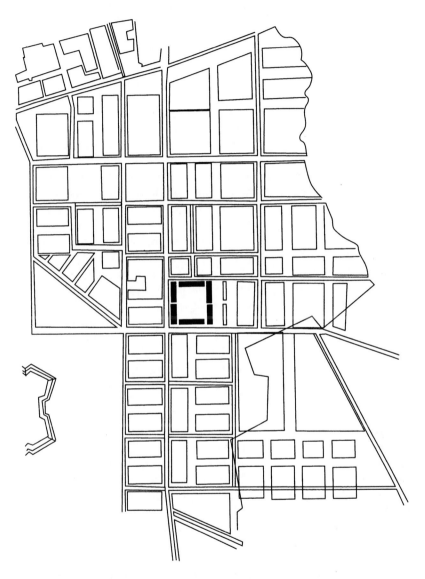

Figure 3. Urban plan of M. N. Kolesnikov, 1866.
Graphic Services, Carleton University.

of delicious fruits.[13] M. A. Terent'ev, a tsarist officer, wrote that houses were constructed in a haphazard, nonsensical pattern. Residents used clay directly from the ground as building material, leading to large, and dangerous, holes in the middle of the roads.[14] Artist V. V. Vereshchagin described early "European" Tashkent as "extremely dirty and dreary, in no way suitable for a European population."[15]

Malaise and fear enveloped the small Russian society of Tashkent in the winter of 1866–67, according to a letter from a resident that appeared in *Moskovskiia Viedomosti*. The writer decried the imperial government's and the public's focus on the economics of expansion and the needs of the Central Asian population, which had caused them to neglect the sorry state of Russians in the region. The departure of tsarist officers and, particularly, Military Governor Romanovskii at the end of the 1866 campaign season had decimated Russian Tashkent's population and had a profound psychological effect: "The meaning of the military governor for Tashkent society is enormous, and depends not on the person, but the situation of those living at such a distance from Russian activities."[16] Local society had grown apathetic. At parties, as four musicians replayed the one song they knew, most attendees played cards, as the departure of officers' wives left very few dance partners. Given the malaise and lack of military leadership, rumors of a joint attack on Russian settlements by the emir of Bukhara and the khan of Khiva proliferated. Stories of the Indian Mutiny of 1857 against British rule reverberated through the Russian community. Only a permanent military and administrative presence and leader could stabilize the Russian presence.

This was the uneven state of Russian Tashkent as K. P. fon Kaufman rode into the central square of the city on November 7, 1867. For the next fourteen years, the first governor-general labored alongside the Russian population to construct a permanent capital city that would symbolize tsarist power and European "civilization" in the region. The years following Kaufman's arrival also marked the development of new cultural traditions that reflected and influenced an evolving colonial society. The first tradition surrounded the arrival itself. Greeting ceremonies applied to the governor-general echoed those given for centuries to the tsars as they traveled through their domains.[17] The style of the ceremony, however, marked the uniqueness of Russian Tashkent. Virtually the entire Russian population, as well as significant numbers of Central Asians, participated, seeking inclusion as well as influence in this new imperial settlement.

Never again would the coming of the tsar's permanent representative to Central Asia be treated in such a haphazard manner as it was on November 7, 1867. Over the 1870s, municipal officials and other representa-

tives of local society devised an elaborate script to greet or bid farewell
to Kaufman and his successors on their frequent trips to central Russia.
Russian Tashkent's first city commandant, E. A. Rossitskii, recruited sappers or prisoners to ensure that incoming roads were in excellent condition and Russian Tashkent pristine for the governor-general's arrival.[18]
Russian merchants maneuvered to ensure a privileged meeting with the
governor-general on the occasions of his arrival. Powerful businessmen
E. V. Kozhevnikov, A. I. Antonov, and Pervushin dispatched emissaries
to greet Kaufman at the village of Chimkent, fifty kilometers away.[19]
These envoys thanked the governor-general for his patronage toward
mercantile interests and requested his presence at the nearby village of
Ak Jar to receive the customary bread and salt from the business community. Kaufman responded by granting an audience to those present.

Other constituents of Russian Tashkent also sought to shape the ceremony. Military administrator V. I. Poltoratskii, a self-proclaimed leading
member of Tashkent society, collected donations to ensure an elaborate
greeting for Kaufman in 1872.[20] He spent weeks planning a ceremony
at an elegant garden on the edge of Tashkent. Eighteen columns gar-
landed with grapevines and flowers decorated the path to the greeting
pavilion, whose walls were draped with murals honoring the feats of
the governor-general. At the pavilion Kaufman received bread and salt
from a leading member of Tashkent society. The military governor, key
officers and bureaucrats, and "first-level" merchants competed for this
honor and Kaufman's ear.[21]

Joining this ceremony were selected Central Asian notables. Representatives from Asian Tashkent sat alongside those of the khan of
Khiva and the emir of Bukhara. The Office of the Governor-General had
undertaken extensive efforts to arrange elections in the Asian city that
produced a municipal board of aksakals to participate in city governance
in 1868. Violent opposition accompanied this process; Kaufman, admit-
ting significant difficulties, nonetheless considered the overall project a
"success."[22] These notables, whose role will be discussed in greater detail
in chapter 3, collected taxes and ostensibly assured peace and stability
in Asian Tashkent.[23] Municipal board leader Sharafii bai Zeinalgabidin
pronounced words of loyalty to the governor-general and the tsar, and
heard Kaufman emphasize his own thankfulness to these local mediators.

After a sumptuous meal, the governor-general mounted his horse
and gathered his Cossack honor guard. The presence of the Cossacks,
the mythically ferocious guardians of the Russian frontier, underlined
the military theme of the next stage of the ceremony. Kaufman followed
a designated route lit with torches and lined with columns of troops

toward the center of Russian Tashkent. According to the official news-paper of the Turkestan province, *Turkestanskiia Viedomosti*, the troops greeted him "with unqualified delight." Cannon shots rang out as the governor-general passed under an arch erected over the Chaul stream. Well-wishers overflowed the streets and shouted hurrahs before the leader offered a prayer of thanks for his safe return and received the blessing of the clergy at the small Iosif-Georgevskii church. Proceeding to his residence, Kaufman offered a "royal thank you" (*tsarskoe spasibo*) to the intermediate civil and military functionaries awaiting him. In the evening, the streets were illuminated and fireworks set off as the city celebrated.

Why did Tashkent Russians invest the arrival of the governor-general with such significance? On the most basic level, the pomp of the ceremony reflected the arduousness of the journey itself. The hardships encountered, and their retelling to friends, families, and colleagues in Tashkent and the metropole, made the trek a foundational event in lo-cal life. The common experience unified Russians from different social and regional backgrounds. It also offered them a sense of uniqueness and self-importance, as pioneers working to foster a new civilization in distant Asian lands.

The route to Tashkent from European Russia passed through two thousand kilometers of harsh steppe and desert territory and lasted anywhere from one to four months. Between the city of Orsk and the Aral Sea, the condition of the road was atrocious: sandy and dusty in the summer, muddy in the spring and fall, and almost invisible under the winter snows. The steppe became increasingly desolate; corrosive, salty soil stung the eyes and inhibited breathing.[24] Travelers then entered the Karakum desert. Kazakh guides directed the traveler to wells and around sand dunes, but carriages frequently stuck in deep deposits of sand, requiring hours of work to be dug out. Camels proved far more reliable than horses at traversing the desert sands, but their slow gait and surly behavior infuriated many travelers.[25] Postal stations, the only form of shelter, were no more than small, dirty huts or tents maintained by local Cossacks or Kazakhs, who often lived elsewhere on the steppe, and remained abandoned for days. Stationmasters, when present, frequently robbed travelers.[26] Dehydration and diarrhea struck frequently. Menno-nites traveling in a caravan to Tashkent in 1880 lost eleven children to disease, in their words, in "the burning hell" of the Karakum.[27]

Russian artist V. V. Vereshchagin claimed that the hazards of travel and the nights spent in "small, stifling, and incredibly dirty huts" forced him and his colleagues to become "new Prometheuses."[28] The compari-son with the Greek god, who sought to bring civilization to the unen-lightened, revealed one meaning of the journey. Many Russians saw the

Figure 4. Greeting of Governor-General S. M. Dukhovskoi, 1898.
Tsentral'nyi Gosudarstvennyi arkhiv kinofotofonodokumentov Uzbekistana.

journey as part of their "civilizing mission," to bring European power and progress to distant Asian lands. An 1866 article in *Golos* stated: "now our fate is clear: Russia has been deemed the Enlightener of Asia."[29] The governor-general embodied the Promethean spirit, as the tsar's representative of "civilization" before the Asian masses.

The passage of the governor-general under the arch into the safety of Russian Tashkent signified the relief Russians felt upon surviving the voyage. Even in its embryonic form, Russian Tashkent appeared to travelers as "heaven on earth."[30] The first novel about Russian Tashkent, by N. N. Karazin, begins by portraying frightened settlers confronting strange animal cries, robbers, and the corpses of less fortunate travelers on their way to the city.[31] *Turkestanskiia Viedomosti* emphasized the rewards that awaited those brave enough to undertake the journey. An 1876 article stated: "we are distanced from Russia . . . by two thousand kilometers of steppe road, and what a road! All who arrive complain . . . but those who persevere see what a fertile, rich region is our Turkestan, where summer has definitively arrived by mid-March, and winter starts no earlier than the end of December and sometimes arrives not at all."[32] Tashkent residents also saw the journey as a rite of passage, asking new arrivals, "How did you enjoy the trip?" and then comparing stories of particular hardships.[33]

The arrival ceremony privileged the governor-general as a symbol of political power, social unity, and colonial uniqueness. Other contemporaries echoed the feelings of Eugene Schuyler, an American diplomat who toured Turkestan in the 1870s, that "[s]hould the governor-general be seen shaking a person warmly by the hand or conversing with him for five or ten minutes, the man so honored immediately becomes a figure in society, and is considered necessarily a rising man and one of great influence."[34] From tsarist bureaucrats and Central Asian notables seeking advancement to traders seeking military contracts, members of colonial society looked to enforce their own interests through association with the leading figure in imperial Tashkent.

Ever-widening circles in Russian Tashkent sought contact with Kaufman to signal their own importance in local society. A newly established city assembly (*duma*) chose the arrival ceremony to petition the governor-general for funds in 1879. The duma's leader, with the opportunity to address Kaufman, stated: "Your excellency, Konstantin Petrovich! Tashkent society, moved by feelings of deep gratitude toward your efforts at developing and strengthening the beginnings of a civilian life (*grazhdanstvennosti*), unanimously ask you to allow in its name . . . [the hiring of] a new teacher of higher education." Municipal authorities awaited the permission of the governor-general, who frequently meddled in city finances, to release 8,200 rubles for the dispatch of a doctor to Tashkent.[35] References to "society" and "civilian life," concepts that will be explored in the next chapter, were used to assert interests and rights by a constituency that sought to broaden the base of power and culture beyond the governor-general.

Kaufman himself, as his choice of route in 1867 made clear, privileged the military aspects of parades and public ceremonies. Never traveling without his honor guard, he fashioned himself a protector of a Russian outpost and a conqueror of surrounding lands.[36] Kaufman retained this role in Tashkent even after tsarist military victories in 1868 and 1873 reduced Bukhara and Khiva, respectively, to semi-independent principalities. Rumors of a "holy war" proliferated in Russian Tashkent, prompting Kaufman on more than one occasion to return to the city in the middle of other campaigns.[37] Anxieties concerning "holy wars" launched by "fanatical Muslims" coursed across the imperial world in the late nineteenth century. European populations feared the savagery of a subject population that they themselves had demonized. Dane Kennedy has argued that European settlers in Africa "were acutely aware of the frailty of their position, and this awareness manifested itself in several particularly vivid forms."[38] Ceremonies that celebrated military prowess assuaged fears of uprisings against imperial power and bound the community under the supervision of its leader.

Throughout his rule, Kaufman worked simultaneously to control and cajole Central Asian notables. Before a welcome following a victory over the emir of Bukhara in May 1868, Kaufman instructed his subordinates to transmit special greetings to leading local elites in Tashkent who had congratulated him for his success. He wrote: "I was very happy to receive evidence that they understand and value the good deeds of the merciful Emperor and the good that the White Tsar brings them. Transmit this in my name, that his Greatness wishes good to all Muslims equal to his other residents."[39] In 1873, Asian Tashkent leaders joined a welcome meal hosted by top tsarist administrators before a large parade, complete with fireworks, to celebrate victory over the khan of Khiva.[40] Central Asian administrators' motives in saluting the governor-general can only be extrapolated; yet their apparent loyalty brought them increased standing with the new imperial leader, something that could be used to their advantage both in relations with Russian administrators and in conflicts within their own community. Celebrating tsarist victories over "fellow" Central Asians, therefore, was not as contradictory as it seemed.

As the arrival ceremony gained a regular character, municipal officials sought to control and to classify participants and the audience. The city commandant assigned separate sites to particular constituencies, and ordered the police chief to ensure these boundaries remained unbreachable.[41] Russian merchants, artisans, and townspeople (*meshchane*), as well as Tatars, and, finally, residents of Asian Tashkent were assigned particular spaces to greet the governor-general as he rode from the outskirts of the city to his house. Local officials used the parade to present a tableau of a well-ordered, peaceful colonial society. Such organization deeply impressed Kaufman's successors. New governor-general N. O. fon Rozenbakh wrote that the scale of the welcome added to his initial favorable impression of the city in 1884.[42] Varvara Dukhovskaia, the wife of Governor-General S. M. Dukhovskoi (1898–1901) remarked that the presence of such a wide cross-section of the local population, particularly the large Central Asian contingent in their "colorful costumes," put the whole family "in excellent spirits." Only an indiscreet word from the police chief on ethnic unrest in the provinces spoiled the effect.[43] The arrival ceremony presented a community in apparent concert, ready to express their loyalty to the governor-general.

Newly arrived governors-general quickly discovered that the arrival ceremony also consisted of appeals from the Russian community.

Russian intellectuals who, for reasons discussed in the next chapter, feuded with the first governor-general's successor, M. G. Cherniaev (1881–84), welcomed Rozenbakh with speeches stressing the need of the new leader to follow Kaufman as a patron of cultural institutions in Russian Tashkent. The city commandant and other leading administrators joined these intellectuals in leading Rozenbakh to Konstantin Petrovich's grave, where the new governor-general, a Lutheran, delighted the crowd by bowing and making the sign of the cross.[44] A tour of the schools opened by Kaufman followed. In 1890, City Commandant S. R. Putintsev employed Governor-General A. B. Vrevskii's inaugural ceremony to emphasize the need for further economic development. Administrators and merchants presented Vrevskii with "useful products of Turkestan": grapes, rice, cotton, and a silkworm.[45] In addition, Vrevskii received gifts from Central Asian artisans, including a silver saltshaker.

*Turkestanskiia Viedomosti* underlined the mass and public character of the ceremonies in the first decades of Russian Tashkent. Its editor, N. A. Maev, took the rare step of personally authoring the reports on the arrival ceremonies. His vivid and extensive descriptions sought to demonstrate the ceremony's impact on both the governor-general and local society. According to Maev, during the arrival ceremony, Kaufman's words of greeting "fell deeply into the soul of each of the trusted sons of the fatherland."[46] By 1890, Maev celebrated the "general, already established celebratory tradition, the meeting of the main leader of the province by Tashkent."[47] The welcome of the governor-general had come a long way since the confused, improvised greeting of Kaufman in 1867.

## Constructing an Imperial City

Governor-General Kaufman expended extensive energy in shaping the urban space of Russian Tashkent. He directed the construction of a modern imperial capital from, in his words, the "temporary, disorderly, miserly" collection of mud huts that he discovered upon his arrival.[48] Kaufman envisaged the city as the embodiment of a "new civilization."[49] He believed European and Russian culture and urbanism would transform Turkestan into a productive and progressive tsarist province, showing the success of Russian empire building to the imperial world.

A true servant of empire, Konstantin Petrovich fon Kaufman came to Tashkent with a background and experience that traveled Europe, Russia, and Asia. His roots traced back to the German region of Schwabia.[50] Konstantin Petrovich's forebears entered the tsarist military as officers and served in Poland in the late eighteenth century. His father adopted the Orthodox faith and settled in St. Petersburg, where he sent his son to the elite military Main Engineering College. Kaufman's first major posting was in the Caucasus, where he engaged in numerous suppressions of tribal and village uprisings over his service from 1843 to 1856. His work earned him a substantial promotion to the director of the Office of the Minister of War in St. Petersburg before he was again called to serve Russia's imperial mission. In 1865, the tsar appointed Kaufman as governor-general of Vilna, a predominantly Polish and Lithuanian province of the empire. His tour there lasted only one year, and Kaufman carried bitter memories of his service, according to colleagues.[51] His efforts to quell the local population's hostility following efforts at Russification had largely failed. Kaufman blamed his failure on Roman Catholic priests, whose doctrinaire attitude prevented them from compromising with imperial authorities. He was said to question whether Poles, as long as they were under the influence of an alien religion, would ever become reconciled to Russian rule.[52]

A. I. Maksheev, a fellow officer and colleague, claimed that Kaufman set out to Turkestan to eradicate Islam. Maksheev asserted that he persuaded the new governor-general that such an attempt was not only folly, but improper, as Catherine the Great herself had supported the religion, even endowing money to a mosque in Bukhara.[53] Due perhaps to this conversation, his own realization of the dangers of forced Russification in Poland, or the activism of Tashkent's Muslim clergy, Kaufman treated Islam with relative delicacy. In the end, he pledged to recognize Islamic law, the *sharia*.[54] Kaufman termed his policy toward Islam one of "disinterest" (*ignorirovanie*), as he claimed not to interfere in the daily functioning of religious schooling or the Islamic legal system. The governor-general, however, worked to reduce the political role of the clergy, abolishing the position of the chief Muslim judge (qazi-kalan) in Tashkent and the spiritual police of the city.[55] He tried on several occasions to introduce Russian teachers into Muslim schools, in what he considered a benign attempt to display the power of European education, but retreated before clerical opposition.[56] In the end, Kaufman decided a simple display of the objective superiority of a "modern" Russia would lead Central Asians to abandon their culture for that of their conquerors.[57] The development of the Russian section of Tashkent would be his contribution to this endeavor.

Kaufman turned his full attention to creating a capital city that would radiate European civilization and Russian power following his defeat of the main forces of the Bukharan emir in 1868. Returning to his capital following the victory, the governor-general found a troubling landscape. Russian bureaucrats and traders, squeezed out of the small central city, had purchased land on its outskirts from local Central Asians. As Rus-

Figure 5. Governor-General K. P. fon Kaufman.
Tsentral'nyi Gosudarstvennyi arkhiv
kinofotofonodokumentov Uzbekistana.

sian Tashkent's boundaries expanded, Kaufman realized the need to ex-
propriate territory to maintain his desire for a "pure" European city.[58] In
December 1869, the governor-general demanded the expulsion of "Sart
intruders" on the edge of the Russian town. Kaufman overruled the
objections of City Commandant V. Iu. Meditskii, who argued that many
of these inhabitants had written deeds.[59] Russian Tashkent's municipal
committee ordered a ban on buildings constructed in the local "Sart"
style, arguing that the walls of these structures, set directly against the
street, recreated the cramped feelings Russians experienced in Asian
Tashkent. Also discouraged were mud huts built with local clay. The
committee empowered city architect I. A. Lekhanov to demolish such
structures and "to try to introduce Russian styles of construction."[60]

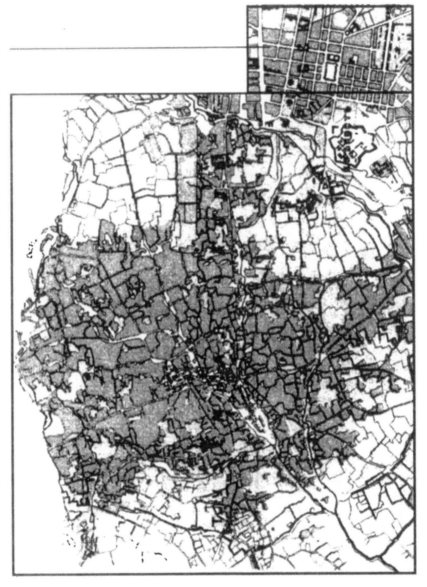

RUSSIAN CITY

ASIAN TASHKENT

Figure 6. Asian Tashkent. Graphic Services, Carleton University.

In March 1870, the governor-general appointed trusted associate F. Ozerov to chair a committee for the administration and construction of the Russian section of Tashkent.[61] The committee's first concern was the role of the Central Asian population in municipal affairs. Ozerov decided to give the locals an inferior status similar to that of Jews in regulations designed for central Russian cities by the Ministry of the Interior. Legal precedent legitimized unequal treatment of the majority population of Tashkent. This status excluded Muslims from the leadership of committees in the Russian city; only Christians could perform this task.[62]

The committee also promoted modern European design models for Russian Tashkent. Ozerov and his colleagues approved the plans of military engineer A. V. Makarov for development of the land to the east of the existing Russian section.[63] Makarov, educated at the Nikolaev Engineering Academy of St. Petersburg, worked to satisfy imperial administrators' desires that their new city become a "little Petersburg."[64] The use of St. Petersburg, the most European of Russian cities, as a model highlighted imperial visions for the new capital. St. Petersburg, according to Richard Wortman, "embodied the idea of regularity, the symmetry, order, and control," which could be transposed against the seeming chaos of Asian Tashkent.[65] Makarov also incorporated trends in western European urban planning, exemplified by the 1850s reconstruction of Paris, which put a premium on symmetry, order, and control against the crowds and chaos of the industrial city.[66] A "little Petersburg," whose style had returned to prominence in Europe, would provide Russians with a sense of superiority and grandeur in the capital of Asian Russia.

Wide boulevards, reminiscent of Nevskii prospect, were the most visible link between Russian Tashkent and St. Petersburg. Their radial-concentric scheme, used most recently in Louis Napoleon III's Paris, also was in evidence in other tsarist frontier cities such as Kherson and Orenburg.[67] Makarov realized the military value of wide radiating boulevards with a point of origination near the Russian fortress, allowing tsarist forces to quickly meet any threats on the city's borders.[68] In Tashkent, these boulevards served another purpose. As the threat of earthquakes prohibited the building of tall structures, Makarov's scheme allowed for close links between state institutions built near the ends of these thoroughfares and central buildings.[69]

Attempts to establish Russian Tashkent as an exclusively European enclave failed. They ignored important roles played by the local population in city life. One of these roles was trade. In 1871, a commission of Russian homeowners near the old Kokandian fortress closed a bazaar run by Central Asian merchants. The commission supported Kaufman's initiative to establish one large trading fair outside the boundaries of

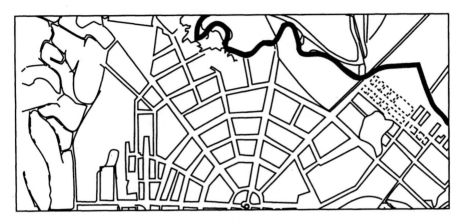

Figure 7. Urban plan of A. V. Makarov, 1870.
Graphic Services, Carleton University.

Russian Tashkent. Despite incentives, including a two-year tax-free period, Central Asian merchants refused to move, and returned to Asian Tashkent.[70] They reemerged in the Russian section as mobile vendors and eventually reestablished their old shops. Some wealthier merchants, as well as Central Asian notables and administrators, began to settle in Russian Tashkent in the early 1870s, without official permission, but apparently without condemnation. Official census data place the number of "Muslims" living in Russian Tashkent in 1875 at 938, or 19 percent of a total population of 4,859.[71]

Other efforts to control and order Russian Tashkent's population met with limited success. Municipal authorities moved soldiers' barracks outside the city center after residents' complaints of "stench" led to the discovery of dirt, garbage, and feces strewn about inside the structures.[72] As Russian Tashkent residents discovered over subsequent years and decades, however, soldiers' behavior within city bounds continued as a disruptive force. City officials, moreover, found themselves powerless to combat the growing number of new settlers, including hundreds of lower-level functionaries, who gathered in the "Samara encampment," a collection of mud huts for those who could not afford to live in the increasingly crowded city center.[73]

Commentators in the early 1870s nonetheless emphasized the dynamism of the new city. Military engineers and architects combined with Russian and Central Asian work *artels* (cooperatives) to realize Makarov's plan. In 1872, N. N. Karazin wrote in the popular St. Petersburg journal *Vsemirnaia Illiustratsiia* that "for six years, a large, completely Russian city has been developing, comparable to many of our governing cities. Long, wide, and straight streets, adorned along their sides by thick poplars, growing not by the day, but by the hour. . . . [A] large, beautiful city is growing literally out of the ground, to the surprise of our new citizens."[74] In 1876, Governor-General Kaufman himself announced the triumphal development of Russian Tashkent in *Turkestanskiia Viedomosti*.[75] Recent construction had eliminated all traces of the once dusty encampment. The wide, straight, tree-lined Vorontsovskii prospect replaced the earthen walls of the Kokandian fortress. The city, already outgrowing its boundaries, would soon stretch east beyond the constructed streets. Ensconced in a rich, fertile province of Turkestan, Tashkent was a city with an unlimited future. (See page 114 for the growth of the city by 1890.)

Amid this dynamic transformation, Kaufman and fellow Russians sought an area of peace and calm. Gardens emerged as vital urban spaces in Russian Tashkent, allowing an escape from the desert environment and heat. Zygmont Bauman has identified the European nineteenth-century garden as a metaphor for the modern, ordered, classified, and useful.[76] Russians followed their counterparts across the colonial world in developing elaborate gardens, creating an aesthetic space that gave a sense of home, or at least one of tranquillity.[77] Russians enjoyed strolls, concerts, and other outdoor activities under the shaded apricot trees of Ming-Uriuk gardens.[78] In the park's inner sanctum, Russian military and administrative elites enjoyed music and fine foods in luxurious surroundings as, according to N. N. Karazin, "ragged" Central Asians and Jews peeked through lattices.[79] N. A. Maev underlined the importance of gardens for Russians in this far-flung environment, as making Russian Tashkent "not Asia, but one of those corners of European Russia, where there still exists sufficient space so that the natural surroundings and buildings do not bump against each other."[80]

Governor-General Kaufman constructed a public garden on his grounds immediately upon his arrival. The garden sought to inspire Russians to create their own green spaces, improving the image of the city and offering a "hygienic aid."[81] Visitors strolled past flowerbeds that bloomed throughout the year, and walked alongside streams that, in places, created the effect of waterfalls. Spectators sat on small hills to view frequent concerts on the theater stage, and saw the governor-general's terrace across a stream, the development of Russian Tashkent at a distance below, and mountains towering above.[82] Children scaled the plentiful fruit trees for cherries and apricots. Kaufman's successors also paid special attention to the garden. Alongside new trails, by 1898 a large fountain placed between the house and garden of the governor-general shot streams of water that showered down to become a swimming pool.[83] A zoo featured animals from European Russia and Central Asia, as bears and tigers occupied neighboring cages. Nature was controlled as part of a modern urban space.

Smaller gardens proliferated in Russian Tashkent. Administrators and officers competed for an annual prize awarded by the governor-general. Residents took advantage of the warm, dry climate and abundant water supply from local streams to plant flowers, plants, and trees. Larger gardens on the city's edge recreated tent-like structures used by the local population to pass away the intense heat of the summer months.[84] Like these gardens, Russian Tashkent itself showed multiple influences from its environment even as its designers sought to project a European face. A scarcity of European building materials and the ability of local homes to stay cool during the summers inspired many Russians to mimic Central Asian architectural styles, using baked clay bricks instead of wood and metal and eschewing windows.[85] Clay-covered willow branches served as roofs. Russian observers noted that these styles not only kept houses cool, but allowed protection against frequent tremors and potentially more serious earthquakes; one of the first attempts to build a two-story structure, by the merchant Khludov, collapsed two months after its completion in 1868.[86]

Official buildings, however, sought to project difference from local styles. Even as the house of the governor-general followed the pattern of low clay dwellings, it was constructed in the Russian "national" style, and resembled a large cottage (*dacha*). By the late 1870s, the importation of fired bricks allowed Russian architects greater range. They favored an eclectic style, then popular in St. Petersburg, which drew from various European architectural trends.[87] The style fit the goal of defining the new city as both Russian and European. Buildings designed by individual architects mixed features that recalled past European empires. V. S. Geintsel'man incorporated baroque and neoclassical styles into the State Bank, constructed in the late 1870s.[88] Geintsel'man's columns evoked the great imperial buildings of Greece and Rome, the antecedents of a modern Europe, also popular models for British architects in colonial India.[89] Geintsel'man's largest project showed an affinity for a different empire. The Spaso-Preobrazhenskii cathedral, erected in the mid-1880s, followed a Byzantine style. The style evoked a specifically Russian imperial past, recalling the myth of Russia as a "Third Rome," after Rome and Byzantium. Significant in the construction was the bell tower, which resembled a minaret so common in Islamic mosques. Ironically, Islamic sites in Asian Tashkent did not include minarets; Geintsel'man appeared to be drawing on a neo-Islamic style also then popular in Europe.[90] The

Figure 8. House of the Governor-General.
Tsentral'nyi Gosudarstvennyi arkhiv
kinofotofonodokumentov Uzbekistana.

cathedral, therefore, represented an odd sort of convergence between
two worlds, adding another dimension to the architectural borrowings
in Russian Tashkent.

Foreign travelers nonetheless imagined Russian Tashkent as part
not of the Asian environment through which they journeyed, but of the
Western world they called home. Eugene Schuyler wrote of the city,

> As I sat on my porch in the bright moonlight, the first night of my ar-
> rival at Tashkent, I could scarcely believe that I was in Central Asia,
> but seemed rather to be in one of the quiet little towns of Central New
> York. The broad, dusty streets, shaded by double rows of trees; the
> sound of rippling water in every direction; the small white houses,
> set a little back from the streets, with trees and a palisade in front; the
> large square, full of turf and flowers, combined to give me this familiar
> impression.[91]

Observers from central Russia echoed this view; the *Russkaia Gazeta* correspondent remarked in 1878 that the city "was taking on an increasingly
European appearance," noting the European-style state control office

Figure 9. State Bank.
Tsentral'nyi Gosudarstvennyi arkhiv
kinofotofonodokumentov Uzbekistana.

and men's gymnasium.[92] French traveler Henri Moser, who visited in 1869 and again in 1883, professed amazement at the changes, calling Russian Tashkent "one of those *tours de force* that only the Russians or Americans know how to execute. It is . . . a pretty and charming little city, with spacious streets, well aligned, lighted in the evenings."[93] A booming cultural life led Moser to pay the ultimate tribute to his hosts, writing that Russian Tashkent reminded him of a "little European capital."[94]

Kaufman's efforts to create a "little European capital" through the implantation of Western culture in fact predated his initial departure from St. Petersburg. Upon his appointment as governor-general, Kaufman sought to compile a repository of Western literature and scholarship for his new capital. He solicited the Imperial Public Library, Imperial Russian Geographic Society, and other organizations in St. Petersburg for duplicate copies of books in their collections.[95] Bernard Cohn has argued that collections of knowledge served a critical role in imperial power, reminding Western populations in the colonies of their own cultural superiority as well as facilitating the classification, and hence the domination, of surrounding peoples and the environment.[96] As donations began

Figure 10. Spaso-Preobrazhenskii Cathedral.
*Aziaskaia Rossiia* (St. Petersburg: Izdanie Pereselencheskogo
Upravlenie, 1914), 1:321.

to arrive in 1868, the governor-general ordered the establishment of a library. Kaufman established a permanent annual subsidy of eight hundred rubles for the institution, and purchased collections of local Russian scholars upon their departure from the region.[97] Later in the decade, a commission of scholars, scientists, and merchants joined Kaufman in planning the collection. By 1880 the library contained 9,734 volumes: 5,018 in Russian and the rest in other European languages. Scientific studies and accounts of adventures and discoveries by Europeans and Russians in the imperial world dominated the collection.[98] These works allowed readers to place themselves in a larger framework of European and Russian imperial endeavors.

To document his community's participation in these endeavors, Kaufman created a record of the Russian experience in Turkestan. Beginning in 1867, the governor-general commissioned the renowned Russian bibliographer V. I. Mezhov to assemble publications on tsarist Central Asia published in Europe, central Russia, and Turkestan.[99] From 1867 to 1888, Mezhov shipped 416 volumes of the *Turkestanskii Sbornik*

(Turkestan Collection) from St. Petersburg to Tashkent. Kaufman kept
in close contact with Mezhov concerning the collection.[100] He sought
scientific and ethnographic studies of the region on the one hand, and
those describing the growth of the Russian population on the other. The
governor-general aimed at two audiences: first, Tashkent Russian educated society, which could measure its renown through reports from the
central press; second, the reading publics of the Russian and European
metropoles, who could witness the progress of the new tsarist regime in
Central Asia. Mezhov distributed comprehensive bibliographies of the
collection throughout Europe. In his statement of purpose, published in
French, Mezhov trumpeted the significance of the Russian conquest and
Russia's newfound status as a great imperial power:

> This collection . . . has a great utility for the residents of a province
> so far away. It is an entire local encyclopedia, containing most of the
> works relative to the history and to different facets of social life, the
> administration, and the economy. This collection is invaluable to the
> province's leaders, all the more so since these people, separated from
> the metropole by impassable steppes must, in many questions of ad-
> ministration, make decisions themselves.
>
> The acquisition of a province such as Turkestan has a great impor-
> tance for Russia. It guarantees our Asian borders against the invasion of
> brigands and has given the conquered country the benefits of European
> civilization. . . . [I]t is hardly surprising that England, vigilant guard-
> ian of its commercial interests, follows with a jealous eye each of our
> steps in the Orient. She sends expeditions and embassies to different
> sovereigns in Central Asia, dreading the invasions of Russia.[101]

The collection emerged as a centerpiece of local intellectual life during
Kaufman's era. Governor-General Rozenbakh halted *Turkestanskii Sbornik* in 1888, citing complaints by local scholars that short, trivial articles in
newspapers were replacing more scientific studies done on Turkestan in
scholarly journals.[102] The wider availability of central scientific journals
appeared to spell the end of the collection; however, in 1907, in an effort
to boost local pride, a committee consisting of librarians and scholars in
Tashkent began once more to gather material.[103] This revival continued
until wartime hardships overwhelmed local society in 1916.

Another of Kaufman's major projects to publicize the progress of
Russian Turkestan was the official weekly newspaper of the Office of the
Governor-General, *Turkestanskiia Viedomosti* (the Turkestan record). For
the first several years of its existence, Kaufman acted as de facto editor,
reading each issue before it went to press.[104] Its inaugural issue on April
28, 1870, eloquently stated the goals the governor-general wished to
pursue for the region, as reflected in the newspaper's mission:

> to allow all to follow the gradual completion of an enormous labor—
> the introduction of civil order, civilization and the full safety of the
> population in a land so long under the yoke of Muslim and Asian des-
> potism. No less important a task for the newspaper is to show also the
> true outlook on the Turkestan province and its importance for Russia.
> . . . Turkestan can be as important for us as India is for Britain, Algeria
> for France.[105]

The first issue sought to establish the pedigree of the Russian community
as a civilizing force. An article titled "Social Life in Tashkent" challenged
recent reports, "falsely spilling from the pens of idle correspondents"
in the central press that Russian Tashkent residents suffered from "high
prices, shortages of all needed goods, fevers, scorpions, earthquakes,
and other horrors." Russians in Tashkent, rather, away from stultifying
national traditions of the metropole, lived "well and free."[106] Tashkent
was a city of the future; lumps of clay transformed, like "mushrooms
after the rain," into new houses. Local and foreign goods existed in
abundance. A new social club contained copies of the best newspapers
and journals from throughout the empire. Russian Tashkent had yet
to define its character, habits, or customs; each citizen could therefore
contribute to a new society.

Kaufman also publicized his province through a large photographic
collection, the *Turkestanskii Al'bom* (Turkestan album). In 1871–72, A. L.
Kun undertook a systematic pictorial study of the region, in imitation of
numerous such collections compiled in British India.[107] Kaufman commissioned six copies of the album, one each for Tsar Alexander II, Tsar-
evitch Alexander Alexandrovich, Grand Prince Vladimir Alexandrovich,
the central branches of the Academy of Sciences, the Imperial Public
Library, and the Russian Geographic Society. The album received great
acclaim. According to the Geographic Society, "it can be maintained
with full confidence that such a photographic collection has never been
collected for any region of Russia."[108] The society praised the detailed
examination of the new peoples of the empire. Decades after its publication, Russian scholars continued to view the album as a monumental
and unequaled task.[109]

*Turkestanskii Al'bom*'s structure counterposed visions of the past,
present, and future of Central Asia. Kun divided his work into four
sections. The first, "archeological," contained photographs of "ancient"
structures in Turkestan, preconquest architecture that focused on the
grand monuments of Samarkand but included mosques and madrasas
in Tashkent. The "historical" section of the collection provided images
of the Russian conquest, particularly photographs of glorious tsarist officers and soldiers. The "ethnographic" section provided posed images

Figure 11. Kukeldash Madrasa, Tashkent. Turkestanskii Al'bom (1872).
Reproduced from Library of Congress.

of various Central Asian peoples and ceremonies. In rigid poses and ceremonial dress, classified by tribe, Central Asians appeared resigned to their new status as subjects, if not curiosities, of the new empire. The ethnographic section showed future promise as well, with photographs of the new Russian cities that would spur these peoples' modernization. Russian Tashkent's state buildings and wide, tree-lined boulevards received pride of place. Potential progress could also be seen in the "industrial" section, which included pictures of cotton, silk, and other industries indigenous to the area. Once modern industry replaced the artisanal Central Asian economy, the region would become a major contributor in the world economy.

The album's design reflected its target audience. The tsar and his family could revel in their new conquest, the peoples and cities on the once great Silk Road, and the glory of tsarist forces. Central scholarly societies could debate the classification of traits and level of cultural and economic development of the new peoples.[110] Kaufman sought to assure the interest and the continuing financing of the imperial enterprise through efforts to display its fruits to political and cultural leaders in St. Petersburg.

Figure 12. Uzbek women: Himet-Ai.
Turkestanskii Al'bom (1872).
Reproduced from Library of Congress.

All of these efforts—the library, the collection, the newspaper, and the album—joined urban planning and architecture to project a powerful, civilized, city, a "little European capital." Kaufman's Russian Tashkent had completed a remarkable development. N. A. Maev noted nonetheless in the St. Petersburg journal *Niva* that while central Russian Tashkent had "a full Russian character" it also carried local, "Turkestani nuances."[111] These nuances created a sense of uniqueness; at the same time, they betrayed a degree of tension between visions of European civilization, Russian society, and Central Asian surroundings. Efforts to impose unity over these tensions, at the same time enforcing specific visions of future imperial society, continued with new ceremonies and rituals that took place on the streets of Tashkent.

Figure 13. House of the military governor. Turkestanskii Al'bom (1872).
Reproduced from Library of Congress.

## Ritual, Identity, and Power

New ceremonies that joined the welcoming of the governor-general played important roles in defining power in an expanding Russian Tashkent, which reached a population of 12,880 in 1890.[112] Intellectual endeavor joined military might as an aspect of imperial authority. Administrators who saw Turkestan as a place to expand cultural and scientific knowledge worked with active and retired military personnel in efforts to shape new rituals. Students, along with women, represented the permanence of the Russian presence. Central Asian notables continued to promote their own goals within these larger spectacles that exuded order and unity. *Turkestanskiia Viedomosti* reported how "all of Tashkent society" participated in ritual parades, endowing residents with a sense of identity. Yet these ceremonies also underlined inequalities inherent in colonial society.

Successful ceremonies honoring Kaufman's conquests inspired ideas of an annual celebration to commemorate the most significant tsarist military victory in the region: the conquest of Tashkent on June 15, 1865. Survivors of the storming first began discussions on honoring the event

Figure 14. Silk production. Unwinding silk on a spool.
Turkestanskii Al'bom (1872). Reproduced from Library of Congress.

in 1872. Hundreds of veterans had chosen to remain in Russian Tashkent, constituting significant numbers of its tailors, shoemakers, carpenters, metalworkers, blacksmiths, and petty traders. Retired military personnel exploited connections within official society.[113] On June 15, 1872, a number of veterans assembled at a common grave on the edge of the Asian city where fallen Russian soldiers were buried. At what was then the garden of a local farmer, they laid the foundation for a monument. Veterans hoped to assert their importance in colonial society.[114]

As a veterans' committee sought official permission to establish a permanent monument, priest A. E. Malov began to hold annual ceremonies at the site. Malov was a participant in Tashkent's storming, renowned for having held the Cross before the enemy in the midst of battle.[115] By 1880, City Commandant Troitskii and other municipal leaders joined the June 15 observance, alongside veterans and significant numbers of spectators. Governor-General Kaufman, despite his fondness for military ceremonies, never attended these services. Kaufman may have been motivated by professional rivalry, hesitant to commemorate an event that focused attention on the general who led the conquest, the "Lion of Tashkent," M. G. Cherniaev. Cherniaev coveted Kaufman's post and remained a constant critic of Turkestan's administration, which he painted as inefficient and corrupt.[116] The governor-general may also have disliked the religious component of the ceremonies. Kaufman had consistently refrained from supporting Orthodox Church activities and had a strained relationship with the head of the Turkestan diocese, Aleksandr.[117] Kaufman preferred the diocese remain the distant city of Vernyi, and did not attend welcoming ceremonies for Aleksandr in Tashkent. Kaufman's views on religion remain elusive. He prohibited missionary work in Turkestan, in accordance with his policy of "disinterest" toward Islam. He feared an Orthodox leader's challenging his authority, even as he asserted the importance of displaying a "Christian civilization" to the local population.[118] During Kaufman's rule, the small, military Iosif-Georgevskii church remained the only Orthodox place of worship in Russian Tashkent, while two mosques served Tatars and local Muslims.

The June 15 ceremony gained momentum in Kaufman's absence and after his death on May 3, 1882. In 1881, acting Governor-General G. A. Kolpakovskii moved services to the Iosif-Georgevskii church and had all the soldiers of the Tashkent garrison array themselves on the opposing central square. Malov, flanked by local clergy, led a public prayer service outside the church, lauding the defenders, past and present, of the empire.[119] The veterans of the stormings of Tashkent then led a parade through the central streets of the Russian city. That evening the whole city was illuminated, and military bands played throughout the night.[120] Cherniaev, appointed Kaufman's successor, revived the dormant committee to erect a monument on the gravesite of the Russian soldiers. Cherniaev was recalled, however, before he could raise the funds to realize the committee's grandiose design, which included a cathedral and burial vault with individual coffins for each of the soldiers.[121]

Governor-General Rozenbakh expanded the scope of the ceremonies. As a Lutheran, Rozenbakh saw the June 15 commemoration as a way to endear himself to Orthodox clergy and other local constituencies.[122] He supported the plans of Tashkent city commandant Putintsev and Syr-Dar'ia military governor N. I. Grodekov for a more modest monument.[123] In 1886, a small chapel was erected over the gravesite, with an iron plaque containing the names of all the victims of the storming, as well as the words "savior" and "crucifixion."[124] The monument's national style emphasized the Russian and Orthodox, rather than European, imperial features of the conquest. The memorial's completion led to a dramatic enlargement of the June 15 observance. A mass procession would now link multiple ceremonies. The 1886 ceremony fixed the protocol that the Russian community observed annually until 1917. The June 15 ceremony presented, for one day, an image of unity supporting the Russian imperial enterprise. The parade's evolution and the roles played by various groups offer important indications of how power was envisioned, constituted, and, within the bounds of a ritual ceremony, contested in colonial society in the later decades of Russian Tashkent.

The 1886 ceremony, commencing at the new monument, was no longer exclusively military in character. Students from local schools in Russian Tashkent faced sixteen squadrons of soldiers in front of the monument. Students had gained an elevated importance under Kaufman's rule. The governor-general had opened primary schools, a gymnasium, a trade school, and a teachers' college in Russian Tashkent.[125] He received weekly reports from school supervisor N. P. Ostroumov on the situation of Russian education in the city.[126] Kaufman regarded education as a symbol of the advantages of "civilization" and students as a sign of permanence for Russian Tashkent. Ostroumov and other intellectuals sought to continue Kaufman's legacy, and securing such a highly visible role for schoolchildren testified to their success.

Russian women, who lit candles surrounding the gravesite, were another distinct group in the ceremony. Women, like students, radiated civilization and permanence. Early Russian administrators in Tashkent had lamented the lack of women in the city. G. P. Fedorov, a leading administrator, wrote of the constant gambling and heavy drinking that proliferated among the male, military society. This changed in 1870, when "many ladies arrived from St. Petersburg. They were very dear, cultured people and instinctively influenced social life for the better."[127] Circles of the dramatic arts, reportedly, replaced drunken card games. Fedorov's musings support the arguments of Penny Edwards that in colonial situations woman was "destined to civilize and police, to inspire and purify, to ennoble and augment all that confronts her."[128] Tashkent writers also mobilized sexual imagery to enforce racial and gender hierarchies. Pashino and Karazin wrote of Russian women's décolleté European fashion, reducing Bukharan emissaries and local traders to senseless blathering.[129] Women represented the attractiveness, perhaps the seductiveness, of European culture. Such formulaic accounts debased Central Asian men, but also objectified Russian women, less important for their actions than for their symbolic worth. Accounts of women's role in the June 15 ceremony emphasized this value, as women bowed to the graves of their male protectors after lighting the candles. Veteran Iu. Iuzhakov wrote in *Turkestanskiia Viedomosti*, "How dear, impressive, and solemn was this act! It produced a thoroughly gratifying impression, it made the soul glad, it fully satisfied a Russian person!"[130]

A long and strictly ordered procession that began at the Russian city center met the welcoming group at the monument. Malov and other clergy led, carrying the church altar cross as well as icons. The

Figure 15. Chapel and grave of Russian soldiers killed in the storming
of Tashkent. *Putevoditel' po Turkestanu i Sredne-Aziatskoi Zheleznoi Dorogi*, ed.
A. I. Dmitriev-Mamonov (St. Petersburg: Tipografiia I. Gol´dberga, 1903), 369.

Holy Synod had granted this ceremony the honored status of an official procession, when sacred objects may be removed from the church.[131] Next came "Christian" members of the city board and duma, as well as tsarist administrators. Representatives of the estate of merchantry (*kupechestvo*) and the estate of townspeople (*meshchanstvo*) followed. Each estate, as across the empire, had official legal status and their own assemblies.[132] After these estates came "city dwellers" (*gorozhane*), likely officially belonging to the peasant estate. This group lacked any official organization, but possessed power by virtue of its ethnicity. At the end of the procession came all Russian soldiers and officers in Tashkent not present at the monument. Their presence displayed military power as literally backing the imperial enterprise.[133]

The procession marched through Russian Tashkent and then crossed the threshold to the Asian city. The two-kilometer-long route through Asian Tashkent to the monument was decorated with flags and, according to observers, lined with spectators. *Turkestanskiia Viedomosti* emphasized the significance of this stage in the parade: "With harmonious songs of holy prayers, the religious procession went forward through the narrow, winding roads of Asian Tashkent. With the development of the procession of June 15, the natives can see how holy and dear the Russian people consider the memory of their brothers fallen in battle."[134] According to N. P. Ostroumov,

> the celebratory procession must have produced a strong impression on the natives. . . . [A]t each intersection of the native city gathered large groups of all ages; women and children watched the parade from the roofs of their houses. Especially for native women it was their one chance to see such a mass of Russian men and women of various ages and social categories. All the natives doubtlessly looked with surprise at such a procession, for which they had no equivalent.[135]

Neither published nor archival sources yielded impressions from these Central Asian observers. One reason for the large crowds was the pressure exerted on the local notables by the Russian authorities. The military governor ordered Central Asian leaders to inform each mahalla head to turn out fifteen to twenty-five people to pay homage to Russian power.[136] Particular instructions informed Central Asian elders of their role in each celebration. Such protocols sought to convince Russian officials, and the public, of their ability to control the Central Asian population.

Veterans of the storming greeted the procession at the monument as a church choir sang "God Save our King in Zion [the tsar]." Malov christened the monument and began prayer services for fallen Russian soldiers:

Christloving Russian soldiers and brothers of Christ! Here is the place where lie many bodies of soldiers, heroically fallen during the stormings of Tashkent, which now flowers under the scepter of our all-powerful monarch; here is the grave of those brave ones, who, unafraid of untold numbers of opponents, remembered one thing: that they were Russian soldiers, that they were blessed.[137]

Governor-General Rozenbakh followed Malov's speech, bowing before the cross and proclaiming that "I am fortunate God has led me to fulfill our debt before our fallen heroes."[138] Religion played an important role in the ceremonies. Orthodoxy was one of the few universal characteristics, if not the only one, associated with a Russian nationality in the mid-nineteenth century, and, as Theodore Weeks has shown, its assertion was particularly important in mixed borderlands.[139] In Tashkent, religion also served as a clear marker between colonizer and colonized. Yet no serious efforts were made to move the Turkestan episcopate to Tashkent, nor did governor-generals after Rozenbakh actively solicit clerical support in administrative matters.[140] June 15 showed the symbolic value of Orthodoxy, but did not result in significant influence for the Church.

Central Asian dignitaries followed the governor-general to the podium. They used the opportunity to underline their own importance in colonial society, as well as to remind tsarist administrators of the terms of their cooperation. Muhiddin Khoja, a leading religious official and city duma member, thanked the Russians for bringing peace, calm, and order to a chaotic land. He emphasized the continued freedoms the local population considered essential: "it has been 21 years since we, Muslims, have been under the protection of the White Tsar and the most powerful state in the world, Russia. . . . From the day of the city's seizure, we have kept freedom of religion, *sharia* courts, full peace and self-rule."[141] *Turkestanskiia Viedomosti*'s publication of these speeches indicated the importance placed on showing the public face and words of local notables. Displays of apparent interethnic harmony, as well as of military force, constituted important elements to reassure the Russian population of its security as well as its superiority.

June 15 remained an honored day in Russian Tashkent, an "invented tradition" that celebrated Russian power and culture and enforced a local identity.[142] Iu. Iuzhakov argued that the procession proved that "in Tashkent beats the Russian heart, and here lives the Russian soul." In 1896, Iuzhakov and others persuaded the municipal administration to make June 15 an official holiday.[143] The ceremony continued to receive prominent coverage in the local press as well as frequent mentions in the metropole as a symbol of Russian imperial might deep in Asia.

Ritual ceremonies continued to evolve in the 1880s. Individuals or constituencies sought to shape the past in order to increase their influence in the present. The body, and the legacy, of Governor-General Kaufman was manipulated for political, cultural, and social ends. Kaufman's mythic status, evident during his reign, continued after he suffered a series of strokes in 1881–82. Announcements of the governor-general's pulse, body temperature, and breath rates appeared in every issue of *Turkestanskiia Viedomosti* before an issue with a black border announced his death on May 11, 1882. The newspaper claimed that Kaufman's name "will never die in Turkestan"; his deeds were too great to be enumerated in a single newspaper issue.[144] Kaufman's body was embalmed, surrounded by plants and flowers, awaiting visits from colleagues and the arrival of his son and wife from central Russia.

Acting Governor-General Kolpakovskii designed a large funeral to signal his own authority, amid fears that Kaufman's death might spark a native uprising or British invasion. On May 17, Kolpakovskii led a procession from the house of the governor-general to central Konstantin square, where Kaufman was to be buried. State employees and soldiers marched behind, on a route decorated with flags and strewn with flowers. *Turkestanskiia Viedomosti* asserted that "without exaggeration, all of Tashkent accompanied the coffin of Kaufman." The burial ceremony itself demonstrated the influence of the intellectuals who surrounded the governor-general. Two scholars delivered the eulogy for the body that was buried in front of the men's gymnasium. N. P. Ostroumov focused on Kaufman's educational efforts. Ethnographer and scientist V. F. Oshanin hailed the governor-general's sponsorship of scientific missions. "This is why," said Oshanin, "the name of this man will . . . always be included in the list of enlighteners."[145] Kaufman's military achievements, meanwhile, went unmentioned. Ostroumov's and Oshanin's speeches, as well as the placement of the body, positioned Kaufman as a patron of intellectual achievement, rather than a simple conqueror.

Governor-General Rozenbakh employed the governor-general's body to cement his status with these intellectuals and the Orthodox community. In 1889, Rozenbakh ordered Kaufman's body reburied in the new Spaso-Preobrazhenskii cathedral.[146] The irony of the new burial site, given the first governor-general's strained relationship with the Orthodox hierarchy, went unmentioned. The 1889 relocation was the grandest ceremonial event in the history of imperial Russian Tashkent. On the eve of the transfer, an honor guard stood watch over Kaufman's corpse. The morning of May 4, 1889, before massive assembled crowds and streets lined by soldiers, Rozenbakh escorted Kaufman's brother and son to the gravesite. A speech from boys' gymnasium teacher A. H.

Ekaterinskii urged "students, parents, and all Christians" to "pay last respects to our honored, dearly loved leader! Let us say from the depths of our soul: 'Farewell to our deeply loved leader, an Orthodox son of the Church and a truly good person!'"[147] A highly structured and massive procession similar in character to the June 15 procession followed the exhumed coffin to the cathedral.[148] At the door, Central Asian dignitaries were forced to leave; the church was a purely Christian space. In the cathedral, speeches saluted the accomplishments of a "biblical, militant, David."[149] Kaufman's colleague, N. V. Dimitrovskii, pledged that "never will the project, so brilliantly started by Konstantin Petrovich, die. Irrepressibly and firmly Turkestan will go forward."[150] A plaque over Kaufman's crypt contained the title by which he would be known to present and future generations: the "Founder of Turkestan" (*ustroitel' Turkestanskogo kraia*). The celestial qualities of the first governor-general endured throughout the tsarist era.[151]

Beside Kaufman's remains in Spaso-Preobrazhenskii cathedral lay those of a Corporal V. V. Obukh, killed in the first, failed storming of Tashkent on October 2, 1864. Kolpakovskii had suggested the transfer of Obukh's remains from the village of Chimkent to the new cathedral.[152] Six years later, Rozenbakh realized the suggestion. Honoring Obukh, killed by successful Central Asian resistance, signaled a desire to demonstrate at once the strength and the vulnerability of a Russian community whose unity needed to extend beyond the realm of ceremony.

Ceremonies, urban design, and cultural initiatives constituted fundamental efforts to express power and define identity in Russian Tashkent. Tsarist officials expended considerable resources to shape the capital city of the tsar's latest conquest. Outside as well as local observers expressed their wonder at how this new urban space, arisen from fields of cotton and clover, could radiate European civilization and Russian power. Ritual ceremonies offered a continued reminder of the structure of this city as well as nurturing a sense of community. Central Asian notables played roles in ceremonies, offering their fealty in exchange for privileged places on the podium. Processions expressed not only unity and order, but also security to a Russian population far removed from the metropole. We lack access to the Central Asian views of these ceremonies, but the fact that many leading indigenous figures took up residence in Russian Tashkent, a phenomenon discussed in greater detail in chapter 5, bore witness to the imperial city and community's allure.

Ceremonies in Russian Tashkent allowed limited contests to structures of power. Central Asian notables used their prominence to deliver a message that imperial power worked in large part because it allowed cultural freedoms for the local population. Russian intellectuals worked to nuance the martial character of the ceremonies, themselves a product of the influence of retired soldiers, to present the imperial mission as one of knowledge as well as military force. In so doing, they sought to elevate their own position within the tsarist administration, and to seek funds for their endeavors. Governor-General Rozenbakh joined these intellectuals in seeking to shape the memory of past events and personages to promote his own legacy. Malov, finally, and other Orthodox Church officials worked to enforce the role of religion in the imperial mission and colonial society.

Public ceremonies and cultural institutions became centerpieces of a new identity that situated Russians as residents of an Asian capital as well as tying them to larger tsarist and imperial worlds. *Turkestanskii Sbornik*, the June 15 conquest, and Kaufman's body, symbols created and recreated by city residents, helped to bestow a unique culture upon Russian Tashkent. "Turkestani nuances" combined European, Russian, and Asian styles of architecture and planning.

Not all city residents, of course, were equally represented in these ceremonies or aspects of urban planning. Russian military parades reminded Central Asian spectators of their subject status. Yet even some of the privileged participants in the June 15 observance, including retired veterans, could not afford to live in the central squares or along the broad boulevards of Kaufman's model city. Church officials faced apparent disregard from leading administrators. The constant need to display military force and create a sense of order and unity in ceremonies and urban space may well have been a product as much of Russian elites' perceived marginality and vulnerability as of power and dominance.

# 2.

## *Educated Society, Identity, and Nationality*

Tashkent Russians reached beyond ceremonies to frame values and roles in colonial society. Leading administrators and intellectuals engaged in a search to define the character and purpose of their endeavors on the frontier, at once part of imperial Europe, tsarist Russia, and colonized Asia. The language and actions of this Russian elite reflected a confidence that they could design a modern, civilized society to serve as a model for imperial Russia and Europe, but also a fear that their distance from the metropole would lead to their neglect by the central state and educated public, dooming the colonial venture in Tashkent.

Russian intellectuals, many of whom served in prominent posts in the tsarist administration, envisioned Tashkent as a city of the future. As Daniel Brower has argued, notable tsarist administrators, whom he labels "cultural enlighteners," saw Turkestan as a laboratory to test new, modern ideas of administration in the wake of the Great Reforms.[1] This chapter will trace the efforts of Russian intellectuals to envision and construct a city and society freed, as they argued, from the stultifying traditions of tsarist state dominance on the one hand, and the violent history of European empire-building on the other. New labels of identity, from Tashkenter to Turkestani, appeared to encapsulate new values associated with this construction of a modern colonial community. Yet local intellectuals found that defining local, national, and imperial identities escaped their control. Officialdom remained divided on the virtues of allowing educated society an independent role outside the bounds of the state. Russians' interactions with Central Asian society challenged the view of a modern, privileged, European colonizer neatly imposing his will and values on the local population and environment. Educated publics in central Russia and the Western world were as likely to portray the building of empire in Tashkent as a sign of continued tsarist and Russian backwardness as they were to see it as a symbol of progress.

The complexities of colonial society and the complicated, shifting relationship between center and periphery undermined stable identities in imperial Tashkent. Pessimism mixed with confidence in the writings of Tashkent Russian intellectuals as they reviewed the recent past and the potential for progress in the decades following the conquest. Characteristics that defined one as a Tashkenter, Turkestani, Russian, and European transformed in the colonial idiom.

## Tashkenters to Turkestanis

Efforts to project Russian Tashkent as a symbol of modern progress went beyond those realized by Governor-General Kaufman. Russian liberals in the city and observers from St. Petersburg imagined a new society and culture that would reflect the dynamism of Alexander II's Great Reforms.[2] Their visions focused on the development of an intellectual society freed from the constraints of the tsarist state.[3] "New Tashkent men" saw themselves as radiating civilization not just to Central Asia, but to central Russia as well.[4] Yet leaders of this quest soon found the meaning of "Tashkenters" appropriated, and sought other labels to define their quest for progress on the periphery.

Who were these men who sought to lead a "civilized" society in Russian Tashkent? The great majority of them served as functionaries. Many, such as *Turkestanskiia Viedomosti* editor N. A. Maev, had begun their careers in active military service and then received a higher education in military or engineering academies. Others were recruited directly from universities. V. F. Oshanin, a naturalist from the physics and mathematical faculty of Moscow University, became the director of a state institute of economic development and the women's gymnasium in Tashkent.[5] The faculty of Eastern languages of St. Petersburg University provided many administrators trained in local languages, ethnography, archaeology, and other intellectual skills.[6] Fresh, young, highly educated Russians served as teachers, doctors, agronomists, economists, zoologists, naturalists, and engineers. N. P. Ostroumov lauded educated Russians who chose to immerse themselves in their work and familiarize themselves with their environment, differentiated from other bureaucrats who saw their service in Turkestan as temporary and worked primarily to enrich themselves or to seek a transfer to a post in European Russia.[7] Those who remained for the long term rose quickly through administrative ranks. They gained a prominent voice in local society through the pages of *Turkestanskiia Viedomosti*, which Maev used as a forum for intellectual discussion, as well as through their attendance at balls, readings, and discussion evenings held by the governor-general and other leading officials.[8]

Russian graduates of civilian and military institutes of higher education, according to Samuel Kassow, were imbued "with new values of public service and liberal education" in the 1860s.[9] Tashkent Russian intellectuals sought to sow these values in their new city. They claimed a role as representatives of a new civil and civilized society, a modern *obshchestvo*. The term, originally applied to the modernizing Western elites who supported Peter the Great's reforms, had evolved to designate elite intellectual society, but retained its progressive sense.[10] By the mid-nineteenth century, the term increasingly became used in opposition to the tsarist autocracy, seen as backward and repressive. Tashkent Russian intellectuals, employed by the regime yet considering themselves public servants, explored the relationship between state and obshchestvo in their creation of what modern observers call a "civil society." In particular, they sought to have an independent obshchestvo, not the state, provide the initiative for social and cultural development, as well as produce policy ideas for adoption by the regime.[11]

Tashkent Russian intellectuals, like their counterparts in the tsarist administration across the empire, traversed unclear boundaries. Harley Balzer, among others, has pointed out the difficulty of separating state and society in late imperial Russia. In so many domains of intellectual activity, the state subsidized professional associations and endeavors. Intellectual societies were therefore as likely to work through the state as against it to seek modernizing reforms. Such a dynamic, according to Balzer, is typical of a "continental pattern" of social development that includes countries such as France and Germany.[12] Russian intellectuals in Tashkent, given the overwhelming presence of the tsarist regime, were acutely aware of potential tensions between the spheres of state and society. The utility of the state, in providing jobs and funds, made them regard it with ambivalence, as a potential progressive as well as regressive force, even as the central regime moved away from modernizing reforms in the 1870s and beyond.[13]

At the same time, intellectuals proved a powerful force in shaping the administration of Turkestan. Governor-General Kaufman promoted those who shared his modernist goals, and allowed them great latitude to develop their own initiatives, including a state museum. Tashkent provided a fresh start for intellectuals exiled from central Russia for clandestine revolutionary activities. P. I. Khomutov, an exile who was a graduate of a medical military academy, rose to the assistant to the director of the Office of the Governor-General.[14] He, along with D. L. Ivanov, another exile who was awarded the responsibility for promoting Turkestan's value in central Russia, headed the most prominent, albeit informal, discussion circle in early Russian Tashkent.

Initial efforts to create a vital public sphere in Russian Tashkent drew the attention of the central press. In the public imagination, Central Asia replaced the Amur, which, as Mark Bassin has shown, had in the early nineteenth century been a site where Russian educated society sought to reform and regenerate the nation.[15] *Russkii Invalid*, the official army newspaper, highlighted a rapidly forming obshchestvo in 1868. An educated public was planning its own projects alongside Governor-General Kaufman's modernizing initiatives. Merchant K. U. Struve's construction of a private meteorological observatory bore witness to an independent intellectual society.[16] *Birzhevyia Viedomosti*, along with other newspapers, lauded the 1869 opening of a public hall as a capstone for an active obshchestvo, which had recently donated one thousand rubles to the building of a library, and up to eleven thousand rubles to build schools.[17] *Russkiia Viedomosti* saw the assembly as a model for the future. Unlike similar institutions in central Russia, this one was not divided by estate, allowing "for common exchanges of thoughts, regardless of differences of sex, status, and rank."[18] An active and egalitarian educated public of "Tashkent men," with "one interested in politics, the other in trade, the next in fine arts" was a force for progress not just on the Asian periphery, but for Russia as a whole.[19]

Other, less flattering portrayals of the periphery also made their way to central Russia. Rumors and newspaper reports of unbridled corruption and venality among Turkestan officers, soldiers, and settlers circulated.[20] These stories caught the ear of M. E. Saltykov-Shchedrin, who was drafting a series of satires simultaneously condemning the tsarist autocracy and the growth of capitalism, both of which he deemed cancers upon the Russian people.[21] Saltykov-Shchedrin decided to use Tashkent to ridicule a state willing to waste precious resources on petty military adventures and a society where greed, an inevitable precursor to exploitative capitalism, predominated. The author changed the setting for his satires from the "City of Idiots" to Tashkent.[22] His article, "What are Tashkenters?" in the October 1869 issue of the journal *Otechest-vennye Zapiski* dismissed the justification for the conquest as Russia's participation in the great European "civilizing mission."[23] Tashkent Russians eschewed science, knowledge, and other hallmarks of European progress, instead educating Central Asians in the practices of extortion, corruption, vice, and greed. One word summed up their attitude:

*zhrat'!*—"gorge [yourselves]!"[24] Saltykov-Shchedrin's repute assured that his imagined characteristics would be forever linked to the label "Tashkenter." Even as the author insisted that one could find "Tashkent gentlemen" [*gospoda tashkenttsy*] throughout Russia, his words caused permanent damage to the city's image.[25]

Eugene Schuyler affirmed many of Saltykov-Shchedrin's critiques.[26] Schuyler described self-absorbed and venal colonizers, isolated from civilization. In Tashkent,

> [s]ociety is . . . divided into cliques and coteries, for though, with the exception of the highest officials, nearly everyone who is there has either come there to avoid his creditors or been sent away to keep out of some scrape, or has come on account of increased pay or the shorter time of service necessary before receiving a pension, or in the hope of making a rapid fortune. . . . People meet, it is true, at the soirees or private theatricals, which are occasionally given at the club, or at the Governor-General's palace, but each coterie keeps apart from the others, and there is nothing like real general social life. These absurd divisions in such a small society, and the fact that Tashkent is looked upon as a temporary place of exile, are very bad for the younger officers and officials. There being few amusements, society being dull and broken up, and their scientific and literary pursuits discouraged or at least not encouraged, the officers have little resource but gambling and drinking, and in many instances young men have utterly ruined themselves, some even having to be sent out of the country—and a man must be bad to be exiled from Tashkent—and others having died or committed suicide. . . . Home is far away, public opinion is lenient or silent, and many allow themselves liberties of conduct which elsewhere they would not have imagined possible.[27]

Schuyler's exposition presented common stereotypes of frontier behavior in the late nineteenth century; his point of comparison with Tashkent was Denver. His writings also betray attempts to critique Russian society as a whole through representations of Tashkent. The American tied common stereotypes of Russia to Tashkent Russians, whose love for potatoes and cabbages outweighed any desire to experiment with new foods, and whose social institutions were backward: "of course there is a club, as stupid and unclublike as all Russian clubs. A bad dinner can be had there everyday."[28]

Schuyler's condemnation of the rampant fraud and maladministration he claimed to have found reignited a central debate over the value and utility of Turkestan. Criticisms of the cost of colonization had appeared in the central Russian press in the late 1860s, putting supporters of the imperial project on the defensive. The liberal newspaper *Golos* defended the conquest of Turkestan against attacks from conservative organs such as *Moskovskiia Viedomosti*.[29] In 1870, *Golos* argued that the officially calculated four-million-ruble deficit in Turkestan was far less than in other areas of the empire, particularly the Far East. The costs of occupation, moreover, should be borne with the realization that spreading European civilization to the Asian East was a "higher calling" for Russia; indeed it was its "very fate."[30] Tashkent Russians needed full central support to fulfill their civilizing mission and bring glory to the empire. Schuyler, in echoing Saltykov-Shchedrin that corruption instead of civilization characterized Russian Tashkent, traced the problem to the highest levels: "it is not only the fact that cases of glaring corruption and venality have occurred, but that these cases, when brought to the Governor-General, have frequently been condoned."[31] His report presented budgetary figures showing that the province of Turkestan was running a seven-million-ruble deficit in 1873.[32] The semiofficial *St. Petersburgskiia Viedomosti* wrote that, even though Schuyler may have been misled by some of Kaufman's enemies, his report deserved the government's full attention.[33] General M. G. Cherniaev, meanwhile, mounted vicious diatribes against Kaufman and the officials who surrounded him in the conservative newspaper *Russkii Mir.* Kaufman's support of widespread corruption, Cherniaev wrote, made a mockery of the civilizing mission.[34] Russian administrators were alienating the indigenous population as well as business interests. Mounting central criticism threatened the scale of the imperial venture.

Saltykov-Shchedrin's and, later, Schuyler's negative images reverberated back to the periphery. Russians hoping to present their new city as a centerpiece of a modern future now saw it portrayed as a symbol of injustice and inequality, characterizing the backwardness of tsarist Russia. "New Tashkent men" had become "Tashkent gentlemen." This shift reflected a growing gloom in central Russia over the fading promise of the Great Reform era and the ability of Russian society to combat autocratic and arbitrary rule.[35] Tashkent Russian intellectuals nonetheless set out to find new labels and characteristics that would identify them as bearers of progress.

N. A. Maev led a renewed charge to develop a positive identity for Russian Tashkent and its population. His mixed background as a soldier, having served in the Crimea during the Russian defeat at the hands of the British, and a scholar, having graduated from the faculty of physics and mathematics in St. Petersburg, emerged clearly in his writings.[36] Maev stressed the complementarity of state power and scientific knowledge in the production of the society Tashkent Russians were seeking to realize. In an article, "Our Situation in Central Asia," published both in St. Petersburg and in Tashkent in 1872, Maev argued that Russians in Turkestan were pursuing a "moral obligation" to develop the untapped wealth of this land effectively and rationally, not for themselves, but for their people, their state, and European civilization.[37] Maev denied that the region would become another frontier where individualism, lawlessness, and corruption dominated. "We are not Americans," he argued.[38] Russians, more measured and careful, would not exploit the land and labor of the local population. Addressing Saltykov-Shchedrin's critique of rapacious capitalism, Maev proposed a model of "administrative guardianship," where state supervision and regulation of private capital would efficiently exploit natural resources.

This model relied upon enlightened administrators who possessed accurate and complete knowledge of the region. Maev admitted that many bureaucrats, military personnel, and traders in Tashkent took little scientific interest in Turkestan. Intellectual society, however, continued to grow. The wide-ranging activities of newly formed scholarly societies in Tashkent demonstrated "our obshchestvo is not asleep."[39] Further intellectual development was critical, lest Central Asians turn their own knowledge of the environment to their benefit and gain the upper hand over the Russian colonizers.[40] If Russians succeeded in their efforts to build a dynamic intellectual society, the rewards could be enormous. Maev argued that Asia's future now belonged to Europe, represented by the "two great powers" of Russia and Great Britain. Ignorance and harshness—the "English race is not distinguished by its gentle and accommodating character," wrote Maev—had prompted the Indian uprising of 1857 and promoted a worldwide questioning of the superiority of European civilization.[41] Turkestan Russians had an opportunity to reverse these errors by deploying knowledge and displaying tolerance, thereby restoring Europe's prominence as well as dominance in Asia.

Tashkent Russian intellectual society had encountered roadblocks in its development, however, underlining limits to a complementary state-society relationship. The Central Asian Scholarly Society began in 1870 as an alternative to the Turkestan Branch of the Imperial Society of Lovers of Natural Sciences, Anthropology, and Ethnography (TOLEAE), which was headed by Governor-General Kaufman and met at his residence. D. L. Ivanov wrote that at meetings of the TOLEAE "[m]any were constrained and deprived of the opportunity to feel at ease, leading several members to detach themselves from this society, considering it an organ of the administration, and to form their own private society."[42] Ivanov gathered other intellectuals, including Maev and those still close to the governor-general, to form a society less directly bound to the state.[43] Lacking private funds, however, Central Asian Scholarly Society members practiced scholarly activities through participation in official civilian and military expeditions.

Society members openly debated the future of Russia in Asia as they discussed statistical, geographical, geological, and ethnographic surveys of the local land and peoples. They criticized official policies, tending to see the state as overly cautious in its efforts to bring progress to Central Asia. An 1870 meeting on surveyor A. V. Kaul'borg's report on the natural geography lands around Lake Issyk-Kul sparked a debate on the potential suitability of these lands for colonization. Society members, seeing potential Russian migrants as civilizers, criticized Kaufman's fears of potential local unrest that led him to limit relocation to Turkestan.[44] In addition to migrants' civilizing influence, members noted that "Russians could gain great trade advantages" by peopling a path, eventually linked by rail, that would join Moscow to Peking and allow reinvention of the Silk Road.[45]

Society members planned to promote their projects to the Russian educated public through publication of their reports in St. Petersburg.[46] Kaufman met these increasingly assertive activities with hostility, however. He used his power not only to deny funding for expeditions or other activities that would promote society efforts, but also to refuse the society an official statute and, in extreme cases, to transfer members outside Tashkent or banish them from Turkestan.[47] Society president A. L. Tatarinov, a military engineer who worked in the Office of the Governor-General, noted that state opposition starved the society of funds, rendering publications impossible and calling its viability into question.[48] Not wishing to challenge his employer further, Tatarinov disbanded the society in 1873.

The overwhelming presence of the imperial state in Turkestan posed difficulties for intellectuals, such as like Tatarinov and Ivanov, seeking an autonomous and influential role for societal actors and organizations. No immediate replacement emerged for the Central Asian Scholarly Society. Many functionaries with higher education schemed to return to central Russia, even as conservatives gained momentum in the tsarist administration in the 1870s and executed the wishes of the reactionary Tsar Alexander III in the 1880s. Leaders of educated society in Russian Tashkent nonetheless continued to press for a greater vanguard role outside the confines of imperial dictate. Striking a balance between state and society emerged as a critical element in Russian intellectuals' quest to display progress through a new label of identity, a "Turkestani."

"Turkestanis" first entered written discourse as those who conquered or supported the conquest of Central Asia. An anniversary of a military victory over Turkmen tribes on July 15, 1870, was a "memorable day for all Turkestanis," according to *Turkestanskiia Viedomosti*.[49] In early years, representations of Turkestanis delineated complementary tasks of conquest and civilization. A gendered element emerged in these tasks through portrayals of the first governor-general and his wife. As Kaufman led his troops to battle, Iulia Mavrikievna fon Kaufmana headed the principal public organization in Russian Tashkent, the Turkestan Charitable Society. One local author presented I. M. Kaufmana's efforts at building civilization as reminding "Turkestanis" of the cultural work enabled by conquest.[50] Women, in elite society as in official ceremonies, continued to serve as markers of European culture in Russian Tashkent. Central and local newspaper correspondents praised their efforts to uphold European civilization through the wearing of the latest fashions from St. Petersburg to Paris.[51]

Russian intellectuals, though not questioning gender hierarchies, sought to overturn a gendered hierarchy that feminized culture and society and privileged the state and military conquest as the domain of the masculine "Turkestani."[52] In 1876, N. A. Maev sought to revitalize societal life and stress its masculinity through the promotion of a new unofficial organization, the Turkestan Hunting Society. Maev recognized hunting's overwhelming popularity among leading officers, part of a European-wide trend in an era when, Harriet Ritvo has argued, "the hunter emerged as both the ideal and definitive type of empire-builder."[53] Hunting allowed European elites in the colonies to practice skills of conquest without harming locals in battle or local women in sexual assaults; it also permitted them, according to John MacKenzie, not to fall prey to "effeminate pleasures" of culture.[54] Hunters in Turkestan pursued tigers and wild boars in the marshes, snow leopards and red deer in the mountains. For military men, Maev wrote, "hunting must be especially stimulating, as nowhere else can be exercised one's love for weapons, measurement with the naked eye . . . , the art of shooting, the ability to overcome all types of obstacles put forth by nature."[55] Maev urged these hunters to use expeditions for more than just shooting. Officers could "advance science, enabling a zoological study of the region." Such endeavors would replace knowledge lost with the demise of the Central Asian Scholarly Society and boost the "weak embryo of civil life" in Tashkent.[56] Displays of Turkestan's exotic fauna across Russia and Europe would tie Russian Tashkent to a succession of strong international organizations capable of uplifting local associational life and the status of the region across the continent. Maev's efforts failed, however. Governor-General Kaufman continued to discourage independent associations, even as he devolved decision-making power in Tashkent.

In 1877, Governor-General Kaufman created a city duma to bring

Tashkent in line with other major urban areas of the empire following municipal acts of the Great Reforms. Kaufman nonetheless imposed many levers to control the body. He appointed the duma's leader, the city head, and reserved the right to refuse duma selections to its six-person executive board. As elsewhere in Russia, a limited and unequal franchise chose representatives. Three tiers of electors were established, based on taxes paid to the state. Finally, in Tashkent, as in other imperial cities such as Kazan, duma membership was divided by race, or more specifically, religion: of seventy-two members, only twenty-four could be "non-Christians." In the first duma, military officers and state administrators predominated, occupying twenty-four of the forty-eight seats allocated to "Christians"; merchants, the next largest group, occupied sixteen seats.[57]

Kaufman meddled constantly in duma affairs, raiding the local budget to fund his own projects. Transcripts of duma meetings in *Turkestanskiia Viedomosti* included frequent calls to the governor-general for funding. The requests highlighted by the newspaper reveal a gendered treatment of the duma, reported to ask for funds for women's schools or a female doctor.[58] At the same time, duma members exercised a measure of power in the city. The duma collected municipal taxes, as well as decided issues of maintenance and property ownership. Duma responsibilities ranged from upkeep of streets and canals to the building of medical clinics and schools.[59]

The status and power of the duma, as well as of the intellectuals who had gained prominent speaking positions at the first governor-general's funeral, rose during the tenure of Kaufman's successor, General Cherniaev. Cherniaev, who had gained the position through connections to conservative allies who ascended to power alongside Tsar Alexander III, arrived determined to reverse trends associated with his predecessor and the Great Reform era.[60] Cherniaev's first target was the city library. A report he commissioned in 1882 defamed the institution, patrons, and employees. V. V. Krestovskii wrote that the small number of subscribers, insufficient to justify the library's existence, read disreputable periodicals, while works on science and exploration remained untouched. Readers preferred the subversive literature of Dobroliubov, Pisarev, Nekrasov, Schiller, and, ironically, Saltykov-Shchedrin, to more worthy Russian works of Turgenev, Dostoevsky, Goncharov, Tolstoi, Ostrovskii, Pushkin, Gogol, and Lermontov. The library head was rumored to distribute censored literature. The reading room had become a place for romantic liaisons.[61] The library defied state laws and hardly supported its reputation as a backbone of European civilization. On the basis of the report, Governor-General Cherniaev ordered the closing of the library "as an independent institution" on January 1, 1883.[62]

City duma members and local intellectuals campaigned to save the library, even as Cherniaev ordered much of the collection sold off at local bazaars.[63] The duma argued that the 1870 reform bill placed libraries under municipal government supervision. The library was the "property not simply of the state, but of society [*obshchestvo*] . . . [which had] the obligation to found and maintain such institutions."[64] Public pressure forced Cherniaev to reopen the library.[65] Duma members also forced the restoration of the collection to the original building in the heart of the city, rather than a decaying structure on the outskirts. Alienation of the governor-general from key intellectuals in the administration facilitated his 1884 removal by the minister of war, ostensibly for aggressive military maneuvers near British-held territory in Afghanistan.

Associational life blossomed in Tashkent in the 1880s and 1890s, as Maev, Ostroumov, Oshanin, and Khomutov formed their own reading circles to integrate a new generation of administrators arriving from across Russia. Civilian and military engineers, including architect V. S. Geintsel'man, opened the Turkestan Technical Society in 1887. Concentrated in state service, associating at work as well as in organizational life, these members of a reinvigorated educated society became a tightly knit group, according to B. V. Lunin.[66] I. I. Popov, an agricultural engineer who traveled throughout Asian Russia while in exile, reported at the beginning of the 1890s that the slowness in gaining St. Petersburg's approval for the many new associations forming in Russian Tashkent had become the greatest frustration for educated society.[67] Author and traveler Evgenii Markov noted the ascendancy of the "knowledgeable, active, and ordered" intellectuals he encountered in the 1890s.[68] Governors-general, who served relatively short terms following Cherniaev's removal, patronized these societies in order to gain the confidence of senior administrators such as G. P. Fedorov, who remained in Turkestan from 1870 to 1906.[69] The emir of Bukhara also donated funds to various societies.

Most prestigious among these new organizations was the Turkestan Branch of the Imperial Russian Geographic Society (TOIRGO), formed in 1896. TOIRGO functioned on a rich budget including substantial private donations. Its ranks included leading intellectuals, businessmen, military officers, colonial officials, and state inspectors, as well as church members.[70] N. G. Mallitskii, who began his career in Turkestan as a history and geography teacher at the Tashkent gymnasium, used TOIRGO as a ladder to climb among Russian Tashkent's elites, eventually assuming the position of city head and editor of *Turkestanskiia Viedomosti.* Mallitskii proudly displayed the new society's influence, in one case writing to the military governor of the neighboring Semirechie province to the east that due to the "ever wider and more useful activities of TOIRGO, you cannot . . . refuse to invite the appearance of this [geographical survey] team [led by Tashkent gymnasium teacher Pavel Diakov] to your region."[71]

Mallitskii's letter to a military governor confirmed a shift in power away from the purely military realm of empire toward the privileging of intellectuals' endeavors. The evolving application of the positive identifier "Turkestani" in the pages of *Turkestanskiia Viedomosti* offered further evidence of this shift. By the 1890s, Turkestanis represented those who chose to settle in the region permanently and foster a prosperous community. Turkestani officials served the public good, helping the poor, seeking to improve standards of living, and promoting a healthy population. N. P. Ostroumov opposed them to the "Tashkenters," now designated as corrupt bureaucrats seeking to enrich themselves even as they sought a quick return to central Russia.[72] Soldiers, meanwhile, gained a new label: an "elder Turkestani" (*staryi Turkestanets*).[73] Military glory was now part of an honored past.

Central Asians did not ascend to the status of a Turkestani during this era. Select notables, parallel to their participation in official ceremonies, also attended meetings of important scholarly societies, sometimes appearing with translators.[74] But, while their names appeared among prominent donors, the leadership of these organizations remained exclusively Russian throughout the imperial period.

By 1894, a newly established private newspaper in Tashkent, *Okraina*, claimed that the burgeoning, influential Tashkent obshchestvo "commonly encountered compliments" in St. Petersburg and "for its liveliness in intellectual interests surpasses almost all cities in European Russia."[75] Intellectual endeavor, symbolizing the new "Turkestani," had emerged as a powerful, positive attribute to a civilized Russian Tashkent. Yet the predominance in these organizations of state officials in these new associational groups—the governor-general was the honorary head of TOIRGO—continued the ambiguous, intertwined relationship between state and society.

## Europeans and Russians

Tashkent Russian intellectuals, as they molded local identities, cast their eyes outward. Russian writers considered themselves participants in a wider nineteenth-century European imperial mission. Their most common point of reference remained British India. Expansion into Central Asia had come dripping with implications for the "Great Game," the contest for influence in the khanates that lay between the ever-shifting Russian frontier and the British Raj. In this game, N. A. Maev and others asserted imperial Tashkent and Turkestan's potential to exhibit not only tsarist might, but Russians' inherent superiority as civilizers. Yet as they trumpeted Russia's potential as a mediator between East and West, members of Russian educated society in Tashkent firmly maintained their identity as Europeans. Increased contact with Central Asians engendered fears of a hybridity that would destroy the boundaries between colonizer and colonized. A coherent national identity, however, was destabilized by poor Russians, whose dirtiness and drunkenness hardly identified them as civilized Europeans.

References to Great Britain and British India permeated the pages of *Turkestanskiia Viedomosti*. The newspaper lauded "Turkestanis" for frustrating repeated British spy missions. Most frequent, however, were articles that compared imperial ventures. The newspaper reprinted articles from the British press that lauded Russia's role, parallel to their own, in bringing civilization to Asia. One from the *Daily Telegraph* ran, "Russians have brought order to where there once was only capriciousness and despotism."[76] Other reprints, printed in a column entitled "News from British India," focused on reports of conflict and local resistance under the Raj.[77] Tashkent Russian administrative and intellectual elites closely followed debates in Great Britain on their potential threat to British India.[78] Efforts to draw favorable comparisons continued throughout the imperial period. In 1897, *Turkestanskiia Viedomosti* began a column "As Others See Us" [the title printed in English]. The periodical jousted with its counterpart in British India, the *Simla News*, over the attitudes of European officials toward the colonized population. Reprints from the *Simla News* critiquing *Turkestanskiia Viedomosti* were published in the latter's pages as a prize of recognition.[79]

Russian writers, meanwhile, expounded on their own unique role as European civilizers in Asia. One author in *Turkestanskiia Viedomosti* noted that, as a people on the borders between Europe and Asia, Russians lacked the "national prejudices" of other Western powers, and sought only peace and harmony between the two continents. In "pointing out the links between all countries," Russians could streamline the entire colonial endeavor.[80] N. P. Ostroumov pointed out Russians' "tender character" in conquering and civilizing Asian peoples.[81] Tashkent could become a model of peaceful integration accomplished by Russians who, having only recently acquired attributes of Western civilization, were ideal transmission belts to Asian peoples who had been part of their empire for centuries.

Yet this special connection, long posited by authors in the metropole, had its limits, and this rhetoric should not be taken at face value, nor should it conceal the exploitative practices that characterized empire as much in Turkestan as elsewhere in the colonized world. Russian uniqueness provided a justification for imperial conquest rather than a guide for colonial policy, as future chapters will demonstrate.[82] The same Russian writers who asserted uniqueness also worked to distance themselves from Asian influence. Remarkably absent in Tashkent was any of the "Eurasianist" or "Asianist" discourse that circulated in the capital among a significant number of the educated public, who saw Russians as a true fusion of East and West.[83] Robert Geraci, in his work on Kazan, has suggested that Russians saw Asian Muslims as too different to contemplate any type of assimilation, much less fusion.[84] Tashkent Russian intellectuals nonetheless sought to adopt selectively elements of local culture, yet all the while feared a hybridity produced by contact in the colonial city.

One prominent sign of Russian distance from Asia, according to local writers, was an inability to adjust to the local environment.[85] Surviving the subtropical climate became at once a misery and a badge of honor. One Russian soldier described the miserable state of troops under the desert sun. Temperatures climbed to forty-six degrees Celsius from June through September. "You breathe fire," wrote the soldier, "as if you were in a large frying-pan."[86] Dangers of heat exposure forced Russians to sleep outside in the cooler night air, where they confronted what became a symbol of the threats of the Central Asian environment: the scorpion. Military journals reported on soldiers' encounters with scorpions; one by E. Shlitter detailed an all-night vigil to capture a creature in his room, which ended when he surprised the "enemy" in a cupboard and stabbed it with a compass.[87]

Russian scientists in Tashkent confirmed the danger of subtropical diseases in invading the "European" Russian body. Lev Kostenko argued that diarrhea and dysentery, affecting almost every soldier in Turkestan and claiming 171 Russians in Tashkent in 1871, threatened the future of colonization.[88] Neither he nor his colleagues believed Russians would adjust to their new environment. Medical researcher P. V. Putilov's 1888 study mimicked European theories that the bodies of northern settlers could not survive the long-term effects of the Asian climate. Russians, who had always lived on cool and shady plains, "thinned out" in the heat. Putilov claimed his study confirmed the "weakness of the Russian people in the matter of acclimatization."[89]

Blood and race, Putilov and others argued, identified Russians as northerners and Europeans. But how, then, could they survive long term in subtropical Asia? Varvara Dukhovskaia believed that Russia's continued inability to manage the environment at the turn of the century provided proof of its continued lag behind Europe. Aside from the heat, Dukhovskaia complained that "bloodsucking mosquitoes ferociously bite me. . . . [T]he stings of flies, almost invisible to the naked eye, cause unbearable itches and inflammations." All Russians suffered from this, yet "at the time when in foreign states all types of peoples are being saved from the ill-effects of the mosquitoes and gnats, our Turkestanis only complain of the consequences of their bites."[90]

Russian chief military medical inspector Okolov had looked to British India to ease the effects of the alien environment on Russian colonizers. In 1878, he proposed the building of a hill station near Tashkent.[91] A thorough search led to the mountain valley of Chimgan, 1,500 meters above sea level, approximately 70 kilometers from the imperial capital. Okolov underlined the restorative advantages of the valley's mild temperatures and crisp mountain air. Governor-General Kaufman designated Chimgan as a sanitarium for ill soldiers in 1879. The sanitarium rapidly evolved into a place of repose for Tashkent Russian elites. Reports of great success treating disease at the hill station spread.[92] Recovered soldiers expanded the barracks, kitchen, and administrative offices. By the late 1880s, senior officers and administrators, including governors-general, summered in the mountain valley. A club and teahouse hosted gatherings of officers and their families. Chimgan became a place to recharge away from the dangers of the local population and environment.

Uninvited civilians also undertook the summer trek to Chimgan, staying in the hills below the military sanitarium. "Everybody who has the means," reported *Turkestanskiia Viedomosti* in 1891, "in the summer escapes from the city."[93] *Russkii Turkestan*, a private newspaper, advocated greater attention to Chimgan's unofficial visitors, equally in need of escape from the frustrations cited by Dukhovskaia to continue as effective colonizers and civilizers. Subsidized transport and inexpensive campsites would avoid the impression that only the "aristocracy" could visit the station.[94] The mountain valley was a place for all "Russian Turkestanis."[95]

Local writers had a far more difficult time defining "Russian" than they did "Turkestani" or "European." Living surrounded by an alien population had not helped to determine common definitions of Russianness. Russian nationality held a precarious space among Turkestan intellectuals and administrators. On the one hand, Russians were proud conquerors and ideal bearers of European civilization. On the other, they continued to be trapped, in terms of culture, history, and geography, between Europe and Asia. An 1882 *Turkestanskiia Viedomosti* article stated concerns about Russians' ability to present themselves as civilized Europeans. The author, "I. D.," used as an example the "horrifying" state of Russian Tashkent's one cemetery. Neglect of the graveyard encouraged Central Asians to steal wooden crosses for firewood and metal ones to fashion household instruments. Animals driven through the cemetery "used this place for their natural needs."[96] I. D. did not condemn Central Asian behavior, arguing in fact that the local population took good care of its own graves. Blame for this situation lay with "[w]e, Russians, in Tashkent [who] approach this situation completely the opposite not only of other peoples, but of Christianity."[97] Local Russian society (obshchestvo) had failed to meet its claim of being "civilized," instead confirming Saltykov-Shchedrin's view of particular morals in imperial Tashkent.

I. D.'s views pinpointed a particular difficulty for Russians in trying to identify with Europe: their religion. Christianity connected Russia to Europe, but also provided a reminder of the different paths the two had taken. In 1866, Lev Kostenko had linked Orthodoxy to a backward Russian state and saw Russian Tashkent as a place where religious freedom would reign.[98] Kostenko was typical of the post-reform intellectuals that considered Orthodoxy as a tradition that needed to be jettisoned in the name of progress.[99] Even as Orthodox Christianity appeared during selected ceremonies as a primary, if not the only, marker of Russian nationhood, Tashkent Russian intellectual elites followed Governor-General Kaufman in viewing their mission as a secular one.[100] Eugene Schuyler joined Western travelers in remarking with surprise the lack of religiosity in Russian Tashkent, stating in 1877 that the one Orthodox church "is quite large enough for present wants, and is somewhat out of repair, a negligence which astonishes the pious Mussulmans [sic], who are also shocked that so few Russians attend Church regularly."[101] Slavophile celebrations of Orthodoxy as a religion that supported the unique values of an organic community based on rural traditions ran counter to the modern, urban society projected in the writings of leading officials and intellectuals in Russian Tashkent.

The few Tashkent Russian writers who used Christianity to connect themselves to a larger European world subsumed mentions of their Orthodox faith. Instead, like Governor-General Kaufman, they propounded their role in a greater Christian mission to spread civilization. General M. A. Terent'ev wrote in the central journal *Viestnik Evropy* in 1875 of the importance for Tashkent Russians of ruling on the basis of "Christian cosmopolitanism," which, vaguely defined as a combination of morality and scientific progress, was "our strength, our glory, and our future."[102] A 1904 *Turkestanskiia Viedomosti* article expanded on this theme, arguing for a Russian mission to realize the "unity of many peoples, eternally hostile to each other, into one grand family on the basis of Christian patience, justice, and humanism."[103] Russians worked as Christian, as well as European, civilizers on the frontier, but what type of Christianity remained unclear.

Alcohol emerged as another marker that symbolized the troubled place of Russianness in imperial Tashkent. Alcohol became an important symbol of distance between Russians and Central Asians on the one hand, and Russians and, ostensibly, Europeans on the other, but hardly a flattering one. Imperial elites lamented the prominence of alcohol in Russian Tashkent. The large number of inebriated soldiers at the main market led Russians to refer to the main market in the city as the "drunken," instead of the Sunday, bazaar. Kaufman, seeking to reverse this image, in 1868 approved plans of medical inspectors to substitute wine or vodka rations given to soldiers with tea. Central newspapers regarded this experiment with interest, but it never gained approval from the minister of war and ended in failure.[104] One writer in 1883 wrote of his anger and shame at the continued dominance of alcohol: "One uncontrollably turns red at the thought that for us [Russians] in the region there are twelve wine and vodka distilleries, eleven breweries, seven wine-making enterprises and hundreds of taverns and other drinking establishments, while there are no bookstores."[105] Russians' love of alcohol was defeating the building of a civilized society.

Alcohol grew in stature as a marker of identity along with the presence of thousands of poor Russians who entered Tashkent in the 1880s. Characterized as dirty, drunk, and lazy, these lower classes were seen among Russian elites as a threat to a progressive, Europeanized identity. As in central Russia, educated society and officialdom counterpoised the *narod* (masses) to a privileged and civilized obshchestvo. Poor Russians became linked to elite anxieties over the precarious state of their nation. The "laziness" of the poor enforced a popular stereotype of Russian sluggishness in Russian Tashkent, which replaced the more common mythology in colonial situations of the "lazy native."[106] As early as 1870, *Turkestanskiia Viedomosti* noted that Central Asians, seeing the rapid construction of the Russian city, "remarked with comic surprise that they in no way expected such energy from a Russian person."[107] In an 1894 article for the St. Petersburg journal *Niva*, N. A. Maev argued that his experience in Tashkent had convinced him that "a Russian person is unable to make use of his/her own labor." As a result, "Russians have always been exploited by foreign nationalities, first the Varangians and Tatars, then the Germans, Jews, Armenians and Sarts."[108] Their "lazy and carefree" character, symbolized by the proverb "to be Russian is to love drink" had made settlers easy prey for teetotaler Muslims.[109] Russians had failed to gain a greater knowledge of their environment and develop a growing economy, as Maev had advocated in 1872.

Maev's views of potential Central Asian "exploitation" of the Russian population derived from another significant, and ambiguous, national trope. Debates over continued Russian failures, and Central Asian success, in trade and business wove their way into the ongoing discourse of nationality. These discussions followed those in central Russia, where, as Thomas C. Owen has argued, non-Russians' prominence in the economy heightened the denigration of capital development.[110] In Tashkent, linking business and capitalism to Central Asians allowed Russian elites to counter representations of greed advanced by Saltykov-Shchedrin. Yet Russians also feared that their apparent weakness in matters of commerce would allow the local population to overturn colonial hierarchies. N. N. Karazin's 1880 article on tsarist Central Asia for the series *Images of Russia* reported on initial success of Russians in implanting civilization, allowing the opening of public activity suppressed by previous khans and emirs.[111] Yet the new "pax Rossica" had engendered an unexpected consequence. Central Asian domination of local trade and business increased even as Russian mercantile interests moved into the region. Karazin's label of "kulak-Sarts," who he claimed were exploiting new Russian migrants, made clear his association between business and exploitation.[112] Karazin, however, aimed his anger at Russian settlers who allowed this exploitation. He decried the "sluggishness and unculturedness" of the primarily peasant population arriving in Turkestan.[113] The author demanded that the state send better quality migrants or properly supply those who arrived. Both the Russian state and Russian people were damaging the quest to spread European civilization to Central Asia.

A less confident Russian national identity mixed with a more positive Turkestani one within imperial Tashkent's educated society in the 1880s–1890s. Images of Russians as "universal civilizers" began to fade before frustrations at failed efforts to locate universal, positive national characteristics and to situate Russia between Europe and Asia. Anxieties over Russia's marginal position grew along with the level of contact between the colonizers and colonized in Tashkent. Instead of establishing differences between European Russians and backward Asian Muslims, relationships across ethnic lines confirmed that the Turkestani Russian was not shielded from external influences.

Determining the significance and outcomes of cross-cultural contacts in a colonial situation is an extremely difficult endeavor. Colonizers' interaction with, and adoption of, aspects of indigenous society and culture can be viewed as an Orientalist enterprise, taking possession of selected aspects of a subject civilization in order to emphasize dominance, or as a deeper cultural hybridity. Tashkent Russians represented their contact with Central Asians in both fashions. Borrowings across cultures occurred at all levels of the social and political spectrum, with multivalent meanings for national identities.

Russian administrators and intellectual elites vaunted their use of Muslim property law in Tashkent. In 1872, Military Governor Golovachev expropriated the Nazar-bia waqf on claims that its owner had gained possession of it illegally, and transferred its 1,200-ruble annual income to the Turkestan Charitable Society. Waqf holdings in Muslim societies are generally awarded to charitable or educational institutions, which gain tax revenue from residents within the bounds of the property to fund their activities. Residents protested this takeover as a violation of Muslim law, which stated that funds should go directly to the poor.[114] *Turkestanskiia Viedomosti* nonetheless presented the revenue as a successful sign of borrowing to aid the (Russian) poor of Tashkent.[115] Russian elites openly displayed other markers of appropriation. They adopted certain local styles of dress, particularly the leather trousers (*chembardi*) that protected against the heat and prickly shrubs that blew across the city during the summer months.[116] The traditional local dish of mutton, rice, and vegetables, *plov*, became a regular part of the Russian diet. N. A. Maev noted that plov's popularity extended across classes, from "intellectuals" to travelers and hunters, who saw it as an excellent staple for long journeys.[117] Tashkent Russians who volunteered for the Russo-Japanese war suggested plov replace their regular rations.[118] Local writers praised efforts to selectively adopt innovations across cultural lines as part of the special nature of Tashkent society.[119]

Maev and other intellectuals worried, however, that Russian lower classes would be unable to distinguish between expropriation and a hybridity that would threaten the boundary between colonizer and colonized.[120] *Turkestanskiia Viedomosti* kept a close watch on possible slippages. Authors decried interchanges of intoxicating substances, with Muslims drinking alcohol and poor Russians, the narod, using hashish and opium.[121] Officer N. S. Lykoshin, who lived for several years in Asian Tashkent and learned the local language—he translated several poems and stories into Russian—condemned any signs of intercultural contact among the lower classes. In his memoir *Half a Life in Turkestan*, Lykoshin decried Russians who exploited a legal statute allowing use of Muslim courts in disputes with the Central Asian population. Lower-class Russians' "carefree and trusting" nature ensnared them in legal contests with "cunning and suspicious" Muslims.[122] Because Central Asians then "hid" in Asian Tashkent, Russian victims believed it would be easier to gain justice through Muslim courts. Lykoshin ridiculed this strategy, as finding a reliable translator for the proceedings was virtually impossible, and court decisions were sure to go against them. This tirade, however, suggested that Russians received satisfactory redress in Muslim courts, and continued to use them throughout the imperial period.

Evoking even more fear was a full acceptance of local culture, in effect "going native." Rare mentions of Russians who wore complete Muslim dress referred to them as drunkards or lunatics.[123] Varvara Dukhovskaia noted that a Russian woman who had asked authorities to convert to Islam was quickly placed in a psychiatric hospital.[124] Intellectuals serving in the administration, including Lykoshin, M. S. Andreev, who studied in Muslim madrasas between stints as a topographer for the state and the Geographic Society, and V. P. Nalivkin, who briefly resigned his commission in 1878 to live in a local village in the Fergana valley as part of the populist "going to the people" movement, were immune from accusations of hybridity.[125] Educated, upper-class Russians apparently had the skills and sense to resist a dangerous mixing that would shift them from Orientalists to Russian-native hybrids.

In St. Petersburg Tsar Alexander III (1881–94) asserted Russian national superiority even as Tashkent Russian educated society displayed concern that ostensible national traits might lead them to damage their status as Europeans and to lose control of the cross-cultural encounter. The tsar's nationalism, favoring an idealized, pre-Petrine past based on "traditional" culture and religion against the modernization efforts of the Great Reform era, found little resonance among Tashkent's progressive elites.[126] One aspect of the tsar's Russification drive that did reverberate in Tashkent, however, was the enforcement of Russian superiority over other—particularly Western, Christian—nations in the empire. Imperial administrators privileged ethnic Russians in a diverse European community that included significant numbers of Poles, Jews, and Germans. Beginning in 1888, Russian Orthodox priests refused to perform burial services for Roman Catholics, mainly Poles.[127] District government functionaries challenged an 1896 Ministry of War decree to allow the building of a Catholic chapel. They argued that granting the request for the 600 Roman Catholics in Tashkent—2,100 including soldiers—would give this minority a better church/ population ratio than the Orthodox Russians. Ministry of War officials overruled this concern and a chapel was built in 1898; local officials, insisted, however that services be performed in Latin or Russian, not the Polish language.

Other European minorities in Tashkent received harsh treatment in the 1880s–90s. In 1889, Military Governor Grodekov began to expel Jews who had broken agreements requiring them to practice a particular profession in exchange for the right to live outside the tsarist pale of settlement.[128] European Jews appealed to the Russian senate, which denied them the inalienable right to live in Turkestan. Russian Tashkent's police chief subsequently exercised strict surveillance over the Jewish population, allowing residence only to those trained and practicing in specific artisanal trades.[129] Yet prominent Jewish merchants evaded these requirements, serving in the city duma as "Christian" deputies and circulating among the elites of Russian Tashkent. They fared better than new German migrants from the Volga and steppe regions, who received a cold welcome from tsarist authorities. Local officials expressed concern over an 1894 "flood" of Germans, who had heard rumors of rich, free land in Turkestan. Governor-General S. M. Dukhovskoi persuaded the Ministry of Finance to assist in covering expenses of a return voyage for the unwelcome Germans.[130]

Concern over their place in imperial society and a modern European world permeated intellectual discourse among educated Russians. Agronomist N. N. Kas'ianov, a former student of Kazan University, placed blame for local pessimism and defensiveness in the early 1890s squarely on the Russian metropole. Before a large 1891 gathering to mark the 135th anniversary of Moscow University, Kas'ianov addressed a "burning question for the intelligentsia of Turkestan."[131] He condemned negative portrayals of the region in the central press, where "any incident or crime . . . is characterized as the result of [Saltykov-Shchedrin's] 'Tashkent morals' or 'Tashkent order.'" Many friends, he claimed, wrote him to ask if rumors of constant disorder or anarchy were true. For Kas'ianov, this was: "Shameful! Unjust!" If more corrupt officials served in Turkestan, this was the fault of the metropole (*metropoliia*), which sent its "freaks" as far away as possible. Russian central elites had lost their desire to explore Turkestan as a model of progress, the policies of the reactionary Alexander III symbolizing Russia's move away from civilization.

"Russian Turkestanis" nonetheless retained their status as chosen "civilizers" of Central Asia, and had successfully developed their own way of life (*byt*).[132] Kas'ianov implored his fellow university graduates to write back to the metropole about the positive characteristics of Tashkent's civilized society (obshchestvo). The following speaker, S. V. Sukhachev, the head of the regional law courts in Tashkent, reminded the audience of their "huge responsibility . . . to advance peaceful cultural life." "Turkestanis" were central participants in "an event of paramount importance in history": the development of European civilization and the expansion of the Russian state to its "natural limits" to the south.[133] Sukhachev as well implored local intellectuals to remember these missions as the center had seemingly lost interest in progress.

These speeches reflected the tenuous balance between a "civilized" European colonial identity, linked to the development of an intellectual "Turkestani" society, and a corrupt, regressive, apathetic colonial identity, linked to Saltykov-Shchedrin's "Tashkenters." Between these visions, Russianness occupied a marginal place, wavering between Europe and Asia, progress and backwardness. Educated society in Russian Tashkent produced a remarkably coherent image of the promise and peril it perceived emerging from the imperial venture. In published periodicals and internal records, leading administrators vaunted Russian Tashkent as a symbol for the nation's future. Even as they disagreed on components of that future, top tsarist officials and intellectuals serving the regime envisioned a dynamic and at least somewhat autonomous society as a basis for new initiatives to realize the potential of Governor-General Kaufman's modern European cityscape.

Ambivalence from central Russian elites and the reactionary reforms of Tsar Alexander III tempered the confidence of leaders of educated society in Russian Tashkent. Poor settlers damaged the image of a civilized colonizer and threatened, through their ignorance, to dissolve the boundaries between a European imperial Russia and a backward Central Asia. Their self-proclaimed status as European civilizers also isolated Russian intellectuals from Maev to Kas'ianov from the majority Central Asians. Even those who immersed themselves in local society and culture refused input from, or cooperation with, Central Asians as they formulated concepts of identity and the "civilizing mission." In the end, stereotypes of lazy and inebriated settlers, cunning and exploitative Central Asians, and arrogant or regressive elites in St. Petersburg solidified a sense of local identity, but precipitated a perception of crisis as privileged Russian Tashkent appeared surrounded by hostile forces. Administrative and intellectual elites who held power in late imperial-era Russian Tashkent focused on countering accusations of backwardness and forces of reaction, rather than broadening the scope of their obshchestvo.

# 3.

## Unstable Boundaries: The Colonial Relationship and the 1892 "Cholera Riot"

On June 24, 1892, a Central Asian crowd crossed the Ankhor canal into the Russian section of Tashkent. The crowd sought to prevent Muhammad Yaqub, Asian Tashkent's chief administrator, from meeting City Commandant Stepan R. Putintsev. Muhammad Yaqub intended to report widespread defiance of tsarist anti-cholera measures, perceived to violate principles of local medicine and culture. The crowd was too late, encountering Putintsev and Muhammad Yaqub together. A few stones and fists flew at the city commandant after he refused demands to lift the measures. Most demonstrators, however, pursued a fleeing Muhammad Yaqub toward the municipal administration building, where they destroyed files used to rule Asian Tashkent. Russian settlers responded to the crowd's actions with force. Clerks, veterans, and an Orthodox cleric joined arriving soldiers in cries of "brothers, beat them." Soldiers and settlers pursued demonstrators trying to return to Asian Tashkent, and attacked any Central Asian they found in the surrounding area. Battered bodies were thrown into the Ankhor canal, with at least eighty dredged up the following day.

Russian actions demonstrated their readiness to commit violence to enforce colonial power. Yet the cholera epidemic and riot also exposed interdependencies in imperial Tashkent. Muhammad Yaqub was one of hundreds of local administrators on whom the Russians depended to keep peace in, and deliver revenue from, Asian Tashkent. Significant numbers of Central Asians, from laborers to wealthy merchants, crossed the Ankhor canal daily. They played critical roles in the local and imperial economy. Russians crossed, albeit less frequently, into the Asian city, not only to purchase goods from local bazaars, but to seek medical care from healers. Tensions between separation and interdependence, as well as between superiority and vulnerability, produced the climate that led to the violence of June 24.

Central Asians themselves worked to navigate the complexities of a colonial relationship that encouraged the exploitation of their land and labor but offered political and economic opportunities. Conciliation maintained an outward peace from 1865 to 1892. Yet alliances across the Ankhor canal were shifting and unstable. A growing awareness of interdependency strengthened Russian efforts to present themselves as inherently different from, and superior to, the "backward" people that they were destined to civilize. Efforts intensified especially as Central Asians proved themselves superior in domains considered modern, including medicine and engineering. Russian demonization of the local population reached new heights following the 1892 riot, blamed on "intrinsic fatalists" who would never accept "civilization."[1] Yet even as the riot engendered harsher measures of rule, tsarist officials realized the necessity of cooperation with local leaders. Damaged nonetheless were Russian elites' hopes that the transformative power of European civilization could make Tashkent Russians and Central Asians into leaders of a changing colonial world.

## Postconquest Asian Tashkent

Central Asians sought to accommodate themselves to tsarist rule following the June 1865 conquest. Tashkent's population was accustomed to outside control, being subject to the khanate of Kokand for decades before the appearance of Russian troops. As discussed in the prologue, local elites had sought to maintain traditions of autonomy under outsiders' rule by striking a deal with General Cherniaev to limit tsarist interference in matters of internal politics, society, and culture. Adjusting to Russian control, however, was not always a smooth process. Even as the urban economy thrived, Central Asian notables, artisans, and day laborers grew aware of growing inequalities between "Russian" and "Asian" populations and cities. Colonial imbalances increased pressure on Central Asian notables. Mediators, as we have seen in chapter 1, gained prominence through their presence at imperial ceremonies, but faced great challenges in simultaneously maintaining the favor of tsarist bureaucrats and wealth, power, and prestige within their own community. Central Asian mediators nonetheless kept a stability, albeit a tenuous one, that maintained outward peace in the city from the conquest to the "cholera riot" of 1892.

Sharafii bai Zeinalgabidin, a Kazan Tatar with close connections to tsarist functionaries, directed efforts to design internal administration in Asian Tashkent that corresponded to the 1867 provisional statute enacted by St. Petersburg to rule Turkestan.[2] Kaufman, despite his policy of "ignorance," had already made important interventions in local politics, most significantly dissolving the position of chief jurist, the qazi-kalan. He also maintained the right to sack any Central Asian in a position of authority. Sharafii bai established an Organizing Commission, which sought to maneuver between local traditions of rule and the demands of the provisional statute. As before the conquest, each of the four districts of Asian Tashkent would be led by aksakals (elders) chosen by prominent community members from each mahalla (neighborhood). Elections, however, replaced consensus as a method of selection. Elections in each mahalla would produce a "fiftier" (*piatdesiatnik*), who would meet to elect not only aksakals, but also qazis (religious judges), who traditionally gained their position through their superior knowledge of the Quran and Islamic law. New rules limited qazis to hear cases in specific regions of the city, and stripped from them the ability to impose the most severe penalties, including death. All elected officials served three-year terms, unless of course imperial administrators chose to strip them of their title.[3] Elected aksakals would also, in conjunction with tsarist authorities, select a head to preside over the city as a whole.

Commission deliberations in 1868 and 1870, and the elections process, faced significant initial resistance. Commission members, according to reports received by Tashkent city commandant E. A. Rossitskii, faced both verbal and physical abuse. One aksakal from the Sebzar district, who served at the time of the conquest, accused the Organizing Commission of "selling out Muslims to the Russians."[4] The greatest protests and unrest surrounded taxation measures. Kaufman charged elected officials with collecting taxes from Asian Tashkent; in return, in addition to a salary paid by the tsarist administration, the officials could keep 6 to 10 percent of the revenues.[5] Crowds led protests at tax collection points. An 1869 petition signed by 287 privileged Central Asians objected to new levies beyond the traditional ones on property (the *kharaj* and *tanap*), which Governor-General Kaufman had originally promised would be the only taxes instituted on the Asian city. Signatories warned that new, "supplementary" taxes would inspire "ill-willed" and "evil" people to disrupt "social peace."[6] Other objections revolved around the quality of elected officials. Reformist bureaucrats in St. Petersburg saw elections as a step toward emancipation and citizenship for Russia's newest subjects.[7] Instead, residents across Asian Tashkent complained that elections fostered any number of vote-rigging schemes, with bribes and wealth replacing deliberations and knowledge as tools and qualifications for qazis and aksakals. Elected officials were seen as beholden to tsarist administrators or wealthy businessmen, Russian or Central Asian, instead of the community as a whole.[8] Such complaints reverberated across Central Asia in response to the 1867 statute, as Virginia Martin notes in her study of Kazakh nomads.[9] Martin also found that elected Kazakh jurists (biys), no longer recognized as having a superior knowledge of the law, lost prestige in the eyes of the community. In Asian Tashkent, residents also complained that new regulations forced them to consult qazis designated for their particular district, against a custom where both sides in a dispute could consult any qazi willing to hear the case. Many inhabitants of Asian Tashkent simply refused to acknowledge elected leaders, instead recognizing the authority of those who had gained community support outside of the electoral process.[10]

Despite dissatisfaction and subterfuge, the system designed by the Organizing Commission remained largely unchanged during the first generation of colonial rule. The continued rapid development of the urban economy may well have muted protests against the colonial administration. Measuring the economic growth of Asian Tashkent through quantitative measures is virtually impossible, given the common evasion of imperial statisticians and efforts to conceal wealth from tax collectors. Official census data nonetheless record a significant population growth of 23 percent from 1872 to 1877, when Asian Tashkent's population reached 51,769 male inhabitants.[11] Numerous attestations of a burgeoning economy also come from contemporary Russian and Central Asian observers. Tashkent, a center of regional trade long before the tsarist conquest, became a collection point for ever-growing quantities of goods to be sent by caravan to Russia. Artisanal shops and small factories in Asian Tashkent opened and closed in rapid succession in the 1870s, as businessmen and guilds adjusted to postconquest markets. Fabrics, clothing, and woodworking proved extremely profitable.[12] Russian Tashkent provided employment and markets. Central Asians began to produce baked bricks, provide labor for construction projects, and generate various goods for settlers, administrators, and tsarist soldiers. Each district of Asian Tashkent chose new areas of specialization, but the boom especially helped the Sheikhantaur section, along the border with the new Russian city.[13] New inhabitants, markets, and knowledge gained from increased contact with Russian business allowed Tashkent to continue its centuries-old role as the economic heart of oasis Central Asia.

Central Asian notables and businessmen endowed portions of this wealth to Islamic religious and educational institutions. In the years following the conquest, Russian observers noted the continued increase in the number of madrasas (religious colleges), which attracted Kazakhs and Tatars as well as locals.[14] A small but significant number of Central Asian notables used the Russian presence to advance their own intellectual horizons. Adeeb Khalid has noted the important role of *Turkestanskiia Viedomosti*'s native-language supplement, *Turkestan Wilayatining Gazeti* (Turkestan District newspaper), in establishing a forum for Central Asian intellectuals seeking to accommodate tsarist rule and examine the region within a global, and imperial, context.[15] N. P. Ostroumov, who edited this supplement beginning in 1883, encouraged debate among local scholars, many of whom he befriended. Increasing numbers of notables began to move in Russian cultural and social circles, attending balls at the governor-general's mansion and meetings of scholarly societies, and entertaining prominent tsarist officials and intellectuals in their homes.

Central Asian notables occupying official positions worked to traverse and mediate between two different, albeit slowly converging, worlds. Their posts made them beholden, to a certain extent, to their colonial overlords. At the same time, the ability of these notables to administer effectively, at once collecting taxes and ensuring peace, as well as to gain sufficient support to win elections, required close attention to the needs and desires of Asian Tashkent residents. Opposition to Russian rule persisted. Tsarist authorities developed an elaborate system of fines for those who failed to show proper respect toward imperial authorities, with the highest penalties reserved for local elites.[16] Kaufman's 1875 campaign against the khanate of Kokand sparked extensive unrest in the Asian city, according to one tsarist soldier. Russians in the markets were treated with hostility, and those in dachas near Asian Tashkent were brought back to the Russian section under military escort.[17] Carts taking goods to Russian Tashkent were destroyed. Not all residents of Asian Tashkent enjoyed the benefits of a growing economy; weavers and day laborers, for example, had difficulty meeting their daily needs.[18] As protests against increased taxation continued among poorer sectors of the population, some Central Asian notables began to complain of discrepancies in expenditures between the Russian and Asian cities. "Muslim" deputies of the inaugural municipal duma protested lavish spending on new projects in Russian Tashkent while their section lacked the most basic services.[19] In this environment, Central Asians involved with the tsarist administration sought to carefully balance cooperation and independence.

Muhiddin Khoja Ishan and Sattar Khan Abdulghaffar oghli chose two different paths as mediators. Muhiddin Khoja, the son of the last qazi-kalan, retained great influence in Asian Tashkent. A wealthy landowner in his own right, he agreed nonetheless to serve as a qazi under conditions imposed by the tsar. His prestige, emanating partially from his father, gained him significant favor among tsarist officials as well as the local population. Muhiddin Khoja led ceremonial delegations and received frequent invitations to social events in the Russian city. Tsarist officials sent him to represent Asian Tashkent at the coronation of Tsar Nicholas II, and he was decorated with the orders of St. Stanislav and St. Anna for his service to the empire.[20] Muhiddin Khoja was careful, however, to keep a degree of distance from the colonizer. He never learned the Russian language. He received European guests in the one and only room in his house decorated in "Russian style," including chairs and a samovar. Muhiddin Khoja's speeches supporting tsarist rule, as in the one cited in chapter 1, sought to remind tsarist officials of promises to maintain Central Asian cultural autonomy. Ostroumov admired Muhiddin Khoja's ability to circulate in a Russian cultural world yet maintain his esteem among conservative Muslims. Traveler Evgenii Markov expressed curiosity at accounts that a man who sported some external signs of assimilation still maintained a "hatred" for Russian control.[21] Unfortunately, we lack records of how Muhiddin Khoja moved within Asian Tashkent, or his own feelings as he steered between these two worlds. We are left to rely on Russian observers to judge his delicate balancing act, though we can be more careful analysts than Ostroumov, who praised Muhiddin Khoja for not falling prey to "typical Asian flattery" of all things associated with Europe and empire.

Sattar Khan also sensed the perils of being recognized as overly friendly with Russian leaders. A qazi who began work in the service of the tsar shortly after the conquest of Tashkent, Sattar Khan learned Russian and occupied various administrative posts across Turkestan. Like Muhiddin Khoja, he gained the confidence of tsarist officials and represented Turkestan Muslims at official gatherings in St. Petersburg, including an 1876 Orientalist Congress. Upon settling in Tashkent in 1881, he assumed residence in the Russian city and decorated his house in European style. He, as well as his wife, wore European clothes, at a time when many Central Asian women in Tashkent wore the veil.[22] Sattar Khan and Ostroumov became close friends and worked together on *Turkestan Wilayatining Gazeti*. The two shared the view of an archaic Central Asian Muslim culture in need of enlightenment, which could be provided by the Russian colonizer.[23] Ostroumov did not directly accuse Sattar Khan of "Central Asian flattery." Yet he noted that Sattar Khan, apparently out of shame, did not visit Asian Tashkent, even during holidays. He sent his sons to be educated in the Russian gymnasium. As Adeeb Khalid notes, Muhiddin Khoja, despite great misgivings, sent one of his sons to the gymnasium, but also trained all of them in Islamic religious texts.

For all their difficulties in accommodating different political and cultural worlds in the early years following the conquest, these Central Asian mediators held important powers. Those who learned the Russian language commanded the ability to selectively interpret intentions, orders, and words between tsarist officials and the Central Asian population. Leading imperial administrators, including Kaufman, noted their frustration at this lack of control.[24] In addition, Russian bureaucrats relied upon these mediators to manage the great majority of the population of Tashkent, to keep peace when fears of local rebellion were never far off. Central Asian mediators found means for both personal advancement and the sheltering of their community from at least some inequities of imperial power.

## Colonial Images and Encounters

Russians asserted their primacy in colonial society through several different channels. One important method of representing and legitimating colonial power involved a disparagement of the Central Asian population. Russian writers represented their Asian neighbors as cultural caricatures rather than complex actors. Central Asians were fanatic or lazy, comedic or somber, stupid or deviously cunning, but never on the same level as the balanced, rational European. Such portrayals echoed those that reverberated across the European-dominated imperial world in the late nineteenth century. Edward Said has recognized the importance of rhetoric and images for Europeans in the colonies to build a "protective enclosure" around them and refute the colonized population's ability to threaten the colonizer's cultural preeminence.[25] Russians used such techniques not only to erect barriers in Tashkent, but to transmit images of their own, and their nation's, superiority and "civilization" to the metropole.

Dirt and disease emerged as primary tropes in Russian discourse. Western imperial images opposing the clean European to the dirty Asian or African paired economic and cultural goals, justifying lesser spending on sanitation and general maintenance for "native" cities, whose residents were deemed inherently incapable of keeping neighborhoods unsoiled.[26] Images of unsanitary Muslims wallowing in filth and carrying illnesses dehumanized the Central Asian population. Dirt, I argue, racialized the colonial relationship, even as Russians generally, though not always, avoided terminologies linked to color and race in characterizing differences with Central Asians.[27]

Powerful images of difference emerged at one of the main public arenas in imperial Tashkent. Horse races, run through the apricot trees of Ming-Uriuk gardens, attracted the attention of the central press for their novel gathering of Russians, Cossacks, Bashkirs, Tatars, Kazakhs, and local Central Asians. A local Russian correspondent for *Syn Otechestva* trumpeted the exoticism of Russia's newest possession in 1868, writing that "the spectacle that entertains Europeans in Tashkent today, you can find only in dreams or in engravings."[28] Most notable were "the sea of Mohammedins (*magometov*), dressed in their long robes with vibrant colours, and standing with philosophical calm and southern inertia."[29] Unlike the other non-Russians, the local "Sart" population, considered unskilled in horsemanship, did not participate in the horse races.[30] Sart boys, however, had their own race on the horse track, after the equine events were finished. *Russkii Invalid* described the race in great detail, as a piece of comedy. It reported that the boys, unlike the horses, lacked the knowledge or discipline to await the starting gun. After numerous false starts, dozens jumped from the crowd to join the race at various intervals, as laughter from the audience mounted. These participants were far more amusing than the horses.[31]

A powerful symbol of difference was presented to the "winner." After, according to the correspondent, a "swarm" of young boys simultaneously crossed the finish line, race officials invited one to join winners of the horse races at the podium. Instead of medals or money, the local boy received a washstand. *Syn Otechestva*'s correspondent reported: "This prize is very valuable, as the dirty-faced little boy will be able to use the result of his victory to his benefit."[32] The race and the presentation counterpoised images of Central Asian inertia, indiscipline, and dirtiness with European order and cleanliness. The race's organization and the correspondent's rhetoric equated Central Asians to animals.

N. N. Karazin elided images of animal and human in his description of executions in Bukhara for the central journal *Vsemirnaia Illiustratsiia*. "Not one bazaar day goes by, where on the squares, in the places used for slaughtering cows, the blood of an unfortunate person, determined guilty by the *sharia*, . . . is not mixed with the blood of oxen and sheep."[33] Karazin's images of mixed animal and human blood, accompanied by grisly drawings, established a contrast between Muslim cruelty in Bukhara and enlightened Russian law in Tashkent. Russians had a duty to spread their superior culture to the region, but Karazin's article also reminded the audience of the dangers faced confronting a hostile population in strange surroundings. Linguist P. I. Pashino's memoirs use dirt to divide Russians and Central Asians as well as to underline hostility to tsarist power. On his first trip through Asian Tashkent in 1867, Pashino described children confronting him with cries of "the

Russian is a rooster" ("*urus-khurus*") and women shaking their fists and hurling insults.[34] Pashino dismissed as backward the opposition of these people, who, he wrote, reveled in filth; the children, after taunting him, returned to play in the same puddles where the local inhabitants had just washed their horses.[35]

Central Asian "dirtiness" also led to associations with disease. This linkage began with one malady that spread quickly among Tashkent Russians, leaving them with reddish marks on their hands and faces. After a few days, the marks, hardened and knotty to the touch, spread to the neck, feet, and other parts of the body. The wounds destroyed skin tissue and produced large scabs, especially on the face. If left untreated, they could last for a year and cause serious disfigurement.[36] Tsarist doctors called this affliction "Tashkent sores." The Russian population, however, preferred the epithet "Sart disease," linking the illness directly to their Central Asian neighbors. The disease was spread through water, which Russians, following Pashino, perceived as a central medium for Central Asians to spread their pollution.

Water grew to symbolize links to Tashkent's Central Asian population and epitomize the vulnerability felt by Russians in their unfamiliar environment. Russian inexperience with desert water delivery systems forced them to rely upon local skills and technology. Before the conquest, Tashkent obtained water through a series of feeder canals from the Chirchik river, sixteen kilometers to the west. Outside a few wells, Russian Tashkent, on the eastern edge of the existing city, received water only after it flowed through conduits alongside the streets and canals of Asian Tashkent. M. A. Terent'ev described Russian anger at this reliance in an 1869 *Russkii Invalid* article:

> [F]or cleanliness [of the water], we are in full dependence upon the Asian canal managers. Supplying of water here is in a primitive state ... through open canals flow sprinklings of dirt, and all sorts of liquids, you see how in the canals horses are bathed or their legs washed ... as canals go through yards, you see other things: the rinsing of laundry, various ablutions of sinning bodies. It [the water] is terrible to drink, terrible to wash in.[37]

Russians deplored this situation, but failed in repeated attempts to change it. In 1868, Military Governor N. N. Golovachev commissioned engineers to build a feeder canal from the Chirchik directly to Russian Tashkent.[38] After a six-year construction project, Russian Orthodox priests blessed the canal in a large public ceremony. *Turkestanskiia Viedomosti* claimed that "[n]othing can speak to the importance of such a construction for the city, where to this time out of necessity unclean water has been received."[39] Yet no water ever flowed. The lead engineer, Kaufman's associate S. K. Ianchevskii, blamed inaccurate instruments for the fact that the canal ran uphill. Imperial administrators conducted multiple, voluminous studies in future years, but none were deemed to guarantee success.[40] Russian officials continued to entrust water delivery to Central Asian managers, now paid a state salary. These managers realized their power. A threatened 1869 strike prompted intervention from the military governor. Canal managers emerged among the best-paid state employees in Tashkent, their annual salary doubling to four hundred rubles between 1868 and 1883.[41] Terent'ev's history of Turkestan, published in 1906, described the continued frustration and resignation of Russian failure to match the local population's technical skills, and subsequent dependence on the "robe-wearers" (*khalatniki*).[42]

Effective local knowledge spread beyond canal management. Even as Tashkent Russians condemned the local population for a lack of hygiene that spread water-borne illnesses, they recognized the skills of Central Asian healers (*tabibs*) in curing these diseases. Asian Tashkent became a source of healing as well as danger, as Russians crossed the Ankhor canal for medical treatment. Military analyst Lev Kostenko wrote that tsarist administrative elites attributed the numbers of Russians seeking treatment in Asian Tashkent to poor settlers' ignorance, based on a mistaken belief that Sarts must be better at curing a disease named after them. Kostenko, however, discovered that Russian physicians confused "Sart disease" with syphilis. By the time the disease was recognized, the sores on the body had hardened and become untreatable.[43] Tabibs immediately treated the disease with a plaster of caustic materials, such as mercuric chloride, mixed with sheep fat and trace oils.[44] Tabibs also gained recognition for their skill in treating guinea worms, which, present in food and water, entered bodies through the digestive system and lodged in the leg. Russian doctors, who extracted a small segment of the worm each day, leading to it often breaking and multiplying, admitted the superior skill of tabibs, who captured and twirled the worm around on a stick, removing it in a single visit.[45]

Central Asian skills in treating disease increased tsarist elites' frustration at their inability to demonstrate superiority in domains considered "civilized." Governor-General Kaufman and other leading officials saw medicine as critical to exhibit European supremacy and benevolence, curing the locals through the latest scientific advances.[46] They considered tabibs as nothing more than "hucksters," whose false claims and ineffective treatments nonetheless allowed them to gain status and wealth.[47] N. A. Maev sought to counter demoralizing effects of apparent local medical skill through an anecdote in *Turkestanskiia Viedomosti*. Maev

Figure 16. Market stalls near Jami Mosque. F. Azadaev, *Tashkent
vo vtoroi polovine XIX veka: Ocherki Sotsial'no-Ekonomicheskoi i Politicheskoi
Istorii* (Tashkent: Izdatel'stvo Akademii Nauk Uzbekskoi SSR, 1959), 169.

claimed that, seeing his limp on the street, a tabib offered to cure it in
three days. Maev led the tabib back to house, where his leg was rubbed
and he was offered four capsules to start his treatment. Upon receiving payment for a full course of medication, the tabib never returned.
What's more, he pocketed a small clock used to show Maev when to
take the first tablets. Such frauds, Maev claimed, were common, and
the newspaper staff "considered it our duty to warn others of this."[48]
Central Asians' skill in medicine was counterbalanced by a lack of other
civilized traits.

Central Asian proficiency in trade and business also forced Russians
in Tashkent to recognize mutual dependencies and vulnerability. Local
shopkeepers' dominance on the streets of Russian Tashkent was a foundational memory for many new arrivals.[49] Russian traders had difficulty
tapping trade networks that supplied relatively cheap, high-quality consumer goods as well as food. By 1868, Central Asian merchants had constructed permanent, European-style stores in the Russian city. Russian
anxiety over this dominance intensified efforts at denigration. Tsarist
soldiers ridiculed Central Asian street vendors' accents and the quality
of their goods, responding to sales pitches of "good milk" with cries
of "a mouse fell in the milk."[50] Correspondents in the local and central

Figure 17. Covered market in Asian Tashkent. *Aziaskaia Rossiia*
(St. Petersburg: Izdanie Pereselencheskogo Upravlenie, 1914), 1:321.

press disparaged Central Asian business success through comparisons
to Jews. D. Borzna reported in *Petersburgskaia Gazeta* that "Sarts, overall,
resemble the Jews, and it seems to me that they are the same tribe: the
type that has a passion for trade and cowardice."[51] Terent'ev explained:
"Sarts are a happy tribe that love money and trade; in this they have
much in common with Jews, having a weak spirit, and are unenviable
horsemen and poor at war. For money a Sart will do anything, especially
if he's poor."[52] Trade, according to this discourse, fostered softness and
dirtied the human spirit. Equating Sarts and Jews continued a centuries-
old discourse of otherness that resonated throughout Europe. Unsullied
by "dirty" business activities, Russian pride could shine forth in honor-
able pursuits, which, for the military newspaper *Russkii Invalid*, meant
combat, war, and conquest.

Central Asian control of trade nonetheless heightened a sense of
weakness. Unprivileged Russians complained that they were at the
mercy of the population they should be dominating. In an 1889 letter in
*Turkestanskiia Viedomosti*, a former tsarist soldier wrote that his and other
Russians' wives needed to beg Central Asian merchants or shoplift to
provide for their families. Forcing Russians to stoop to this level should

provoke "moral disquietude . . . this also offends our 'national pride.'"[53] The letter, one of the few published by the newspaper, indicated that such concerns had penetrated official elites. The stated desire to avoid dirtying their hands with commerce meshed poorly with the hope to control the local economy for the good of the empire.

Water, medical care, and basic goods lay outside direct Russian control. Officials or settlers could appropriate resources through negotiation or coercion, but still relied on the local population for daily necessities. Yet interdependence should not conceal a fundamental imbalance in the colonial city. Power, flowing from the soldiers' barracks on the outskirts of town, was regularly displayed in numerous ceremonies. Russians across the social spectrum practiced extortion and robbery. Military Governor Golovachev filled prisons with Central Asians who refused to pay his frequent "extraordinary" supplemental levies; officials at all levels designed new tax measures to be applied to Asian Tashkent.[54] Russian workers and soldiers regularly stole goods from Central Asian stores or farms.[55] Local writers trumpeted the variety of get-rich-quick schemes developed by Russian officers and businessmen at the expense of the colonized population.[56] Colonial exploitation operated alongside fears of unsettled hierarchies of power in Tashkent.

## Treating Cholera: A Deadly Opportunity

Cholera exposed the nature of imperial power in as well as the scale of interdependence in Tashkent. Dirt, pollution, and an epidemic disease all connected through the medium of water. R. J. Morris has argued that nineteenth-century battles against cholera were "a test of social cohesion . . . it was to watch the trust and cooperation between different parts of society strained to the utmost."[57] In 1892, cholera produced the most violent episode in the history of imperial Tashkent, one that marked important shifts in imperial policy in the city and region and became emblazoned in Russian and Central Asian memories.

Cholera had concerned Russian officials even before the first epidemic in imperial Turkestan, in 1872. The disease had made frequent previous appearances to the region, the last in 1847. Epidemics had continued westward toward Russia and Europe, killing hundreds of thousands globally.[58] Cholera struck quickly, without warning, with often fatal consequences.[59] Its course was gruesome; a victim feeling perfectly well could be dead within five hours. A vague feeling of anxiety and unwellness quickly yielded to violent spasms of vomiting and diarrhea. Grayish liquid stools were involuntarily expelled from the body. Intense seizures and a burning thirst followed, before a deep lethargy set in and the pulse faded. Muscular cramps could contort the body once more, but the victim at this point was near death, the face sunken and cadaverous, the lips puckered and blue. Death from cardiac and renal failure quickly resulted.[60] Cholera's ghastly course was only one factor that enhanced panic about the disease. European and Islamic medicine recognized that cholera most frequently afflicted those who lived in unhygienic conditions, and both underlined the need for effective sanitary measures. Yet cholera struck with "irregularity and caprice," defying social and geographic boundaries, becoming, in the minds of European contemporaries, "disorder itself."[61] Colonial situations magnified the disease's disruptive impact. In striking a small number of colonizers, in particular soldiers, cholera could alter the tenuous balance of power.[62]

Its origins also magnified cholera's significance. The bacterium, spreading to Europe from the South Asian subcontinent, symbolized the dangers of a primitive East. For Russian administrators and professionals, the inability to stem frequent cholera outbreaks had been an embarrassing marker of backwardness in comparison with the rest of Europe, which had avoided many recent pandemics.[63] To defeat cholera at its source would represent a great victory for scientific progress. Success would elevate tsarist officials and the imperial enterprise, as cholera was perceived across the imperial world as a curse, a penalty paid for the adventures of colonialism. Imperial functionaries solicited "rational and active" measures against the disease, but a divided state and medical establishment failed to provide them in the early years of Russian Tashkent.[64]

Russian officials trod carefully when cholera first arrived in Turkestan. Governor-General Kaufman enacted anti-cholera committees throughout the region, with instructions to follow the most recent measures in force in European cities.[65] Fearing a threat to his imperial capital, Kaufman focused on Asian Tashkent, where five medical stations were established. Leading a visit to Asian Tashkent at the height of the epidemic, Kaufman credited Sheikhantaur district aksakal Mulla Sultan Muhammad with "courage" for his purchase of European equipment for a cholera station and his work there himself as panic reigned.[66] The governor-general nonetheless also feared local reaction to Russian-run clinics. Seeking to avoid potential unrest at an unstable period, he had ordered that "ill natives are not to be taken [to cholera stations] against their wishes."[67] His visit sought to assure leading elders and judges of the voluntary nature of anti-cholera measures.

The 1872 epidemic ravaged both Russian and Asian Tashkent. Official statistics recorded 241 Russian deaths, including 189 soldiers, and 2,349 Muslim fatalities.[68] In 1873, the city commandant launched a study on the course and effects of the disease. Russian officials visiting Asian

Tashkent argued that intense crowding influenced death rates.[69] But the municipal doctor focused on the seventy graveyards scattered through the city. He considered these graveyards dangerous as, in accordance with prevailing miasmatic theories of disease, polluted air could arise from an improperly buried corpse and waft as far as Russian Tashkent.[70] The focus on graveyards, and threats to the health of the Russian city, continued among tsarist officials even as theories of disease changed.

Excitement over subsequent medical advances against cholera mixed with trepidation in Russian Tashkent. Robert Koch's extensive experiments around Calcutta in 1883 isolated a pure culture of the germ "comma bacillus," the cause of cholera. The discovery caused a sensation. German politicians feted Koch as a national hero, bringing glory to their country as the one that had used modern science to isolate the Asiatic disease.[71] Tashkent Russian medical officials revised measures to reflect Koch's anti-cholera recommendations, which centered on close supervision of water sources as well as strict disinfection and quarantine protocols. Municipal doctor K. K. Kazanskii, however, realized the implications of Koch's discovery that the cholera bacterium replicated most easily in water.[72] Kazanskii warned that canals could become primary conduits for the disease to Russian Tashkent. The doctor, discounting Central Asian experience with water-borne diseases, claimed that Russians were now inextricably bound to a "local population, characterized by its fatalism."[73]

Fears of the "dirty" Central Asian intensified following Koch's discoveries. Kazanskii pointed to the 1872 cholera epidemic, where, he stated, Central Asians were left to die in the streets, as evidence of their "indifference towards matters of life and death."[74] I. A. Shishmarev, in an 1891 article in *Turkestanskiia Viedomosti*, discounted Kazanskii's belief that more interventionist measures by tsarist administrators may have saved Russian as well as Central Asian lives in 1872, given the apathy of the one hundred thousand "ignorant" residents of Asian Tashkent. Shishmarev registered his disgust at Central Asians' leaving refuse strewn throughout the streets and washing their dishes and dipping body parts into canal water yet to flow into Russian Tashkent. The Russian officer, combining miasmatic and Koch's theories of disease, argued that elements of local dirtiness, in particular leaving corpses in shallow graves in the center of the Asian city, were especially dangerous as they polluted air and water. He stated that with "such a neighbor . . . the Russian city will never enjoy health, especially as it is downwind." How, he asked, would the "native administration, jointly with ours, cope with the might of a visiting epidemic, for example cholera . . . ? The disaster would be huge!"[75]

Shishmarev's fear of the "native administration" reflected a discomfort with continued reliance on Central Asian notables. This indirect system of rule had undergone recent strains. In 1887, Central Asian deputies in the city duma unsuccessfully opposed a plan to double revenues for the development of the Russian city through increased taxation, primarily on Asian Tashkent. This would exacerbate a fiscal imbalance that saw, in 1884, of a total municipal budget of 150,000 rubles, only 4,000 to 5,000 rubles spent on the Asian city.[76] Central Asian notables increased their participation in numerous schemes to conceal property and wealth from tsarist census takers.[77] Military Governor N. I. Grodekov replaced the entire leadership of Asian Tashkent in retribution. Central Asian duma representatives continued to protest inequities in spending. City board member Maksud Khoja argued that the Russian administration was purposefully neglecting the sanitary and maintenance needs of Asian Tashkent.[78] Following a failed effort to obtain greater Central Asian representation on the board, he raised the threat of widespread resistance. Inattention to Asian Tashkent's needs, Maksud Khoja argued, "causes the locals to make fun of the duma and is provoking dark conversations in meeting-places, which of course for us, as deputies, is extremely undesirable."[79] Agreeing with Shishmarev that the local administration had failed to improve sanitation in Asian Tashkent, Maksud Khoja placed the blame on poor funding by Russian administrators, which was threatening peace and stability in the colonial city.

Growing tensions over health and sanitation exposed rifts in imperial society. Confidence that Koch's measures could protect Tashkent against a future cholera outbreak mixed with concern over the continued poor state of medical, health, and sanitation services in the Asian city. Anger and threats mounted from both sides of the Ankhor canal in the late 1880s. Central Asian mediators—those who served in the duma as well as those who occupied official positions in Asian Tashkent—faced mounting pressures as cholera approached.

## The Epidemic and Riot of 1892

News that the dreaded cholera bacterium was again moving toward Tashkent came with the June 2, 1892, issue of *Turkestanskiia Viedomosti*. The article struck an optimistic tone. "Fortunately, the work of Paster [Louis Pasteur] and Kokh [Robert Koch] on microorganisms, including cholera, give hope."[80] Following reports of a cholera outbreak in Afghanistan in March, an extraordinary meeting of the Syr-Dar'ia Oblast Committee of Public Health had ordered oblast Doctor Okolov to prepare an interventionist plan based on Koch's theories.[81] Okolov commanded a thorough cleaning of all canals and close supervision of the water supply in Russian and Asian Tashkent. Disinfectant solutions were mixed. Sanitary officials stood ready to supervise designated sections of the Russian and Asian cities, each of which would have its own cholera barracks. A vital task was to ensure that ill people or dead bodies did not contact canal or ground water.[82] Such measures would enjoy success, according to the newspaper, as long as "society itself, having gained a full understanding [of their] significance, will work in a friendly way with the administration."[83] Tashkent residents were urged to read "Notes on Cholera," distributed in Russian and "native" languages. Thus prepared, the administration and the population would "await our turn for cholera with hope in the mercy of God, with faith in science, and with courageous determination not to fall before the enemy."[84]

The 1892 cholera epidemic produced a rich base of source material to investigate the colonial relationship. Syr-Dar'ia district court officials launched a detailed investigation of the causes and events of the June 24 riot. Court secretaries interrogated scores of Russian and Central Asian witnesses. Another series of interrogations formed the basis of a fall 1892 military trial of sixty Central Asians relating to the riot. Certainly, the voices that appear are heavily mediated. Central Asian complaints about the anti-cholera measures appear formulaic, and witnesses denied direct participation in demonstrations. Testimony nonetheless detailed how the measures violated Muslim beliefs and how opposition built. Given the dearth of Central Asian voices available to historians of the period, the interrogations offer a unique opportunity to view cultural differences and dynamics of power and resistance from both sides of Tashkent.[85]

One important detail that emerges from the planning of the anti-cholera measures was the absence of any participation from the local Central Asian population. The Committee of Public Health was composed of Russian officers and functionaries, as well as one Kazakh, Tashkent city doctor Khamafiia Mirza Aliev Batyrshin. Batyrshin, trained in Orenburg, played an important role in local society, having served alongside Sharafii bai Zeinalgabidin as "Muslim" members of the inaugural city board. Their presence signaled Russian officials' initial distrust of indigenous Tashkent residents and their desire to use Muslims already socialized to the empire. Batyrshin and Zeinalgabidin maintained their own distance from Central Asian society. Both shared a belief in their own role as "enlighteners" of Central Asians, and the assumption of local dirtiness and backwardness.[86] Yet Batyrshin had campaigned in the 1880s for greater funds for Asian Tashkent, including the construction of a hospital.[87] Officials from Asian Tashkent remained isolated from the commission, with no input on planned measures on their side of the Ankhor canal nor on protection of the shared water supply.

The absence of Central Asian representation did not prevent duma member N. I. Mandel'shtam from launching into a tirade against Asian Tashkent's "complete lack of preparedness" for a cholera epidemic at a May 7 duma session.[88] Mandel'shtam, who had recently voted down increased funding for the Asian city, used the argument of a lack of infrastructure to justify a plan that would see the Russian section, one-fifth the size, receive sixteen cholera barracks as opposed to just four for Asian Tashkent.[89] In the end, by the time the epidemic struck, only one barrack had been established in the Asian city, in the Sheikhantaur district that bordered Russian Tashkent.

On June 2, as *Turkestanskiia Viedomosti* announced the imminent arrival of the disease, incidents of which had spread throughout surrounding regions, the city board established medical observation points on main roads into Tashkent.[90] One leading official, however, did not see his presence necessary in the besieged capital. Governor-General A. B. Vrevskii decamped Tashkent for Chimgan and his annual vacation on June 7. Cholera came to Tashkent that same day. After manifesting symptoms of the disease, the widow of Russian settler Aleksandr Khudinkov, recently arrived from Samarkand, went to the military hospital, where city doctor Batyrshin pronounced her ill with cholera. Batyrshin placed her in quarantine and sent officials to disinfect her apartment before notifying administrators that the bacterium had penetrated city limits.[91]

Despite cholera's initial appearance in the Russian section, City Commandant Putintsev focused his attention on Asian Tashkent as he implemented recommendations of the district medical committee. Putintsev dispatched dozens of Russian "medical assistants" across the Ankhor canal to search for residents with cholera symptoms.[92] In a marked departure from 1872, their mandate was broad: to deliver ill people or dead bodies to clinics or cholera stations, regardless of the wishes of the sick or the family members of the ill or dead.[93] Officials at these stations could then begin disinfection and quarantine protocols. Tsarist General M. A. Terent'ev later blamed the actions of these inspectors, often young and inexperienced clerks with no medical training, for raising tension in the days preceding the riot. "Dressed in officers' clothes," he wrote, "these gentlemen [*gospoda*] appeared with the police at the homes of the natives and . . . entered the women's quarters, and under the pretext of observing its cleanliness allowed themselves to take various liberties with the women . . . in the presence of their fathers and mothers."[94] Either Central Asian accounts of the anger that precipitated the June 24 demonstration remained silent on this point during interrogations or their testimony was not recorded. This silence remains a mystery, difficult to interpret. Russian officials nonetheless agreed following June 24 to local demands to alter search protocols, issuing written orders banning the invasion of homes.

Central Asian testimony did condemn numerous other effects of the measures. These included the requirement to bring the victim of any illness, or any cadaver, immediately to Russian medical clinics or cholera stations, or at least to notify the police. Movement of the ill or dead anywhere else was forbidden. Another measure required even the healthy to restrict their movements, banning travel outside the suburbs of Tashkent.[95] Asian Tashkent resident Seiful Mir Alimov detailed hostility toward these procedures in his testimony before tsarist authorities. Residents resented the presence of tsarist officials. Seiful Mir Alimov declared that the antagonism of the population grew when medical officials dispatched the ill to a clinic: "sending the ill away caused unhappiness, as the ill then died there, and their treatment took place away from their family. But expressions of our unhappiness brought no results."[96]

The protocol for handling the ill contravened a number of local practices. Residents of Asian Tashkent received home visits and immediate treatments of herb broths and poultices, animal and mineral oils, and other products applied by a "healer father."[97] Evidence of Central Asian responses to the epidemic is scanty. Russian officials reported that many of the wealthy opened their own houses to serve as clinics.[98] The measures that stirred the greatest reaction concerned the treatment of the dead. The city commandant had ordered Muhammad Yaqub, the head aksakal of Asian Tashkent, upon pain of imprisonment, to enforce provisions banning the movement of all cadavers without a tsarist official's supervision and requiring cholera victims to be buried at a special graveyard outside city limits. Large funeral processions were banned. The ritual Islamic cleansing of the body could be performed only at the graveside.[99]

Measures concerning corpses contravened local and Islamic practices, which, during an epidemic, emphasized sanitary protection as well as religious custom. Corpses underwent careful washing, using water from special wells. Sheets covered the body completely. Special attendants then washed the entire room. Funeral processions, during which the body was carried by hand out of respect for the dead, also contained special measures. Those carrying the corpse followed a thorough washing procedure after arrival at the graveyard. Finally, healers ordered the family of the dead to wait three extra days before serving meals for friends and relatives to mark the victim's memory.[100] No evidence exists, however, to show that Russians in Tashkent took account of the sanitary value of these practices in 1892.

Muhammad Yaqub, in his testimony to tsarist authorities, argued that adherence to established traditions made tsarist measures impossible to enforce. In 1890, the Asian city held seventy-four graveyards, reflecting the high degree of mahalla identification.[101] One Muslim observer noted the "particular unhappiness at having to bury the dead away from families."[102] By providing only one cholera graveyard outside the bounds of the geographically largest city in the Russian empire, Putintsev made it extremely difficult to continue the practice of carrying the victim by hand to the grave. Mullas hesitated to venture outside their own districts, complicating mourners' efforts to find a figure to offer prayers easing the transition of the deceased from this world to the next.[103] Execution of the measures also raised the frustration of local residents. Russian sanitary officials took days before inspecting bodies, violating Muslim customs that demand a quick burial.[104] Given such pressures, according to Muhammad Yaqub, "it was completely understandable that among the population arose the wish to conceal ill or dead bodies."[105]

Interventionist measures placed strains upon a ruling mechanism rendered extremely fragile by recent maneuverings of the imperial regime. In spring 1892, for reasons that are unclear, Military Governor Grodekov replaced head aksakal Inogam Khoja, from the Sebzar district, with Muhammad Yaqub, then leading aksakal of the Sheikhantaur district.[106] The removal followed a five-year period during which Inogam Khoja had placed family members and Sebzar associates in all leading posts. He secured the goodwill of Russian officials through restoring order following the 1887 tax protests, assuring ample tax collections, and facilitating the participation of select Russian officials in business schemes in Asian Tashkent.[107] Inogam Khoja retained influence following his removal. City Commandant Putintsev continued frequent visits to the former senior aksakal's home.[108] Muhammad Yaqub claimed that Putintsev forbade him from making personnel changes in Asian Tashkent, forcing him to rely on Inogam Khoja's associates. The city commandant enforced these limitations, the head aksakal argued, as well as strict anti-cholera measures, to trigger an uprising and reinstall his friend as leader of Asian Tashkent. This argument underlined the complex relationship between Russian and Central Asian elites. Imperial practice made senior officials of Asian Tashkent responsible to their tsarist overlords and precluded interaction with the local population that tsarist officials and Muhammad Yaqub later saw as so lacking in the days leading up to the riot.

As cholera victims mounted, with more than a dozen deaths daily by mid-June, so did Central Asian anger toward the anti-cholera measures.[109] Bodies awaiting inspection lay decomposing in the summer heat. Medical inspectors violated Muslim custom that forbade men from touching the dead bodies of women.[110] Rumors attributed sinister goals to Russian intervention. Cholera frequently prompted rumors in afflicted regions by residents laying blame for the havoc wreaked by the disease. The dispossessed employed the bacterium as a medium to express anger at their place in the social structure. Rumors, according to Donald Horowitz, consolidate frustration at identifiable targets and heighten the potential for violence.[111] In Asian Tashkent, stories condemned the tsarist state and Russian medical practices. One rumor involved a plot to poison the Ankhor canal.[112] Fears of diseases imported through water between the two cities were not limited to the colonizer.

Rumors and discontent coalesced into open protests. Mirza Rajab Muhammadov, a contractor, informed the Office of the Governor-General on June 18 that protesters were circulating a petition, destined for the Russian Senate, demanding the anti-cholera measures' revocation.[113] On June 20, aksakal Mulla Sadyk convened a meeting of political and religious leaders at the Khanak mosque. He testified that the meeting emerged from cries for help from the poor, for "the new cemetery was far away, and it was difficult to bring their dead there."[114] The crowd heard speeches on the measures' contravention of Islamic law, the sharia. The meeting elected three deputies to negotiate with the city commandant.[115] Another rally was held at the Tallak mosque on June 22. Central Asian witnesses claimed that only nonviolent protest measures were discussed. Leaders sought to work within the legal framework of imperial rule. Yet their resolve to bypass the head aksakal violated colonial practice. Muhammad Yaqub accordingly sent word of rising discontent to Putintsev. The city commandant was wrestling with a growing epidemic in Russian Tashkent as well, with a record nine deaths on June 22. N. A. Maev offered a grim assessment of the situation. He blamed poor Russian settlers who used water that had become tainted while it was passing through Asian Tashkent and who refused to visit anti-cholera situations.[116] To contain the widening disease, Putintsev decided that Central Asian recalcitrance required a direct response.

Putintsev rode out from his apartment to the heart of Asian Tashkent as dawn broke on June 23, the hottest day of the year. He arrived at the central Jami mosque near the end of prayer services marking the *Qurban-bayram* holiday.[117] Speaking in the local language before a crowd of several thousand, Putintsev insisted that anti-cholera measures had been instituted following the latest scientific knowledge. Rumors that Russians were poisoning the local population were complete nonsense. Putintsev stated that "Russians do not have any reason to hurt natives; had they, they could have exterminated them much earlier." Rather than arousing protest, anti-cholera policies should allow "the natives themselves to see how the White Tsar watches over them."[118] Putintsev then left the stage to join Muhammad Yaqub and other aksakals for tea inside the mosque.

The city commandant's words offered no hope of softening the anti-cholera measures. Years of neglect toward the sanitary state of Asian Tashkent undercut his argument concerning the attention of the "White Tsar," a term that itself implied a racial division.[119] The word "exterminate" provided a reminder that subjugation and violence lay at the heart of colonial rule. Putintsev dismissed Sebzar district aksakal Kamalbek's warnings of mounting local anger and warned that he expected nothing less than full compliance with and enforcement of the anti-cholera measures.[120]

Putintsev's stance and a worsening of the epidemic precipitated an explosion of "unauthorized" burials on the night of June 23. Subterfuge had emerged as a tactic early in the epidemic. Muslims concealed persons afflicted by any disease from the authorities or bribed Russian medical inspectors for a certificate that the illness contracted was not cholera. Muslim clerics and police officers supervised burials of bodies, not yet examined by the authorities, in regular graveyards.[121] Shortly after 1 A.M., police officer Ahmed Khoja reported three unauthorized burials in the Zebok mahalla to Muhammad Yaqub. Ahmed Khoja later testified that, upon his return to the mahalla, a crowd that included several elders, believing he planned to exhume the bodies, forced him to retreat. Muhammad Yaqub testified that he heard several similar reports from police on the morning of June 24. He claimed that the officers, allies of Inogam Khoja, may have been inciting crowds to provoke a coup in the Asian city. The senior aksakal, asserting fear for his safety, crossed the Ankhor canal to seek Putintsev's authority.[122]

Muhammad Yaqub departed shortly before the arrival at his house of a crowd, led by aksakals Ahmed Khoja Abdurashid Khojin and Iakup Khoja Iusup Khoja, seeking a public renunciation of the anti-cholera measures. Witnesses reported hearing angry threats directed at not only Muhammad Yaqub, but also Seid Karim, a Central Asian serving on the city board.[123] Once the crowd discovered the flight of Muhammad Yaqub, it pursued him into Russian Tashkent.

No firsthand testimony exists surrounding the crowd's decision to cross the Ankhor canal. The goal of the protesters—to corral Muhammad Yaqub before he met Putintsev—was consistent with previous strategies of avoiding direct confrontation with Russian authorities. Never, however, had a Central Asian protest stretched to Russian Tashkent. V. Zykin has argued that the high numbers in the crowd of day laborers, hurt by the ban on movement around the city, indicated the primacy of economic motives.[124] Certainly, the ban had a significant economic impact, preventing these laborers from earning money at the height of the cotton harvest season. The testimony analyzed below, however, reveals

Central Asian opposition centered on other measures in force during the epidemic and shows an awareness of ethnic and cultural differences that legitimated colonial power.

Witness testimony to district and military courts varied significantly on the mood and intentions of the crowd, estimated from two hundred to two thousand. Central Asians working for the tsarist administration reported the most hostile words, including, "slaughter the senior aksakal or the city commandant!"[125] Musa Magomet Rustambaev, an Asian Tashkent resident working as a police officer in the Russian city, claimed that he warned the crowd of the consequences of its actions: "I said 'Muslims, what are you doing? Be careful! For your actions the poor will die! Tashkent will die!'"[126] It is unclear whether demonstrators made a conscious decision to limit inflammatory comments to fellow Central Asians, or whether those reporting such statements sought to make the crowd appear hostile in contrast to their own "loyal" behavior.

Russian observers painted a calmer picture of the protest. Many thought the crowd in search of supplies to celebrate Qurban-bayram. G. P. Fedorov reported that Russians watched the demonstration with curiosity.[127] M. A. Putianin, a retired assessor, queried one demonstrator on the reason for the march. The reply came: "[There is] a big row: Muhammad Yaqub is not allowing burials, threatening to exhume bodies, and is reporting us."[128] Medical assistant Lepikhin mixed with the crowd, and reported coming to no harm.[129] Initial Russian nonchalance indicated a level of comfort with cross-cultural contact in Tashkent virtually absent from other public or archival sources of the era. Settlers and Central Asians came together for economic and personal relationships. Many Russians understood some vocabulary of the local language. As long as the crowd, apparently seeking to settle scores with one of its own, seemed not to threaten the balance of imperial power, it was perceived as relatively harmless. N. I. Gal'kin, however, noted that demonstrators seemed well aware of their potential vulnerability as well as the ethno-religious character of the demonstration, shouting to Central Asian street merchants, "Muslims—join us!"[130]

Not long after traversing the Ankhor canal, the crowd unexpectedly ran into Putintsev and Muhammad Yaqub, who were heading back to Asian Tashkent to verify rumors of unauthorized burials. Muhammad Yaqub berated the crowd for crossing the Ankhor canal. According to the city commandant, "from the crowd began cries, that the aksakal was not allowing burials and was poisoning the water in the streams" followed by "give us the aksakal, and we will beat him."[131] Demonstrators pursued Muhammad Yaqub to the city administration building, with Putintsev following.

Limited violence accompanied the pursuit. The account that depicts the crowd as most hostile comes from Central Asian police officer Seid Ahmad Shaikbaev, who claimed that demonstrators beat and robbed him. Putintsev, hearing complaints against supposed Russian efforts to poison the Ankhor canal, reported that a few crowd members attempted to punch him before others intervened to stop the attack.[132] No other testimony recounted any attacks on Russians; Seid Ahmad Shaikbaev's account again seemingly emphasizes demonstrators' efforts to strike at those seen as collaborating with Russian rule. Putintsev felt comfortable enough to await alone the arrival of the military summoned by his assistants.[133]

The crowd's subsequent acts can be read as a desire for greater autonomy for Asian Tashkent. Inside the administration building, protesters, after searching for Muhammad Yaqub, who apparently was hiding in a cabinet, gathered in the rooms that handled the affairs of the Asian city. One Russian observer reported cries of "Give us Sart [local] law, we don't need Russian!"[134] They dumped ink over signed orders and destroyed documents and issues of *Turkestanskiia Viedomosti*.[135] Demonstrators then surrounded the city commandant, and, according to his testimony, demanded expulsion of all Russian personnel from Asian Tashkent. Central Asians never mentioned this demand, perhaps seeking to shield themselves from accusations of sedition. Protesters demonstrated their sensitivity to legal practices, producing a document that demanded the revocation of all anti-cholera measures. Multiple cries of "Sign!" were aimed at Putintsev.

Failing to find Muhammad Yaqub or secure Putintsev's signature, the crowd was dispersing when a few unarmed soldiers of a musical company arrived. Their presence sparked the Russian reaction. Quiescence before the Central Asian incursion into the municipal administration building turned to violence. Russian settlers, witnessing the direct challenge to imperial rule, moved with soldiers toward the crowd, attacking with fists and sticks even before troops led by Military Governor Grodekov arrived. G. P. Fedorov, an official in the Office of the Governor-General, stated that the invasion of the municipal administration building betrayed the protestors as "dirty street vagabonds" exploiting cholera to beat up Russians.[136] A lethal carnage ensued. As Donald Horowitz argued, in ethnic riots, this was no "lighthearted or ritualized test of strength—it was deadly serious."[137] Russian soldiers and settlers used violence to enforce the boundary between colonizer and colonized.

Testimony of witnesses and observer accounts demonstrate the divisions exposed by the riot. Nobody who was interviewed or who recorded the event blamed it on economic pressure or the paranoia or madness of a population unsure of where cholera would strike next. The

Russian attack became a deadly statement against not just the demonstrators, but any Central Asian present in the Russian city. Cries rang out of "Beat the Sarts until they fall!"[138] Gal'kin noted that Russians rallied around an Orthodox priest, Zolotov, who implored them to tear up wooden fences and use the posts as weapons.[139] Zolotov symbolized the conflict of religions, which was also highlighted by Kurbam Badaev, a translator for Grodekov. Badaev reported that his efforts to get Central Asians in the Urdu bazaar—on the border between the two sections—to return to Asian Tashkent were met with cries of "we are [treated as] the infidel [*kafiry*]."[140] Russians dragged Central Asian shopkeepers from their stalls and attacked them alongside the retreating crowd. Several accounts blamed Military Governor Grodekov for further inciting violence with actions such as yelling, "Russian brothers, arm yourselves with anything and beat them."[141] Battered and dead bodies, estimated at between eighty and one hundred, were then thrown into the Ankhor canal. The act closed a circle of association between disease, water, and the "dirty" Central Asian. A cordon prevented any more crossings into the city.[142]

Grodekov, meanwhile, led his troops into Asian Tashkent and opened fire on a peaceful gathering outside the Jami mosque, killing at least ten. The shootings served as a message to those in the Asian city that the tsarist state would employ deadly force to enforce domination.[143] No Russians in Asian Tashkent had come to harm; A. I. Mandel'shtam, a doctor at a clinic in the city, reported traveling and working in June 24 without incident. Four infantry squadrons and two Cossack companies nonetheless remained in the center of the Asian city. Grodekov ordered the deputy city commandant to establish a list of "influential Muslims" and arrest them, regardless of their involvement in the protest.[144] The military governor believed notables merited collective punishment for failure to make their population obey the tsarist state.

Municipal officials did not fulfill Grodekov's request. Political elites on both sides of the Ankhor canal sought conciliation in the wake of the violence. Tsarist officials and aksakals, worried about the riot's unmediated nature, worked to assuage tensions and prevent a repeat of an incident that might threaten their privileged status. On June 30, the Office of the Governor-General arranged a reconciliation ceremony. Fourteen leading aksakals crossed the Ankhor canal to meet Governor-General Vrevskii, recently returned from Chimgan, and a host of leading tsarist officials. Abdul Kasym presented a petition with one thousand signatures pledging "boundless loyalty" to the tsar. The regrettable incident of June 24, caused by "mindless fools" interested only in toppling Muhammad Yaqub, would never be repeated.[145] "Signed with tears," the petition ostensibly assured the subject population's loyalty.

Russian and Central Asian leaders worked to control the meanings of the riot as well as prevent a repeat of violence. The ceremony avoided any implication of ethno-cultural division. Rather, the riot was presented as an action of pawns in a contest for power between Muhammad Yaqub and the man he replaced, Inogam Khoja. Internal politics in Asian Tashkent provided convenient cover for Russian authorities and local mediators to deflect attention away from troubling implications of ethnic discord.

Tsarist officials offered significant rewards for pledges of loyalty. Governor-General Vrevskii withdrew troops from Asian Tashkent in response to arguments that locals, afraid to enter the streets, could not attend mosque services to pray for the tsar.[146] Most remarkably, Russian colonial authorities ceased enforcement of all anti-cholera measures in Asian Tashkent, despite a severe worsening of the epidemic.[147] The image of the "dirty Muslim" now justified separation instead of intervention. Vrevskii claimed to fear that tsarist officials and soldiers in Asian Tashkent would be more susceptible to the cholera bacterium. This new policy sparked dissension. Grodekov demanded the measures' restoration, arguing that the Asian city had become a "hearth of cholera infection," but to no avail.[148] Faith in science as a transformative tool withered before the prospect of a loss of colonial control.

The tsarist military tribunal portrayed the riot as flowing from poor leadership from selected Russian and Central Asian administrators.[149] Putintsev and Grodekov were sacked for failure to recognize the gravity of Central Asian anger toward the anti-cholera measures and curb the violence of June 24. Central Asian leaders were punished selectively. Chief prosecutor Reinbot did not charge aksakals involved in demonstrations prior to June 24, calling the circulating of petitions and election of deputies "completely legal" under Russian law.[150] Of the sixty Central Asians charged, thirty-five were released. Among eight who received a death sentence—later commuted by the minister of war—was Inogam Khoja, the former senior aksakal, who was by all accounts at his home the entire day of the riot. Yet his conviction bolstered the public interpretation of the riot flowing from Asian Tashkent's internal politics. Among others who received death sentences were aksakals Ahmed Khoja Abdurashid Khoja and Iakup Khoja Iusup Khoja, charged with forming the crowd and inciting it to "violence, theft, and murder."[151] The trial produced an image of ethnic relations provisionally damaged by a confluence of flawed personnel and poisoned political relationships. Over Reinbot's protestations, none of the Russian civilians involved in the riot were charged, despite evidence presented of wanton killings.

A growing sense of suspicion and hostility accompanied Russian efforts at accommodation. Governor-General Vrevskii, shortly after honoring Abdul Kasym and withdrawing Russian troops, abolished the position of head aksakal in favor of a Russian commandant. Many of the aksakals and religious judges serving on June 24, including Muhiddin Khoja, lost their positions. The governor-general also applied to the minister of war for a statute of emergency rule. He labeled the June 24 demonstrators a "black, malevolent" force. Their riotous actions were "a reflection of the true character" of all Central Asians who, due to their Muslim faith, are "hostile to us in principle." Any pretext, such as cholera, could mobilize instigators to rouse the "primitive" native of the population to opposition.[152] Vrevskii argued that Russian "humanitarian laws" betrayed weakness to a population that recognized only unbridled power.[153] Images of the dark, backward, and fanatic Muslim justified an extension of administrative control.

The minister of war approved Vrevskii's request. A September 1, 1892, decree ordered a temporary state of emergency in the city and district of Tashkent, as well as two other districts of the Syr-Dar'ia oblast and the Fergana valley. The state of emergency allowed officials to rule "administratively" on violations of any law, to forbid any public or private meeting, to close any trading or industrial establishment, and to forbid anyone entrance into the region.[154] Vrevskii had argued that such measures would not only quell unrest, but allow for a more aggressive collection of tax revenues, decreasing Turkestan's reliance on the center. Imperial officials used these new powers to assert control over Asian Tashkent. Soldiers and police mounted a series of raids on local teahouses in 1892–93, arresting those "without passports, without a determined occupation, and involved in carousing or gambling."[155] Despite resistance that frequently turned violent, scores of Central Asians were arrested and dozens of teahouses in the city closed. The minister of war turned down some other requests made by the governor-general and Military Governor Grodekov, including the exile of all "troublesome" Central Asians from Tashkent and the ability to appoint personally all aksakals of the Asian city, rather than have them selected through Russian-sponsored elections. But the emergency statute proved a powerful and permanent legacy of the cholera epidemic and riot, as ministers of war granted annual renewals until 1917.

Local Russian writers, mainly former officers, presented the cholera epidemic as a seminal event that altered relations in Tashkent. *Turkestanskiia Viedomosti* now commonly decried Muslims as "dark" and "blackened." In 1913, G. P. Fedorov wrote that the invasion of the municipal administration building set off a "panicked fear" as settlers realized the "reality that a 200,000-strong [*sic*] fanaticized population could at any time slaughter all of us like chickens."[156] The image of the "fanatic Muslim," which had waned following the completion of tsarist military campaigns in the late 1870s, reemerged in Russian society. Lieutenant General Terent'ev's account of the riot in 1906 described the Muslim crowd as determined to prosecute a holy war (*ghazavat*) and applauded Grodekov's shooting of Muslims in the Asian city on June 24 as a reprisal.[157] He depicted Russian townsmen "joining in the hunt" for Central Asians.[158] Fedorov universally condemned the residents and the city of Asian Tashkent. "The natives . . . live in unimaginable filth in the most unsanitary conditions. They lack the notion of even the most elementary demands of cleanliness. . . . You can judge, what a favorable climate cholera found in that huge, stinking sewer of a city."[159] Fedorov ignored official statistics that, although they must be viewed with skepticism given efforts by poor Russians as well as Central Asians to evade official measures, indicated equal rates of death, proportionally, on each side of Tashkent, with a listing of 1,462 Muslim, 217 Russian civilian, and 87 Russian military cholera fatalities.[160]

Public efforts to encourage accommodation and promote the superiority of European science did continue following the riot. On April 7, 1893, Governor-General Vrevskii visited Asian Tashkent on Qurban-bayram. Pomp and circumstance surrounded the visit, as Vrevskii rode through a massive arch in the city center bearing the words "welcome" and headed, accompanied by a large crowd, toward the cholera graveyard.[161] There, he paid respects to Abdul Kasym, who died shortly after offering the petition of loyalty. Vrevskii then presented medals and awards to all those holding administrative positions in Asian Tashkent. A new generation of mediators, it was hoped, would restore stability. Some who had served in 1892 returned to good graces, including Muhiddin Khoja, who went on to attend Tsar Nicholas II's coronation in 1894. Yet the abolition of the post of head aksakal and the imposition of emergency rule bore witness to the diminished trust in Central Asian notables.[162] The visit also sought to restore shaken beliefs in the superiority of Russian medicine. On an inspection of the men's and women's clinics staffed by Russian doctors, Vrevskii admonished spectators to seek care for any illness there.[163] He sought to accomplish what the epidemic had failed to do: convince Central Asians of the effectiveness of European medical care.

The unrest of 1892 nonetheless once more altered Russian elites' discourse and strategies toward public health as well as the Central Asian population. Language of the "dirty Muslim" continued now to legitimate an isolationist instead of an interventionist strategy. Terent'ev wrote bitterly of post-1892 Russian attitudes, which had shifted from one of trying to help the local population to one of saying "you do not want our care, therefore as many as you like will die."[164] Imperial authorities instituted no invasive measures during the next appearance of the cholera virus, in 1908. Municipal doctor A. Shvarts wrote then that "the main principles in the struggle against cholera in the native section had been firmly established: do not interfere with either religious or cultural conventions of the natives."[165] Shvarts blamed Central Asians for the failure of Russian progress. Even wealthy notables who consulted Russian physicians refused their help when afflicted with cholera. If this was the case, Shvarts argued: "What could you expect from the dark masses of the backward natives, who, rarely coming into contact with Russians, are hardened fanatics and intrinsic fatalists?"[166] Dismissive of any value of local medicine, Shvarts presented the locals as incapable of absorbing aspects of "civilization." Gone was the redemptive language of a generation earlier.

The events surrounding the "cholera riot" upheld inequalities while underlining the intricacies of Russian colonial society in Tashkent. Violence was confirmed as the ultimate arbiter between colonizer and colonized. At the same time, colonial officials realized the necessity of cooperation with the local population. Central Asian mediators assured stability, businessmen brought trade, engineers supplied water, and residents provided taxes and labor. These contacts continued, and indeed intensified, as both Russian and Asian Tashkent developed at a rapid pace. Russians, frustrated by the interdependencies of colonial rule, strengthened the demonization and racialization of the colonized population. The year 1892 became a powerful example of where ethnic divisions, characteristics, and power were most clearly distilled. Central Asian success in having anti-cholera measures lifted was seen as ultimate proof of their backwardness. The dance between separation and dependence, dominance and vulnerability, grew more difficult to perform following the epidemic and bloodshed of the cholera riot.

Damaged in this new discourse was the enthusiasm of the "civilizing mission." Russians failed to employ the tools of European science to thwart cholera as it approached Europe. Efforts to distance themselves from Central Asians and the Slavic poor hardly restored the hubris of Russian administrators and writers. In the "cholera riot," Central Asians acted with restraint and employed efforts accepted at the time as more "civilized" than the Russians involved in the violence. A study of this riot should prompt questioning of common assumptions of cholera crowds, particularly but not exclusively non-Western, as driven by madness.[167] It also highlights the fragile nature of colonial control, on a razor's edge between accommodation and violence. The complexities of imperial rule confronted colonial officials and Russian elites, whose isolation of the subalterns they hoped to transform only intensified their own sense of alienation from progress and "civilization."

# 4.

# *Migration, Class, and Colonialism*

"The growth of Tashkent has engendered the development of a proletariat, the inevitable evil of all European societies, the dark, reverse side of our civilization. It will be easier to combat this evil now, before it lays its tenacious roots."[1] N. A. Maev printed this warning in *Turkestanskiia Viedomosti* following the migration of increasing numbers of poor Russians in the early 1880s. The author bristled at the appearance of these newcomers, identified by their hungry faces, ragged dress, and mud shacks on the edge of Russian Tashkent. His article reflected tsarist administrators' and intellectuals' fears that this underclass threatened a self-image of Russians as representatives of a superior European civilization. A "proletariat" could also spark class conflict in Tashkent, fragmenting minority Russians in full view of the colonized Central Asians.

Fears of lower-class Russian migrants in Tashkent predated the formation of an organized proletariat.[2] The 1848 revolutions and incidents of social conflict across the continent heightened suspicion of the urban underprivileged among European elites, including those in Russia.[3] Concerns over the poor's blurring the boundary between privileged Russians and backward Central Asians intensified anxieties among Maev and his colleagues. Such worries outweighed hopes that increased numbers of settlers would engender greater security for the entire Russian community. Just as with the Central Asians, poor settlers became foils against which Russian writers and officials defined ideas of progress and civilization. Such a strategy mirrored elite attitudes toward the peasantry in central Russia, where, Cathy Frierson has argued, denigratory language served to assist a "process of self-definition."[4] To bind themselves together as a colonial elite, officers, intellectuals, merchants, professionals, and other privileged Russians employed discourse and policies alienating the poor. These efforts produced tensions and unforeseen results. Neglect of the Russian poor worsened their condition and increased their contacts with the Central Asian population, evoking fears of hybridity and miscegenation. Prostitution emerged as an important issue in Russian Tashkent, defying boundaries of race, class, and gender, and exemplifying the lack of control felt by imperial elites toward subject groups.

Russian workers and other plebeian settlers played critical roles in the development of imperial Tashkent. Tsarist officials and mercantile elites, even as they professed opposition to increased migration, tailored policies and hiring practices that attracted poor Russians from the metropole. Cotton processing and other industries sparked a boom in Tashkent in the 1880s. Railways that linked the city to central Russia in the late 1890s and 1900s accelerated growth. Along with the railway came railway workers. Highly skilled as well as schooled in the language of class, these workers at once profited from colonial power and protested their subordinate status and distance from tsarist elites. Activist railway workers spread their own brand of socialist ideology during the 1905 revolution, one that fixed themselves as prime agents of progress against a corrupt tsarist regime but denied equality to the colonized Central Asians. These workers also distanced themselves from the unskilled and uncultured poor of the Russian suburbs, in so doing affirming their own claim to privilege and "civilization."

## The "Proletariat": Fracturing the Settler Community?

Russian Tashkent rapidly expanded in the decades following the conquest. Small numbers of Slavic artisans and construction workers, drawn by the promise of higher salaries or the opportunity to escape creditors, arrived in the early 1870s.[5] In 1872, the first census of Russian Tashkent's urban population counted 628 "workers" among a civilian population of 2,073. Russians composed a bare majority of these workers, with the rest designated as Muslims and Jews.[6] Subsequent censuses divided the local population by religious affiliation and the official tsarist social categories of *sosloviia* (estates).[7] The city commandant's 1877 census, which included military personnel, counted 13,236 Orthodox Christians, 652 other Christians, and 618 Jews in the Russian city. The census recorded 2,518 meshchane (townspeople), a *soslovie* (estate) that, in cities throughout Russia, included many workers. Conspicuously absent from the census was the largest soslovie in Russia, the peasantry, which also furnished urban labor.[8] In neglecting this category, census takers may have sought to dissimulate lower-class, rural origins of their population and reinforce the idea of their community as one of progress and privilege.

Former peasants nonetheless composed part of the largest category of the 1877 census: tsarist soldiers. The census counted 9,123 active personnel as well as 1,812 military retirees. Retired soldiers constituted a significant segment of Russian Tashkent's labor force. They worked as tailors, shoemakers, carpenters, metalworkers, blacksmiths, and petty traders.[9] Tsarist officials offered housing benefits for former soldiers, who could provide military support to the regime and offered a ready-made, "domestic" working class in Russian Tashkent.[10] Yet soldiers' and ex-soldiers' behavior disquieted leading tsarist officials. They gained a reputation for indiscriminate drinking, gambling, and frequenting of prostitutes. G. P. Fedorov complained that displays of "debauchery" attracted young Central Asians, who witnessed the "seamy side" of Russian civilization.[11]

Policies of economic development assured needs for Russian workers would increase. Governor-General Kaufman envisioned the city as Turkestan's industrial center, at first to process the cotton that he planned as the primary export good.[12] In 1871, Kaufman dispatched representatives as far afield as Texas to find the seed best suited for machine spinning. By the end of the decade, transplanted strains of American upland cotton sparked an economic surge. Russian and Central Asian businessmen profited from favorable taxation and tariff polices to organize cotton farms and induce local farmers to grow the plant.[13] Large Moscow and Vladimir firms opened operations and rough-processing factories across Turkestan. Imperial officials took advantage of the new trade; French traveler Henri Moser, visiting Tashkent in 1882, wrote "there is . . . a true cotton fever; officers are quitting their posts to take up this new occupation. The new enterprises are achieving a rate of profitability of one hundred percent."[14] Governor-General N. O. fon Rozenbakh gave away American seeds and hosted at his mansion annual congresses of cotton growers. Rozenbakh claimed that yields increased fifteenfold during his tenure, from 20,000 to 300,000 *pudy*.[15]

Cotton development propelled efforts to recruit wageworkers. Russian merchants had relied primarily on ex-soldier and Central Asian labor for earlier ventures that included beer, wine, tobacco, brick, and leather factories.[16] Rough-processing cotton plants, a number of which opened in the mid-1880s, demanded skilled workers to operate expensive new machinery. Russian and Central Asian owners alike preferred Russian labor, as they perceived Central Asians as less willing and less suited to work in a factory environment. Word of jobs and opportunities spread to European Russia, attracting several hundred migrants annually in the 1880s.

Tsarist officials treated new migrants of imperial society with neglect. By the 1880s, as increasing numbers of soldiers remained in Turkestan to exploit new opportunities, the Office of the Governor-General ceased the policy of giving them lots in the city center.[17] Retired soldiers joined skilled and unskilled labor migrants who had gathered pell-mell on the dusty, undeveloped edges of the city, called the "New Settlement." As the settlement swelled, the city board in late 1883 sent a fact-finding mission, which discovered "astonishing things, successfully cooped up for the past eight years."[18] Bars and houses of prostitution, designed for the "greater amusement" of inhabitants, proliferated. "Monstrous amounts of waste" were strewn about these institutions, and the entire quarter. The committee recommended the closure and rapid disinfection of several establishments, to reduce moral and physical dangers for Tashkent inhabitants, yet it recommended no measures to improve the sanitary or living conditions of the quarter as a whole.

Of greatest concern to the committee was the significant Central Asian presence in the New Settlement. It noted that Central Asians owned many of the dirtier bars and brothels, which were "infecting" poor Russians who visited. Worse, Central Asian men, "on periodic binges," not only had developed a fondness for alcohol, but consorted with Russian women, particularly prostitutes.[19] Tashkent Russian officials obsessed about such liaisons and appeared to conceal the results of these unions.[20] Archival sources, official statistics, and the local press are eerily silent on long-term relationships or marriage between Russians and Central Asians, or the existence of "mixed" children. Only allusions to Russian soldiers taking "temporary" Central Asian wives are present in settler memoirs.[21] One article in a 1913 newspaper describes a local Muslim beaten to death by a Russian whose wife had "paid [the Muslim] a visit."[22] No solid evidence exists to discuss mixed marriages or miscegenation; the danger such unions posed to the visions of colonial superiority may have forced their dissimulation.

Prostitution turned tsarist officials' attention toward the New Settlement. Officials had banned brothels, seen as damaging to an image of European moral superiority, from the city center in 1873.[23] Police nonetheless registered one hundred prostitutes in 1876, twenty Russians and eighty Central Asians, the latter largely consisting of women cast out of family networks.[24] In 1888, City Commandant Smirnov declared the presence of "teahouses," Central Asian–owned establishments that served as fronts for prostitution, the most serious problem in the New

Settlement. He proposed their removal to an unpopulated northeast corner of Tashkent. An ensuing commission of leading municipal and district leaders recommended the transfer of all prostitutes to one area of no more than twenty houses, surrounded by a wall four stories high, with police guarding the one entrance and exit.[25] This effort failed, however, after legal officials of the Syr-Dar'ia district claimed they lacked proper authority to move existing businesses. Dangers of prostitution and miscegenation concerned tsarist officials and commentators in Tashkent's Russian press throughout the imperial period. Russian female prostitutes destroyed the image of Russian women as paragons of European culture, guardians of the separation between civilization and the wild spaces of the periphery.

Continued disregard of the New Settlement encouraged the mixing so condemned by tsarist officials. Central Asians, men and women, not only participated in prostitution, but also became the main sellers of food, water, and other products. Russian merchants as well as officials rarely visited the suburbs, outside of participation in occasional committees that condemned its sanitary state. The isolation and poverty of New Settlement, as distinct from the city center, continued.

N. A. Maev attempted to overcome this neglect in 1884. In the pages of *Turkestanskiia Viedomosti*, he heaped praise upon O. I. fon Rozenbakha, the governor-general's wife who served as head of the Turkestan Charitable Society. Rozenbakha's care for poor Russian women proved that upper-class females could restore the boundaries between ethnic groups their less fortunate sisters were violating. Rozenbakha now sought to aid the growing number of young, desperate, hungry, men in Russian Tashkent, referred to by Maev as the proletariat. Rozenbakha and Turkestan Bishop Neofit had recently officially opened the Tashkent Night Shelter and Dining Hall. Prominent merchant N. I. Ivanov served the first meal. Maev lauded the coming together of "all of Tashkent society," ready to play a momentous role in demonstrating how "to eliminate the proletariat as a root evil corroding the lowest strata of European society."[26]

Maev employed an ambiguous tone toward these "younger brothers, whom many are inclined to look upon with aversion and contempt."[27] Contempt for poor settlers had precipitated important policy measures, including the 1883 decision to recruit Central Asians, seen as more peaceful and disciplined, instead of Russians as police officers for central Russian Tashkent.[28] Maev decried the dirtiness, raggedness, and drunkenness that made many of these younger brothers "renegades" and threatened to destroy "intelligent society."[29] The "proletariat," which he contrasted later in his article to the "moral poor," appeared as a foil to define a "cultured" settler society. Sergei Idanov, writing in the following issue of *Turkestanskiia Viedomosti*, approved of the night shelter, as giving the poor beds and food would assist in the "protection of the health of the densely-populated city, Tashkent, from cholera, typhus, and other diseases."[30] Yet he condemned the New Settlement, which, just like the Asian city, was a contaminating force that threatened the image and health of central Russian Tashkent.

Imperial authorities sought to constrain industrial development as well as new working-class migrants in the mid-1880s. The city board decried the numbers of new factories that spewed foul-smelling air into central Russian Tashkent. A series of administrative orders relegated factories to the city's periphery.[31] Efforts to restrict the number of poor migrants in Russian Tashkent were addressed through a decree by Tsar Alexander III on June 12, 1886, that limited Russian migrants to rural areas of Turkestan. Governor-General Vrevskii and Syr-Dar'ia military governor Grodekov saw peasant settlers as important tools in colonization plans.[32] Migration, however, was a complex process that ultimately proved beyond the capabilities of tsarist officialdom to control.

Peasant migrants, many arriving without the approval of tsarist authorities, often refused to settle in villages or designated land plots.[33] Significant numbers found work in Russian Tashkent, designated as a transit station for migrants awaiting guides to take them to the countryside. By the late 1880s, after land ran out in nearby Chimkent and Aulie-Ata, where agricultural conditions proved most similar to those in Russia, increasing numbers of peasants assigned to more barren regions of Turkestan gave up farming and came to Tashkent.[34] In 1890, when the category "workers" reappeared in censuses, the Oblast Statistical Committee recorded 1,926 workers in Russian Tashkent of a total population of 17,988 nonmilitary personnel.[35] The cotton industry employed 1,340 of these workers, which included those in paint and dye, linen, furniture, upholstery, glass, and metal-making factories.[36] This figure excluded counts of other groups likely to be included among the "proletariat": the peasant soslovie, at 1,118, and former soldiers, numbering 1,412. Workers and the other lower classes constituted a significant share of the settler urban population alongside the military and bureaucrats.

Writers in *Turkestanskiia Viedomosti* decried the effects of a growing Russian Tashkent. Foul-smelling waste or dust and dirt whipped up by frequent winds rendered impassable entire streets of the New Settlement, renamed the Zachaulinskoi district of Tashkent.[37] The Chaul canal, like the Ankhor canal to the west, designated the boundary between the central Russian city and its less "civilized" districts. One midlevel functionary complained that rising land prices had forced him and

Figure 18. Russian Tashkent in 1890. 1. Voskresenskii Bazaar;
2. House of the Governor-General; 3. City Library and Museum;
4. Men's and Women's Gymnasiums; 5. Military barracks and camps;
6. Cemetery. Graphic Services, Carleton University.

many of his colleagues to live beyond the Chaul. He related difficulties in finding quality domestic help, as cooks and maids did not want to be at the mercy of itinerant Central Asian traders. Officials pleaded for the duma to realize that not only the poor lived beyond the Chaul canal and to pay more attention to the region.[38]

Municipal authorities' neglect of the suburbs stretched well into the twentieth century, drawing the attention of observers from central Rus-

Figure 19. Lagernyi Prospekt. Tsentral'nyi Gosudarstvennyi
arkhiv kinofotofonodokumentov Uzbekistana.

sia. Even as medical stations staffed by Russian doctors opened in Asian
Tashkent, Zachaulinskoi residents complained that money apportioned
by the duma for a medical clinic in their district went instead for top
bureaucrats' office furniture.[39] In 1910, Senator K. K. Palen, inspecting Turkestan for the Imperial Senate, sharply criticized local officials
in Tashkent for complete inattentiveness to city planning beyond the
center.[40] A lack of municipal social services condemned these areas to a
permanent unsanitary condition. The suburbs' dirt and narrow streets
made transportation extremely difficult, further increasing the isolation
of the margins from central Russian Tashkent.

Spatial and cultural isolation characterized the treatment of migrant
lower classes by leading officials, writers, and other elites in the city
center. Yet interconnections in local society between these constituencies, as between Russians and Central Asians, became clear in the early
1890s. Thousands of refugees fleeing disease and famine in European
Russia arrived in Turkestan in 1891–92. Their appearance in the center
and the suburbs of Russian Tashkent hardened boundaries between the
privileged and unprivileged as it became clear that the city could not
isolate itself from growing social problems endemic to central Russia.

## Hardened Boundaries

The migratory wave of the early 1890s overwhelmed imperial officials' settlement efforts. In the 1880s, regional authorities undertook land surveying in the spring, working to find fertile soil and allotments for peasant migrants in the summer. Migrants could thus travel to Turkestan during favorable springtime conditions and plant crops before the winter. The 1891 famine, however, drove thousands of migrants across the Karakum desert in the blazing summer heat. Most arrived without farming implements or cattle; others sold their possessions for food. As district officials had already distributed surveyed plots, these migrants could only file requests for plots the following year. In the meantime, they established a squatter camp on the empty fields proposed for Governor-General Kaufman's trade fair twenty years earlier.[41] Governor-General Vrevskii demanded that the minister of interior halt all migration to Turkestan, complaining in October that one thousand migrant families had arrived in Syr-Dar'ia oblast the previous month, and officials were warning of another thousand en route to Tashkent. At present, 180 families in Tashkent had no food or lodging, and no land allotments could be given before winter. Vrevskii demanded as well that the ministry dispatch personnel to assist with the crisis.[42] The scale of the famine across Russia overwhelmed central authorities, however, and Vrevskii's requests fell on deaf ears.

City doctors warned that growing squatter camps could rapidly become breeding grounds for typhoid and cholera. Vrevskii formed a migration committee under City Commandant Putintsev to address the issue.[43] Putintsev began by renting vacant apartments throughout the city for migrant families. City center residents resisted this initiative. They had previously delivered multiple complaints to authorities that central squares, once the gathering place of officers, administrators, and their families, were now filled with ragged, dirty Russians asking for money or work, and buskers playing for donations.[44] One landlord, Ivan Postinov, held the migration committee responsible for damage that the "hungry ones" had caused in rented apartments.[45] Other petitions forced Putintsev to hire a doctor to tour all migrant apartments and report on their sanitary conditions.[46] In the late fall of 1891, Putintsev moved migrants to an abandoned military barracks on the edge of town. Despite concerns over disease, he placed four hundred in a building designed for one hundred soldiers. The migration committee established a labor exchange, principally for the hiring of domestic servants, perpetually in short supply in Russian Tashkent, and employed a handful of migrants in public works. The Committee also solicited donations from Tashkent residents; Central Asians, including several duma members, were among the largest donors.[47] Their philanthropy continued a tradition of donating to Russian charitable causes. Central Asian elites likely shared worries over the destabilizing potential of these migrants.

The crisis worsened in 1892, as refugee numbers ballooned to five thousand by March. Awaiting allotments or searching for work, these migrants squatted on summer dachas of leading officials. Military Governor Golovachev urged these newcomers be expelled, but district survey teams experienced difficulties in finding unused land plots that could be successfully irrigated.[48] By spring, only one new village, Cherniaevskoe, with fifty plots had been established. Most Russian peasants who struck out looking for their own land returned, unable to grasp the intricacies of irrigated farming.[49] Fears of Russian migrants increased as news of cholera spread in 1892. In May, the migration committee established a medical observation station outside Tashkent and required peasants to report there instead of the city to receive land allotments or social assistance. The station included a camp where peasants, if needed, were expected to spend the winter. Thousands of migrants arrived at the station over the summer and fall of 1892. The governor-general funded free meals in a distant city park for those peasants who pledged to leave Tashkent once an allotment was found for them.[50]

Tsarist officials' perception of the Russian poor as threats to the health of colonial society intensified as cholera struck. Fears of the poor's spreading disease dated back to the 1872 cholera epidemic, when the official report blamed Russian "lower classes" (*prostoi klass narod*) for passing the epidemic in a drunken state rather than following sanitary regulations.[51] Worries that the poor's behavior facilitated cholera's spread in Russian Tashkent was one of the factors that pushed City Commandant Putintsev across the Ankhor canal to address Central Asians on the necessity of following official measures against the disease, precipitating the June violence. As the epidemic continued in August 1892, K. Proskupiakov, the head of the Tashkent military hospital, described his frustration with "commoners" who displayed "extreme distrust towards doctors' orders" and defied anti-cholera measures, which remained in place in the Russian city.[52] City doctor K. Shul'gin's official report on the epidemic condemned the Russian poor for refusing to visit medical personnel and following "folk treatments," including the consumption of pepper brandy. Death rates among plebeian Russians, he stated, were higher than for the local population.[53]

Poor Russians, though not prosecuted for any role in the "cholera riot," received blame in the military trial of fall 1892. One lieutenant stated that, as officers were focused on making arrests, "townspeople and others belonging to lower castes beat one Sart to death and threw him in the river."[54] The trial's official account censured Grodekov for inciting the "riffraff" (sbrod) of central Russian Tashkent.[55] Governor-General Vrevskii cited the threat of Russian "commoners" to the political order of the city and region in his appeal for an emergency statute. Vrevskii claimed the forces of defiance and resistance unleashed by the epidemic and riot could lead to "malicious individuals from the Russian population" joining Muslims in a revolutionary coalition.[56]

Intensified disparagement of the Russian poor extended beyond official circles in the months and years following the cholera epidemic. Okraina, a new private newspaper, heralded by its editors as "the organ of a growing civilian intellectual society in Russian Tashkent," defined itself and its readership against the lower classes of the Russian city.[57] Okraina began an "investigative" series on the Turkestan Charitable Society's night shelter in March 1894. The newspaper condemned the shelter for encouraging the poor to stay in Tashkent. As a result, "people are noticing in the city representatives of a different class of people, completely lacking any resemblance to usual city inhabitants." The "vulgar" poor, prompted by rumors that "you needed only a shovel or a rake to find work and strike it rich beyond the Chaul canal," had come to live off the riches of colonial society.[58] Failing to find such wealth, they slept in night shelter beds or outside in the warm Tashkent air.[59] Okraina expounded on the poor's role in destroying the esthetics of Russian Tashkent: "Returning [from begging in the city center] to a den in their lair, located mostly on the outskirts, the vagabonds, if they are drunk (and drunkenness can be considered their normal state) without fail collapse halfway along their way, wherever they find a resting place." This "barefoot brigade" had progressed to robbery of wealthy Russians, whose clothes and goods they sold to "Jews and Sarts" in exchange for alcohol. Okraina claimed that for "most residents, the words 'zachaulintsy' [those living beyond the Chaul canal] and 'thief' are synonyms."[60]

Views of the poor evolved from a group that, although alien and uncultured, deserved a chance at redemption to a criminal force destined to engage in vice and lawlessness. Stephen P. Frank has argued that the cholera epidemic that spread throughout central Russia in 1892, on the heels of the famine, hardened attitudes of elite urban Russians toward a peasantry already viewed as suffering from "moral and physical degeneration."[61] For Okraina, the urban Russian poor symbolized the failure to create a modern city and nation. Following 1892, poor Russians in Tashkent gained an image as a force that subverted Russian efforts to implement scientific knowledge. Residents of the underprivileged suburbs, preferring to associate with non-Russians, "began gradually to lose, both morally and physically, their human form."[62]

Efforts to expel poor Russians from Tashkent expanded in 1893. Regional land surveyors extended efforts to construct irrigation canals and showed a new willingness to usurp Central Asian farmers' land, establishing seventeen new settler villages.[63] *Turkestanskiia Viedomosti* hailed the new wave of rural colonization as a great success, one that should arouse pride in any "true Russian person."[64] Russian lower-class migrants could serve their more "natural" role as peasant settlers of Central Asia, furthering national and state interests. Governor-General S. M. Dukhovskoi ejected former soldiers, part of *Okraina's* condemned "barefoot brigade," from Tashkent. Honored veterans of the Khivan war were offered free passage out of town.[65]

Prostitution emerged again as a major issue, tying together race, class, and gender. Military Governor Grodekov revived the plan to create a walled-off district of brothels, pointing to record high numbers of soldiers suffering from syphilis; fifty-nine had come to the military hospital in one week in 1893.[66] The military governor feared that syphilis would be passed on to soldiers' wives and become a scourge in the imperial city. Residents on the borders of the Zachaulinskoi district filed numerous petitions demanding the expulsion of prostitutes who, they claimed, were driving down property values.[67] Letters focused on Central Asian participation in prostitution, perhaps in the hope that the threat of miscegenation would prompt official intervention. *Russkii Turkestan,* a private newspaper begun in 1898, condemned prostitution for attracting "native waste" from Asian Tashkent, and supported its removal to an isolated region.[68]

In 1899, the city commandant focused on political impacts of uncontrolled mixing between Russians and Central Asians, warning the military governor that "natives . . . are becoming increasingly involved with unreliable elements of the Russian population, who could have a seriously damaging influence. . . . Natives could either fall under the sway of their fanatics, or various newcomers from the Russian population."[69] Warnings of interethnic collaboration, though unaccompanied by evidence, proved useful in allowing governor-generals to justify annual renewals of the state of emergency over Tashkent.

Economic growth continued to attract workers in the 1890s, albeit not in substantial numbers. An 1898 census conducted by the Regional Statistical Committee found 333 enterprises in Tashkent employing 1,880 workers. These numbers remained below those of tsarist functionaries and Central Asian "artisans," the two most numerous groups in Tashkent according to the 1897 all-union census.[70] The Fergana valley competed with Tashkent as a site to locate rough-processing factories for the cotton industry.[71] *Russkii Turkestan* declared local factory life still in an "embryonic" state in 1899, but noted an absence of any labor strife.[72] Class conflict had yet to arrive. The construction of a railway to the city, however, transformed images and realities of class relations and economic development in imperial Tashkent.

## The Railway: Hopes and Fears Realized

Governor-General Kaufman recognized the economic and military importance of a railway link between the metropole and Tashkent from the earliest days of his rule.[73] As Daniel Brower has argued, Kaufman and other officials in Tashkent believed the railway would "embod[y] imperial integration and colonial progress."[74] The governor-general's commissioning of several surveys and tireless lobbying in St. Petersburg proved fruitless, however. Minister of war D. A. Miliutin could not justify the enormous cost of the project. In 1879, military considerations motivated the building of a smaller, two-hundred-kilometer line from the Caspian Sea port of Krasnovodsk to Kizil Arvat, a military post at the center of the efforts to subdue Turcoman tribes. In the mid 1880s, railway director M. N. Annenkov ordered its extension to Samarkand following fears that British troops were planning to invade the region from Afghanistan.[75] Once completed in 1888, the railway tracks lay tantalizingly close to the city of Tashkent.

The new railroad, according to one contemporary, "demonstrated its enormous and invaluable service to Turkestan, particularly in the economic realm."[76] Cotton was transported far more easily to the metropole; exports quadrupled from 873,092 *pudy* in 1888 to 3,588,025 *pudy* in 1893.[77] Turkestan residents received sugar, kerosene, wood, iron, and construction materials from the line, now dubbed the Transcaspian Railway. Governor-General Rozenbakh employed rising trade figures to argue for the expansion of the railroad to Tashkent. A leading merchant, N. I. Reshetnikov, proposed to extend the line using private funds.[78] Lobbying efforts bore fruit, as on May 27, 1895, the ministers of war and the interior ordered the state control office to release funds to continue the Transcaspian railway to Tashkent, with a branch line to the cotton-rich Fergana valley.

As surveyors plotted the new route, minister of war A. N. Kuropatkin envisioned a more direct link to Turkestan. Kuropatkin considered a direct line a strategic and military necessity against potential incursions by British or Chinese soldiers. Turkestan's growing economy was also marshaled as evidence of the potential utility of a new railway. Beginning in 1898, the War Ministry lobbied the tsar for a line from European

Russia to Orenburg and Tashkent. Nicholas II approved the plan in 1900, and the "Orenburg-Tashkent" railway was completed in 1906. Officials and elites in Russian Tashkent celebrated their new importance to St. Petersburg.[79]

Extending railways across the deserts proved a mammoth task. Labor recruitment altered the composition of the working classes in Tashkent and Turkestan. Chief engineer A. I. Ursati at first employed cheaper Central Asian labor to build the railway, but low wages and horrible conditions quickly drove away workers. Local villagers also opposed the route, which cut through farms and canals.[80] Ursati turned to railway battalions of conscripted soldiers, but their numbers proved insufficient. Forced to recruit more expensive Russian free labor, Ursati approached landless migrant peasants and remaining unemployed former soldiers in Tashkent. Then he sought workers from rail lines across the empire. Railway workers were a migratory group, with a high degree of turn-over as workers sought better economic conditions.[81] Ursati offered recruits a salary 10 to 15 percent higher than in central Russia, free transportation and fuel supplies, and, in 1899, a bonus equivalent to three months' wages to offset moving expenses. These tactics lured hundreds from central Russia.

Minister of war Kuropatkin approved the extra payments, believing that the recruitment of Russian workers has "an extreme political importance, as hiring natives as employees was harmful and dangerous."[82] Heeding this policy, Governor-General Dukhovskoi required that any Central Asian employed on the line receive his personal approval. When track laying was completed, 5,094 Russians worked on the Orenburg-Tashkent line, compared to 948 locals. Russians received significantly higher wages, with even unskilled workers earning double the salary of their Central Asian counterparts.[83] Skilled workers, almost exclusively Russian, earned far more.

Wage differentials perpetuated boundaries between the labor forces of the colonizer and colonized. Nonpayment of wages, however, affected Russians and Central Asians alike. Krasnovodsk, the starting point for the Transcaspian line, now renamed the Central Asian Railway, experienced sporadic strikes from 1894. Hundreds of workers struck in Samarkand in 1899. Their refusal to return to work until their wages were paid and working conditions improved sparked police intervention. Railway workers struck in Tashkent in April 1899, the first labor action against the state in the city.[84]

Tashkent railway workers found themselves isolated from official elites, as well as newly arrived professionals involved in railway construction. The building of the Tashkent railway station epitomized and reinforced a class divide. Ursati placed the railway station far from the city center, sparing it the pollution of the engines and the presence of lower-class Russian as well as Central Asian passengers. Ursati envisioned his station, located beyond the Zachaulinskoi district, as a new, modern neighborhood for the city's outskirts.[85] Employees' housing reflected a clear hierarchy. Administrators, medical personnel, and agents were placed at the station's head, white-collar employees of the telegraph, traction, and line services along its axes, and the other functionaries in a group of houses at the end of a surrounding square. The Blagoveshchenskaia church, capable of holding five hundred worshipers, was built on the station square. A school for employees' children arrived a few years later. No room in this community was offered to railway workers. Unable to afford dwellings in the city center, these workers found housing in the Zachaulinskoi district.[86] Some lived in Asian Tashkent, where rents were lower.[87] Differential housing policies made clear the isolation of the "proletariat."

Leading tsarist officials worried about the reaction of the new residents they planned to isolate. Turkestan proved a popular destination for skilled workers in Russia blacklisted from previous employment for labor protests or revolutionary activities. Some members of the Turkestan railway battalions enlisted only after their dismissal from other work for political reasons.[88] Following the 1899 strike, they formed reading circles and discussed relations of class. Governor-General N. A. Ivanov warned St. Petersburg of potential consequences of worker activism. Railway workers could become the weak link in the solidarity of the Russian community. Their education and philosophies made them a more imminent threat than earlier lower-class migrants. Ivanov wrote to the minister of war,

> [Sowing disorder and opposition to the state] is hardly unthinkable in such centers as Tashkent where a significant number of railway workers are collected, and there can be no doubt that any such event would considerably shake the certainty of the native population that the Russian people are inseparable, a strongly unified force, selflessly obeying the will of the MIGHTY TSAR [sic].[89]

Ivanov's warnings increased in urgency as railway workers made contact with political exiles. St. Petersburg had designated Tashkent a place of exile in the 1890s. Governor-General Dukhovskoi accepted the policy from 1894 to 1898, as long as the minister of war renewed the state of emergency for the city. Ivanov argued that railway workers and exiles were a corrosive mix. Many of these exiles were in fact railway workers, including V. D. Korniushin, expelled from Kazan for the publication and distribution of Social Democratic Party materials. Korniushin took a job at the Central Asian railway and renewed his socialist activities, establishing an underground print shop in Russian Tashkent.[90] Municipal authorities reported on worker-exile cooperation, including the sending of "agitators" to schools to "corrupt" Russian youth.[91]

Minister of the interior V. K. von Pleve rejected Ivanov's concerns. Turkestan continued to serve as a dumping ground for exiles, and underground opposition to the regime burgeoned. Central policies were working against the interest of tsarist officials in Tashkent. The railway, envisioned as a symbol of progress, now threatened to sow disorder in Russian Tashkent and Turkestan. Its importance—even before the completion of the Orenburg-Tashkent line, the Central Asian Railway had become a vital cog in local and regional economies—endowed railway workers with significant power.[92]

The railway station emerged as a growing site of contestation at the turn of the century. Railway stations, as places where all members of the public mix, have provided particular challenges to stratified colonial societies.[93] Whereas most regimes have been concerned primarily with enforcing the separation of colonizer and colonized, however, imperial authorities and the private press in Tashkent were more anxious about the destabilizing potential of their "own" workers and lower classes. The Russian press condemned railway workers' apparent increasingly irreverent and disorderly behavior at the station and in the wagons. *Russkii Turkestan* criticized railway workers, and all workers who rode the railway. Workers, "demonstrating their immaturity," clung to, and swung on, entrances and exits to the railway cars both while the train was in motion and in the station. Their "most unpleasant way of relating to the public" seemed all the more improper in the presence of the large number of women at the station.[94] Railway workers, betraying their lower-class origins, despoiled both the order of the station and the cultural values of Tashkent elite society, referred to as the "public [*publika*]." Reporter Ivan Pliat noted that Russian railway workers treated Central Asians, forced due to crowding to occupy passageways between cars, in a "rude and disturbing manner," threatening to spark interethnic conflict.[95]

*Russkii Turkestan* asserted that the railway had allowed threats to "civilized" society to penetrate the heart of the city. Voskresenskii bazaar had become a haunt for criminals from central Russia. Iakov Girienko, who had fled Khar'kov prison, where he was serving time for thefts and murder, had moved to Tashkent to evade authorities. He became a renowned pillager of caravans at the bazaar. Girienko's actions testified to the fact that "Russian criminals consider Tashkent to be the new El Dorado."[96] In a 1904 article entitled "Tashkent Slums," recent migrants were noted to be living in empty stalls in Voskresenskii bazaar, surrounded by their own waste, debris left by merchants, and horse and camel excrement. Russians were dangerously living shoulder-to-shoulder with other peoples, from Armenian cooks to Muslim watchmakers.[97] Though condemning municipal officials for their inability to assist the poor, writers in *Russkii Turkestan* saved their bile for the lower classes, including peasants who came to Russian Tashkent on market days, where they mixed with other poor and criminal elements, selling their goods to buy alcohol, which reduced them to "zombies" (*ne zhivoi chelovek*).[98]

Frustration and concern over the poor and workers of Tashkent did not result in increased social assistance. The Turkestan Charitable Society remained the one principal philanthropic organization in Tashkent. After the 1892 crisis, no state organization such as the migration committee attended to these new migrants. Unlike in central Russian cities, no reform movement emerged that preached the "modern" values of mutual assistance.[99] Once the elites of Russian Tashkent had failed to play a vanguard role in creating a modern society without a "proletariat," the poor became a counterpoint to demonstrate the civilized nature of tsarist officials, merchants, and intellectuals and a threat to mix with the colonized Central Asians.

## Railway Worker Activism

Railway workers led efforts to challenge tsarist elite control in Russian Tashkent. Highly educated and compensated, with skills vital to the functioning of the local economy, they fit what Mark Steinberg has defined as "vanguard" workers. Railway worker activists considered themselves a part of the working class, but placed themselves in a leading role.[100] These activists developed strategies of exclusion to differentiate themselves from the unskilled laborers and peasants of Russian Tashkent's suburbs as well as the Central Asian population, groups they perceived as "uncivilized."[101]

Russian railway workers chafed at their place in the colonial city. Imperial officials, despite offering higher wages than in the metropole, followed central Russian authorities in limiting railway worker rights and privileges.[102] Russian railway workers received far fewer perquisites than their counterparts serving in British India, who obtained high wages, privileged housing, and educational institutes that differentiated them from other "poor Whites" in the colony.[103] Railway worker activists increased subversive activities in the early twentieth century through underground organizations and the publication of socialist literature. They sought to advance their own position in imperial Tashkent as well as to become leaders a modern socialist society.

At the same time, many of these workers participated in cultural events that included Russian Tashkent's elites. Worker activists made frequent appearances at concerts, plays, and readings of classic literature. They made contacts with a small group of radical intellectuals, the Pushkin Society, composed of midlevel functionaries, some white-collar railway personnel, and newspaper employees, from publishers to printers. Pushkin Society members offered public readings of literature before large crowds of workers at the railway station.[104] Railway worker performances and plays at the station attracted large numbers of the privileged elite from the city center.[105] Worker activists convinced railway administrators to support the building of a teahouse to hold these crowds, arguing that it would be more beneficial for workers to attend cultural performances than spend time in bars.[106] These activists aspired to distance themselves from negative associations with the "proletariat" and to share several of the same values—sobriety, industriousness, and respectability—preached by leading elites as "civilized."

Railway workers who were leaders of the Social Democratic Party in Tashkent joined Pushkin Society members in condemning the slaughter of unarmed protesters by tsarist troops in St. Petersburg on January 9, 1905. Imperial authorities had unsuccessfully attempted to conceal the events of "Bloody Sunday." V. D. Korniushin and other socialist leaders in the city, as elsewhere in Russia, hoped that news of the slaughter would unite a wide coalition of social forces against the tsarist regime.[107] Korniushin and exile G. Shavdiia led efforts to create a "Unified Group" of Socialist Revolutionary and Social Democratic circles in Tashkent to coordinate activity against the tsarist regime. Their initial efforts focused on railway workers, considered the most activist radical group in imperial Tashkent.

Railway workers initiated a one-day strike on February 19, the anniversary of Alexander II's 1861 Emancipation Proclamation. Demands echoed those from vanguard workers across Russia in the weeks following Bloody Sunday. In addition to workplace-condition and monetary demands, railway workers sought greater respect for their skills and position in society. They demanded consultation on all station matters, and that administrators address them by the formal "*vy*" (you) instead of the informal "*ty*."[108] Strike leaders also demanded support on cultural matters, including guaranteed public readings as well as administration support for a library.

Strike leaders battled imperial authorities and railway administrators over who represented progress and order in Tashkent. As administrators rejected the manifesto, Governor-General Ivanov, citing rumors of potentially violent "worker disturbances," ordered squads of Cossacks to patrol the city center and the railway station. The newspaper *Samarkand* later reported that tensions ran so high "parents were not letting their children go to school, anticipating conflicts in the streets."[109] *Russkii Turkestan*, which supported the strikers, published an article entitled "Stop Gossiping," which chastised Russian society for succumbing to malicious innuendo about "dark" proletariat unrest. Special frustration was reserved for Pushkin Society members, who appeared swayed despite the fact that the "absurdity of these rumors is clear to any person with even the least bit of culture."[110] "Cultured" people must understand that forces of disorder are not workers, "quietly walking the streets" for better conditions, but the regime, which employed "dark individuals who enjoyed terrorizing the population and exploiting panic to rob people and houses" in the name of stopping the strike.[111]

Railway workers remained isolated in imperial Tashkent, however. Printers had returned to work following a brief sympathy strike February 20–21. Strike leaders emphasized a corporate identity for railway workers, as part of a movement spreading across lines and stations throughout the empire.[112] But significant numbers returned to work on February 22, when railway director N. A. Ul'ianin brought in railway battalions from Ashkabad to break the strike. In the following weeks, Ul'ianin sacked strike leaders and revoked their rights to free travel, moves that met with approval from imperial administrators and silence from the rest of Russian society in Tashkent.[113]

Railway workers took a more moderate position in the following months, turning away from socialist exiles Shavdiia and Korniushin and choosing a railway station accountant, A. P. Gol'bert, to head their union. Gol'bert advised railway workers to stay on the job as a wave of strikes swept Tashkent in June 1905.[114] Tramway employees, retail workers, bakers, and clerks, as well as workers in the cotton-cleaning and tobacco industries, issued demands for shorter hours and better working conditions, in addition to freedom of assembly, in separate work stoppages. Strikers, however, never coordinated their actions, and the gains from these actions varied widely between groups.

Gol'bert focused on political protests, as he saw the regime vulnerable to accusations of acting against progress and "civilization." He sought alliances with liberal administrators and other members of elite society rather than the less skilled workers in Tashkent. Hundreds of railway workers marched to the city center on July 16 to protest the announcement of the weak, limited-franchise "Bulygin duma" instead of the powerful, democratic legislative body promised by the tsar in the wake of public outcry over Bloody Sunday.[115] Gol'bert, however, ordered the crowd to return to the railway station when Cossack forces scuffled with workers. He and other worker activists began a campaign to portray themselves as representatives of peace and order against a violent, arbitrary tsarist regime.

## *Russkii Turkestan* and the Language of the Colonial Revolution

Railway worker activists developed these arguments through the pages of the daily newspaper *Russkii Turkestan*. Articles that presented activist workers as guardians of stability and agents of progress in Tashkent accompanied condemnations of the tsarist regime and statements of principles reprinted from central socialist newspapers.[116] In presenting themselves as advocates of a more egalitarian society, however, these worker activists revealed their own hierarchical vision. Poor workers joined elites as targets of their contempt. Central Asians were portrayed as a subject group that deserved better protection, but not full citizenship, in a modern socialist Tashkent.

*Russkii Turkestan* condemned unjust treatment of Central Asians as a sign of the backwardness and repressiveness of the tsarist regime. Writers blamed the administration for sanctioning, if not encouraging, "hooligan" behavior against the local population. In so doing, they borrowed discourse from central Russia, where "hooligans" (*khuligany*) symbolized fear of growing disorder and chaos and became yardsticks against which "civilized" behavior could be measured.[117] In *Russkii Turkestan*, hooligans were not the semi-urbanized peasants portrayed in the central press, but rather military scribes or other lower state officials. Their targets were not elite society, but Central Asians. In a typical case, described as being "practiced in wide measure," hooligans beat one local merchant to the point of disfigurement.[118] Venal behaviors perpetrated by state functionaries proliferated under the noses of the governor-general and leading administrators. Police, often present during the violence, refused to intervene.

Railway worker activists decried abuse of Central Asians by their employers or professionals on the railway lines as well. One writer condemned the Central Asian Railway for its use of special "Muslim wagons," so crowded that "even sardines in a tin felt more free."[119] Another article attacked railway engineers, the frequent target of worker scorn for their superior comportment and refusal to support the February strike. On July 20, on the platform of the nearby Tiumen-aryk station, station engineer Bartasevich beat up Kazakh Jurab Karabaev, who had punched one of the engineer's dogs that had tried to bite him. The author criticized Bartasevich's "arrogance," which refuted engineers' self-image as models of propriety. "Could not the railway engineer better carry his rank with greater correctness than to chase . . . after a Kazakh who had courageously defended himself from an animal attack?" In a mocking tone, the author argued that his display should prompt a questioning of the civilized values of tsarist elites: "Citizen engineer hoped to demonstrate his military readiness, bravery, and illustrate the superiority of a cultured people in front of a free son of the steppe—a Kazakh—and it must be said that he fulfilled his task brilliantly."[120] This report, alongside others of attacks and injustices committed by tsarist elites, from soldiers to doctors to Orthodox priests, displayed the extent to which Russians had strayed from the values of European civilization they claimed to be bringing to Turkestan.[121]

Central Asians appeared in these stories uniquely as helpless victims. Absent from *Russkii Turkestan* was any discussion of the social and political inequities of empire. Social Democrats and other worker activists did not elicit the participation of Central Asians in revolutionary activity. Pamphlets were published only in the Russian language, and not one Central Asian served on railway worker groups or strike committees, or wrote for the newspaper that identified itself as the agent of the repressed. A rare article that pondered the potential of growing revolutionary activity among the local population ended on an ominous note. The author noted with approval the large number of arrests of Muslims for petty crimes against colonial authorities, in particular for refusing to perform symbolic gestures of submission. Local police had even jailed duma member Seid Karim for refusing to remove his hat in front of officers. Perhaps, noted the author, Muslims suffering under Russian criminals in the state apparatus had become aware of their repression. Still, they remained a "semi-barbaric" people yet to benefit from the "civilizing mission" of Russia.[122] This status justified their exclusion from a revolutionary coalition and from equal participation in a socialist society.

Exclusionary rhetoric in *Russkii Turkestan* extended beyond Central Asians. Women and Jews had their roles in revolutionary activities subsumed. Women played prominent roles in Tashkent during 1905. One female Jewish worker, Rubenshtein, spoke frequently at rallies at the railway station and on the streets of Russian Tashkent.[123] Another woman, Ryss', was elected as one of the four members of the October Strike Committee. Maria Lezina, the live-in partner of railway worker

Andrei Livchenko, assisted a scheme to assassinate the governor-general and the police chief of Russian Tashkent in 1906.[124] Large numbers of Jews, worker S. Anfinov wrote in his memoir of the revolution, played prominent roles in revolutionary activities.[125] Yet women and Jews appeared in *Russkii Turkestan* uniquely as victims of hooligan behavior. Women fended off frequent attacks from hooligans, who blocked their paths and shouted vulgarities, only through loud screams and cries.[126] Russian male workers protected Jewish shopkeepers—regular victims of hooligan attacks—through the organizing of self-defense patrols against pogroms, which were occurring in cities across the empire.[127] Activist writers highlighted the superior revolutionary qualities of the Russian male worker. Their silence on women's and Jews' roles in revolutionary activity may also have been a political strategy, to counter official reports that socialist agitation was the result of women and non-Russians, both outsiders to civilized society.[128]

After agents of imperial power, the urban settler poor received the harshest treatment in *Russkii Turkestan*. Socialist writers followed other Tashkent publications in denigrating the behavior, appearance, and values of the zachaulintsy. The suburban poor frequented bars, teahouses, and other "places of vice," abusing alcohol and hashish and horrifying respectable "family types," the skilled workers forced to live alongside them.[129] Other articles reported the Zachaulinskoi district as the source of the hooligans who attacked women, Jews, and Central Asians. Commentators in *Russkii Turkestan,* as had imperial elites, found the poor's behavior threatening to inverse boundaries between the "civilized" colonizer and the "backward" colonized. The newspaper reported that successful Central Asian efforts to prevent the establishment of "teahouses," in actuality fronts for prostitution, in Asian Tashkent demonstrated "the natives who we, Russians, consider below us in moral terms, are now above us, protecting themselves and their families from the corrupting influence of such establishments, tolerated by a 'cultured people.'"[130] Poor Russians' appetite for vice, meanwhile, allowed unscrupulous Central Asian merchants to expand operations in the Zachaulinskoi district.

Reports in *Russkii Turkestan* hinted that tension between more privileged workers and the unskilled poor was mutual. One article reported an incident where drunkards hurled insults at railway workers refusing to offer them cigarettes, mockingly crying out "there goes another 'lord.'"[131] Joan Neuberger has argued that, in St. Petersburg, hooligan behavior expressed defiance and mockery, openly declaring an "uncultured" way of life.[132] If this was the case in Russian Tashkent, activist railway workers made an attractive target on the streets of the suburbs.

They dressed more "respectably" and preferred the cultural circles of the elite. *Russkii Turkestan*, ignoring in its issues the plight of the dispossessed in the suburbs, just as it did in Asian Tashkent, nonetheless reported their staging of the play "Poverty Is Not a Vice" in early 1905. The newspaper noted how workers, in both the performance and the crowd, mixed freely with the cultured public who had come to enjoy the performance.[133] Identification with this "public" proved as important to worker activists' self-image as the differentiation of themselves from the urban poor.

## The 1905 Revolution in Tashkent: Unity and Discord

Russian railway workers joined the October 1905 general strike called by the All-Russian Union of Railway Workers. The demands issued by the Central Bureau of the union on October 9 combined the workplace issues that Tashkent railway workers struck for in February with cultural and political ones, which centered on improvements in health and education, civil liberties, and an effective, representative constituent assembly.[134] The strike began in Tashkent on October 15.

As across the empire, October 1905 in Russian Tashkent proved to be the pinnacle of cooperation among anti-tsarist forces. The local branch of the Union of Engineers and Technicians joined the strike, along with white-collar employees, middle managers, and telegraphers, who had suffered from significant layoffs earlier in the month.[135] A. P. Gol'bert headed a twenty-one-member strike committee. On October 17, the committee ordered a mass rally from the railway station to the city center. Syr-Dar'ia military governor I. I. Fedotov mustered Cossacks to combat the crowd, yet hesitated upon seeing at the head of the demonstration the chief engineer of the Central Asian Railway, N. O. Shpakovskii. The military governor exclaimed, "Where are you leading this dark mass? You are an official in the service of the crown!"[136]

The united opposition of railway workers, engineers, and functionaries displayed its power. Workers unloaded from wagons only those goods they considered essential.[137] The strike committee occupied the telegraph office, receiving news of the October Manifesto even before the Office of the Governor-General did so. In a mass rally outside the railway station on October 18, Gol'bert and other committee members announced the tsar's promise of a powerful, elected duma and the granting of civil rights. Strikers called for further concessions, notably an amnesty for all political prisoners. Acting governor-general V. V. Sakharov still awaited his copy, writing to minister of war A. F. Rediger that "the lack of an official version of the Manifesto of October 17 is having an extremely unfavorable effect on the popular masses. Uprisings among workers and strikes have not stopped."[138] The strike committee prepared to meet at the city duma at 5 P.M. on October 18 to discuss reforms to the "whole of Tashkent society." Alerted to Sakharov's intention to use Cossacks to break up the meeting, railway workers met instead at the city circus. Sakharov nonetheless ordered an attack on those who had not been apprised of the move. Cossacks posted outside the duma moved into a crowd with batons, killing two and wounding thirty-eight.[139]

The killings energized anti-tsarist forces. The October 20 funeral of the coach driver and trader killed attracted the largest rally to date in Tashkent. City duma and city board members headed a procession that included officers, students, intellectuals, bureaucrats, traders, and workers.[140] Gol'bert and other railway workers approached activists in the Pushkin Society and other intellectual groups to unite opposition to the regime through the formation of the "Committee to Organize Rallies and Public Readings." Two thousand five hundred spectators, mostly workers, attended a public session of the city duma the following day. Railway workers cheered the decision to send a telegram to Prime Minister Sergei Iu. Witte requesting the sacking of Military Governor Fedotov, deemed responsible for the bloodshed, the immediate institution of a new state duma based upon democratic principles, and the freeing of all political prisoners.[141] Yet only twenty-four of the seventy-two city duma members had attended the meeting. A full November 7 session of the city duma rewrote the still unsent telegram to express its "loyalty to the Tsar and its appreciation for the granting of the October Manifesto."[142] Fear of further disorder among railway workers and soldiers dominated duma deliberations. Governor-General Sakharov, emboldened by this support, as well as by a telegram from internal affairs minister A. F. Trepov to crush all opposition, sent Cossacks on the streets of Tashkent.[143]

*Sredneaziatskaia Zhizn'*, a private newspaper started in November 1905, stressed the increasing danger posed by malcontent railway workers, apparently now considering armed opposition to the regime. The newspaper mocked the designation "intellectual proletariat" as a contradiction in terms.[144] A November mutiny within the Tashkent garrison that was bloodily suppressed further alarmed privileged society.[145] The radical intellectuals who worked with Gol'bert in October refused to support a renewed railway strike in November, despite the latter's pleas that strikers were working for the "general good."[146] Lacking support from the engineers and functionaries, railway workers found their latest strike easily broken. Governor-General Sakharov arrested *Russkii Turkestan's* editor, M. V. Morozov, other Social Democrats, and strike committee and other railway worker activists. Gol'bert momentarily escaped incarceration by jumping through a window at the approach of police and fleeing to a nearby railway station. On November 29, the Russian Senate ratified a tsarist decree placing the Central Asian and Orenburg-Tashkent railways under martial law.

Worker activists in Tashkent, as across the empire, shifted from a "collaborationist" to an "isolationist" position in 1906.[147] Railway workers were aware of their power in local society. The railroad had become Tashkent's economic heart and the crucial link between metropole and periphery. This retreat to a corporate identity nonetheless showed the fragility of links between workers and liberal professionals (who will be discussed in the next chapter) opposed to the tsar, as well as among workers themselves, who, except for October, never coordinated labor protests.

Massive firings of activist workers followed the failed November 1905 strike. Cossacks and soldiers occupied permanent postings at the railway station. Railway director Ul'ianin replaced those fired with unemployed laborers who had completed the new Orenburg-Tashkent line or who had been sacked for opposition activities earlier in the year, at a fraction of their wages.[148] He pressured replacements to join his own "Union of Legality and Order." Efforts to isolate Tashkent workers culminated with all worker travel to central Russia being suspended during known congresses of the All-Russian Union of Railway Workers.

Railway worker activism reignited, albeit on a smaller scale, in a May 1906 protest against chief engineer Shpakovskii. Shpakovskii's decision to fine workers who attended May 1 holiday celebrations produced a heated meeting following the issuing of paychecks three weeks later. One worker approached the engineer, and, in a common symbol of Russian worker protest, threw a coal sack over his head and held it there for two minutes.[149] Worker anger at Ul'ianin, responsible for the firing of hundreds of workers, and Shpakovskii, who had distanced himself from talk of a "worker family" following the issuing of the October Manifesto, had intensified in previous months. As William Rosenberg and Diane Koenker have argued, worker anger and solidarity appeared particularly strong when directed against individual personalities.[150] Workers refused to name the perpetrators even after Ul'ianin closed the railway shops and threatened to fire all labor on June 3. Yet efforts to find soldiers capable of running the trains failed, and railway battalions refused to replace the strikers. On June 26, Ul'ianin announced that workers would be taken back without conditions.[151] Workers offered victory speeches outside the closed shop gates.

Social Democratic leaders, in an electoral pamphlet published in *Russkii Turkestan*, argued that the sack placed over Shpakovskii's head was a "revolutionary symbol, directly threatening the basis of the Constitutional Monarchy."[152] Party leaders nonetheless urged the replacement of such spontaneous acts with more organized forms of resistance, and successfully used worker frustration to form independent councils, or soviets, at the railway station, with each shop selecting one representative.[153]

Divisions between activist leaders and the rank-and-file emerged in July. In a sign of a strong regional identity that crossed class lines in Russian Tashkent, a diverse crowd of hundreds protested tsarist authorities' attempts to send eighteen soldiers convicted in the November 1905 mutiny to St. Petersburg in preparation for internal exile. Red flags, revolutionary songs, and chants of "Down with shackles! It's time to remove all fetters!" greeted the mutineers as they arrived, under police escort, at the railway station. Railway workers blockaded the train by placing wagon ramps on the tracks and sabotaging one of the sections ahead as the crowd, estimated by Cossack officer A. Rudyi at four to five thousand, continued to grow.[154] A. Gol'bert and M. V. Morozov, released from prison and still editor of *Russkii Turkestan*, sought to calm the crowd. Fearing violence, Morozov pleaded, "[i]f you think of releasing [the soldiers], then await the troops, ready to mow them down with weapons and there will be blood spilt in vain."[155] Protesters surrounded Morozov and Gol'bert, who ordered the train blockades removed, accusing them of being traitors. Armed sappers tried to come to the defense of the mutineers, but Cossack forces assured the train left as scheduled.

The incident at the station damaged railway worker solidarity. Morozov and Gol'bert saw their standing significantly reduced. Morozov issued an apologia for his actions in *Russkii Turkestan*, writing that he had seen a huge number of troops moving toward the railway station and claiming the crowd lacked the "decisiveness to give their own lives," necessary to triumph in a violent confrontation.[156] "Organized workers" needed to recognize the significant numbers of women and children in the crowd. Morozov also issued other condemnations of "unorganized" worker behavior, including "crowd justice" (*samosud*) and attacks of adversaries on the shop floor. Railway workers needed to demonstrate their *kulturnost'* ("culturedness") to the rest of society. Later issues of *Russkii Turkestan* warned railway workers against theft of company property and encouraged them to set examples by not taking second jobs at a time of high unemployment.[157] The July incident provided fodder for *Sredneaziatskaia Zhizn'*, which wrote that "organizers and the most active participants of these events, incapable of critiques and analysis, in the vortex of vicious crimes, at the moment of serious danger shamefully run, turning their backs on the crowd."[158]

Following July, worker activism retreated to shop-floor issues. Railway workers took control of "expert commissions," designed as a joint initiative between lower management and workers to channel protest. Commission workers targeted for demotion or dismissal brigade leaders and foremen who had abused their power over workers.[159] Many of those targeted were opponents of the revolutionary movement.

The remaining unjailed Social Democrats in Turkestan revised their goals following the failure of broad-based protest. In July 1906, V. V. Bykovskii, newly elected leader of the party, invited railway worker activists from throughout the region to a secret congress to approve a Tashkent branch of the All-Russian railway union. Thirty-four delegates approved new tactics that featured clandestine work. Delegates rejected proposals to form soviets in favor of small, centralized local railway committees. Bykovskii backed the small-cell model, arguing that "due to local conditions it is necessary to work out completely autonomous tactics."[160] "Local conditions" referred to the majority Central Asian population, whom Russian activists feared might take over a more open soviet. Images of the backward Central Asian proliferated in the socialist press as Muslim notables supported suppression of the revolutionary movement. *Russkii Turkestan* argued that Russians must keep power in order to push the "inert mass" of the native population to acquire "culture" so that they may act responsibly in society.[161] Commentators dismissed Central Asian revolutionary efforts in 1905, which will be discussed in the next chapter, as qualitatively different from their own struggle, as the locals had yet to acquire the "beginnings of civilization."[162]

Russian railway workers increasingly engaged in unsanctioned protest tactics. Ignoring the admonitions of *Russkii Turkestan*, they participated in numerous armament thefts from railway cars.[163] In November 1906, acting governor-general Shpitzberg wrote that "at the railway station constantly gather groups of railway workers and city hooligans, whose conduct is sufficiently alarming that it is dangerous for the public, and particularly for officers, to appear on the platform."[164] Murders of railway personnel known for their hostile attitude toward workers began, with suspects escaping before their potential arrest.[165] The official welcoming ceremony for new governor-general N. I. Grodekov in January 1907 was held at the nearby station of Keles, instead of Tashkent, for fear of worker demonstrations and potential sabotage

Following his arrival, Grodekov dismissed hundreds of railway workers suspected of revolutionary activity.[166] Harsher state policies softened the attitude of liberal elites toward these workers. *Na Rubezhe*, a newspaper that succeeded *Sredneaziatskaia Zhizn'* in 1908, claimed that poor working conditions and low salaries justified incidents of theft by railway station weighers trying to support their families. The newspaper published a letter from a railway metalworker, who wrote, "conditions are as bad as Siberia—justified complaints of existing disorder are apathetically dealt with [by the authorities]; legal demands are oppressed, sometimes resisted and frequently the results of such 'human' relations are the depriving of these laborers their needed morsel of bread."[167] State officials wrestled with the issue of "disorderly" railway workers, who were now gaining support in the post-1905 years. One project floated in 1910 involved the replacing of all conductors and shop workers by reserve soldiers. This effort to return to the early days of imperial Tashkent, when soldiers formed the bulk of the Russian labor force, failed, given the numbers and skills needed to maintain the two lines operating out of the city. Railway workers considered themselves a "proletariat," which had, as N. A. Maev feared in 1884, laid their "tenacious roots" in the imperial city.

Tashkent Russian elites, and, later, railway workers, marginalized the Slavic poor in large part to overcome their own anxieties over cultural, social, and spatial isolation. Beginning in the 1870s, elite efforts to condemn and isolate plebeian settlers sought to enforce the image of central Russian Tashkent as an oasis of European progress, one that could prosper without a proletariat. Tsarist officials and intellectuals viewed poor migrant settlers not as a counterweight to the Central Asian majority or as a sign of successful economic development, but as a danger to the image of Russians as bearers of European culture and civilization. In many ways, Asian Tashkent and the suburbs of Russian Tashkent merged in the imagination of the privileged society of the Russian city. Parallel segregation of these two subject groups nonetheless encouraged images and realities of interethnic mixing and miscegenation, which, as the attention to prostitution showed, continued to trouble tsarist officials. After 1892, boundaries along lines of class as well as race hardened, as tsarist elites no longer saw the settler poor as capable of redemption. The rhetoric of the "civilizing mission" was not stretched to them. Social polarization extended to characterizing as the "proletariat" the educated railway workers whose skills became vital to a burgeoning colonial economy in the 1890s and 1900s.

Railway workers led efforts to resist subordinate status and create a socialist society in Russian Tashkent. Yet activists occupied a liminal position in the Russian city. Sharing cultural values and some elements of visions of progress with tsarist elites, railway worker activists and socialist writers also condemned the settler poor, as well as Central Asians, as threats to a modern, civilized society. Their vision of socialism excluded these constituencies' participation as equals. Dreams of revolutionary unity among the "proletariat," however defined, remained illusory throughout 1905. By the following year, tensions mounted even within the ranks of railway workers, whose corporate identity and economic importance gave them a measure of power in Russian Tashkent. Yet these tensions did not invalidate *Russkii Turkestan*'s criticisms of tsarist officialdom, at the center as well as in the imperial city. St. Petersburg, through its policies of sending unwanted migrants on the one hand and blocking political reforms on the other, contributed to multiple ruptures in colonial society that stretched beyond lines of class.

# 5.

# The Predicaments of "Progress," 1905–1914

On November 24, 1905, the Tashkent newspaper *Sredneaziatskaia Zhizn'* featured an article entitled "Down with Progress." Its author stressed the dangers of recent political changes to Russia's quest to bring "culture" and "civilization" to Central Asia.[1] The October Manifesto's provision for direct elections threatened to transfer political power in Turkestan to the overwhelming Central Asian majority. Such a development, it was argued, would place the region in the hands of a population characterized by "religious fanaticism and crude superstition, and a complete absence of understanding of the necessity of enlightenment." Russians, as the "higher race," needed to complete their mission to spread "civilization" to the "dark" Muslim masses before the implementation of democratic reforms.[2]

The article's strong language revealed growing concerns among overlapping strata of Tashkent Russian administrators, intellectuals, and commercial interests toward emerging concepts of progress in the tsarist empire. In 1905, Central Asians, as had railway workers, seized upon empire-wide ideas of a free press and democratic representative government to assert their own interests in colonial society. Imperial elites struggled to reconcile their stated adherence to the civilizing mission with their continued denial of equal political rights to the colonized majority. Over the next decade, the vision of a Russian mission to spread European culture to Central Asia foundered. The causes, however, were not those feared by the author of "Down with Progress." They lay instead with policies drafted in St. Petersburg. The tsar's turn away from democratic provisions of the October Manifesto painted imperial officials in Tashkent as well as in the metropole as forces of backwardness instead of modern civilization. Other central policies subsequent to the manifesto, particularly the dispatch of hundreds of thousands of Slavic migrants to Central Asia and the relegation of the region to a producer of raw materials, particularly cotton, imperiled the image and practice of tsarist rule. Effects of these policies seemed to redound to the advantage of Central Asian farmers and businessmen, profiting as impoverished new settlers were flooding Russian Tashkent.

Anxieties over the future of Russian colonial rule grew even as railway links sparked sustained urban development and economic growth. Russian writers and administrators decried capital development as dirty and ugly, and continued to link it to the Central Asian population. Yet St. Petersburg, Moscow, and local Russian business interests alike benefited from economic expansion, and the balance of colonial power continued to favor representatives of the tsarist state. Repression of the local population continued, if not strengthened, as Russian liberal forces lamented their inability to represent or spread progress across Tashkent and Turkestan.

Social and cultural tensions, as well as contests over political power and visions of progress, intensified on both sides of the Ankhor canal. Young Central Asian intellectuals, calling themselves "Jadids," or "new-method thinkers," challenged Islamic clerical elites with their own concept of progress. Central Asian commercial interests supported this movement, which adhered to many of the concepts of civilization preached by Russian elites. Economic growth offered new paths to power and influence in Asian Tashkent. Jadids remained small in numbers, condemned by the Islamic clergy, yet their intellectual energy signaled a new dynamism in local society and concerned Russian administrative and intellectual elites, already questioning who was the colonizer and who was the colonized in early-twentieth-century Tashkent.

## 1905: The Beginning or End of Progress?

As across the empire, the provisions of the October Manifesto, once they became known in Tashkent, mollified Russian liberal forces—primarily white-collar workers in the bureaucracy and professions—who had joined strident anti-government protests in October 1905. Engineer Shpakovskii, abandoning his alliance with striking railway workers, led a "rush to organize" for civic activity and democratic elections for a duma (state assembly). Shpakovskii steered his Union of Engineers and Technicians toward the branch of the new Constitutional Democratic

(*Kadet*) Party that formed in Tashkent.[3] Leading the Kadet party was
G. S. Reiser, one of the former editors of *Russkii Turkestan*.[4] Reiser and
other leading intellectuals who had been pushed out from the newspaper began the publication of *Sredneaziatskaia Zhizn,'* which advocated
acceptance of the October Manifesto as a basis for political reform and
condemned the "dangerous" radicalism of railway workers.[5] Its inaugural issue, much like that of the private newspaper *Okraina* in 1894,
argued that local Russian intellectuals would lead Tashkent, Turkestan,
and the entire empire along the road to progress.[6] Russian liberals envisioned taking leading roles in bringing the rule of law to a region still
under emergency statute and then reducing, if not eliminating, political
or legal distinctions based on estate or ethnicity. Their efforts would enable achievements, including universal literacy and education, aimed
at local Russians as well as Central Asians. Planning for elections to the
state duma, these intellectuals, now self-designated the "intelligentsia,"
supported "vanguard elements" that would widen democratic reforms
throughout the tsarist empire.[7]

Tsarist administrators took advantage of the reduction in revolutionary activity. By early November, forces loyal to the administration
had gained control of the city duma as the October general strike lost
momentum, with merchants opening their stores and activist railway
workers increasingly isolated. Yet provisions of the October Manifesto
posed significant problems for tsarist administrators. Leading officials
had no will to allow statewide reforms to threaten Russians' hold on political power in Turkestan. Their solution to the issue of a democratically
elected state duma involved the division of "natives" (*tuzemtsy*) and
"non-natives" into separate electoral franchises. Despite the preponder-
ance of the "native" population, which comprised over 90 percent of the
population of Turkestan, each franchise would elect one representative.
Gerrymandering allowed for the appearance of representative government, all the while denying equal rights to the Central Asian majority.

Russian liberals and socialists in Tashkent reacted with uncertainty
to this system, which represented a clear violation of the "four-tailed"
(equal, direct, universal, and secret) system of elections, which they had
demanded for the empire as a whole in the revolution of 1905. In October
and early November, as society-wide forces held daily mass meetings
on the future of Russia at the Tashkent circus, Shpakovskii and his engineers, Russian liberal state employees, and railway workers all rejected
the demands of Seid Azim and other Muslim deputies for a "four-tailed"
franchise for the Tashkent city duma. They agreed only to abolish Statute
64 of the Administration of the Turkestan Province, which allowed Russian administrators and police sweeping powers of imprisonment and

the right to levy arbitrary fines on the local Muslim population.[8] The socialist *Russkii Turkestan*, which had previously condemned any alteration of the "four-tailed" franchise as an attack upon human dignity, an affront to progress, and a symbol of the injustices of tsarist rule, approved of the tsarist administrators' electoral scheme to the state duma in January 1906.[9] The newspaper, paralleling the language of the author of "Down with Progress," argued that Central Asians, "uncultured, conservative, and backward," lacked the consciousness necessary to participate as equals in a modern socialist society.[10]

Several Russian liberal intellectuals remained troubled by tsarist officials' breach of the four-tailed franchise. St. Petersburg Kadet party leaders had taken a clear position against "national chauvinism," one shared by other liberal forces and Social Democrats.[11] A special interparty meeting hosted by the Tashkent Constitutional Democrats on January 4, 1906, addressed the issue of voting rights for the Central Asian population. At the meeting, Tashkent Kadet leader Reiser echoed the majority view supporting separate franchises, arguing that Muslims and Russians had "extreme" differences in culture.[12] Other voices justified separation on the grounds that it was to the benefit of the colonized; one delegate, Meier, argued that Russians were "guests" in the region, and needed to allow the native population representatives to address questions and problems that specifically affected them.[13]

Such arguments, which avoided mention of the demographic inequality of the planned franchises, demonstrated unease at depriving the local population of the voting rights Russian liberals had struggled themselves to realize. A more direct voice at the meeting did condemn the intended electoral scheme as a "clear breach of the principles of equal voting."[14] Reiser and Meier joined other Kadets to reject the views of N. G. Mallitskii, a prominent Orientalist scholar and editor of *Turkestanskiia Viedomosti*, that the Muslim population, having no experience at popular elections and dominated by aristocrats and the bourgeoisie, should be deprived of representation completely. Mallitskii in fact proved unique among the speakers in justifying unequal voting rights on the basis of common practice in "enlightened" European colonial states, using Algeria as an example. Denial of equal voting rights in imperial regions, he argued, would bring Russia closer to Europe.[15] Yet fears abounded among Kadet leaders that a violation of the "four-tailed" franchise would establish Tashkent and Turkestan as "backward" areas within the empire. Liberals argued that traditions of ethnic tolerance and multiethnicity were at the center of Russian strength and civilization, proving Russia as a superior imperial nation to Europe. Reiser justified limiting local voting rights by the fact the Muslim population was extremely conservative and would send representatives that would roll back modern reforms.[16] Mallitskii and Reiser agreed that the denial of rights to the Central Asian population should only be temporary, until the "civilizing mission" was complete.

The abandonment of democratic principles placed Russian liberals and radicals in an awkward position. Progressive forces in Tashkent, as across the tsarist empire, lost momentum in following years to more conservative alignments. Members of the so-called People's Progressive Party, many of whom were present at the January interparty meeting, preached an aggressive Russian nationalism. Party members targeted not only Central Asians, but "Jews, Poles, and Caucasians" who sought to bring disorder to the empire.[17] They countered the vision among liberal tsarist elites, expressed powerfully in *Turkestanskiia Viedomosti* in 1904, that the lack of a "national consciousness" was a source of strength for Russians as they attempted to complete their historical imperial mission to bring progress to Asia.[18] *Sredneaziatskaia Zhizn'* regretted in January 1907 the "petty squabbles" that absorbed "progressive" political parties, to the benefit of conservatives and socialists, who used, respectively, nationality and class as organizing principles to divide society. Seeing conservative and socialist strength as duma elections approached, the newspaper argued that "preelection agitation in Tashkent shows how little Russian society is ready for conscious political activity."[19] Democracy had exposed the backwardness rather than the progress of Russian society.

Central Asian political leaders had withdrawn from cooperation with liberal and socialist forces following rejection of their demands for "four-tailed" elections to the city duma. Seid Azim and other Central Asian deputies instead returned to their support of the imperial state, a partner seen as less likely to enact reforms that might threaten the position of Asian Tashkent's notables. In late October, Central Asian deputies in the duma demanded, in a joint letter to the governor-general, that imperial administrators restore Cossack police to the streets of the Russian city, despite their recent killing of two unarmed protesters.[20] On November 2, Central Asian deputy Khakimbek Nazarov presented the proposal to the entire duma. One Russian deputy, Serov, invited Nazarov to "take the Cossacks with him to the old [Asian] city, so that he could feel on his own back the force of a Cossack nightstick."[21] Khakimbek Nazarov's proposal passed by a vote of twenty-one to ten, prompting Serov to congratulate the "natives" for their "victory." Tsarist administrators cheered the support of Central Asian elites, who had grown adept at managing votes in the duma.[22] City head V. N. Rybushkin withdrew extra officers who had been posted at crossing points between the Russian and Asian cities in order to prevent contact between potential anti-government forces.[23] G. P. Fedorov, director of the Office of the Governor-General, believed that the failure of revolutionary forces to attract Central Asians to their cause confirmed their ultimate defeat.

Seid Azim's and Khakimbek Nazarov's actions provided Russian liberals with examples of reactionary Central Asians to justify unequal franchises, but these figures represented only one local response to the events of 1905. Central Asians were far from the passive observers in the revolution that the contemporary Russian press and subsequent histori- cal studies have made them out to be.[24] The events of 1905 marked the debut on the political stage of the modernist Central Asian intellectuals, the Jadids, who took advantage of press freedoms following the Octo- ber Manifesto to publicize their own vision of progress in Tashkent and Turkestan. Jadids used platforms not only in the local-language supple- ment of *Turkestanskiia Viedomosti*, entitled *Turkistan Wilayatining Gazeti* (Turkestan District Newspaper), but in two independent publications, *Taraqqi* (Progress) and *Khurshid* (Sun).[25] In these newspapers and other fora, Jadid writers offered searching critiques of Islamic society and culture as well as colonial rule.

Adeeb Khalid has argued that Central Asian Jadids focused on com- plementary efforts to modernize their own society and throw off their imperial overlords. They formed part of a larger movement for Islam- ic renewal at the turn of the twentieth century, though Central Asian Jadidism had its own unique features. Educated in local Islamic colleges, the madrasas, these intellectuals had, through travel or study, come into contact with Islamic modernist thinkers from Egypt to India, and had gained an "awareness of the world." They believed that they had a moral duty to lift Central Asian society from what they perceived as its cultural isolation, which had led to stultification and ignorance.[26] Visions of renewal varied widely between thinkers, but what united these Jadids was a belief in historical change and in "progress," or *taraqqi*, which con- notes also ideas of growth and development.[27]

Jadids, expressing admiration for many of the same aspects of Euro- pean progress so vaunted by Russian administrators and liberal elites claiming participation in the civilizing mission, sought to apply, in the words of Edward Lazzerini, the "mentality of modernism" to Islam and Central Asia.[28] Their belief that knowledge was universal instead of culturally specific allowed them to intertwine ideas and practices from Europe and Asia, particularly in education. The term "jadid" originated with the name for "new-method" schools arising across the Islamic world in the late nineteenth century.[29] Beginning with an emphasis upon functional literacy—learning the Arabic alphabet phonetically instead of syllabically, by rote—these schools expanded to adopt many features of contemporary European education. Munawwar Qari Abdurrashid Khan oghli, who pioneered new-method schools in Tashkent, opening the first in 1901, taught arithmetic, geography, and history. Jadid schools stressed the history of Islam in their teachings, weaving its cultural achievements into a modern curriculum, with the goal of making the sharia and the religion compatible with modern knowledge.

Activism and the new freedoms of 1905 allowed Jadids to spread ideas of progress beyond the doors of their small number of schools. *Taraqqi* advocated wholesale reform of Islamic educational systems and greater openness from the Islamic clergy.[30] Jadids saw Islam as an important marker of cultural identity and a vital component of regional history, but desacralized the religion, separating strict religious practice from state and society. They envisioned no social or political leadership role for the spiritual authorities, a vision that distanced them even from reformist clerics who questioned the conservative practice of taqlid, which strictly bound followers to their leaders' dictates.[31] *Taraqqi* and *Khurshid* further advocated that Muslims turn away from tradition to science, and modernize many facets of their society, from infrastructure to medicine.[32] By early 1906, *Taraqqi* turned its attacks to tsarist bureaucrats who sought to stifle the promises of the October Manifesto. Imperial officials quickly began to harass the newspaper's editors, and closed the paper after seventeen issues.[33]

Islamic clerics supported tsarist actions. Asian Tashkent's mullas and qazis saw *Taraqqi* as supporting the liberal policies of Seid Azim and the more "Russianized" elites of the Sheikhantaur district, which bordered Russian Tashkent. Religious leaders demanded the closing of *Khurshid* as well, a demand fulfilled by tsarist police at the end of 1906.[34] The clergy viewed the Jadids as impetuous youth disastrously drawing local society away from its traditions. The Jadids were indeed young—most in their twenties at the time of the 1905 revolution—but the main source of conflict centered on their view of Islam in politics, society, and culture. Jadids saw themselves as leaders of a new nation (*watan*), a political unit modeled upon European lines that would offer modern group identities to replace local ones affiliated with family, tribe, or religion, as well as ones such as "Sart," which, used by Russians to refer to the local settled population, now served as a pejorative. Central Asian Jadids nonetheless conceived their watan, which they called *Turan*, as coterminous with the boundaries of Russian Turkestan.

Jadids' focus on building their own watan isolated them from the Tatar and Azerbaijani Turk-led All-Russian Muslim Movement. The All-Russian Muslim Movement had not solicited Central Asian participation in its two 1905 congresses, designed to mobilize the sixteen million Muslims of the tsarist empire into an effective political unity. This neglect intensified Central Asian anger toward perceived Tatar high-handedness.[35] Tatar intellectuals viewed their presence in Central Asia as part of their own Turkic civilizing mission and lived separately from the local population.[36] Russian officials favored Tatars as translators and in other positions where they could be used as mediators with the local population. In any case, Jadidism, by the 1905 revolution, had become a complex phenomenon, varying by thinker and region, leaving little to unify Muslim modernists across the Russian empire.

Despite their disappointment over undemocratic electoral franchises, Tashkent Jadids, along with other sectors of society in the Asian city, saw state duma elections as an opportunity to make their own mark on the all-Union political scene and demonstrate the modernizing potential of Muslim Turkestan to the empire.[37] Jadid participation in a series of complex preliminary elections for the duma produced an electoral board of a new generation of local notables and businessmen sympathetic to their causes, including Seid Karim, the nephew of Seid Azim, Arif Khoja Azis Khojaev, Karimdat Shamsutdinov, and Arifjan Malabaev. Jadid hopes to represent Turkestan in the duma were buoyed by tsarist officials' insistence that electoral rolls be published only in Russian, a language that most of them had mastered.[38] Confusion over the application of separate franchises, however, delayed elections in Turkestan beyond the life of the first state duma, which was dissolved by Nicholas II in July 1906.

Elections for the second duma evoked strong feelings throughout Asian Tashkent, involving new actors besides the Jadids and the traditional elites. An official report of a September 12 meeting at the Jami mosque to choose one delegate from the city discussed at length a protest by Makhdi Khoja Khorum Khojaev and Sultan Khoja Inogam Khojaev, who led several demonstrators, yelling, "We do not need a duma! Only the rich are elected to the duma!"[39] The crowd, which included artisans, cried, "I have given a petition; people are overburdened by taxes!" A large group roughed up a Russian police officer overseeing the elections.[40] This protest offers a tantalizing hint at potential social discord in Asian Tashkent, but available sources do not mention any other manifestations during the era. As other police dragged away Makhdi Khoja, who was later classified as "mentally ill," the meeting continued. Several candidates chosen by eligible voters withdrew, for reasons unknown, with the position finally taken by Abdulwahid Qari, an instructor at a Tashkent madrasa. Abdulwahid Qari attended the sessions of the second all-Union duma, though he had no discernible impact.[41] Hopes that central authorities would act to address regional grievances, including the removal of Statute 64, evaporated. Central Asians gained no increased political rights. St. Petersburg deprived Turkestan, as well as several other border and non-Russian regions of the empire, of state duma representation altogether following the "Stolypin coup" of 1907, which drastically reduced the franchise for the assembly and emphasized the turn of the tsarist state toward reaction.[42]

Jadids shared their disappointment with Russian liberal forces; the two groups, increasingly isolated from circles of power, circulated in similar social and intellectual worlds, participating in learned societies in the Russian city.[43] Beginning in 1906, the Jadids also shared growing suspicions of revolutionary workers. *Taraqqi* advocated a stronger police presence in Tashkent, believing that revolutionary and criminal activity, which they did not distinguish, threatened the stability of colonial society.[44] *Tujjor* (Merchant), an apolitical newspaper published by Seid Karim, noted perpetual disorder on railway lines and deteriorating relations between Russian workers and Central Asians. Yet the newspaper had no kind words for the Russian police, asking for their replacement with Persians or Kazakhs.[45] Central Asians sought to take security into their own hands; merchants began to request firearms from the tsarist authorities, stating their fear of transporting money or precious goods into Russian areas given the current climate of disorder.[46]

Central Asians nonetheless continued to campaign for greater political rights. Emerging as the leader of local deputies in the city duma was Arif Khoja Azis Khojaev, the son-in-law of Muhiddin Khoja, who had died in 1902. Arif Khoja had already amassed a fortune approaching one million rubles, and lived in opulence in Russian Tashkent, in a residence divided into "Russian" and "Asian" sections.[47] Along with Seid Karim, Arif Khoja represented a new generation of Central Asian mediators. Both spoke Russian fluently, had traveled extensively throughout Europe, and were very wealthy. Both, like the Jadids, were suspicious of Russian revolutionary activity but active proponents of Central Asian liberties and privileges. Arif Khoja made an impassioned call for greater equality in a speech before the city duma in November 1906. He argued that the "role of natives in producing wealth is no less than that of Russians; only in participation in matters of city government are we unequal."[48] He demanded that all revenues generated in Asian Tashkent stay there, as inequitable distribution led to Central Asians' being able to enjoy "civilization" only in the Russian city. The civilizing mission would be complete only when Asian Tashkent had modern symbols and institutions such as street lights and hospitals.[49] Arif Khoja, along with the Jadids and others, continued criticisms of imperial rule and colonial society following the suspension of duma representation for Turkestan and the closure of *Tujjor* in 1908. Mass support for their activities was unclear; none of the Central Asian periodicals spawned by the freedoms of 1905 ever achieved widespread circulation, being published in runs of two to three hundred.[50] The willingness of Tashkent Central Asians to intervene in imperial politics nonetheless debunked myths, spread across the Russian political spectrum, of their society as unable to understand, much less exploit, freedoms seemingly offered in the wake of the October Manifesto.

## Colony and Colonialism, 1906–1914

As revolutionary fervor and public demonstrations dissipated throughout 1906, tsarist officials and Russian commercial elites regained a sense of optimism about the future of the imperial city. *Sredneaziatskaia Zhizn'*, even as it lamented political reaction in the center, celebrated the economic opportunities now afforded by the completion of the Orenburg-Tashkent railway.[51] An internal report in early 1906 alerted Prime Minister Sergei Witte to the value of developing the numerous valuable resources of Turkestan, from cotton to tobacco to oil.[52] Russians in Tashkent envisioned the building of new factories that could process these materials before sending them to Russia and, eventually, to Europe. European investors were already demonstrating their interest in the region, with a Belgian company winning a concession to construct a tramway in Tashkent. In 1908, *Turkestanskiia Viedomosti* boasted that the Orenburg-Tashkent railway was fulfilling all the expectations of the Russian population, placing Tashkent on the cusp of becoming a vital regional, national, and international hub, the "St. Petersburg" of Asian Russia.[53]

The railway provided dangers as well as opportunities for Russian official and commercial elites. In 1905, striking railway workers had exploited their ability to strangle the city, cutting off trade and supplies that now came almost uniquely by rail. Lower-class migrants arriving by the hundreds on the Orenburg-Tashkent line emerged as another threat in 1906. Their appearance mocked tsarist officials' efforts to limit migration, which had intensified since 1892; in 1897, Governor-General Vrevskii had banned rural as well as urban colonization in Turkestan.[54] Administrators feared that any migration would disturb the fragile balance of power in the region, as Russian settlers could not be trusted to avoid behavior that might provoke Central Asian resistance. Russian migrants had nonetheless continued to arrive, and the combination of the direct rail line and unemployment at the center sparked the 1906 wave.[55] Many recent migrants were among the thousands, seeking employment,

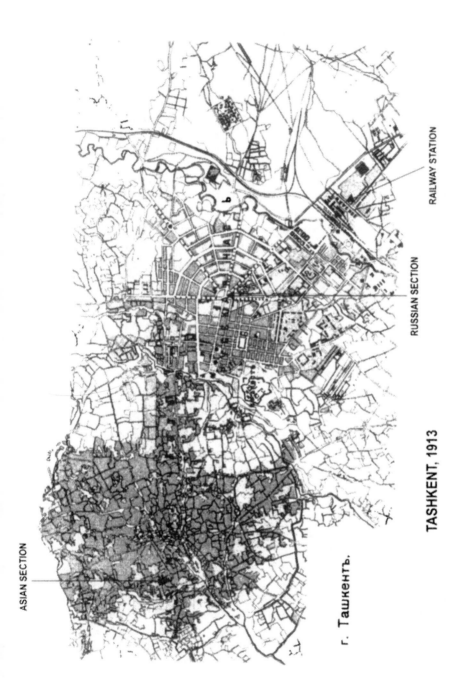

ASIAN SECTION

RAILWAY STATION

RUSSIAN SECTION

г. Ташкентъ.

**TASHKENT, 1913**

Figure 20. Russian Tashkent, 1913. *Aziaskaia Rossiia* (St. Petersburg:
Izdanie Pereselencheskogo Upravlenie, 1914), Atlas Plate 60, Figure 9.1.

who crowded the central labor market in Voskresenskii bazaar. In May, the Syr-Dar'ia district administration reported that migrants had occupied all vacant housing. The city duma opened debate on a yet another measure to ban movement to Tashkent. Lower-class Russians were begging Central Asian employers for work. Tsarist officials claimed working with these new arrivals was a "moral torment."[56]

Attitudes and policies toward migration sharpened discord between center and periphery. By the turn of the century, ministries in St. Petersburg viewed Turkestan as an ideal home for increasing numbers of Russian subjects. In 1899, minister of war A. N. Kuropatkin hailed the potential for the region's "Russification" due to railway construction.[57] A large Russian presence, he argued, would secure Turkestan against incursions from British troops. St. Petersburg officials were also beginning to view Asiatic Russia as a "safety valve" for the perceived problem of a land shortage in the central regions of the empire. In 1906–1907, Prime Minister P. A. Stolypin forged a comprehensive plan to open Siberia, the Kazakh steppe, and Turkestan to the Russian peasantry. Stolypin funneled millions of rubles to the state Resettlement Administration, with the goal of transferring millions of peasants eastward and southward.[58] Stolypin's policies to transform the future of farming in Russia, simultaneously creating a new class of farmers liberated from the traditional peasant commune and assuring the future of Russia in Asian lands, caught the attention of metropolitan elites.[59] The central press reported extensively on colonization efforts. A new monthly journal dedicated exclusively to the issue, *Questions of Colonization* (*Voprosy Kolonizatsii*), was launched. Tsarist officials and Russian writers in St. Petersburg and Moscow saw the settlement of the Asian frontier as playing a crucial role in their national future.[60]

Some administrators and intellectuals in Russian Tashkent, anxious to gain notoriety in central Russia, shelved their reservations over increased migration and embraced their role in fulfilling a national mission. Enthusiasm percolated as well among Russians from Turkestan studying at institutes of higher education in St. Petersburg, who had formed their own association (*zemliachestvo*). Dov Yaroshevski has argued that these students placed importance on using their region to serve their home country.[61] In Tashkent, one *Sredneaziatskaia Zhizn'* writer saw new migrants as necessary to prevent Central Asians from "colonizing" lands made far more valuable due to the railway link with central Russia.[62] *Na Rubezhe*, another private newspaper, reported on the "stunning success" of migration in the Syr-Dar'ia oblast, which would assure the future of an independent farming class in a Christian, Russian society for the indefinite future.[63] Tours by high-ranking central officials, culminating in the visit of the minister of agriculture A. V. Krivoshein

Figure 21. Kaufman Boulevard, 1917. Tsentral'nyi Gosudarstvennyi
arkhiv kinofotofonodokumentov Uzbekistana.

in 1912, aroused great excitement in the Office of the Governor-General.
The region would be afforded the opportunity to spearhead Russian
development.[64]

A new generation of Russian intellectuals believed that this migratory wave could be handled effectively, using new knowledge gained
from recent explorations and studies on the periphery. *Sredneaziatskaia
Zhizn'* argued that new lands could be found for farming through "scientific" methods as long as officials relied on "academic" relations.[65] The
newspaper lauded the Turkestan Agricultural Society, led by district
agronomist R. R. Shreder, who aggressively criticized the unscientific
behavior of resettlement officials in attributing land allotments during
meetings, often held at the house of the governor-general. The local
press reported on society debates and administrators solicited briefings
from the society on the needs of the province. Other scholarly societies,
including the Turkestan branch of the Imperial Russian Geographic
Society, lent their own efforts to locating land for colonization.[66] A growing civic culture offered the potential to overcome the problems that
had surfaced during previous waves of migration to Turkestan.

Hopes that new colonists would elevate the Russian imperial enterprise quickly began to fade, however. Syr-Dar'ia district officials rushed
to find allotments for peasants from southern regions of the empire,
believing experience working in warmer climates would smooth their
transition to Turkestan.[67] Regardless of their place of origin, however,

new migrants preferred to grow food instead of valuable export goods and proved unable to master the intricacies of irrigation in a subtropical climate. They failed to fulfill Stolypin's dream of a new entrepreneurial class. By early 1907, substantial numbers of Russian peasants, their attempts to farm having failed, returned to Tashkent in search of work.[68] Peasant migrants' attributes, in the words of the Syr-Dar'ia Regional Statistical Committee's 1912 annual report, made them "less desirable" as additions to Russian Turkestan.[69]

Russian migrants were also destabilizing the countryside. New settlers seized land from Central Asian villagers, triggering resistance. By 1909, increasing rural violence led the office of the Syr-Dar'ia military governor to foresee a general breakdown in order.[70] "Crimes against the administrative order" had increased from 255 to 1,367 annually in the rural areas of the Syr-Dar'ia oblast from 1906 to 1910.[71] Conversely, other Russian colonists were selling their lots to Central Asian farmers, who irrigated the land and employed the settlers as sharecroppers.[72] Many of these Russian peasants did then grow export goods, particularly cotton, but not at all in the way imperial officials had envisaged. Instead of forming a solid, peaceful, prosperous, independent class of farmers, migrants were attacking or submitting to the colonized population, threatening the fragile balance of colonial superiority and stability.

The imperious behavior of central officials further upset this balance. On December 19, 1910, the Main Administration of Land Settlement and Agriculture, determined to enforce St. Petersburg's desire to intensify the pace of settlement, took direct control of the entire colonization process. Agents were armed with changes to the statute for governing Turkestan, which now allowed any land "deemed in excess" of the needs of the local population to be freed for settlement. Statistical survey commissions openly expropriated lands acknowledged as belonging to Central Asian villagers or on nomadic routes. Krivoshein, in his 1912 tour of Turkestan, ignored statistics of rising violence in the countryside and envisaged huge irrigation projects that would precede the arrival of 1,500,000 Russian peasants.[73] Numbers of migrants were growing significantly; in 1912 alone, 18,821 arrived in the Syr-Dar'ia oblast, a substantial percentage of the total number of 46,795 Russian peasants working in the region.[74]

Commentators in the Tashkent Russian press expressed their frustration with the continuing parade of migrants through the central railway station. *Na Rubezhe* condemned the "huge crowds" of peasants who, after noisily descending on offices of resettlement authorities in failed attempts to find land, took up begging, destroying the peace of privileged inhabitants of the Russian city.[75] *Turkestanskiia Viedomosti* echoed this view; one article stated: "Passenger trains are bringing to Tashkent the unemployed, coming from hungry provinces in the hope of finding any kind of work. Many under the category of 'independent migrants' are staying at the waystation and some are living under the open sky. This whole mass comes to Voskresenskii bazaar, where there are no jobs."[76] Anger at poor outsiders was surmounting pride at fulfilling a national destiny.

*Turkestanskiia Viedomosti* avoided placing direct blame on central policies for the undesired presence of poor migrants. Tsarist officials in Turkestan, in their own pleas to the center, stressed the number of settlers who had come without official permission, even if they were encouraged by the nationwide propaganda campaign of the Resettlement Administration.[77] Yet frustrations with central policies in the post-1905 years grew among local administrators, particularly as the consequences of the limited economic role envisioned by the metropole for Turkestan became clear. Central officials as well as businessmen saw Turkestan not as a center of diverse new industries, but as a supplier of raw cotton. Senator K. K. Palen, on an inspection of the province in 1908, made his opinion clear: "[The growth of cotton] has already been extremely profitable for the nation, as by creating an internal cotton market, Russia will not be dependent on various foreign trusts and arbitrary prices for cotton, established by the London and American markets, but will be in position to regulate prices itself. Moreover, money now wasted for buying foreign cotton will no longer go abroad, but stay within the country."[78] Taxation and tariff policies set in St. Petersburg favored cotton. By 1909, twenty major investors, including the leader of the Moscow Exchange Committee, G. A. Krestovnikov, and the "Young Industrialist" P. P. Riabushinskii, formed the Moscow Irrigation Company, with plans to irrigate hundreds of thousands of *desiatins* of land. Tsarist officials and merchants alike saw Turkestan cotton as having the potential to provide cheap inputs to Russian textile factories, vaulting them past their Polish rivals.[79] Exports, now shipped directly by rail to Russia, more than tripled, from 5 million to 18.5 million *pudy* from 1900 to 1915.[80] Turkestan played a critical but narrow role in the future of the Russian economy.

Governor-General A. V. Samsonov surveyed these developments with concern. Exploiting the region as a cotton producer hindered the development of a diversified economy. Samsonov called upon Russian industrialists, entrepreneurs, traders, and "representatives of Russian culture" to recognize the potential of Turkestan as a center for secondary, productive industry as well as for exports and internal trade.[81] The Turkestan Agricultural Society, which had originally worked to find new land suitable for cotton growing, claimed by 1911 that territory to

support the planting of cotton had been exhausted. Any further planting risked destroying the surrounding environment, as irrigating barren
fields would draw water away from existing canals.[82] In St. Petersburg,
Prince V. I. Masal'skii, an agent of the Main Administration of Land
Settlement and Agriculture, admitted in 1912 that Russians had as yet
failed to master the intricacies of irrigation.[83] A rapacious desire for this
water-intensive crop threatened the present and future of all agriculture
in Turkestan.

District statisticians also began to express misgivings concerning the
increased land allotted to cotton. In the Syr-Dar'ia oblast, the land dedicated to cotton production increased sevenfold, from 11,019 to 76,276
*desiatins* from 1903 to 1913.[84] The Syr-Dar'ia Regional Statistical Committee stated in its annual report that at present the "district is no more
than a vast market of raw materials, and at the same time, a place for
the sale of goods from Russian factories."[85] A young Turkestan, at the
mercy of central economic policy, had become no more than a "colony"
(*koloniia*) of Russia.[86]

Employing "colony" in place of other terms in use for their region
among Tashkent Russians, including "province" (*krai*), "outlying region" (*okraina*) or "homeland" (*rodina*), was significant in contemporary
Russian discourse. As early as the 1880s, Siberian regionalists used the
term as a pejorative to describe the results of central policies that shipped
raw goods directly to the metropole, preventing the development of a
balanced economy.[87] Works of these regionalists had grown extremely
popular among Turkestan Russians studying in St. Petersburg, who
shared concerns over central "expansionist" policies.[88] "Koloniia" came
to symbolize the dependence of a region upon a center ignorant of its
needs.[89] In addition to frustration over economic policies, central political actions drew criticism. The newspaper *Tashkentskii Kur'er* argued in
1908 that the absence of local self-government—a reference to the fact
that Turkestan still lacked such governing organs (*zemstvo*) granted elsewhere in the empire during the Great Reform era—and with the loss of
representation in a reformed state duma made it difficult to decide the
migration question rationally and determine a future economic direc-
tion.[90]

The Syr-Dar'ia Statistical Committee allocated blame for Turkestan's
status as a "colony" to the Central Asian population as well as the central government. Since the conquest, tsarist officials in Turkestan had
introduced new cottonseeds, grapes, and tobacco, as well as teaching
the local population improved harvesting techniques. Yet these efforts,
as well as investment capital from Russia, had only a minimal effect.
Beaten down by "centuries of oppression," local peasants had proven

unable to grasp the skills necessary to build a diversified economy through intensive agriculture.[91] The report, silent on the failure of Russian peasants to do the same, presented the indigenous population as an antipode to progress.

## Islam and Progress, 1906–14

Russian anxieties about the future development of Turkestan grew intertwined with representations of Central Asians in the early twentieth century. Tensions over increased migration, cotton production, and economic development underscored the intricacies and uncertainties of the relationship between colonizer and colonized. Debates over the status of the local population proliferated in the Russian press in Tashkent between 1906 and 1914. Arguments illuminated the complexity of Russian attitudes not only toward Central Asians, but also toward the metropole, toward progress, toward modernity itself. Central Asians also grappled with the rapid changes produced by cultural and economic shifts in the post-1905 years.

Even while casting Central Asians in an image of backwardness, district statisticians recognized the need for their participation in the development of a modern, industrialized economy. The idea of an incomplete civilizing mission was studied with increased urgency in the post-1905 years. Blame was spread, from the local population, who refused to accept modern knowledge, to the Russians themselves, who had failed to transfer the tools of progress. The author of "Down with Progress," even while trumpeting Russian accomplishments in the region, stated that civilization is known only "by hearsay to most of the Russian population."[92] *Turkestanskiia Viedomosti* and *Sredneaziatskaia Zhizn'* chided Russian administrators and intellectuals who refused to learn local languages, making them unable to spread modern ideas to the Muslims.[93] *Sredneaziatskaia Zhizn'* argued that this "indifference" was preventing the region's "normal development."[94] Evgenii Markov reported that Russian jurists in Tashkent believed, similarly to Arif Khoja, that the inequalities of colonial rule deepened a divide between Russians and Central Asians, in this case causing a collapse of the latter's morals.[95]

In March 1906, another essay studying the relationship between Russians, Central Asians, and civilization appeared in *Sredneaziatskaia Zhizn'*. Entitled "Down with Bachas," the article argued that Russian tastes for the exotic were directly responsible for the reappearance of one of the most repulsive elements of local culture: *bachas*, Muslim dancing boys who performed for male audiences in local teahouses. Islamic priests, characterized as the most fanatical and ignorant segments of the population, had agreed with tsarist authorities following the conquest to institute a ban on the practice to protect against pederasty. Wealthy Russians, however, had begun hiring dancing boys to perform at local exhibitions, and their presence was once again ubiquitous in Tashkent.[96] In terms of politics, a 1908 *Tashkentskii Kur'er* article criticized the central Russian state for not allowing even a token Central Asian presence in the duma. Were the Russians leading Central Asians forward or backward in time?[97]

Alongside these views grew a belief among local Russian writers that Central Asians possessed certain civilized qualities absent among the European population of Tashkent. Even as N. G. Mallitskii sought to deny voting rights to Central Asians in January 1906, he lauded their "cultured, industrious, honourable, and peaceful" traditions.[98] One Russian who lived in Asian Tashkent espoused that city's virtues, noting the low rate of crime as well as the patience and discipline of his neighbors. Central Asians knew how to live in peace, as a community, unlike the fractured Russians.[99] A. I. Dobrosmyslov, in his history of the city published in 1912, noted that the Asian city, with double the population, required fewer police officers than Russian Tashkent.[100] Others argued that Tashkent Muslims, urbanized and familiar with a complex, capitalist economy through Silk Road trade, possessed a superior work ethic to many settlers.[101] Sales of Russian peasant land back to local Central Asians confirmed the perception of the latter's adeptness at exploiting colonial rule.[102]

Such views strengthened the stereotype of superior Central Asian business acumen, which had now led to their domination of the economy. One article, entitled "A Possible Future for Tashkent," in *Turkestanskiia Viedomosti* in 1903 discussed the "danger of economic enslavement [of Russian settlers] to Sarts, Bukharan Jews, and Tatars."[103] All that was necessary for life, the author argued, was in the hands of the tuzemtsy (natives), who had mastered the increasing complexity of the local economy following the arrival of the railway better than the Russians themselves. Policies favoring cotton growth were perceived to tighten Central Asian economic control. A new Central Asian middle class, known as the *chistachi*, had emerged as intermediaries delivering cotton from farmers to business.[104] Central Asian businessmen had, by concentrating rough-processing plants near the sources of the best cotton in Fergana, industrialized this area before Tashkent.[105] Dobrosmyslov warned, "[S]oon, we Russians, due to our laziness and absence of entrepreneurship, will be in full dependence on the local Jews and Muslims."[106]

The development of the cotton economy had strengthened Central Asian business elites, alongside their Russian, Jewish, and German counterparts, at the beginning of the century. Isabek Khakimbatov, Bakijan Dadajanov, and Akram Khoja joined Arif Khoja as among the wealthiest cotton barons in Tashkent.[107] Advertisements in Russian newspapers confirmed the perception of the colonized population as shrewder businessmen; one seeking investors for a new oil company gave pride of place among its board members to Arif Khoja, whose name appeared larger and in bold over those of his Russian counterparts.[108]

Press articles mocked Central Asian commercial successes, allaying Russian concerns over the importance of capital by linking the pursuit of profit to immorality.[109] A 1909 *Na Rubezhe* piece condemned as hypocritical Central Asian elites who opposed the planned move of brothels from the suburbs of the Russian city to the Chimkent road, which abutted the western edge of Asian Tashkent. Muslim claims of concern toward the sanitary and moral dangers of moving prostitutes so close to the Asian city were but a smokescreen for business owners worried about a loss of "enormous profits." *Na Rubezhe* claimed these owners had determined that Muslim men, the majority of the clients, and Muslim women, the majority of the prostitutes, would be less likely to use or work at brothels so close to their friends and neighbors. Central Asian elites' hunger for money led them to promote "depravity."[110] A city duma decision to grant exclusive advertising rights to Seid Azim sparked fears over the combined power of business and Muslims to threaten cultured society. Petitions to the municipal government complained about the proliferation of placards that turned Russian Tashkent into one giant bazaar.[111] Advertisements for cigarettes and drinks blanketed landmarks of civilization, such as Kaufman square and the many schools of the Russian city. Placards offended the "eyes and esthetic sense of residents."[112]

Criticizing through racializing capitalism reflected continuing doubts of many among the Russian elites as to the compatibility of capitalism and a "civilized" culture. Representations of business as controlled by non-Russians were ubiquitous in the post-1905 local press. Cartoons in the satirical journal *Turkestanskii Kara-Kurt* represented capitalists as Central Asians, or, perhaps, as Jewish.[113] At once powerful and greedy, they had local residents at their mercy. The chaos of the market fit poorly with the sense of order and peace envisioned by the first planners of the Russian city. Tsarist officials shared doubts about unrestrained capital development; intervention from authorities in St. Petersburg and Tashkent, each determined to direct economic growth, pushed many leading Moscow industrialists to abandon their designs for Turkestan.[114]

Representations of Central Asian economic control concealed as much as they revealed about the role of Russians in the local and regional economy. Dobrosmyslov, even as he argued that Russians were edging toward full dependence on the colonized population, admitted the role in Tashkent of powerful Russian business interests, including the Shlishel-burg and Tverskii manufacturing companies and the Moscow Trading Industrial Association as well as Russian conglomerates.[115] In the post-1905 climate, following feelings of unease at denying Central Asians democratic rights, Russians concealed another axis of colonial domination by trumpeting Central Asian business success. Claims that the local population had gained economically from Russian rule allowed an accomplishment for the civilizing mission, at the same time distancing a modern Russian identity from the chaos and inequities of capital gain.

The sense of incompatibility between "culturedness" (kulturnost') and capitalism prompted a questioning of what were once regarded as centerpieces of a modern society. The railway had brought turmoil as well as benefits to Tashkent. The Orenburg-Tashkent line delivered tens of thousands of unwelcome migrants. Closer linkages between the metropole and Turkestan had placed the latter in a dependent position, no longer self-sufficient in food as cotton replaced grain.[116] Prices for foodstuffs skyrocketed. Similar phenomena in Siberia, as Stephen Marks has argued, had led regionalists to question the value of a railway.[117] One writer in Turkestanskii Kur'er in 1913 argued that the railroad was allowing all of the region's natural wealth to be exported and exploited.[118] Residents also wondered at the esthetics and the efficiency of the dirty, slow-moving engines that pulled in and out of Tashkent station. Were these machines, asked one author, really an improvement over the caravans of camels that had supplied Tashkent so well for decades?[119] What were the benefits of this changing economy that Russian elites had for so long desired?

Local writer Evgenii Fedorov questioned the motivations, effectiveness, and outcomes of nineteenth-century imperialism in light of these uncertainties in a 1909 article in Na Rubezhe. Fedorov tied his views of changes in Tashkent to contemporary European criticisms of imperialism exemplified by J. A. Hobson's renowned 1902 work, Imperialism: A Study. Imperial conquest, Fedorov argued, was primarily driven not by the "civilizing mission," but by the desire of metropolitan elites to gain new markets for European products. Fedorov, however, was principally concerned with the effects of conquest on the conquered peoples. The colonized populations of European territories, particularly Muslims, he argued, had quickly adapted to this new economic system. Not only were they sharing in colonial development, but they threatened soon to surpass their colonizers.

Fedorov, unlike previous critics, linked apparent Central Asian business success to cultural progress. Europeans, exclaimed the author, must renounce the view that Muslim societies were incapable of cultural development. Islam, like Christianity, underwent cyclical progressions of reaction and change, and Muslim societies worldwide, after a period of stasis, were actively meeting the challenges posed by European civilization. Russians in Tashkent were witnesses to this phenomenon: "Take for example our Sarts . . . the energy and receptiveness with which they have developed their trade, allowing them to acquire the cultural accomplishments of the Europeans." Not only could local Muslims acquire European culture, but they are "capable of finding their own path, and leaving us only with sadness to note . . . that we, who sowed the first seeds of progress, may remain behind them."[120]

Fedorov expressed a profound ambivalence at the apparent Central Asian resurgence. On the one hand, this identified a certain degree of success in spreading civilization. On the other, as Central Asians progressed, they shattered boundaries between colonizer and colonized, exploding the rationale and the imbalance of power that motivated and maintained European imperialism. This dilemma echoed across the colonial world in the early twentieth century. Alice Conklin has argued that French "republican universalism" at once conditioned a belief in an inherently superior metropolitan French civilization and also a belief that this civilization could lift the colonized worldwide to the same level as the colonizers. These tensions were never fully resolved.[121] Elsewhere in the Russian empire, Yuri Slezkine has noted a profound ambivalence among imperial elites toward linear concepts of progress at the turn of the century, as the colonized population refused to play the role of grateful subordinates and the basic contradiction of the civilizing mission became apparent.[122] In Tashkent, Muslim progress was at once a sign of success and of failure for local Russians in the age of empire.

Evolving representations of Russian imperial rule and the cultured and prosperous Central Asian therefore reflected intertwined international, national, and local understandings of empire. As Hobson's criticisms of empire echoed across Europe, liberals and socialists cast a new critical eye on imperial expansion, seen as potentially exploitative and dehumanizing.[123] The defeat of "European" Russia by "Asian" Japan in the Russo-Japanese War, discussed in great detail by the Tashkent press, demoralized Slavic elites across the tsarist empire and uplifted hopes of Asian peoples, from Turkey to Iran, of the possibility of throwing off European control.[124] In Tashkent, skepticism toward the tenets of nineteenth-century empire also reflected social and cultural changes within the Asian city itself. Evidence suggests that Asian Tashkent profited from the colonial economy in the post-1905 years. Artisans and laborers in the city supplied goods, such as clothing, utensils, and tools, for a society engaged more than ever in the trade of cotton.[125] The population of Asian Tashkent increased significantly, from 107,705 in 1890 to 141,047 in 1908, according to official censuses.[126] Whether the growth reflected primarily increased opportunities for employment or the growing number of Muslim peasants dispossessed from their land is uncertain. Many of the newcomers found work as poorly paid, unskilled or day laborers in the new cotton-cleaning or other factories of the city, often working directly under Russian overseers. Dobrosmyslov, however, noted the vitality of the Asian city, citing European architectural features that sprouted in the wealthier parts of town; many Central Asian businessmen were also investing in land in Russian Tashkent.[127] Mallitskii compared the city to the textile center of Moscow.[128] The colonial economy appeared to have improved the economic prospects of many in Asian Tashkent, though many worked for wages far below those received by Russians across the Ankhor canal.[129]

Central Asian deputies vigorously, if not always successfully, defended the interests of Asian Tashkent at the city duma. Of twenty-seven meetings in 1907–1908, Muslim deputies were in the majority eight times, and on other occasions equaled or fell slightly below the number of "Christian" representatives, which included one Pole, four Germans, and three Jews as well as Russians. Senator Palen, in his review of the duma for central authorities, noted, however disingenuously, that continuing petitions of Muslim deputies complaining of unequal representation were unjustified, given their ability to defend their interests through high attendance and vigorous debate. Palen claimed that the Muslims, effectively controlled by Arif Khoja, formed the single most effective bloc against disorganized Christian representatives.[130] Muslim deputies gained some successes in their endeavors, notably by dictating the route of Tashkent's new tramway system, allowing it to connect the Russian and Asian cities in 1908. The duma also acted as a forum to express discontent with actions of colonial officials.[131] One deputy argued in 1913 that arbitrary taxation, violence, and exploitation of colonized labor had reached "the most extreme limits possible."[132] Duma members failed in their paramount tasks, however, of obtaining equal representation to the assembly and equal government spending per capita for the Russian and Asian cities.

Central Asian Jadids continued their efforts to adapt Western notions of culture and education in the post-1905 years. Tashkent Jadids Munawwar Qari and allies such as Abdullah Awlani used their schools, as well as public plays and discussion circles, to spread their ideas.[133] Jadids, not unlike Russian liberals of the era, looked inward to find fault within a society they saw as having strayed from a path toward modern civilization. Among Jadid targets were practices of pederasty (directed against the bachas) and the seclusion of women, both attacked by Russian writers who sought to demonstrate Central Asian backwardness and depravity. Jadids also attacked forms of "irrational" wastefulness and extravagance in local society, particularly grandiose ritual celebrations for circumcisions, weddings, and deaths that threatened to bankrupt poor families. Criticism also continued to focus on the Islamic clergy, whose conservatism prevented local society from gaining the knowledge to combat tsarist rule. Jadids also attacked elements of European culture not considered progressive. As did Russian modernists, Jadids found particularly odious influences of alcohol, gambling, and prostitution that, they claimed, seeped from the settler population into local culture. A new Jadid newspaper, *Sada-yi Turkestan*, which began publication in 1914, approved traditional religious courts' harsh treatments of Muslim drunkards who indulged their habit in the Russian city, hoping to escape sanction.[134] Jadids aggressively explored their marginal status, between Europe and Asia, to include the characteristics of both societies that would best bring about "progress."

Constructing a modern culture was necessary to remove the inequalities and humiliation of colonial rule. Jadids viewed themselves as locked in a ferocious struggle, where a failure to adapt to and combat the features of European power threatened to destroy Islamic society and culture. Munawwar Qari shared a feeling of "impending doom" in the post-1905 years: the numbers of Jadids and their schools remained small, with students across Turkestan numbering eight thousand, as compared to over one hundred thousand in the traditional system;[135] ideas of progress had met with hostility from conservative elites; and the revolutionary momentum of 1905 had dimmed. The Jadids' world was replete with tensions. Even as thoughts of battle with imperial Europe drove them, many not only acquired European knowledge, but also moved in Russian social circles and maintained residences in the Russian city. Power, Adeeb Khalid argues, attracted Jadids, who associated with the colonizer as they sought to lift their own society from its backwardness.[136] This attraction extended to others who sought leadership of Asian Tashkent. The Russian-trained lawyer Ubaydallah Khojaev, editor of *Sada-yi Turkestan*, participated in Russian rituals honoring the tsar and empire and held his own ceremonies of loyalty in Asian Tashkent.[137] Khojaev and many Jadids hoped that displays of loyalty would convince the metropole to grant improved political and legal status to the local Central Asians.

Wealthy Central Asian businessmen and traders, many of them young and ambitious, supported these efforts. *Sada-yi Turkestan* lauded the "young businessmen" whose contributions of time and money had allowed the construction and operation of many Jadid schools in the Asian city, as well as the operation of their own newspaper.[138] Jadids, viewing capital as a useful tool to combat Russian superiority, expressed less of the doubt present among Russian intellectuals toward the incompatibility of capital accumulation and modernity. Unable to gain government posts, Jadids themselves moved in business circles; Munawwar Qari, for example, ran a bookstore. Mahmud Behubdi forcefully expressed his desire that Muslims should pursue financial gain, stating, "may God increase [their wealth]!"[139] Accumulation, however, was viewed as an absolute good only when it benefited the entire Muslim community. "Young businessmen" who whittled away their savings gambling or supported extravagant ritual feasts came under sharp attack from the Jadids.[140]

As reformist ideas gained currency in Asian Tashkent, Russian intellectuals sought ways to uphold the superiority of European culture. Evgenii Fedorov took comfort in one feature of progress that clearly still favored Europe: the status of women. In a 1910 article entitled "Respect Women!" Fedorov argued that Russian women, free to play important roles in society, had imitated the roles of Greeks and Romans in imperial territories, "propelling men to heroism and great feats."[141] Islamic women, behind the veil, subject to polygamous marriages, and enclosed in separate women's quarters, lacked the ability to contribute to their culture. Their disgraceful treatment also displayed the distance Muslims would still need to travel to catch up to all aspects of European progress. *Turkestanskiia Viedomosti* lauded the public and progressive role of Russian female physicians who practiced in Turkestan, many in clinics that served Central Asian women.[142] A. Almatinskaia, a Russian feminist writer, argued, however, in *Turkestanskii Kur'er* that Russian women in Tashkent lagged behind their sisters in western Europe, preferring to play an assigned role as "objects of luxury," symbols of European fashion and culture rather than helpers of less privileged Russian and Muslim women, who could be led to "a new path" of equality between the sexes.[143] Memoirs of Russian elite women who followed their officer-husbands to Tashkent are replete with their own frustrations at being isolated from a society dominated by male-centered activities such as hunting and military drills. Princess Anatole Marie Bariatinsky wrote of long periods "sitting at my window—about the only thing to do in this dead-alive place."[144] Jadids, nonetheless, ardent advocates for equal rights as well as sensitive to Russian criticism, worked forcefully to end Central Asian women's isolation, condemning polygyny and the veil and opening their schools to both sexes.[145]

New ideas and energy across the Islamic world caused great anxiety among Tashkent administrators. Agents of the tsarist secret police, the *Okhrana,* who had established their presence following the 1905 revolution, reported closely on Turkish and Tatar visitors to the city. After the Young Turk revolution of 1908, agents claimed that itinerant priests and modernist intellectuals were working to foment Panturkic or Panislamic ideologies that threatened the empire's integrity.[146] Municipal authorities, likely more aware of the Jadids' desire to emphasize local reforms over internationalist tendencies, were less consumed by such fears. Jadid schools generally, but not always, received official approval for their texts and curricula.[147] At the same time, Russian city commandant N. K. Kalmakov wrote to the Syr-Dar'ia regional administration in 1909 requesting the banning of a new local voluntary society, "Assistance." Kalmakov asserted that this secular charitable society, under Jadid leadership, was in violation of statutes of the sharia. He reminded regional officials of his responsibilities to head off any potential future conflict in Tashkent, and worried that internal struggles within the Central Asian community might destabilize the city as a whole.[148] As Adeeb Khalid has argued, tsarist officials, wary of phenomena they did not understand, sought to keep Jadids on a "short leash."[149]

Russian fears of being outpaced by the colonized rested on a credible foundation, even if they concealed substantial profits and domination. Jadids and local commercial interests saw opportunity where many Russian intellectuals forecast decline. Axes of power, however, still clearly favored the Russians, who exploited the local population through corruption, extortion, and violence. "Supplementary taxes" continued to line the pockets of colonial officials; *Sada-yi Turkestan* reported on police beatings of Asian Tashkent residents who refused to pay their obligations.[150] Archival and press sources offer evidence of everyday violence against the colonized majority. One local merchant took police who attacked him in a bazaar in the Russian city to court, but thrashings either by or in the presence of tsarist officials were noted in the local press as commonplace.[151] Russian medical personnel could refuse to assist Central Asians, leading in at least one case to the death of a local.[152] Russian power forced degrees of accommodation, even as it inspired resistance, from the Jadids just as it had from the local notables, who accepted salaries from and delivered taxation revenue to tsarist authorities, and the ulama, who pledged loyalty to the tsar in exchange for pledges of religious and cultural autonomy. The various understandings reached between Central Asians and Russians, as well as divisions within the Central Asian community, forestalled a unified resistance against imperial power in the tsarist era.

Imperial power, however, provided cold comfort to Russian administrators and intellectuals in the post-1905 years. Tashkent Russian concerns reflected growing doubts across Europe over the value and morality of empire as well as, in the words of Cathy Frierson, a growing "fin-de-siècle despondency" within the tsarist empire as forces of progress appeared stalled by reaction from above and ignorance from below.[153] Tashkent Russian liberals demonstrated unease at denying political equality to Central Asians, cloaking their desire to maintain colonial privilege through a condemnation of Central Asian backwardness. Tensions mounted between center and periphery, as tsarist administrators in St. Petersburg at best ignored, and at worst deliberately acted against, the interests of Tashkent Russians. New Slavic migrants, a result of central policies, displayed their inferiority to Central Asian farmers and slotted themselves below local traders and businessmen in evolving social hierarchies. Central Asians were alternately using and demanding the tools of progress, from capital development to representative government, originally brought by the colonizer. Russians in Tashkent, as a consequence, began to ask who was colonizing and who was civilizing whom?

Tashkent Russians confronted paradoxes inherent in building a "modern" colonial state in the early twentieth century. The "civilizing mission," whose success was the stated goal of all major European colonial powers, would destroy the rationale for colonial power, that there are "higher" and "lower" races. Colonized populations worldwide, as they adapted to colonial rule, exposed the fallacy of inherent divisions between peoples through their enterprise and ability to offer effective resistance. Europeans struggled to reconcile colonial rule with ideas of representative government and democracy. Many had begun to criticize the rapaciousness of their states on the periphery, which seemed to have very little in common with the civilization and culture that they claimed to be spreading.

The marginal status of Russia in Europe exacerbated the impact of these paradoxes in Turkestan. Hopeful that their actions in Tashkent would help to overcome centuries of perceived Russian backwardness, Russian administrative and intellectual elites experienced great frustration when these expectations appeared doomed. Russia appeared to lack not only the ideas of progress that had enabled the coming to power of the Young Turks, but the power that a modernizing state such as Japan had wielded in the Russo-Japanese War. Even as Tashkent developed rapidly, with the railway and tramway sparking new economic growth, discussions in all of the major periodicals in the Russian city focused on the issue of Russia's decline as a progressive imperial power and the failure to realize the hopes of the first generation of empire builders in Central Asia.

# 6.

## War, Empire, and Society, 1914–1916

A large crowd of Russian women gathered around the store of local merchant Paizu Umirzakov in the early morning of October 22, 1916. Rumors had circulated that Umirzakov was withholding large supplies of meat, then in extremely short supply in Russian Tashkent. Angry that the merchant had not yet appeared, members of the crowd agitated to destroy the store. Police intervened to protect Umirzakov's property. A scuffle then ensued, as the women, through threats and blows, successfully resisted arrest. For the moment, however, the store was preserved.[1]

This incident deeply disturbed imperial officials. Violent demonstrations by Russian women in previous months had frayed crucial relationships that bound local society in Tashkent. Police, duma representatives, and tsarist functionaries despaired of resolving issues that had provoked this unrest. Wartime policies, dictated in Petrograd (as St. Petersburg was renamed during the war), diverted supplies of basic goods headed to Turkestan, no longer self-sufficient in food, to the front. Pleas from local officials for greater attention to the fragility of the empire's periphery went unanswered. Central demands for Central Asian manpower for the war effort prompted a riot in Tashkent, and a rebellion across Turkestan, beginning in June 1916. As military defeats mounted at the front, control of the streets on both sides of Tashkent grew increasingly uncertain.

A sense of vulnerability, a fear of marginalization, an awareness of isolation pervaded wartime Tashkent, from the corridors of imperial power to the dusty outskirts of the Russian and Asian cities. The war had begun with optimism, as Russian and Central Asian politicians, businessmen, and intellectuals, as well as imperial officials, saw opportunities to prove Tashkent's importance to the metropole. They hoped support for the war effort, including the production of cotton, a vital wartime good, would be repaid with greater central attention and support at the war's end. Multiple constituencies within colonial society, from minority European nationalities and Central Asian notables, to, later, Slavic prisoners of war from the Austro-Hungarian Empire gained visibility and prestige through their roles in wartime society. The dislocations of the war years, however, compelled subordinate groups to speak and act clearly and forcefully. As Russian lower-class women targeted Central Asian merchants, imperial officials, and other males opposing them, small traders and residents of Asian Tashkent asserted their own power on the streets. Linkages as well as tensions coalesced along and across boundaries of race, class, and gender, the "multiple axes of domination and subordination" that drove imperial rule.[2] As after the 1892 cholera riot, fear of losing control of the city forced imperial elites to launch multiple investigations and inquiries into dissatisfaction and unrest. Their records offer us the voices, albeit mediated, of the less privileged groups in colonial society.[3] Russian elites struggled to restore power and prestige, slipping since the turn of the century, before their inability to provide basic goods to the population of Tashkent.

## Wartime Strains, 1914–16

Patriotic rallies in Russian Tashkent greeted news of tsarist support for its traditional Serbian ally against an impending Austro-Hungarian invasion in July 1914.[4] Pro-war demonstrators gathered in front of a new monument to former Governor-General Kaufman, where speakers reminded the Russian audience of their own role in helping the country gain the status of a power capable of bringing "peace" and "civilization" to troubled areas of the world.[5] Reports of attendance, however, placed the numbers in the low hundreds from a Russian population numbering at least 58,000, hardly on the scale of other public rituals in the city.[6]

Gauging the opinions of Tashkent Russian society toward the war at this stage is difficult. Some evidence indicates that the desire to serve in the army was less than overwhelming. Russians who had been born in Turkestan or who moved there before the age of sixteen were exempt from the draft according to an early-twentieth-century provision to encourage migration. Press reports suggest that many Tashkent Russians either refused to serve or "swapped" passports in various schemes to avoid conscription, prompting calls from self-described "patriots" to revoke the status.[7] Support for the war effort, however, meant more than serving at the front, and involved a complex set of motives and goals for different individuals and groups in Tashkent.

The sight of the desperate faces of refugees fleeing battlefields in Poland and Galicia initiated Tashkent residents into World War I. These refugees were a fraction of the several million inhabitants of the tsarist empire's western provinces who decamped eastward in 1914–15, a movement that minister of agriculture Krivoshein, citing a lack of resettlement resources, likened to the apocalypse.[8] Reactions to refugees varied wildly across the empire, but officials and private citizens in Russian Tashkent greeted the first waves, arriving by rail in late 1914, with sympathy. City duma members worked to fulfill "needs of our brothers of the fatherland, deprived of shelter and property as a consequence of the advance of our enemy."[9] As refugee numbers reached six thousand by summer 1915, Governor-General F. M. Martson sought to distribute them across Turkestan. Russian women and minority European nationalities in Tashkent led efforts to form voluntary organizations to assist refugees and lobby imperial officials for resources.

Wives of prominent tsarist officials, headed by E. D. Galkina, the spouse of the Syr-Dar'ia military governor, formed the Tashkent Women's Committee in late 1914. Fundraisers for local soldiers at the front and refugees accumulated eighteen thousand rubles in January 1916 alone. The committee received prominent coverage in the local press, which highlighted women in their traditional roles as supporting men who had gone on to great deeds at the front or poor families who needed charity and attention.[10] Another women's organization, the Tat'iana Committee, an extension of the empire-wide Tat'iana Committee for the Relief of War Victims, worked exclusively with refugees.[11] In St. Petersburg and Moscow, the Tat'iana Committee attracted the patronage of prominent wealthy women and assigned funds directly to local branches, also headed by women. This independent source of financing frustrated local officials throughout the empire, who could not bend the committee to their will.[12] In Tashkent, the Tat'iana Committee gained a reputation for greater efficiency than official institutions; *Turkestanskii Kur'er* praised the women of the committee for their "heroic efforts," as opposed to duma paralysis, as the numbers of refugees reached fourteen thousand in late 1915.[13] Committee members managed feeding stations and found housing for refugees far superior to the disease- and insect-ridden barracks opened by the duma, as well as provided employment, operating their own sewing and furniture-making factories. The number of refugees under the Tat'iana Committee's care remains unclear, as members—perhaps as a sign of independence—did not share information with local officials.[14]

Other voluntary societies operated along lines of nationality. Polish, Jewish, and Latvian committees raised funds within their own communities to receive compatriots displaced from their homelands. They fed refugees and boarded them with local families. They also formed labor exchanges to find work for the new arrivals. Committees gained public exposure and coverage in the local press through these activities, as well as through ubiquitous fundraising events, including flea markets, concerts, and public lectures. The Polish committee opened their own school and hospital for their refugees at the end of 1915.[15] Altruism and nationalism blended in these initiatives. Minority groups used their newfound visibility to assert their interests in local society and overcome some of the divisions wrought by Russification policies enacted across the empire in the 1890s. Poles overcame years of resistance from the city duma toward building a Roman Catholic cathedral, receiving a five-thousand-ruble interest-free loan even as economic difficulties intensified in Tashkent.[16] The status of minority nationalities as well as privileged women rose as they assisted in dealing with strains in wartime Tashkent.

Prisoners of war flooded into Turkestan at a rate greater than refugees in 1914–15. By the end of September 1914, 3,952 prisoners had reached the province, as the tsarist government sought to send them far from the front.[17] The Office of the Governor-General constructed camps throughout the region, including one, designed to house several thousands, forty kilometers outside of Tashkent. Prisoners, overwhelmingly from the Austro-Hungarian Empire, were also lodged in former soldiers' barracks within the bounds of the Russian city. Officials saw their supervision as a patriotic duty. Russian businessmen saw these young, skilled Europeans as an ideal labor force. *Turkestanskii Kur'er* urged authorities to make a maximum number of prisoners available for work. They could forestall a labor shortage created by those serving at the front, preventing the need to promote women or Central Asians to skilled labor positions. The newspaper worried that soon even unskilled Kazakh nomads would be in a position to demand higher wages for service.[18]

Tsarist officials and Russian intellectuals, with the encouragement of the Ministry of Internal Affairs, relished the opportunity to switch the allegiance of captured Austro-Hungarian Slavs, including Poles, Czechs, Slovaks, Serbs, Croats, and Ruthenians, to the tsarist empire. A 1915 policy allowed Slavic prisoners to mix freely with the civilians of Tashkent on day leaves from camps.[19] On June 7, the Tashkent branch of the All-Russian Society for the Guardianship of Slavic Prisoners of War opened its doors. Educators, including regional schools inspector N. P. Ostroumov, offered courses on the Russian language, as well as on the history, economy, and geography of the tsarist empire. Priest A. Pokrovskii spoke in glowing terms of the potential "merger of peoples of related Slavic tribes with our fatherland."[20] The local press glorified the new school as performing a new type of "civilizing mission." For Ostroumov and other intellectuals, even more was at stake. The wide curriculum of courses allowed them to discuss their program as a "little university."[21] Their efforts presaged an extensive campaign that lasted throughout and beyond the war: lobbying Petrograd, and later Moscow, to construct and certify a local university, a move that would confirm Tashkent's status as a leading city in the empire.[22]

Imperial officials offered extensive privileges to fellow officers of opposing armies. Austro-Hungarian officers stayed at the best hotel in town, the recently constructed National. They received supplies from subsidized state food stores without having to wait in line. As late as 1917, prisoner-of-war officers received luxury goods, such as plum jam and cream.[23] Officers and soldiers walked the streets of Tashkent in their uniforms, even participating in military parades. These privileges annoyed some Tashkent Russians. One writer wondered if detainees were taking unfair advantage of the civilization that the city ostensibly embodied. "U. R.," writing in *Turkestanskii Kur'er* in 1916, complained that German and Austro-Hungarian combatants strolled the streets of Tashkent, drinking tea in Muslim teahouses and listening to nightly concerts in the park. Those confined to camps received full rations and performed only light labor, still enjoying a higher standard of living than local Russians and Central Asians. "Delighted," prisoners hoped to remain permanently in the "Russian tropics." Russians in German camps, meanwhile, were treated with disdain, given microscopic food rations, and performed backbreaking labor in filthy conditions.[24] This imbalance was a national insult to Russian troops and civilians as well as a drain on the central treasury, as prison care cost over two million rubles annually.

Accounts from foreign observers and archival evidence paint a harsher picture of prison life in Turkestan. Jerome Davis, an American who visited the main prison outside Tashkent in 1916, agreed with local parlance that referred to it as the "death camp."[25] Davis reported that the installation, meant to hold ten thousand prisoners, was now home to more than twenty-five thousand. Malaria and typhus ran rampant, claiming fifteen to eighty prisoners daily. A. H. Brun, a Dane who traveled to Tashkent to care for prisoners of war in 1917, reported insufficient food supplies, a lack of clothing, and appalling sanitary conditions in the camps.[26] Camp commanders' continual complaints of shortages and poor conditions were ignored by regional officials.[27] Great hardship characterized the existence of the majority of prisoners, even as selected detainees profited from their status as European fighters and skilled labor.

The arrival of tens of thousands of prisoners of war and refugees exacerbated a growing crisis of food supplies in Tashkent and Turkestan. Central policies continued to drive Turkestan farmers away from food production. In October 1914, leading figures in the Ministries of Agriculture, Internal Affairs, and Trade and Industry banded together to seek ways to raise the production of cotton, an essential ingredient in munitions as well as textiles. A Central Cotton Commission, established to coordinate growth and shipments with buyers and factories in Central Asia, allowed prices to rise until they had reached triple their prewar value by early 1915.[28] Commercial interests responded by pressuring local farmers to grow cotton. Farmers realized that imperial officials were under central orders to supply food products to the front, and feared requisitions. The amount of land dedicated to cotton in Turkestan increased 13 percent in 1914–15 alone.[29]

Once 1915 planting goals had been reached, a reformed Central Cotton Commission moved to regulate prices, setting them on July 1 at twenty-four rubles per *pud*, below the market price of thirty-one rubles.[30] The fall of cotton prices wounded the industry, impoverished farmers, and lowered the available revenue for the state to tax. More serious, however, was the mounting deficit in food supplies. Food production fell across Turkestan, from the Syr-Dar'ia oblast to the richest grain-growing region, the Semirechie to the east, where decreases were due not only to cotton planting but Russian peasants' leaving their fields to fight in the war.[31] Turkestan, self-sufficient in food before the enactment of earlier central policies favoring cotton, saw its need for imported grain rise from 2.4 to 6.7 million *pudy* over 1914–15.[32] Receiving food from elsewhere in Russia posed significant challenges. The tsarist government prioritized the supply of the front lines as the conscription of railway workers and furious competition among state agencies for train cars placed the Russian internal transport system in chaos.[33]

Food shortages first struck Turkestan in March 1915. Flour and potatoes disappeared from local markets. Members of the city duma, responsible for the food supply, blamed shortages on temporary transport difficulties. Duma head N. G. Mallitskii called a meeting of wholesalers and millers to discuss shortages, but representatives had no immediate remedies, claiming their suppliers had switched over to growing cotton.[34] Mallitskii urged intermediaries to examine ways to bring more locally grown food to the city. The center could no longer be depended upon to help Turkestan.[35]

Blame for shortages soon shifted to local traders. Governor-General F. M. Martson accused Central Asian merchants of withholding supplies to effect a permanent rise in prices. Martson ordered police to requisition one thousand *pudy* of potatoes from wholesalers and merchants and sell them at official fixed prices (*taksa*). The duma had set fixed prices for staple goods in 1893, along with creating a special police force to supervise supplies and prices in the bazaars. But the measures were largely ignored, with only the worst quality goods being sold at official rates.[36] In the most notable case of a previous food shortage, during the 1905 revolution, the duma abolished fixed prices in an effort to bring goods back to Tashkent.[37] Nonetheless, the establishment of such rates, one year after the 1892 cholera riot, and their reactivation in 1915, reflected concerns over Central Asian traders' ability to control food supplies. *Turkestanskii Kur'er* hailed Martson's action as overcoming Central Asian "greed."[38] The exploitative power of Central Asian traders had become a popular trope in the local press; a 1912 *Turkestanskiia Viedomosti* article accused Central Asians of defiance of imperial authority and profiteering for their "habit" of restricting supplies of foodstuffs essential to Russians during the holidays of Christmas and Easter.[39] Muslim traders could create shortages without inconveniencing their own people, who did not eat pork or beef. They would sell only to their "preferred" Russian customers at rates significantly higher than official prices. The newspaper expressed "admiration" for this mastering of market mechanisms and anger toward Russian authorities, unable to offer alternative supplies.[40] As a result, Russians faced a threat to not only their power, but their culture; other articles foresaw Russians forced to abandon their foods for lamb and rice.[41]

Duma members in 1915 ignored calls for strict enforcement of fixed prices. The growing influence of Russian, German, and Jewish businessmen, now the largest occupational faction among "Christian" duma members, may have played a role in this decision. Many, along with their Central Asian counterparts, owned stores in Russian and Asian Tashkent and had significant interests across the region.[42] As shortages worsened, the duma dispatched purchasing agents to grain-growing regions of the empire, such as Samara and Orenburg. Prices continued to rise across the empire, however, and transport problems increased. Duma meetings offered sympathy, but no solutions, to complaints that rises in food costs no longer allowed junior bureaucrats to earn a "living wage."[43]

Central Asian duma members were acutely conscious of the social and ethnic implications of food shortages. Articles in the Tashkent Russian press blamed neither the war nor central policy for food shortages, but duma apathy and the tyranny of local traders, who held the city "at their mercy."[44] Arif Khoja, one of duma's wealthiest members, lobbied the body to take a more active role in food procurement. His efforts were crucial in the October 30, 1915, formation of the Tashkent provision committee (*prodovol'stvennyi komitet*). Committee members were given "extreme" powers, including spending revenues for food without reporting to the duma. Arif Khoja lobbied his friends to make contributions to the committee. Arif Khan Azis Khojinov donated five thousand *pudy* of grain on November 2. By January 1916, Arif Khoja was funding the committee from his pocket, donating fifty-five thousand rubles that month alone.[45] His efforts, however, could not prevent worsening shortages and inflation.[46]

Anger in Russian Tashkent at duma policies intensified. The press condemned the favoring of refugees and prisoners of war, who received coupons for provision committee–run stores, where goods were sold at fixed rates. Meanwhile, police at the bazaars, which served the bulk of Russian inhabitants, stood by idly as traders sold goods far above fixed prices.[47] Frustration mounted among Russian women consumers. Local police and the Okhrana reported women in food lines expressing anger at refugees, who received food while refusing to work, and prisoners of war, who rudely pushed them aside.[48] In January 1916, the city board stationed police at points where food was distributed to refugees, at times dispensing goods at undisclosed locations. Okhrana reports cited mounting tension among traders, who responded to cries of speculation with threats that they would charge even higher, "Moscow prices" for goods.[49] Russian Tashkent's bazaars brewed with discontent as winter continued.

## The "Women's Riot" (babii bunt) of 1916

Lower-class women, responding to shortages and inflation, instigated food riots throughout the tsarist empire in 1915–16. Barbara Alpern Engel has argued that these women drew on "long-standing notions of justice that included the right to subsistence and the affordability of essential goods even in times of crisis."[50] For Engel, a deeply moral motivation and sense of community, perhaps drawn from feelings of solidarity developed in the villages of peasant Russia, influenced women's decision to riot. Women were also alienated by the effects of wartime. Entering the workforce, they earned a fraction of men's wages.[51] Russian lower-class women in Tashkent experienced these hardships; their riots, however, illustrate a wider anger at a transforming, and, for them, deteriorating, colonial economic system as well as a failure to gain access to the benefits of imperial rule. As John Bohstedt has argued in his studies of British food riots, grievances leading to such events course through, and alter, the community as a whole.[52]

Russian lower-class women received little sympathy from Tashkent Russian elites in 1915–16. Imperial authorities, as they would do throughout the war, viewed tension in the bazaar through the lens of gender and ethnic stereotypes. In late 1915, Russian police officers accompanied reports outlining growing women's frustration at shortages and high prices with statements that their cries were but "ordinary female reproaches."[53] The Russian press published demeaning images of Russian lower-class women, whose reliance on Central Asian traders represented an embarrassing inversion of colonial power.[54] As rumors of Central Asian merchants' concealing goods to charge higher prices spread, however, tsarist officials began to shadow food shipments from warehouses, generally in Asian Tashkent, to bazaars in the Russian city. Ironically, it was a police decision to intervene in food sales that sparked the riot.

On February 28, 1916, officer R. N. Aleksandrovskii received an anonymous phone call informing him that hidden stocks of potatoes had been discovered at the shops of Mir Paizu Mir Akbarov and two other Muslim merchants in the suburban Staro-Gospital'nyi bazaar. The caller urged Aleksandrovskii to locate these concealed potatoes and sell them, at the official rates, to a hungry population. At the scene, Aleksandrovskii and two other officers discovered five hundred *pudy* of potatoes in the merchants' cellars.[55] While he fined the merchants, officers supervised sales of the potatoes at the official rate of three kopecks per *funt*, well below the current market rate of seven kopecks. Half of the stocks were depleted when the officers departed, telling angry customers in line that the rest would be sold the following morning.

News of cheap potatoes spread throughout the Russian city. A large crowd had gathered at the bazaar by early morning, purchasing the rest of the stock by 7 A.M. Several hundred women demanded more potatoes from merchants and police. Receiving no response, the women smashed on the ground or placed in their baskets goods from storefronts beside where they stood. More women shoppers flowed into the bazaar, yelling at police and merchants that "life was impossible" under present conditions.[56] Small groups, crying "beat" and "destroy," entered stores and stalls to take or destroy merchandise. Ethnic undertones became clear when one of the Central Asian merchants loaded his goods on a cart and attempted to drive off toward the Asian city. Demonstrators threw stones at him, and, according to several witnesses, yelled that "Sart trader-dogs" were refusing to sell goods to Russians.[57] Some women, however, sought to combat this anger; trader Abdulla Magometov noted that a few of the original demonstrators ran to his shop near the Staro-Gospital'nyi bazaar, warning Muslim merchants of the anger against them and advising them to abandon their stores quickly.[58]

Women rioters' attacks spread throughout the bazaar as police officers and tsarist soldiers awaited the arrival of Syr-Dar'ia military governor S. A. Geppener. Geppener, pulling up in his automobile, gathered the women about him, urging loyalty to the fatherland and calm at a difficult time. He invited the crowd to choose representatives for face-to-face discussions on the food problem. Quiet prevailed until demonstrator Irina Tolstikova hurled vegetables at Geppener's car and shouted "beat the fatsos" ("*bei, ikh, tolstopuzykh*").[59] Attacks resumed, as police and soldiers stood aside. Only Russian trader A. M. Klevantsov had his store spared, as he brought his children in front of the store window and tearfully begged demonstrators not to reduce his family to poverty.[60]

Small bands of women, approximately two thousand in all, fanned throughout the Russian city, attacking the stores and stalls of Central Asian merchants. Russian traders, sensing the ethnic character of the riot, appeared openly in front of their stores. One was warned, however, that he would receive a "visit" the following day.[61] Several of the roving bands united at the central Voskresenskii bazaar in mid-afternoon. Once more, Geppener attempted to soothe the crowd. On this occasion, demonstrator Natalia Arzamastseva interrupted his speech, telling the women that no one need listen to him. Several threw plates at the military governor, who quickly retreated. After destroying stalls identified as owned by Muslims, the crowd returned home for the dinner hour.

Police officers and soldiers were ready when women gathered the following morning at Staro-Gospital'nyi bazaar with a particular target: a Jewish storekeeper, Tsiperson, who had gained a reputation of ostensibly cheating customers. An attack on his store was followed once more by a wider riot. Officers and soldiers varied in their reactions: some assisted the women in attacking stores, others did nothing, and still others arrested demonstrators.[62] Facing an angry crowd at the central police station that refused to disperse after a dousing with fire hoses, Police Chief S. O. Kochan released imprisoned women demonstrators. But police and soldiers united to head off a potential incursion of women into Asian Tashkent. Police officer Kharchaev first spotted a group heading toward the Asian city, crying, "Sarts must be beaten."[63] Asian Tashkent's police chief, N. E. Kolesnikov, arrested eight women who refused to retreat from the border of the Asian city and sent word to all available Cossack units to guard the boundary between the two sides of Tashkent. Kolesnikov feared that any crossing of boundaries might ignite a wider conflagration.

Tensions remained high even as the rioting ended on March 1. Soldiers and police patrolled the streets. Duma members convened an emergency session to discuss the issue of food shortages. Geppener, touring Staro-Gospital'nyi bazaar, met the scorn of Russian women, one of whom cried out, "Ah, our godson, you have come once more, you have forgotten how, at the Voskresenskii bazaar, we christened you with plates?"[64] Shortages intertwined with questions of status and dignity in a disturbance that exposed and shaped issues of colonial power and control in wartime Tashkent.

Russian women's actions, and their testimony given to judicial investigator V. Dorogokupets, indicated the strength of the image of the greedy, powerful, Muslim speculator. Rioters believed Central Asian traders had the capacity to manipulate the city's food supply, creating "shortages" through withholding reserves of goods. Women tore apart walls and floors of shops, looking for secret passages where goods, particularly potatoes, might be stored. Police professed shock at the preparation and tenacity of the rioters, who used bolt cutters and hammers to break into back rooms.[65] Local traders acknowledged holding small reserves for future sale, but denied any role in speculation, blaming rising prices on wholesalers as shipments of imported food dwindled.

Rioters admitted their desire to "teach a lesson" to the colonized Central Asian population. Natalia Golodova stated that "we [Russians] need to beat up Sarts, so they will not succeed in bothering [*trogat'*] us. I decided to beat one up that had insulted me in the past."[66] Several demonstrators, as well as Central Asian merchants, noted that Russian soldiers assisted them in these beatings.[67] Women rioters, however, placed blame as well on tsarist officials for their perceived support of Central Asian merchants. Before the riot, police were seen to intervene on the side of these merchants instead of Russian women, in defiance of ethnic boundaries of colonial privilege.

Although rioters attacked Central Asian stores indiscriminately, they were more selective with those owned by members of other ethnic groups. Aleksandra Sorotskova testified that the crucial factor determining whether and how to attack these stores was the means of the owner. Demonstrators vigorously debated owners' backgrounds and family situations; some Jewish and Armenian stores were ransacked and others spared. In the case of poorer shopkeepers, women offered to pay reduced amounts for the goods they were taking.[68] Women were aware of the social nature of their protest, but their differentiation between wealthy and unwealthy merchants did not extend to Central Asians, who were universally condemned.

Rioters identified gender as another motivating factor in their attacks.

Women argued that imperial officials favored male prisoners of war as well as Central Asian merchants over them. Issues of gender equality had arisen not long before the riot; in a January 1916 strike, female tramway workers demanded equal wages and working conditions with their male counterparts.[69] One of the rioters, Bezen, pointed to this heritage as evidence that women were best suited to rise up against deprivations, as men were not capable of proper organization.[70] Women merchants were the last to have their stores attacked, and faced no violence from the crowd. Educated women asserted gender rights as a prime motivation in the riot. Aleksandra Orlova stated to the investigator that "I wanted to teach women how we need to battle against men and achieve equal rights. I am a follower of this idea and therefore took part in the attack on stores."[71] Anna Stepanova defied the law and protocol by flippantly using the casual "ty" form of speech toward Police Chief Kochan, for which she was rapidly arrested, and later fined two hundred rubles.[72] Yet the actions, and inaction, of male police and soldiers had allowed the riot to spread, within the limits of Russian Tashkent. Poor Russian men joined in beatings of Central Asians and ate food that women threw from stores. The riot exposed connections as well as cleavages across lines of gender and class.

Participants in the riot viewed their grievances from a local perspective, placing blame primarily on Central Asian merchants and male officials in Tashkent instead of wartime strains or imperial policies favoring cotton. Women remained alienated from these larger events, and Military Governor Geppener's calls for loyalty had little effect. As across the empire, Hubertus Jahn has argued, the regime failed to integrate women successfully into wartime propaganda.[73] Imperial authorities, for their part, saw the Tashkent riots akin to others across the empire, rather than shaped by local factors. Police accused "outside instigator" Nina Parovskaia, a Pole, of directing the riot, leading the crowd to new stores, to which she would point and cry, "Destroy!" Officer F. N. Kliutko claimed that two weeks earlier Parovskaia had helped instigate food riots in Baku, which left nine people dead.[74] Kliutko testified that Parovskaia's military medals convinced women that such riots were sanctioned by the tsar. Parovskaia, despite denying participation in the riots, was accused, alongside "outsider" female refugees, of the most serious crimes. Blaming "outsiders," a common tactic across the empire, allowed authorities to evade questions of local tensions, evident in the testimony of demonstrators and merchants alike, exposed by the riot.

Blaming refugee outsiders also served the interests of imperial officials who, by spring 1916, felt overwhelmed by the scale of new arrivals. An Okhrana report that blamed refugees for the intensity of the Tashkent food riots precipitated a decision by the Ministry of Internal

Affairs, fearful of ethnic conflict, to move refugees from Turkestan to other areas of Russia.[75] On March 8, Governor-General Martson, citing food shortages, ordered fifty-seven thousand refugees resettled to Volga and Ural regions. Refugee assistance groups, particularly those serving minority nationalities, continued to assist new arrivals coming against government orders.

Governor-General Martson expressed grave concern at the destabilizing influence of shortages in the imperial city. He personally attended spring duma meetings, when food supply issues dominated discussion. Provision committee head I. M. Ufimtsev argued that local authorities could do little to address scarcities, given the impossibility of procuring railway cars to bring supplies to Tashkent. The committee promised nonetheless to become involved in wholesale trade and to increase its network of stores. Arif Khoja and others pledged to find ways to improve local food production, reopening a mill on the outskirts of Tashkent and asking the assistance of Turkestan Agricultural Society head R. R. Shreder to improve grain yields on local farms not growing cotton.[76] Other duma members continued to blame the crisis on "speculators" who created "artificial" shortages. A faction of traders insisted that eliminating fixed prices would resolve the issue. Lacking consensus, the duma adopted no concrete measures to battle shortages, much to the consternation of the local press. The duma avoided any mention of ethnic and gender issues involved in the riot, claiming any effective solutions were beyond its control.[77] Only merchants' own decision to reduce prices, and an increase in arrests of those violating fixed rates, kept the streets calm in subsequent weeks.[78]

Tsarist officials, meanwhile, condemned rioters' actions. Martson published an appeal in Tashkent newspapers that recognized current hardships but denounced the riots as pogroms and mob protests (*protesta-samosuda*) that threatened to tear apart local society.[79] Rioters failed, unlike the great mass of the common people, to endure their hardship out of loyalty to the homeland. Martson wrote that even factory workers, who had a history of class conflict and "felt the disruption on the course of their economic life no less," remained patient and loyal, recognizing the travails of wartime.[80] His appeal wove discourses of gender and class to condemn female, disloyal "simple people" as unreliable subjects. Unlike the response to the 1892 cholera riot, tsarist authorities focused their arrests on Russians who perpetrated, in this case, nonlethal violence, rather than on Central Asian "instigators." A military tribunal imprisoned fifty-six women, but none of the men who assisted them, as "political criminals." Most were released two months later, ostensibly in order to relieve prison overcrowding. Nine, however, identified as the principal instigators, remained in prison until early 1917.[81]

Reactions to the riot indicated nervousness among male elites about the now unpredictable behavior of lower-class women. Martson's appeal betrayed shock that women would violate their traditional role of holders of civilized values. On March 4, 1916, *Turkestanskiia Viedomosti* condemned newfound female aggressiveness, stretching to the rude behavior of women tramway drivers. Women, placed in more public roles due to the war, "needed to be taught simple courtesies in relations with the public." Once lauded as heralds of culture, these women had shown themselves capable of extreme "coarseness." Of particular concern for the author was that, as trams operated in Asian Tashkent, Muslims would witness, and perhaps replicate, crass female behavior. The article ended by condemning women's liberation movements, asking sarcastically, "Is this the way 'the woman question' has been resolved?"[82] *Turkestanskii Kur'er* attacked women tramway drivers who flirted with young soldiers while treating other customers rudely. Although flirting was "in a woman's nature," rude and uncivilized comportment, particularly the spitting of sunflower seeds on the tram floors, symbolized the deterioration of appropriate gender roles.[83] Another article admitted, however, that wartime exigencies necessitated the presence of women in public jobs such as couriers, lamplighters, and even security guards. Having Russian women in these positions was still preferable to allowing Central Asians to gain advancement in the labor market.[84]

Russian women continued to exercise their power in the bazaars in 1916. Selected attacks on merchants believed to be hiding stockpiles, along with an influx of locally grown fruits and vegetables, kept prices from rising in the summer. Such actions, however, disturbed the fragile relationship between colonizer and colonized as well as the balance of the colonial economy. By mid-1916, Central Asian traders were leaving Russian Tashkent entirely, claiming to authorities that they were tired of being "beaten up by Russian women."[85] Wartime strains on the local level, as well as central policies toward the empire's Muslims, led to the first lethal demonstrations in Tashkent since the cholera riot of 1892.

## The Central Asian Response to War

Central Asian notables in Tashkent initially envisioned opportunities for themselves and their community when the First World War erupted. Jadids were particularly enthusiastic, offering words and poems of devotion in support of the war.[86] Along with Central Asian businessmen and Russian-educated liberal Muslim professionals, Jadids hoped their support of Russia even after the entry of the Ottoman empire as an opponent would ease fears of Panislamism and Panturkism and pave the way for equal Muslim rights.[87] Jadid leader Mahmud Khoja Behbudi and the lawyer Ubaydallah Khojaev sponsored fundraising events for tsarist soldiers, including many Central Asians, fighting at the front. One event in August 1914 raised forty-five thousand rubles, far more than amounts donated at individual fundraisers of the Tashkent Women's Committee.[88] Jadids pioneered a parallel Muslim Women's Committee, though the fact that it met only in the Russian city indicated limits to its scope.[89]

Central Asian elites donated portions of their profits from the cotton boom in the early months of the war to loyalist causes. Hardships greeted the majority of the local population, however. Exempt from conscription due to tsarist fears of disloyalty, all Central Asian Muslims faced a compensatory war tax of 21 percent levied by the Ministry of Finance. Ministry officials also requested "voluntary" contributions in kind or in money to the war effort. Tsarist officials, especially in rural areas, seized on this "suggestion" to levy further duties, most of which went into their own pockets.[90] No significant recorded protests, however, greeted these measures' implementation.

In the wake of the 1916 women's riot, Governor-General Marston sought to assure Tashkent's Central Asian elites of continued tsarist backing, and also to raise money for the war effort. On March 3, he invited twenty notables, including administrators, judges, and businessmen, to his home. Martson's case for Central Asians to support the war effort echoed the Jadid press. Russia, he argued, was a country worth protecting, as it aimed to secure equality for all faiths and nationalities. The governor-general sought contributions to the latest government fundraising effort of military loans, and argued that such loans, as "good deeds," overrode provisions of the sharia forbidding usury. Tashkent notables pledged not only to support the loan program, but to recruit other wealthy Muslims to the cause. Money bought them audiences at the highest level of imperial power.

Cooperation from Central Asian notables, and a lack of reaction to the beatings suffered by Russian women, altered stereotypes of the "fanatic Muslim" that had coursed through Russian discourse in Tashkent. The local press now portrayed Muslims as passive and childlike, under full control of leaders who had expressed their loyalty to the tsar. After the women's riot, Muslim men were presented as under the thumb of not only Russian women, but their own wives. *Turkestanskiia Viedomosti* amusedly described Muslim males needing to slave away at work to satisfy wives' demands for new clothing, fearing that failure would end their marriage.[91] Substituting emasculation for fanaticism comforted Russian readers at a time when wartime strains had increased tensions within colonial society, but produced disastrous consequences in following months.

In late June 1916, the tsarist general staff, facing serious manpower shortages, ordered the mobilization of Muslims in the Caucasus and Central Asia for rearguard duty, freeing up more soldiers for active combat.[92] Tsar Nicholas II signed the decree, made without consultation in the affected regions, on June 25. On July 2, regional military governors discussed the order, which required the conscription of 250,000 males, ages nineteen to forty-three, from Turkestan. Concerns expressed at the beginning of the meeting, revolving around the high number of draftees, approximately 8 percent of the male population, and the timing of the order, at the height of the cotton season, dissipated before the image of the passive Muslim. Fergana Oblast governor A. I. Gippius noted that the method of selection of recruits was crucial: "The mood of the mass depends on the so-called leaders of the population: mullas, honored individuals, etc. If these are taken [in the draft] . . . then an unfavorable mood will be created." Syr-Dar'ia military governor N. I. Galkin, as well as other officers present, agreed that if leaders were not directly affected, Muslim masses would unquestioningly recognize their "natural duty" to obey.[93]

Central Asian reactions to the draft order exposed the fallacy of these beliefs. On July 4, even before its public announcement, news of conscription spread to the city of Khojent, where a riot of the local population resulted in the deaths of dozens of tsarist officials, Central Asian administrators, and demonstrators.[94] News of the draft, the riot, and its violent suppression stiffened local opposition by the time the order was publicly issued on July 8.[95] In Tashkent, Central Asian notables informed the Asian city's Police Chief Kolesnikov of the depth of the opposition to the draft measure. News of the events in Khojent had sparked animated debates across Asian Tashkent, with conclusions reached that breaking up families was an unacceptable condition, an insult to their "way of life."[96] Kolesnikov reported that these notables suggested the substitution of draft measures with extra monetary contributions, so as not to risk violence in the city.

Russian Tashkent's Police Chief Kochan, ignoring this advice, began the process of conscription with a briefing of Central Asian administrators at a mosque in the Sheikhantaur district of the Asian city. Okhrana evidence had suggested that this district, bordering Russian Tashkent and home to many of the wealthier traders and mediators, might be most responsive to the draft.[97] Kochan informed administrators that they would be responsible for drawing up lists of draftees and presenting the candidates for service. The police chief, however, garnered frustration by presenting shifting figures of the number of conscripts required, as well as being unclear as to what salaries or supplies recruits might expect.[98] A

July 10 private meeting of Central Asian notables expressed opposition to the draft, fearing that it would impact particularly harshly the poor, so reliant upon the day-to-day wages of the male household earner. Katta Khoja Baba Khojaev and Seid Ahmed Khoja Seid Karimbaev, two of the closest confidantes of Police Chief Kolesnikov, decreed the draft "unnecessary" and warned of resistance.[99] Central Asian administrators not publicly opposing the draft were receiving threatening, unsigned letters warning them not to cooperate with tsarist authorities.

On July 11, a crowd seeking to prevent a meeting of neighborhood elders to draw up conscription lists gathered at the police administration building in Asian Tashkent. Women, the largest and most vocal contingent of these demonstrators, cried for *dod* (justice) and insisted that they would not surrender male family members to the authorities.[100] Men yelled, "We will not go, we will die here." Several thousand surrounded the building, many throwing rocks as police deputies surveyed the crowd from the rooftop. As demonstrators pushed toward the courtyard, a Central Asian police officer fell to his death. Kolesnikov, arriving at that moment with a squadron of Cossacks, shot a demonstrator he claimed was surging toward him, setting off a volley of Cossack gunfire. The shots killed nine demonstrators, including one woman; the crowd, however, dispersed only hours after the initial demonstration.[101]

Little evidence exists on Central Asian reactions to the July 11 violence. Tashkent resident Turar Rysqulov, who later joined the Soviet government, describes a class-based division of Asian Tashkent into pro- and anti-Russian elements. According to Rysqulov, "bourgeois" traders and administrators, as well as supporters of the draft from the more prosperous Sheikhantaur district, opposed working-class elements from the poorer Sebzar and Kukcha quarters, who had the most to lose from the draft of wage earners.[102] Documentary evidence challenges this facile division, as Kolesnikov noted local elites' heated opposition to the draft and their concern over effects on the city's poor.[103] Marianne Kamp has identified a gendered element to protests, with Central Asian women determined to protect their husbands during the lucrative cotton-picking season.[104] Central Asian duma members boycotted the July 13 and 15 duma sessions to protest the deadly tsarist reaction, which they contrasted to quiescence during the Russian women's riot.[105] But Central Asian notables feared that continuing resistance to the conscription orders might trigger an even more violent reaction from tsarist forces and, potentially, Russian civilians. News of a bloody riot in the city of Jizak on July 16, where demonstrators killed several Russian officers and forced Russian inhabitants to flee the city, demonstrated the depth of local anger. On July 17, Governor-General Martson declared martial law.

One week later, the newspaper *Ferganskaia Oblast' Viedomosti* reported that unspecified "leaders" of the Asian city of Tashkent, fearful of mass violence, had thrown their support behind conscription and promised that the population of their city would fulfill their obligations.

The support of Central Asian notables, relied upon to draw up draft lists and convince Muslims to serve, was crucial to the success of the conscription project. Tsarist authorities remained convinced that Central Asian masses would follow their religious and political leaders. In one of the more bizarre incidents of Russian colonial rule in Turkestan, Fergana military governor Gippius decided himself to impersonate an Islamic priest. Believing mullas were telling worshippers that agreeing to conscription violated Islamic beliefs, Gippius decided, after consultations with "scholars and Muslims," to read publicly sections of the Quran that indicated that Muslims must "obey the regime." In front of thousands assembled in Namangan, Gippius donned a Muslim robe and skullcap, kissed the Quran, and read his selections, to the indignation of a large number of Russians, who quickly left the crowd.[106]

Fear gripped the Russian community of Tashkent as news of anti-draft riots spread. D. I. Manzhara, a Russian worker, recalled that police, soldiers, and lower-ranking officers spread rumors that agents from Germany and Turkey had arrived to direct a revolt and that thousands of armed Muslims were marching toward Tashkent, massacring all Russians found in their path.[107] Tashkent, however, remained quiet, especially after the tsar agreed, in the wake of growing uprisings, to postpone the implementation of the draft until September 15.

In July, Tsar Nicholas II dispatched A. N. Kuropatkin to stop the violence and execute the draft in his role as the new governor-general of Turkestan. Tashkent Russians hailed the appointment, in July, of one of "ours." Kuropatkin had served in tsarist campaigns to conquer the region. *Turkestanskii Kur'er* believed that he had an innate understanding, as a "native Turkestani," of Central Asia. Like the first governor-general, K. P. fon Kaufman, whom he served alongside, Kuropatkin could restore harmony among peoples after a turbulent time.[108] Tsarist authorities, easing Kuropatkin's task, had reduced the number of draftees required from Turkestan from 250,000 to 180,000. The tsar had also given Kuropatkin control over Cossack battalions that had recently served on the front. In diametric opposition to the goals of the conscription order, the draft now required the center to reduce its frontline troop strength.

Kuropatkin intensified the courting of Central Asian elites in order to establish peace and reinstitute conscription. He formed "native committees" in cities and villages across Turkestan in late August, asking members to decide the most peaceful way to implement the draft. Sacked were officers, including Gippius and Syr-Dar'ia military governor Galkin, for their failure to gain local support. Traveling widely to supervise these committees, Kuropatkin showed members great deference. His kissing the hand of Kokand committee chair A. Mahmudov produced, according to a reporter from *Turkestanskiia Viedomosti*, "a tempest of ecstasy from the surrounding population."[109]

Significant salaries and prestige attracted Central Asian notables to serve. Ubaydallah Khojaev led the Tashkent draft committee, serving with seventeen other Asian city residents chosen in local elections. Khojaev held open, public meetings in the city duma and became a frequent visitor to the governor-general's mansion for meetings and lavish banquets.[110] Kuropatkin agreed to the committee's first request, for twenty thousand rubles to purchase clothes for new recruits, and funded a newspaper in Asian Tashkent under Khojaev's editorship.[111] In the longer term, Khojaev and other members of these "native committees" hoped that their participation would demonstrate their ability to work in a reformed, modern political system they believed would emerge after the war.[112]

The decision to hold meetings uniquely in Russian Tashkent, however, likely demonstrated the unease many members felt at their reception on the other side of the Ankhor canal. Resistance to the mobilization of rearguard labor continued in the fall of 1916, most notably in the Kazakh steppe regions to the north. Protests were intimately tied to large-scale Russian colonization since 1905. Massive armies of Kazakhs and Kyrgyz fought imperial power. In the end, more Russian troops were killed suppressing the rebellion than died during the initial conquest of the steppe and Central Asia.[113] In central regions of Turkestan, however, including the Samarkand, Fergana, and the Syr-Dar'ia oblasts, further violence was largely avoided. The "native committees" presented Muslims for rearguard service without engendering open resistance to tsarist rule.

Kuropatkin worked to give draft supporters significant prestige in Tashkent. Conscripts turned into public celebrities. A September 17 parade through the Russian town honored the first echelon of Central Asians to report for labor duty. Russian flags flew alongside portraits of the tsar. The draftees reportedly cried *"Ura"* as they passed Kaufman's monument. On September 29, two reporters in the Asian city wrote of the joy of natives off to the labor force, crying, "Long live the White Tsar!"[114] Such words acted to soothe the Russian community as much as demonstrate Central Asian support for the draft. Russian writers lauded the efforts of conscripts, evidence of a new spirit of cooperation in imperial Tashkent. *Turkestanskii Kur'er* reported workers in Kiev, Khar'kov, and Odessa were staffing bakeries, factories, and other enterprises essential to maintaining the home front. For the first time, Muslims were referred to as "Turkestanis" and as "ours," appropriate representatives to illustrate the successes of the "colony" in "civilizing" its native population.[115] Russian articles also described the conscripts' wonder at their new European environment and mused that they would transfer this knowledge back to their families.[116]

Other articles demonstrated a concern that the conscription project was not running so smoothly. *Turkestanskiia Viedomosti*, in its Russian and native-language editions, implored families of conscript workers to disregard a "bombardment" of appeals for money based on claims of hardship. Work brigade leader Musakhan' Mirzakhonov wrote that the authorities fully satisfied material needs for all workers. Dispatches of money were "unnecessary, and even dangerous" and could spark "licentiousness."[117] Set against the backdrop of continuing violent resistance to the draft, which prompted a new rebellion in the Semirechie region to the east, these warnings provided ominous portents of continued regional instability. Rumors spread once more of Muslim bands marching toward Tashkent, intent on slaughtering Russian settlers.[118]

The draft had become the latest central initiative to damage local relationships and imperil colonial rule. Added to the tensions surrounding the draft were continuing shortages of food supplies that resulted in smaller-scale street disturbances. Conflict along lines of class and gender intensified alongside that between colonizer and colonized in the fall of 1916. Alliances maintaining stability proved fragile in the face of growing central demands and local suffering.

## Coping with Wartime

Governor-General Kuropatkin expended considerable energy to reassure the Russian population of Tashkent of their safety. Following honorifics applied to him, Kuropatkin mobilized the image of courageous, powerful European "Turkestani" males. The governor-general led numerous military parades through the streets of Russian Tashkent in late 1916. *Turkestanskiia Viedomosti* reported on these processions with an enthusiasm once reserved for the anniversary of the June 15 conquest. "Huge crowds of people" lined the streets, listened to military music, and cheered "*Ura*" to the passing troops. Kuropatkin surveyed the companies and pronounced: "Do you see our defenders? They are many. Go home and sleep safely!"[119] Slavic prisoners of war, recruited as defenders of Russian Tashkent, participated in the processions. Stories of new Turkestani heroes abounded in 1916. Honorifics to soldiers born or raised in the region worked to instill a sense of loyalty to a metropole that had appeared in recent years to be acting against the interests of Tashkent Russian society. Imperial officials repatriated the bodies of "native Turkestanis" and held large funerals in their honor, with processions that wove through city streets before open services at the Spaso-Preobrazhenskii cathedral.[120] *Turkestanskiia Viedomosti* praised a new "spirit" among the Russian youth of Turkestan who were running away from home in their desire "to fight the Germans."[121]

At the same time, social tensions within the Russian community increased. Imperial officials and Russian press commentators began to distinguish between "genuine" refugees fleeing the battlefields of Poland, the Baltics, and Ukraine, and other migrants, mostly ethnic Russians, who arrived during the war.[122] *Turkestanskii Kur'er* reported on the activities of various "foreign" criminal gangs, including the "Samara Five." *Turkestanskiia Viedomosti* castigated outsiders in an article blaming a recent murder on a gang from Tambov. Once able to leave their doors unlocked, Tashkent residents were now forced to act as "*Sherlok-Kholmtsy*," ever vigilant against crime.[123] Food shortages and other wartime tensions reignited prewar suspicions toward new migrants.

Food shortages worsened dramatically over the course of 1916. Largely due to the rebellion, fall grain production in the Semirechie and steppe regions decreased by 23 percent.[124] Kazakh and Kyrgyz raids also threatened shipments of foodstuffs coming to Tashkent via rail. In October, provision committee members announced that only one month of grain reserves remained, with no guarantee that more stocks could be purchased before the winter. A more immediate problem involved prices, which had quadrupled over the course of the year.[125]

In the bazaars, women increased protests against rising prices and their unequal status in obtaining food. Crowds in October objected to privileges given to prisoners of war and threatened trading police, provision committee store clerks, and Central Asian traders with violence if their needs for food were not met. Okhrana agents chastised imperial authorities for preferential food policies toward prisoners and warned of the radicalization of soldiers' wives, ready to wreak havoc on the streets of Tashkent. If this happened, soldiers might join their spouses, posing a serious threat to the stability of the imperial city.[126] After the October 22 demonstration outside the food store of Paizu Umirzakov, Syr-Dar'ia military governor Madritov published warnings and toured the city to inform potential rioters of dire consequences that awaited them.

A November 9 strike by women tramway drivers brought calls in the duma for an immediate response, lest Russian Tashkent's women launch massive disturbances, as Central Asian discontent over the draft still simmered. The next day, duma members announced preliminary rationing plans for basic goods, including fuel, bread, meat, and sugar.[127] The duma ordered the regional Statistical Committee to conduct a census to determine the number of rationing cards to be issued. Fear of another major riot overcame significant duma opposition to rationing, even as some members protested rewarding women's ability "to inconvenience the public" for selfish ends.[128]

Russian elites also reconsidered their relationship with Central Asians in light of wartime events, but did not alter their views of a distinct colonizer and colonized. On September 14, 1916, the Turkestan Branch of the Imperial Geographic Society debated the nature of the "Sart." P. E. Kuznetsov and other Orientalists defended their position that cowardice and a love of peace characterized the local population. Governor-General Kuropatkin and others disagreed, arguing in the wake of the rebellion that Sarts had a history of resistance to alien power, beginning with defense of Tashkent in 1865. Yet their resistance proved futile before European military superiority. Kuropatkin judged military strength as the ultimate measure of a culture's level of progress. By his measure, even if the civilizing mission were successful, Central Asians could aspire to be no more than a "worthy son" of Russia.[129] The meeting also discussed the ostensible Central Asian love for trade and money. N. G. Mallitskii argued that the local population, though trailing Jews in the desire for acquisitiveness, had an inherent talent in capital gain.[130] Russian duma members repeated arguments that Central Asian merchants were deliberately withholding from the open market goods consumed primarily by Russians, including cabbage and potatoes. On October 28, these members contended that huge quantities were concealed in storehouses in the Asian city, beyond the reach of the Russian consumer, in order to create the image of a crisis and gain huge profits.[131]

Scarcity and the rebellion facilitated further subjection of the local population. On November 7, Russian duma members proposed to abolish the positions of aksakal and replace aksakals with Russian officials. Central Asian duma members offered vociferous resistance to this proposal, which violated principles and practices of the colonial relationship in place since the conquest. Mejid-Khan protested "in the name of the entire native population," arguing that conservation of traditional political structures remained necessary to link Central Asians to colonial power. Ubaydallah Khojaev argued that the aksakals played a social and cultural as well as a political role, and traditions dictated these be maintained. In the end, the twenty-two "Christians" in the duma voted to replace the aksakals, and the twenty-two Muslims voted to maintain the position. Mallitskii, as duma head, broke the tie in favor of replacing the aksakals.[132]

The rationing system was the next major issue to divide "Christian" and "native" deputies. Central Asians, when they had earlier joined a duma majority rejecting rationing, decreed that any such plan, if enacted, must treat Russian and Asian Tashkent equally.[133] Yet even at this point, Russian deputies wondered how a unitary system could work when one culture consumed beef and the other, mutton. Europeans and Central Asians, they argued, favored different types of grains and breads, and used sugar for different purposes. Indeed, on November 10, after the duma had voted in favor of rationing, city head Mallitskii announced that "practical difficulties" prevented its introduction to both sides of Tashkent. Only those living in the Russian city and Russians in Asian Tashkent would receive ration cards.[134] Mallitskii further infuriated Central Asian deputies by announcing that a special tax on flatbread (*non*, or *lepeshki*), a staple of local diets but not generally eaten by Russians, would finance the rationing plan.[135] Ubaydallah Khojaev and other Central Asian representatives condemned the efforts of a reconstructed provision committee under Ia. Ia. Korolev for its exclusive focus on the Russian population and its neglect toward other goods, particularly lamb, consumed primarily by Central Asians. P. I. Dolinskii represented the Russian view that traders held substantial stocks of food in Asian Tashkent. The duma session of December 9 degenerated into name-calling, with Central Asian deputies demanding that Dolinskii retract his "insulting words."[136] "Christian" deputies, including Russians, Jews, Germans, and Poles, carried the vote to limit distribution of ration cards.

Central Asian deputies saw their power in the duma disappear as the European representatives now attended in sufficient numbers to guarantee a majority and voted as a bloc. Duma members from Asian Tashkent petitioned the Office of the Governor-General to include the local population in rationing, but without success. Yet having worked so closely with imperial authorities over the course of the year, liberal intellectuals such as U. Khojaev and the Jadids found it difficult to contemplate an open break with their overlords, and continued to work within the colonial system.

Rationing, instead of calming tensions, created new divisions, even within Russian Tashkent. *Turkestanskiia Viedomosti* claimed to have discovered a new source of instability: the woman (*baba*) speculator. The newspaper reported that Russian women, having obtained rationed goods such as sugar, went immediately to bazaars in Tashkent or nearby cities to sell them at higher prices.[137] Russian women were cooperating with Central Asian traders to maximize profits; the two groups, once mortal enemies, had now found common cause in acting against the regime.

Even as Kuropatkin's troops suppressed the rebellions of 1916 across the steppe and Turkestan, city head Mallitskii expressed his deepening concerns about the prospects for social peace in Tashkent. Rationing could not conceal the fact that the city, quite simply, lacked the supplies of basic goods to get through the winter. Even if rumors of concealed stocks in Asian Tashkent were proven true, the provision committee, despite sending agents to Orenburg, Samara, and the Caucasus, was unable to procure significant stocks of food. Mallitskii's warnings of dire consequences if the city could not obtain food from central Russia were greeted with silence by agriculture minister N. M. Bulatov.[138]

Wartime presented initial opportunities for several constituencies in imperial Tashkent, thousands of kilometers from the front lines. Changes in the region's economy, as well as its demography, boosted Central Asian businessmen selling cotton, minority European nationalities sheltering refugees, and employers cheering a new, "white" labor pool of prisoners of war. Even the 1916 rebellion offered Central Asian notables the chance to prove their ultimate loyalty to the empire, and hopefully gain momentum for equal rights in Turkestan. Overall, however, as the conflict stretched on, central demands strained relationships and exposed fault lines in colonial society. Policies designed in St. Petersburg had already stripped Turkestan of self-sufficiency in food, and were now demanding not only cotton but also extra taxes, and finally bodies. An already fragile balance along lines of gender and class, as well as ethnicity, evaporated. Conflicts broke out in both Asian and Russian Tashkent, aimed not only at tsarist authorities, but also at other seemingly privileged groups, from local notables suspected of collaboration with the imperial regime to men accused of enforcing gender hierarchies in the city. Violent protests in the streets and unprecedented polarization in local political institutions threatened to undermine the image as well as the reality of a stable imperial regime. Kuropatkin's efforts to foster solidarity behind the European soldier and the city duma's rationing plan only served to crystallize inequalities. Already wounded discourses of the civilizing mission and the frontier as a site of progress faded as competition for scarce resources intensified and military force grew in importance. Pleas for central support went unanswered. Tashkent and Turkestan, which had proven a drain instead of a boon to the empire's wartime efforts, faced a winter of shortages and discontent.

# 7.

# Exploiters or Exploited? Russian Workers and Colonial Rule, 1917–1918

Social tensions in Tashkent, as across the Russian empire, exploded in the revolutions of 1917. The colonial environment posed special challenges for Russians and Central Asians alike. In the aftermath of the sudden collapse of tsarist power, Tashkent Russians struggled to reconcile post-tsarist emancipation with their continued positions of privilege. Central Asian notables led their community in efforts to realize democracy and equal rights. Emerging as the most powerful constituency in 1917, Russian skilled workers sought to balance their own language of revolutionary socialism with one that recognized and extended their power over Central Asians in the workplace and the political arena. Growing food shortages and political uncertainty at the center sharpened local conflicts within an increasingly polarized society.

As revolutionary hopes eroded, multiple constituencies within colonial society sought power and access to scarce goods. Struggles were far more complex than between the Provisional Government, educated society, and assorted allies on the one hand and workers, soldiers, and soviets on the other in a system contemporaries and contemporary historians of the Russian empire characterize as "dual power."[1] In Tashkent, conservative Russians extended their cooperation with the Muslim ulama against forces of change on both sides of the Ankhor canal. The Jadids also sought the ulama's assistance to assert Central Asian rights in a revolutionary society. Russian workers turned to imperial soldiers and Austro-Hungarian prisoners of war, but hesitated crossing lines of race or gender to build a broad-based revolutionary coalition. All these constituencies sought cooperation with Petrograd, but also eyed the center with distrust. A desire to grasp the fruits of imperial power from the central government and its local allies motivated the Tashkent soviet to seize effective control even before the Bolshevik revolution, as the empire crumbled from the outside in.

Class, as Orlando Figes and Boris Kolonitskii have argued, succeeded as a discourse across the empire in 1917 largely because of its flexibility and ability to unite grievances and accommodate multiple images of the future.[2] Leaders of the Tashkent soviet cast Russian workers, soldiers, and selected others as the exploited, not just by former tsarist elites, but also by Central Asian notables and merchants as well as the central Provisional Government. Tashkent Russian socialists used class as a racial and a gendered attribute.[3] Dividing as well as uniting, class was employed to justify differential access to scarce goods, particularly food, in a period of chaos and collapse.[4] Creating class divisions, however, did not consolidate support for the Tashkent soviet as it seized power in 1917. Railway workers, Red Guards, and other key constituencies of soviet power undermined soviet rule, enforcing their own power and privileges in revolutionary Central Asia.[5]

## Privileges and Politics of Russian
## Skilled Workers, 1908–1917

Russian workers reaped substantial benefits in tsarist Turkestan. Since the conquest, Russian labor filled positions of authority in the workplace, receiving higher pay than Central Asians, who served almost exclusively as unskilled workers in the factories and other enterprises of Russian Tashkent. Employers favored Russians to operate industrial machinery and build a diversified modern economy, particularly following the construction of the railway. The strict hierarchy of labor struck Senator K. K. Palen, traveling through Turkestan to investigate the causes of the 1905 revolution. Palen reported that Russian skilled workers were not repressed, but privileged. According to the senator,

> The contingent of workers engaged in the manufacturing industry of Turkestan consists of the following two categories, extremely un-equal in number: the first, a small number of personnel of technically educated foremen and head workers, consisting of Russians and in general Europeans, and a few from the native [tuzemtsy] population, formerly simple workers, who have acquired technical techniques in one or another method of production; the second, a large number of second-level lower workers, consisting mainly of natives and a small number of Europeans, primarily underage workers. The contingent of the first category, firmly settled in the province, are extremely limited, and replacing them from within the locality entails great difficulties for

factory owners. Therefore workers of this category are distinguished by high rates and larger demands to management, as a result of which, nowhere, possibly, do owners give workers higher concessions, than here.[6]

European managers and Russian workers enhanced profits through plots to fleece Central Asians who worked in the factories and industrial enterprises of Tashkent. D. I. Manzhara, a railway worker who arrived in the city in 1912, quickly learned the intricate methods employed by Russians to victimize local labor. Sector heads, foremen, and senior workers organized *troikas* (groups of three) of "hustlers" to bribe translators to misstate pay rates, allowing them to dispatch smaller sums of money to Central Asian workers and pocket the difference. Manzhara states that "politically conscious" Russians who protested such practices were chased away as seditionists.[7]

Perquisites for Russian workers extended even further. Unskilled laborers could rise to positions of authority in the workplace in three to four years, ahead of Central Asians who had worked there far longer. Opportunities to rapidly develop skills that would improve pay ranks throughout the empire, as well as low unemployment, enticed Manzhara and others to Turkestan. Russians dominated elite labor professions, including railway workers, metalworkers, miners, and printers. The numbers of Russian industrial workers grew to nearly five thousand by the eve of the war.[8]

Railway workers, intense opponents of the regime in 1905, emerged slowly thereafter as pillars of colonial power. Imperial authorities, facing a lack of support from the metropole and unruly peasant settlers, as well as increased activism among Central Asians and, later, Russian women, solicited skilled Russian workers as allies and tempted them with the benefits of colonial privilege. Land resettlement recruiters offered railway workers arable plots of land across Turkestan; many used their high wages to hire peasant labor, and developed crops for extra income. Others used their wages to buy into business schemes, including a new rail line to the cotton plantations of Fergana.[9] In the war years, when their importance was magnified given supply scarcities and transport difficulties with the center, railway workers received special workplace meals from their employers even as food shortages worsened. Continued high wages allowed many skilled workers to retain domestic servants throughout the war.[10]

Worker activism dimmed considerably in the years before and during World War I. Manzhara noted high worker support for the war effort, as imperial authorities held weekly services at the railway station in support of the tsar, the empire, and the war. After the women's riots in 1916,

Okhrana officials ensured that workers who protested wartime hard-ships were transferred away from Tashkent.[11] Manzhara, in his desire to locate pre-1917 worker activism, could only argue that the impetus for the February–March 1916 riot stemmed from women who "uncon-ditionally manifested the internalization of the revolutionary mood of workers."[12] The socialist newspaper *Nasha Gazeta* expressed support for World War I as late as June 1917.[13]

Revolutionary activism, however, quickly infected the railway shops of Tashkent following the tsarist regime's collapse in late February 1917. Working conditions on the railways and in the factories were dangerous, and the grievances that had prompted the 1905 unrest remained unad-dressed. But the rush to organize involved as much a move to protect, if not build upon, existing privileges as to address their complaints as an exploited class. Russian skilled workers had found a solid place within the hierarchies of post-1905 Tashkent. The need to repel challenges from other subordinate groups as well as stake their claim in a post-tsarist or-der confronted the members of the new Tashkent soviet, which gathered workers' deputies on March 2, 1917.

## The Establishment of Soviet Power

.A hurried affair, the inaugural meeting of the Tashkent soviet consisted of only thirty-five workers from the Central Asian railway, who elected the technician I. I. Bel'kov as leader. Word of the tsar's abdication and the formation of the Provisional Government on Feb. 27, 1917, had only just reached Tashkent, after a failed effort by Governor-General Kuropatkin to conceal the news. Public organizations, as across the Russian empire, "sprang up like mushrooms after the rain."[14] Corporate groups from doctors to shop assistants, from lawyers to "functionaries of various professions," attended a March 3 duma meeting, which voted to estab-lish a nineteen-member Executive Committee of Public Organizations to run the "sociopolitical and economic life of the city." Russian power was reflected in the composition of the committee, which included only two Central Asians, lawyers Ubaydallah Khojaev and Tashpolad Narbuta-bekov, to act as mediators with the majority population.[15] The Tashkent soviet, which pledged to take active roles in all aspects of city life, in-cluded no representatives from Asian Tashkent despite vows to "gather all uncoordinated proletarian elements."[16]

Central Asians nonetheless viewed the post-tsarist era as one of great promise. Local poet Sirajiddin Makhdum Sidqi published mass-circula-tion pamphlets in popular verse extolling a new epoch of freedom and liberty.[17] Meetings to discuss the future state attracted thousands across

Asian Tashkent, and inspired Ubaydallah Khojaev, as well as Munaw-war Qari and other Jadids active since the 1916 draft mobilization, to organize a Tashkent Muslim Council (*Tashkand Shura-yi-Islamiya*). Central Asian notables, not only Jadids, sought self-administration for Asian Tashkent and participation in the political life of Turkestan as equals with the "former" Russian colonizers.

In the heady days following the revolution, any number of new political and social orders appeared possible. A March 10 parade marked the apogee of this optimism. Russian workers marched with red flags promoting greater worker rights. Soldiers wore red ribbons and sang the Marseillaise.[18] Following were local Central Asians—not just notables, but thousands who marched enthusiastically through the streets of the Russian city, ready to claim their own share of power. Russian and Central Asian orators spoke words of optimism and loyalty before the crowd. Governor-General Kuropatkin, still in office, ended with the words "Long live a great free Russia." French archeologist Joseph Castagné, witnessing this display of fraternity, observed that "what a funny people are these Russians, who can make a revolution without spilling a drop of blood."[19]

Optimism for a new political order paralleled a reprieve in the food crisis, as greater supplies of meat flowed into Tashkent than at any other time since 1914. Like the unity of the March 10 parade, however, the promise of plentiful food in Tashkent's bazaars proved ephemeral. The meat came only due to frosts and drought that had ruined most of the spring crops, making it impossible for farmers to feed their animals.[20] By late April, district authorities were urging farmers to grow food instead of cotton to avoid a severe crisis. Railway workers outside of Tashkent were seizing goods transported through their stations destined for the city.[21] Meanwhile, purchasing agents for the Russian army and wholesale traders from central Russia were outbidding the city duma and local buyers for the scant supplies available in Turkestan.[22] For many Russians in Tashkent, however, shortages still appeared to be the work of unscrupulous Central Asian traders, hiding secret stocks of goods in order to inflate prices.[23]

Asian Tashkent's suffering from food shortages was worsening, as purchasing agents from central Russia had taken huge supplies of mutton from Turkestan. Meat traders warned local authorities that consumers in the Asian city's bazaars were becoming restive.[24] Central Asian anger focused on the city duma, which excluded the local population from rationing even as evidence mounted that Asian Tashkent's poor were going hungry. Under questioning by Central Asian duma members, Asian Tashkent police chief Tikhotskii admitted that he saw signs of starvation, but as long as he continued to witness plentiful supplies of bread in restaurants and teahouses, he was suspicious of any reports of widespread hunger.[25] Grain that did reach Tashkent, meanwhile, went exclusively to the Russian city.

The Tashkent soviet intervened in the food issue in late March, forming an independent provision commission to battle "trader-marauders."[26] Yet this body, ostensibly formed to protect class interests, quickly developed a racial element: "trader-marauders" were discussed uniquely as Central Asians. Central Asian workers who formed a Muslim branch of the Social Democratic party, meanwhile, found advances toward the Tashkent soviet rebuffed.[27] The soviet's Russian leaders had already focused on gaining greater power from former tsarist authorities; on March 28, separate worker and soldier soviets merged in a bid to oust Governor-General Kuropatkin. Decrying his failure to overcome the power of "speculators," soviet leaders arrested Kuropatkin on March 31.[28]

No tears were shed for the departure of the tsar's appointee. *Turkestanskii Kur'er*, generally hostile to the soviet, saluted the move as the culmination of the true "Tashkent revolution."[29] Soviet leaders nonetheless sought to convince Petrograd's Provisional Government to approve the arrest. In so doing, they played on fears of another Central Asian uprising. The Provisional Government had already shown itself sensitive to the issue by canceling the 1916 draft order of Russian Muslims and offering an amnesty to all those who participated in the ensuing rebellion.[30] Soviet leaders claimed to have evidence that Kuropatkin was arming Russian peasant settlers in the eastern Semirechie region of Turkestan in a "provocation of interethnic tension."[31] On April 6, the Provisional Government ordered Kuropatkin not to protest his arrest and expulsion from the city.[32] Soviet leaders painted themselves, to Petrograd at least, as defenders of order and harmony in post-tsarist colonial society.

As 1917 went on, central authority grew less relevant for residents of both Russian and Asian Tashkent. Following Kuropatkin's removal, the Provisional Government dispatched state duma member N. N. Shchepkin, along with four Russian and four Tatar Muslim associates, to Tashkent to oversee Turkestan until the election of a Constituent Assembly.[33] This Turkestan Commission (*Turkkom*), with no experience in the region, no clear mandate to govern, and no ability to provide concrete assistance, saw itself ignored by local organs of power and vilified by the local press. These unelected representatives were condemned as more likely to siphon valuable resources from Turkestan than to rule with local interests in mind. Central Asians resented the presence of patronizing Tatars. On May 6, Shchepkin asked to be recalled by the

Provisional Government.[34] In his place came a respected "Turkestani," V. P. Nalivkin. Nalivkin had served in the Kokandian and Khivan campaigns, and had spent several years living in a Central Asian village in the 1870s, motivated by the populist "to the people" movement. His hatred of corruption led him to resign from the tsarist administration in 1901, but he remained in Turkestan, gaining state duma election as a Social Democrat.[35] Provisional Government hopes that Nalivkin's eclectic beliefs and experiences would bind him to colonial society proved misplaced. The Turkkom still could not deliver assistance to a hungry city. G. I. Broido, head of the soldiers' section of the Tashkent soviet, decried the centrally appointed body in the metropolitan *Utro Rossii* on June 15, 1917, claiming, "We expected a lot from the committee, but quickly realized that our hopes were ill-founded. . . . Turkestan is now undergoing a very intense crisis of provisions. . . . The committee, however, has limited itself to sending telegrams to the Provisional Government. The response is always the same: 'No bread is coming.'"[36]

The Tashkent soviet, meanwhile, accumulated power in the Russian city at the expense of a disorganized duma and committee of public organizations. As elsewhere in Russia during this period, the soviet proved the most aggressive in taking charge of social affairs, holding arbitration hearings on labor and other matters, offering assistance to unemployed workers, and supervising the distribution of various supplies, especially those transported by rail, throughout the city and region.[37] By early summer, soviet leaders were mimicking the elite behavior of their former rulers. The Tashkent soviet held exclusive concerts with "renowned artists" at the Khiva theater. Members of the regional Turkestan soviet began to mount hunting expeditions from the dacha of the military governor, which they now controlled.[38] Yet their open denunciations of both local traders and the Turkkom for failing to resolve the food crisis placed the soviet in a position of searching for a solution that had eluded previous municipal bodies over the past years. Given the structure of the colonial economy, the irresponsiveness of the center, and continuing poor harvests, this search would force the soviet to navigate a complex web of interests and conflicts in a volatile postrevolutionary society.

## Food, Society, and Revolution

As a consequence of the failed spring harvest, by mid-April queues at bread stores reached four hours in Russian Tashkent.[39] City duma provision committee members extended rationing to bread, but once more excluded the Central Asian population. City head N. G. Mallitskii, in response to an outcry from Muslim duma members, proposed creating a separate provision committee for the Asian city, but without any funds. Muslim deputy Gani Khan argued in response that "we are not against the formation of a [separate] provision committee, but open the road to us, give us supplies then we will organize a committee; otherwise such a committee would be useless."[40] Beliefs nonetheless persisted that Central Asians had substantial stocks of food concealed. Speakers at the Tashkent soviet accused Central Asian peasants of participating in a conspiracy alongside traders, burying grain in fields throughout the district, and then plowing over the holes and sowing cotton to avoid detection.[41] Images of the Muslim exploiter expressed in the duma and the soviet illustrated intensified ethnic cleavages as shortages worsened.

A women's food riot in July 1917 awoke Tashkent soviet leaders to the complexity of the food supply situation. Before July, soviet delegates had played an "oversight" role on various food committees, focusing on feeding Russian industrial workers and prisoners of war, and ignoring not only Central Asians, but Russian women.[42] Soviet leaders, as had tsarist elites, saw women's roles as domestic. Deputies to an April regional assembly declared industrial work, "dangerous for the organism," undesirable for women.[43] Discussion of women's rights was limited to those concerned with maternity leave and family issues, and ignored women's role as consumers. Absent themselves from soviet meetings or the pages of the official newspaper of the soviet, *Nasha Gazeta*, women expressed their power in colonial society through a July 3–4 riot against Central Asian merchants and opposing police officers at the central Voskresenskii bazaar. As in 1916, police, soldiers, and other males joined the riot, attacking Central Asian merchants and seizing their supplies.[44] Alarmed by the disturbance's scale and uncontrolled nature, the Tashkent soviet led efforts to develop a temporary committee of public safety to return order to the streets of the Russian city. Soviet leaders, like tsarist elites one year previous, saw rioters as "simple" women, whose anarchic tendencies "could be exploited by the dark forces of counter-revolution." The spectacle of soldiers joining the riot caused deep concern, as they might be influenced by "politically unsophisticated" citizens to rebel, threatening internal solidarity and the war effort that the soviet heartily supported.[45]

Soviet leaders also expressed great concern at the desertion from Russian Tashkent of Central Asian merchants, who claimed "Russian soldiers are taking, Russian women are destroying, and the authorities are nowhere; it is impossible to trade."[46] The soviet invited a representative of the Tashkent Muslim Council to participate on the committee of safety and pledged to act decisively against any "calls to action placing one group of the population against another."[47] Committee patrols defended Central Asian merchants, and melons and vegetables returned to the streets of Russian Tashkent by July 18, though lowered fixed prices established by the committee were ignored.[48]

The July events initiated a brief soviet drive to find allies in Asian Tashkent. *Nasha Gazeta* reported on any new bodies showing "flickers of a proletarian consciousness."[49] Adeeb Khalid has argued that the artisanal nature of labor in the Asian city did not allow for an easy transposition of Marxist class categories.[50] Even so, Muslim conscript workers returning from the 1916 draft, who established an Asian city soviet, failed to form significant links with their Russian counterpart. Soviet members retained their view of the Central Asians as either class enemies or incapable of class consciousness. Any recognition of Central Asians as equal in class status would presage their inclusion in a revolutionary coalition and necessitate a surrender of imperial privileges that had become so central to Russian skilled workers in Turkestan.

In Asian Tashkent, politics focused initially on internal power struggles. Clerical elites formed their own organization, the Society of Ulama (*Ulama Jamiyati*), to combat early Jadid successes in political mobilization, which had culminated in the election of Munawwar Qari as president of the First Turkestan Muslim Congress, a broad-based assembly of notables held in Tashkent April 16–22, 1917. Ulama representatives abandoned the Tashkent Muslim Council and intensified portrayals of the Jadids as impetuous youth threatening the foundations of Muslim culture and society.[51] In this struggle, each group sought allies on the other side of the Ankhor canal. Ulama representatives initiated contact with former leading tsarist officials and Russian businessmen in an effort to conserve pre-1917 hierarchies of power. The Muslim Council allied with the liberal, anti-soviet Russian Householders Union.[52] Russian sources are conspicuously silent on their cooperation with Central Asian political groups, but both sides realized the importance of alliances in this uncertain period.

Political maneuvering intensified as elections to a reformed city duma in August approached. The city board had announced its intention to hold these elections, according to the orders of the Provisional Government, based on the "four-tailed" franchise. Mallitskii proclaimed his vehement opposition, arguing again that Muslim society was too backward to grasp ideas of democracy. Liberal representatives of "public organizations" in Tashkent, while not opposing the franchise, sought separate dumas for Russian and Asian Tashkent as a recognition of their "two different economic systems."[53] The board, however, rejected this argument. Administrators may have felt bound by the Provisional Government decree, may have been unwilling to risk opposition from a now highly politicized Asian community, or very well may have had a sincere commitment to full democracy in a post-tsarist era.

Election results, announced on August 3, demonstrated the political mobilization of Asian Tashkent and the strength of the Society of Ulama, which received 40,302 votes, the largest of any political party, and 62 seats, an absolute majority of the 112 seats in the new duma. The liberal Muslim Council gained 11 seats. In Russian Tashkent, parties loyal to the Tashkent soviet dominated. The Socialist Revolutionaries won 24 seats from 15,753 votes; the Social Democrats obtained 5 seats. *Turkestanskii Kur'er* wrote that the Socialist Revolutionary success stemmed from a campaign waged around local issues, such as improving the food supply, housing, and education, as opposed to Social Democrats' stressing the importance of proletarian internationalism.[54] A number of other minor parties filled out the duma.[55]

Ulama success produced an outcry in Russian Tashkent. *Turkestanskiia Viedomosti*, now operating under the auspices of the Turkkom, regarded the electoral outcome as a result of the "noxious" influence of the ulama on the "undifferentiated native mass."[56] The ulama's tactical decision, in a clear sign of the continuing colonial legacy, to nominate Russian conservative industrialist A. N. Iakomovich as city head only enhanced suspicions among socialist workers about a reactionary alliance designed to doom the revolution.[57] *Turkestanskii Kur'er* decried the ability of the "the most backward party" in Tashkent to gain power, but chided Russians for their low turnout (60 percent). They were only lucky that, while virtually all of the Muslim males voted, no Muslim women participated in the election, which would have further reduced Russian representation.[58]

Soviet meetings in following days featured speakers who castigated as class enemies the mulla, a leader of a closed, ignorant culture and religion, and the *bai*. Russians in the soviet used the term "bai," which generally indicated village landholding elites, as a pejorative to designate either a "feudal" lord or "bourgeois" trader or aristocrat. Soviet delegates claimed the power of bais and mullas signaled either a society mired, according to Marxist parlance, in a backward feudal stage of development or one at the early stages of capitalism, when an internal dialectic of class opposition had yet to arise. Sanjar Asfendiarov, a Kazakh socialist who had been working in the Asian city, noted in *Nasha Gazeta* how the "dark masses of the native proletariat find themselves in slavelike dependence on the all-powerful *bais*."[59] The term "bai" came to include even Central Asian petty traders, who were greeted by Russians with cries of "Hey, bai, what evil are you up to?"[60] G. M. Tsviling, one of the Tashkent soviet leaders, argued that "reactionary bosses," merchants and mullas, were controlling Muslim duma representatives.[61] Poems in *Nasha Gazeta* and *Turkestanskiia Viedomosti* mocked the "zombie-like chanting" that followed the "call of the mulla."[62] Concern that "[Muslim] marauders will run us over" led for renewed calls for separate dumas for Russian and Asian Tashkent.[63]

Central Asian political activism was on display again on August 19, when tens of thousands crossed the border into Russian Tashkent to protest the slaughter of Kazakhs by Russian settlers in the Semirechie.[64] Demonstrators gathered in front of Turkkom headquarters, and, ignoring Nalivkin's cries that an investigation was underway, yelled, "We did not come here to listen to past history. Give us a clear answer. . . . It's been six months since freedom was declared, but the government has not given a thought to [the Muslims of Semirechie]. This is because the blood flowing in Semirechie is Muslim blood and Turkic blood."[65] The crowd then repeated demands for a disarming of the settlers and a stop to the bloodshed before the regional Turkestan soviet. Shouting "equality and brotherhood," the demonstrators, along with an unspecified number of Russians, then marched to Kaufman square to hear speeches denouncing Russian rule.[66]

Such a spectacle far surpassed the last Central Asian protest in Russian Tashkent, which had been met by deadly violence, in 1892. In this case, strangely, the Russian press and published memoirs avoid any mention of reactions to the event, perhaps because it was so profoundly unsettling. Or perhaps this was because attention was on the food crisis, which reached critical levels because intense heat had scorched and ruined most of the local grain crop.[67] Provision committee agents dispersed across Russia, Persia, and Afghanistan to search for food, instructed that "[h]unger threatens. We need heroic measures of struggle."[68] The struggle for food became profoundly implicated in Tashkent's intense social, political, and ethnic struggle in coming weeks and months.

Russian railway workers and soldiers began their own requisitions in late August, targeting Central Asians at the Tashkent railway station. Perhaps seeking to restore ethnic hierarchies following the August 19 demonstration, or simply frustrated with the failure of the city provision committee to supply basic goods, these workers and soldiers rifled through passenger baggage and railway cars.[69] The Tashkent soviet and the committee for public safety condemned and banned these unauthorized requisitions, but offered no solutions for the worsening crisis. On September 10, the municipal provision committee halved rations to skilled workers, which sent Russian women and men into the streets of Tashkent in protest.[70] Turkkom member I. N. Shendrikov asked Petrograd to send soldiers as well as food to suppress a potential mutiny.[71]

The same day as the ration reductions, Central Asian peasants crowd-ed the Tashkent railway station, buying and selling provisions in prepa-ration for the holiday of the Feast of the Sacrifice. Rumors shot through the Russian city that traders and peasants were conspiring to empty the city of food and send their purchases to the semi-independent emirate of Bukhara. On September 11, soldiers of the First and Second Siberian Reg-iments, in violation of committee of public safety orders, surrounded the railway station and began searches and confiscations from all Muslims present, detaining them for hours.[72] Soldiers and some railway workers planned citywide requisitions, seeking, in Manzhara's words, "to shake down the Sarts."[73] The Turkkom and duma ordered loyal soldiers and police to guard the boundaries between the two cities.

After heated debate, the Tashkent soviet executive committee (*ispolkom*) outvoted its leadership and supported a plan to initiate req-uisitions from Asian Tashkent. A. D. Chicherin, the new soviet leader, looked to seize political power as well.[74] Chicherin's actions may have been guided by the "July Days" debacle in Petrograd, when central Bolshevik refusal to support a worker bid for greater power almost de-stroyed the party. He and his supporters may also have seen their task as relatively easy, as they faced an unpopular ulama-dominated duma and an isolated, "foreign" Turkkom. Yet the Tashkent soviet had no support on the other side of the Ankhor canal, and, as former soviet leader I. Ia. Pershin recognized, seizing power in an atmosphere of ethnic violence threatened severe damage to a city where connections between Russian and Asian Tashkent made the two cities, and the two communities, interdependent.

## October in September: The Tashkent Revolution

Soviet leaders convened a meeting of thousands of workers and soldiers at the suburban Aleksandrovskii Park on September 12. The meeting elected railway worker I. I. Tobolin as head of a fourteen-member pro-visional Revolutionary Committee (*Revkom*) to guide Tashkent through an "acute food crisis."[75] Resolutions authorized the Revkom to execute, in the name of the Tashkent soviet, immediate requisitions from "capi-talists" throughout the city. The crowd also charged the Revkom with taking full oversight over organs of production and distribution of basic goods.

As the Revkom gained the loyalty of Tashkent soldiers, Turkkom leader Nalivkin telegraphed to Petrograd that "[i]n Tashkent excesses of workers and soldiers are occurring, there is an attack on the native town."[76] Provisional Government leader A. F. Kerenskii, raised in Tashkent and sensitive to the issue of ethnic tensions, labeled the takeover a "criminal act" and dispatched General P. A. Korovichenko from Kazan with a company of soldiers on a "punitive expedition."[77] Korovichenko arrived in Tashkent on September 24, but the soviet and Revkom retained effective control over the Russian city. Chicherin and other leaders backed away from pledges to mount requisitions in Asian Tashkent, but angry crowds were themselves assaulting merchants and seizing goods. Not one wagon of grain from central Russia arrived in Tashkent in October.[78] Companies of soldiers petitioned the soviet to expel Korovichenko, who, they claimed, protected "insolent criminals" engaged in speculation.[79] On October 25, two days before the fall of the Provisional Government was known in Turkestan, the presidium of the Tashkent soviet voted to support an armed confrontation. Soldiers, primarily of the First and Second Siberian regiments, railway workers, and a significant contingent of Hungarian prisoners of war battled troops loyal to the Provisional Government. After a week, the Tashkent soviet gained the upper hand, and arrested Korovichenko and other senior military officers on October 31.[80]

Tashkent soviet leaders still had no effective mechanism to control the Asian city, however. Ubaydallah Khojaev and other Jadids had formed an alliance with the more moderate leaders of the regional Turkestan soviet, but the latter had fled Tashkent for the Fergana valley after refusing to support the September *putsch*.[81] Ulama leaders, still in charge of the duma, ignored the soviet takeover of Tashkent and proposed the creation of a new Turkestan Commission, composed of both Russians and Muslims, to act as a caretaker government until the election of a Constituent Assembly.[82] Tashkent soviet leaders, unreceptive to any form of power sharing, sought instead to unite the Russian-speaking population of Turkestan behind soviet rule. At a regional congress of soviets November 15–22, Kh. L. Vainshtein, secretary of the Tashkent soviet, evoked images of the mulla and bai to argue that "no democratic organizations," much less revolutionary class organizations, existed among the local population.[83] Muslims' "slave-like" dependence on their leaders precluded them from becoming effective participants in soviet power. Such attitudes, however, were not shared unanimously. Russian deputies from outside Tashkent argued that excluding Central Asians from power would lead them, not unjustifiably, to see soviet leaders as demagogues. Passive, not to mention active, opposition from 98 percent of the population would be enough to doom the effective practice of power in Turkestan.[84]

In the end, the congress, consisting uniquely of Europeans, voted 97 to 17 that the inclusion of Muslims in the organs of higher regional revolutionary power appears at the present moment unacceptable, in view both of the fully undetermined relationship between the native population and the Soviet of soldiers', workers', and peasants' deputies, and that among the native population there are no class proletarian organizations, the representatives of which would be welcome in the organs of higher regional revolutionary power.[85]

Class was used to exclude the entire colonized population from political equality in soviet Turkestan.

The use of the term "higher regional revolutionary power" left some room for maneuver. At the local level, Russian deputies sought relationships across ethnic lines that would assure their own superiority and regional stability. Central Asians' political mobilization over the course of the year, however, testified to their desires to throw off the fetters of colonial rule and participate in a new state only on an equal, democratic footing. Against the backdrop of an worsening supply crisis, Russian workers chose to ignore socialist internationalist ideology and the politics of coalition building.

## Famine, Food, and Force in Postrevolutionary Tashkent, 1917–1918

Civil war raging on the steppe isolated Turkestan from central Russia. Anti-Bolshevik Cossack leader Ataman Dutov blockaded all rail links into the region.[86] Facing seclusion and shortages, soviet leaders struggled to maintain power within the Russian community as well as dominance over the Central Asian majority. The Tashkent soviet turned to force, killing tens of thousands of Tashkent and Turkestan residents, primarily but not exclusively Central Asians, to maintain their mastery over the city and region.

A wave of spontaneous requisitions and violence swept across Tashkent in late October. Workers and soldiers commandeered food and valuables from anyone deemed "hostile" to the new regime, killing hundreds in Russian Tashkent.[87] In late November, soldiers murdered the imprisoned General Korovichenko.[88] Soviet leaders, fearing violence spiraling out of its control, worked to focus the population's attention on Asian Tashkent, where seizures and requisitions could take place without threatening the peace of the Russian city. I. I. Tobolin chaired a newly formed requisitions committee, with the goal of finding food "hidden with the goal of speculation."[89] Playing on the myth of the Central Asian speculator, soviet leaders anticipated widespread and successful searches of Asian Tashkent, all the while preparing for resistance.

Requisitions began on December 4, 1917. Teams of ten, including some Kazakh and Tatar Muslim representatives, fanned out across Asian Tashkent, protected by soldiers and a newly formed Red Guard. Teams delivered confiscated goods to designated drop-off points in squares, where carts then bore the supplies to Russian Tashkent's warehouses. The requisitions, however, fell short of soviet goals. The committee never produced a count of the goods seized during the December 4–6 requisitions, which led soviet member Boris Gudovich to argue that there was in fact little excess food in Asian Tashkent. Other soviet members believed that workers and soldiers had pilfered requisitioned goods.[90] Meanwhile, former soviet leader Tsviling noted that the "zeal" of the requisition squads had contributed to a "nervous state" among the residents of Asian Tashkent.[91] On December 6, Central Asian workers and artisans appeared before the Tashkent soviet and demanded a halt to requisitions, which were provoking, in their words, an "abnormal mood among the residents of the old city."[92] These delegates also protested the continuation of a rationing system that denied food to Central Asians.

In Asian Tashkent, a massive December rally hailed a new Turkestan Autonomous Government. Cries of "long live an autonomous Turkestan" and words of future equality supported the body created by the Jadid-dominated Fourth Extraordinary Regional Muslim Congress, which met, along with moderate Russian organizations disenfranchised by the soviet, in Kokand.[93] Jadids solicited funds from wealthy businessmen to finance the fledging body, designed to rule until the election of a Constituent Assembly, and began efforts to organize a militia.[94] The "Kokand Autonomy," as it became known, guaranteed a one-third Russian representation in the assembly, even though Russians composed less than 10 percent of the population.[95] Autonomist leaders, however, were under no illusions as to their reception by the soviet regime.

Central Asian mobilization unsettled soviet officials, who immediately appointed two Muslim members, Mirza Ahmed Mirhadybaev and Mulla Bahram Nor Muhamedov, to its ranks.[96] Russian intellectuals, writing in independent newspapers, warned that Soviet "imperialist behavior" justified Muslim protests against a Russian proletariat that had proven itself "uncivilized."[97] In part to forestall a massive demonstration planned the next day, soviet leaders voted on December 12 to "recognize the right of self-determination" for the Muslim population. Speakers recommended that soviet leaders join the rally for Muslim equality to signal "a new beginning" in ethnic relations.[98] Even as proclamations of support for the Central Asian population reached their apex, however, the Tashkent soviet quietly passed a decree dissolving the ulama-dominated city duma. Soldiers patrolled the borders of Russian and Asian Tashkent to impress the local population with the balance of armed power.[99]

Tens of thousands of Central Asian demonstrators overwhelmed the soldiers, who did not fire on the peaceful crowd, and entered Russian Tashkent on December 13. Joined by numerous Russians, they protested in front of government buildings, demanding equality. A prison raid freed several tsarist officers before troops loyal to the soviet opened fire, killing over one hundred.[100] The crowd dispersed, but the consequences of the massive demonstration were made clear at a December 15 meeting, when railway workers sanctioned the Tashkent soviet for its inability to maintain the integrity of the boundaries of the Russian city. Soviet leaders were already beginning to see their authority slip away as Red Guards had decided to undertake requisitions and arrest "speculators" without soviet approval and railway workers were openly confiscating supplies along lines for their own use.[101] I. I. Tobolin and other soviet leaders once again turned against the local Asian population. Another round of requisitions began in late December, and a cordon was established around Asian Tashkent in response to reports in *Nasha Gazeta* that food was being secretly shuttled in and out of the city.[102] In fact, in Asian Tashkent, bakeries were mixing chalk with flour, and several cases of starvation had been reported.[103] Soviet leaders countered such evidence with claims that the bai was denying food even to his "own" people in order to make profits from speculation. Yet requisitions again provided little, and the daily bread ration in Russian Tashkent for workers was halved one more time, from 0.5 to 0.25 *funt*.

In the meantime, the Tashkent soviet was preparing for a military confrontation with the Turkestan Autonomous Government. Reports in *Nasha Gazeta* of huge grain stocks around Kokand provided justification for a conflict with a body the Tashkent soviet was determined to crush. Soviet leaders began to arm Russians in Kokand and stepped up recruitment of prisoners of war in late December. Danish Red Cross delegate A. H. Brun accused Tashkent soviet leaders of deliberately starving thirty-eight thousand prisoners in order to compel them to join the Red Guard.[104] German prisoner Gustav Krist reported that this effort was hugely successful, as former prisoners of war composed nearly half of the fighting forces loyal to soviet power.[105]

The soviet attack on Kokand on February 14, 1918, began with cannons and machine guns that fired indiscriminately into crowds in the city, killing thousands. Next, according to one account, "all the stores, trading firms, and rows of stalls in the old city were looted, as well as all banks, and all private, more or less decent apartments. Safes . . . were broken open and emptied. The thieves gathered their plundered goods on carts and drove them to the railway and the fortress [where Russian troops were housed]."[106] Soviet leaders in Tashkent expressed joy at the "cleansing" of the Turkestan Autonomous Government, but professed shock at the scale of deaths.[107] News that soldiers were selling looted heirlooms in Tashkent bazaars evoked nervousness that local Muslims might become aware of the scale of destruction in Kokand.[108] But the Kokand attack had proven the ability of the Tashkent soviet to mount an effective, large-scale military operation. As during the imperial period, Russian leaders in Turkestan had responded to a growing sense of vulnerability with violence. Central Asians saw their desire and opportunity for greater political and social rights evaporate before Russian aggressiveness.

Soviet efforts to feed Russian Tashkent in early 1918 faced subversion by the body's most ardent backers. One grain shipment that managed to break Dutov's blockade saw only one of twelve wagons arrive full, the rest stolen by railway workers and Red Guards. Soldiers maintained a constant ring to forbid the exit of food from Asian Tashkent, but suspended requisitions due to the chaos caused by the arrival of thousands of emaciated Kazakh nomads. Settler expropriation of their herds following the 1916 rebellion combined with the drought the following year to leave the Kazakhs with few animals and not enough food to survive the winter.[109] One recent study estimates that 30 percent of the nomadic population of Turkestan died during the winter of 1917–18.[110] Seeking food in the cities, massive numbers tried to reach Tashkent, with hundreds, weakened by disease, dying at railway stations en route. Soviet authorities forced those who arrived at the railway station in Russian Tashkent to the Asian city. Bodies of dead migrants accumulated on the streets.

Leaders of the Tashkent and Turkestan soviets condemned these Kazakh arrivals. Castagné reported Turkestan soviet head F. I. Kolesov yelling, "Let them stuff themselves with their autonomy; I will not give them one bite of bread!"[111] Soviet leaders only discussed fanciful suggestions of evacuating Kazakhs, and perhaps other Tashkent residents, to the Aral Sea, with its plentiful fish stocks. The plight of these Kazakhs, however, mobilized Russian intellectuals, who had been marginalized by soviet power. Many of these, including Mallitskii, had stayed active in public life as state employees, as well as coordinating plans to open a university in Tashkent.[112] Their opposition to soviet power was signaled by a strike of high municipal employees in January, which prompted a strong rebuke from *Nasha Gazeta*.[113] Intellectuals including R. R. Shreder took up the cause of the Kazakhs, organizing a "Turkestan Public Committee to Help the Hungry." *Novyi Turkestan*, an "independent socialist newspaper," praised Shreder's efforts and condemned the Tashkent soviet for a "basic lack of humanity" in refusing to take the bodies on the streets to a hospital or gravesite.[114] In February, the union of municipal employees voted to donate one percent of their salaries to help the starving Kazakhs. Tashkent soviet leaders chafed at these "separatist actions," but as the scale of victims grew, they allowed philanthropic efforts to continue. By early March 1918, twelve hundred refugees were in the committee's care. Soviet-run neighborhood committees, meanwhile, refused to feed Kazakhs who remained in Russian Tashkent, and urged the soviet to expel these interlopers.[115] As fears of cholera and typhus mounted, the Tashkent soviet established its own feeding station in Asian Tashkent, where Arif Khoja and other Muslim businessmen were coordinating efforts to assist the hungry, having opened a canteen to feed three thousand daily.[116]

In the months following the Kokand invasion, Tashkent soviet leaders saw the greatest threats to their power come from their own ostensible supporters. Foreign diplomats reported almost nightly gunfire in the suburbs of the Russian city as Red Guards battled residents for food and goods.[117] *Nasha Gazeta* reported in April that "due to daily robberies and murders, loyal residents [of Russian Tashkent] can not live peacefully." The soviet was soliciting volunteers for a new militia to stop the "audacious attacks and beastly murders" committed by "criminals" who were slaughtering entire families.[118] Details on the nature of these attacks and murders remain elusive, due largely to the inaccessibility of police and party archival records for this period. Records of Tashkent soviet meetings nonetheless register frequent complaints against the Red Guard, whose drunken attacks and shootings left residents "literally terrorized."[119] Railway workers, meanwhile, had established their own provision committee, which fed Russians only. Members told Central Asians to return home "to take care of their families."[120] Their committee confiscated goods arriving by wagon from the city. The soviet executive committee wrote that "these separate actions . . . violate all proper workings of the administrative apparatus. . . . [A]ll questions of requisitions must go through the ispolkom, which is the main organ of soviet power in Tashkent."[121]

Railway workers nonetheless continued to compete with the soviet for food, sending grain agents across the empire and threatening to strike if not given textiles to exchange with local farmers. They also demanded the opening of peace negotiations with Ataman Dutov, to end his blockade of the region. Railway worker delegate A. Mameliuk successfully defended these "separatist" actions at a July 1918 congress of provision committees, arguing against Tashkent soviet delegates' claims of "unfairness." Mameliuk argued that hungry railway workers, physically unable to perform their duties, would effectively deny the whole region of bread.[122]

Several other worker bodies subsequently formed their own provision committees, over the complaints of *Sovetskii Turkestan*, the newspaper of the executive of the Turkestan soviet, that such initiatives were "pitting workers against each other."[123] Teachers and printers sent purchasing agents as far as the Caucasus, and metal workers began to operate soap, textile, and leather enterprises to supply barter goods for food collection.[124] Soviet leaders balanced their frustration at independent collections with fear of provoking opposition from workers already suffering privations of war and drought. The Tashkent soviet ispolkom decided not to ban these independent committees, reverting to policing more egregious inequalities that might arise, including one incident when the union of bakers and confectioners used their privileged position in the food production line to take eight times the amount of rationed wheat.[125]

Independent committees favored male workers at the expense of women, less likely to gain access to union and enterprise supplies and more reliant on goods rationed by the soviet. Anger at continuing ration cuts erupted in April. A women's protest in front of committee offices demanding "Flour for Easter!" turned violent, with one demonstrator shouting a "woman should be head of the provision committee!"[126] The women dispersed only when each given three *funty* of flour. Provision committee bureaucrats replaced Central Asian merchants as the main targets of Russian women, who stalked these functionaries on their way home from work. The provision committee board wrote to the Tashkent soviet ispolkom on May 24, 1918, that "it is difficult to carry out our work with the necessary intensity when employees of the administration must labor under the threat of a *samosud* of a hungry crowd."[127]

Asian Tashkent continued to suffer disproportionately, with regular deaths from starvation throughout spring 1918. Central Asian notables worked to manage the crisis. The dissolved city duma met secretly in the Asian city, and traders funded charitable organizations to feed specific neighborhoods.[128] These initiatives only confirmed to the Russian press that "everything can be found" in the Asian city. The scale of efforts to feed the poor in Asian Tashkent, reported *Svobodnyi Turkestan*, proved the success of the local Central Asians in finding and purchasing essential goods when necessary.[129] *Novyi Turkestan* reported on the "professional poor" of Asian Tashkent, accentuating their suffering to gain access to the substantial stocks of food accumulated by their elites.[130] Even as these stories were counterpoised by others reporting on starvation deaths in Asian Tashkent, they fed the complementary myths of the successful Muslim businessman and hidden stocks of foodstuffs.

The addition of hundreds of Russian refugees from Bukhara in March 1918 pushed the Tashkent soviet once more to consider requisitions from the Asian city. These refugees were a product of the failed effort of Turkestan soviet leader Kolesov to overthrow the Bukharan emir, an event that heightened ethnic tensions across the region, including Tashkent.[131] Requisition teams discovered that Central Asians had become more assertive defending their property. Previously, victims of requisitions had bombarded the Tashkent soviet with petitions, using class language to demand restitution. Wood seller Mir Azval Mir Karimov argued in January that requisitions taken from him were unjust, as "he worked without hired labor . . . sold to the poor and [did] not engage in speculation." He claimed to be exploited by richer wholesalers.[132] More direct confrontations now ensued. Provision committee member Okulov reported that local residents surrounded his squad, berating and threatening it for taking goods from the poor rather than "speculators."[133] Central Asians had learned well the vocabulary of class. Soviet leaders, smarting from their failure in Bukhara, feared catalyzing more resistance and again retreated from requisitions.

Efforts to assure Russian supremacy in provision matters continued, however. The Tashkent soviet condemned "separatist actions" of Muslim members of the Turkestan Public Committee to Help the Hungry for plans to donate food to the Asian city, saying that all residents must realize that the Tashkent soviet was "the factual master of the situation, in both the Russian and the Asian cities."[134] Yet soviet efforts to form a branch in Asian Tashkent were farcical. Russian leaders never trusted their counterparts, purging the "old city" soviet on multiple occasions and refusing to provide requested funding for children's shelters, canteens, and medical assistance.[135] Writers in the soviet press continued to portray local lower classes as sheeplike followers of Muslim elites. One poem in *Sovetskii Turkestan* portrayed the bai as a political as well as an economic manipulator:

> The bai is angry, everyone is roused from their homes
> Even the women are herded into public places
> As the bai has yet to see his "autonomy"
> clever, clever bai![136]

In the absence of an effective Asian city soviet, local notables ruled Asian Tashkent as best they could. The Asian city's leaders faced a new government not only determined to enforce inequality between colonizer and colonized, but also unwilling to entrust mediators with previously held tasks, such as sharing, even inequitably, revenue. Violence became an everyday instead of an extraordinary tool of power. Heated rhetoric and violent actions along ethnic lines, however, failed to unite even Russian workers and soldiers behind the soviet.

Russian workers' and soldiers' desire to guard colonial identities and privileges surmounted class solidarity and revolutionary emancipation in Tashkent. Class became a tool to exclude Central Asians and other subject groups, including all Russian women, as well as leading functionaries tied to tsarist-era elites. Skilled Russian workers sought to extend their already advantaged position, adding political power to their economic importance. But they faced a far more complicated landscape than their colonial predecessors. The metropole, already considered unresponsive to the needs of Tashkent and Turkestan, now became virtually irrelevant, unable or unwilling to supply the region with needed resources. Food shortages, due in large part to colonial policies that encouraged cotton growth, sparked intense competition for supplies, and heightened ethnic tensions. The Central Asian population, after a decade of political activism, stood ready in 1917 to reject the inequities of colonialism and participate as full citizens in a future democratic society. Leaders from modernist Jadids to the conservative ulama participated in the city duma and other political organs with the goal of achieving a free, postcolonial, autonomous region. Combined with the unwillingness of the Tashkent soviet to find a mediating cohort in Asian Tashkent, these factors produced great violence. The Tashkent soviet's appropriation of resources and repression of Central Asians across Turkestan displayed its military primacy, but did not bring together the settler population. Railway workers and soldiers defied soviet authority in their search for food supplies, even as they supported and mimicked soviet policies against the Central Asian population, as well as other Russians. Chaos and colonial legacies gained the attention of the central Bolshevik party, which sought to restore Turkestan as an important economic contributor to the central economy and employ it as a springboard to a wider socialist revolution.

# 8.

## "Under a Soviet Roof": City, Country, and Center, 1918–1923

Former tsarist officials, adventurists, and kulaks, in the name of the class struggle, have effected the most preposterous schemes upon the local population. . . . This continuation of colonial politics has led directly to the enslavement of the native poor; until this ceases the local population will not come around to supporting soviet power by themselves, but will act in their own interests. In power alongside these colonial elements are the native exploiting elites who instead of helping the laboring masses in terms of national-cultural and class self-determination, practice intense exploitation of them, bringing all the traditions of feudal methods of oppression: bribery, thefts, and personal terror, all "under a soviet roof."[1]

This summer 1920 analysis by the Central Committee of the Russian Communist Party revealed continuing frustration at Tashkent Russians' ability to maintain imperial privileges even as Bolshevik representatives from Moscow purged and arrested hundreds for "colonialist attitudes" (*kolonizatorstvo*) and sought to elevate non-elite Central Asians to positions of power.[2] During 1918–23, violent confrontations in the soviets, streets, and villages of Tashkent and Turkestan unfolded over conflicts between center and periphery and colonizers and colonized. Tensions also worked along other axes, particularly an urban versus rural one. The desperate search for food and basic supplies catalyzed a bewildering and complex array of micro-constituencies outside of state control. As did the revolution, the civil war era in Turkestan unfolded according to its own dynamic. Communist and imperialist ideologies mixed with scarcity and isolation on the one hand and a legacy of interdependencies fostered by colonial society on the other. Central as well as local officials strained to assert their authority and to build foundations for a new state underneath the "soviet roof" that succeeded imperial Russia.

A multifaceted struggle, against a backdrop of intricate relationships on the ground, modifies contemporary historiographical views, which portray an eventually triumphant center seeking balance, and a degree of tolerance, as it struggled against parochial Russian and Central Asian regionalists and masses polarized along ethnic lines.[3] Central Bolsheviks held their own imperial stereotypes and prejudices. Local Russians and Central Asians sought compromise as well as conflict. Power and violence nonetheless characterized the period, highlighted by the struggle for food. In the end, the main mission of central Bolshevik emissaries was less about ethnic equality and other features of modern socialist progress, and more about restoring a cotton economy to restart idling factories in central Russia.

## 1917–1918: A Distant Center

Tashkent Russian frustration with the center had grown as food shortages worsened in early 1917. Unable to procure food elsewhere in the empire, Turkestan residents saw central army purchasing agents and wholesale traders outbidding local buyers and provision committees, then delivering the scant supplies to the front or major cities in European Russia.[4] Central buyers flooded the region following the decision of the Petrograd Provisional Government not to include Turkestan in its grain monopoly.[5] Competition, driving up prices, persuaded many farmers to grow food instead of cotton, which was still subject to fixed prices. Cotton production declined by 36 percent in 1917.[6] Drought, however, prevented any rise in food supplies. Turkkom head Nalivkin's pleas for more deliveries to combat an "inescapable famine" in Turkestan were met with silence; by August 1917 grain was not even reaching Petrograd.[7]

Tashkent soviet leaders, despite pleading for greater assistance from the new Bolshevik government, doubted that the center would prove a reliable ally. On November 20, 1917, as the Turkestan congress of soviets debated excluding the local population from political power, V. I. Lenin issued a proclamation "To All Muslim Toilers of Russia and the East." The proclamation urged Muslims of Soviet Russia to lead the colonized populations of Asia in overthrowing European colonial rule.[8] Lenin saw the Muslim poor, not Russian workers, as the new vanguard force in Central Asia. The blockade that separated central Russia from Turkestan made supporting this vision difficult, however. Lenin and

I. V. Stalin, the head of the People's Commissariat on Nationality Affairs (*Narkomnats*), wavered as to whether to endorse the Russian-worker-led Tashkent soviet or the Kokand autonomy as a successor to the Provisional Government. The latter had appealed to the center to dissolve the "chauvinist" soviet as per Lenin's policy favoring self-determination for non-Russian peoples. Stalin declined to take a firm position, stating that "[t]he soviets are autonomous in their internal affairs and discharge their duties by leaning upon their own actual forces. The native proletarians of Turkestan, therefore, should not appeal to the central Soviet power . . . but should themselves dissolve [the Turkestan and Tashkent soviets] by force, if such a force is available to the Muslim proletarians and peasants."[9] Stalin's endorsement of force favored the Tashkent soviet, which had a far superior military, but his ambivalent statement, added to Lenin's speech, signaled that the Bolsheviks could not be relied upon to preserve the colonial privileges that had played a central role in the uprising of Russian workers and soldiers in Turkestan.

Lenin's and Stalin's words, combined with continued silence toward the pleas of F. I. Kolesov, leader of the Turkestan soviet, to break Ataman Dutov's blockade and feed Turkestan produced an atmosphere of open disdain among the Tashkent soviet elite toward the center.[10] A. H. Brun, who had received a telegram signed by Lenin and Trotskii banning the recruitment of former prisoners of war into the Red Army, was told by Kolesov in January 1918 that the capital "is so very far away we do what seems right for us."[11] Delegates to the Fourth Regional Congress of Soviets, fearing Bolshevik support for a Central Asian–led government, issued a statement that read: "Considering the economic, cultural, national, and everyday peculiarities of the region, the congress considers necessary the formation of an autonomous Turkestan within the borders of a democratic Russia."[12] Leadership of this autonomy, vague in form, was limited to the working classes, with the implication that Central Asians lacked the development and consciousness to be "workers."[13] Socialist Revolutionary leader Cherneskii declared in *Svobodnyi Turkestan* on January 24 that such formal documents were unnecessary, as "we already have autonomy, since we do not communicate with Petrograd, and as for the administration of Turkestan, we administer it ourselves."[14]

Concerned by such declarations, Narkomnats dispatched P. A. Kobozev to lead a delegation to restore central authority in Turkestan. Successfully running Dutov's blockade, these representatives planned to force the inclusion of Central Asians in the Tashkent and Turkestan soviets, taking a step to fulfilling Lenin's dream of a Muslim revolutionary vanguard.[15] Kobozev confronted soviet leaders at the Fifth Regional

Congress of Soviets in April 1918. He opened the congress by reading a letter of greetings signed by Lenin and Stalin, which declared support for autonomy but requested the dispatch of an embassy to Moscow "to determine the relations of the government of your regions with the [central administration]."[16] Regional soviet leaders exploited this letter to declare a "Turkestan Autonomous Soviet Republic" and create a Turkestan Central Executive Committee (*TurkTsIK*) with the unique right to enact legislation within the province as well the prerogative to overrule any federal decrees to take effect within Turkestan.[17] Congress leaders balanced this rejection of central primacy by electing Kobozev as first head of the TurkTsIK. Kobozev, with Stalin's assistance, had managed to deliver more than one hundred wagons of grain to Tashkent through the blockade in April, reminding delegates of the potential benefits of central support.[18] In Moscow, Tashkent soviet delegate Troitskii justified the declaration of autonomy as necessary "given the mass of financial and economic problems that could be decided only by local authorities." He received assurances from Narkomnats that a strong soviet central state would assist in the region's industrialization.[19]

Kobozev, meanwhile, used his position to increase Central Asian participation in the Turkestan soviet republic. Ten Central Asians joined the thirty-six-person Council of People's Commissars (*sovnarkom*), which became the executive wing of the TurkTsIK. Kobozev established a regional Commissariat of Nationalities (*Turkkomnats*) and called for regional conferences to draw the local population toward soviet power.[20] Political opportunities attracted Central Asians. Many, including Jadids Munawwar Qari and Tursun Khojaev, admired the emancipatory and anticolonial rhetoric of Communism and shared Lenin's view of the need to create modern nations for the repressed peoples of the empire.[21] Nizametdin Khojaev, the former Tashkent spokesperson for the defeated Kokand Autonomy, joined the soviet government to uplift "dark" Central Asians, whom he and many Jadids saw as people in need of enlightenment.[22] Turar Rysqulov, a Kazakh who rose from a poor family to gain a place at a teacher's institute in Tashkent, became the most prominent local representative in soviet power. Declaring his unconditional allegiance to Bolshevism, Rysqulov emerged as Kobozev's chief ally at the age of twenty-four. Rysqulov argued that only the active guidance of a Central Asian vanguard elite could raise the level of the backward masses and allow productive participation in a new Communist order.[23]

Early efforts to include the Central Asian population in soviet power enjoyed limited success. Russian-dominated regional and local soviets resisted enacting political equality. Continued halfhearted efforts to establish an effective "Old City" soviet in Asian Tashkent were driven more by a desire to keep the existing Tashkent soviet purely ethnically Russian. *Nasha Gazeta* illuminated the attitude of Russian soviet members on July 14, 1918, arguing that "we cannot forget our status as conquerors and we must occupy an important position in the republic which befits our importance. . . . Our relations with the natives could never be one that prevails between equals."[24]

## City and Countryside, 1918–1919

Strains between Russians and Central Asians increased following Kobozev's early initiatives. Ataman Dutov's blockade of Turkestan tightened in May, heightening competition for local food supplies. Russians fanned out across the countryside. Turar Rysqulov characterized requisition squads, particularly army ones, as "drunk and violent . . . taking whatever suited them." They contributed to an "atmosphere of animosity" between Muslim party conference delegates and "comrade Russians."[25] Forced requisitions were drawing Central Asian peasants toward an anti-soviet movement, designated by its opponents as the *Basmachi* (bandits). The Basmachi included a wide range of opposition: Jadids and former leaders of the Kokand Autonomy who mistrusted soviet power, mullas calling for a holy war, landowners whose holdings had been seized by Russian peasants, and villagers, in many cases on the brink of starvation.[26] Basmachi leaders explored the possibility of alliances with Russian opposition to the soviet regime, particularly a conspiratorial officer group called the Turkestan Military Organization, but these efforts fizzled as violence increased in 1918–19.[27] Basmachi groups defended local villagers and attacked food collection agents, soldiers, and supply lines across Turkestan.[28] Requisitions and draught produced hunger and starvation among hundreds of thousands of peasants.[29] The Fergana valley, where an estimated 30 percent of the population died in 1918 alone, became the center of Basmachi operations. By summer 1919, the region was virtually cut off from soviet control.[30]

Violence was frequent and widespread. The Tashkent soviet confiscated food and animals from Kazakh nomads to the north, driving hundreds, starving, into Tashkent, and provoking a massive flight to Afghanistan and China.[31] Turar Rysqulov formed the Central Commission for the Struggle against Hunger (*Komgolod*) in November 1918 to assist the Kazakhs, but faced hostility from Russian-dominated provision committees. The latest wave of migrant Kazakhs once again inflated the number of hungry in Asian Tashkent, which stood officially at 26,000 in January 1919. Deaths from hunger were common.[32] Tashkent soviet officials refused to share requisitions that had allowed the raising of daily grain rations for Russian inhabitants, and closed hospitals to the ill from the Asian city.[33]

Alongside the violence, collection agents from Russian Tashkent's unions, enterprises, and even individual neighborhoods used barter and contractual agreements to obtain food from Central Asian and Russian peasants. These unofficial methods, as well as the rising bloodshed, prompted soviet officials to seek to plan harvests and food collections. Planning, however, was no less chaotic. Different organs within the TurkTsIK, district, local, and even railway soviets all devised independent designs.[34] Agents and squads from these organizations competed to convince peasants to adhere to their plans. Railway worker cooperatives proved most successful in pursuing agreements with village leaders, promising monetary payments and quality barter goods in exchange for food.[35] Tashkent railway workers offered products from tobacco and boot factories as well as bakeries they had taken over, and complemented foodstuffs obtained from villagers with produce from large tomato and fruit gardens on the outskirts of the city.[36] Metalworkers, following this example, appropriated soap, textile, and leather manufacturing enterprises in order to obtain barter goods.[37]

Frustrated by their inability to control the food supply, TurkTsIK leaders resorted to an acerbic anti-rural discourse that associated the peasantry, Russian or Central Asian, with subversive activities and linked their submission to an ultimate soviet victory. The attack began at the Seventh Congress of Soviets in March 1919, when the TurkTsIK food directorate blamed the "complete darkness" of Russian and Central Asian peasants in the fertile steppe regions of northern Turkestan for their refusal to oppose Ataman Dutov and their unwillingness to hand their grain over to soviet authorities.[38] Muslim peasants, directorate delegates argued, "thanks to their lack of political consciousness and age-old slavelike dependence on bais and capitalists, are deluding themselves, dying from hunger and becoming scoundrels, victims of their own appetite."[39] Even more frustrating were Russian peasant robber bands that were stealing food from Central Asian villagers, inflaming ethnic tensions as well as reducing the amount available to cities.

TurkTsIK food directorate head A. A. Kazakov employed such reports to introduce a grain monopoly on June 4, 1919.[40] Local soviets used the monopoly to justify increased collections. In the Tashkent district, agents came with revolvers to demand not only grain, but horses, and other goods that were never paid for nor returned.[41] City officials worried that such measures would increase Basmachi activity on the edges of Tashkent. Equally serious, the monopoly decreased the amount of goods available in the city, as local soviets were hoarding grain for themselves.[42] In a rare occurrence, the soviets of Russian and Asian Tashkent issued a joint protest against the monopoly, which stifled private trade, an important supplement to rations in the Russian section and the only food distribution mechanism in the Asian city.[43] The 1919 grain monopoly highlighted the interdependency between city and country in early Soviet Turkestan. But it failed to halt chaos in food collections or distribution. Hundreds of thousands of Central Asian peasants were starving. Basmachi forces were operating within fifty kilometers of Tashkent. Kobozev's inability to restore order compelled Moscow to send a more powerful commission to Turkestan, a region viewed as essential to the revolutionary designs and economic health of Soviet Russia.

## The Turkkomissiia: Enshrining Equality?

Orchestras, festivities, and welcome speeches greeted the arrival from Moscow of a new Turkestan Commission (*Turkkomissiia*), with a staff of nearly one hundred, on November 4, 1919.[44] Recalling the arrival of the first governor-general, the ceremonies signaled the region's elevated status under a new regime. Turkkomissiia head Shalva Eliava was nonetheless determined to differentiate himself from representatives of the tsar. As one of their first public acts, Turkkomissiia leaders ordered the removal of the statue honoring Governor-General Kaufman. A hammer and sickle replaced the most visible symbol of colonial rule in the last years of tsarist Tashkent.

Optimism permeated the arrival of the commission. On September 13, Red Army forces led by M. V. Frunze, now a member of the Turkkomissiia, had defeated Dutov's forces and restored all links between central Russia and Turkestan. Local political actors hoped that supplies of food and other vital goods would accompany the arrival of the high-level commission. Rising party stars Eliava, Frunze, V. V. Kuibyshev, F. I. Goloshchekin, Ia. E. Rudzutak and G. I. Bokii represented the central executive committee of the soviet state and the central committee of the Communist Party. Initial goodwill toward the commission, however, reflected vague hopes rather than any concrete understanding of its mission.

Turkkomissiia members arrived following a year of tumult. In January 1919, K. P. Osipov, the Turkestan soviet's commissar of war, attempted a coup in a conspiracy involving former tsarist officers.[45] Fragmentary evidence suggests conservative elements in Asian Tashkent and the head of the Tashkent railway workers' soviet, V. E. Agapov, who was resisting state efforts to curb the body's autonomy, also supported the coup.[46] Osipov, whose own motives remain unclear, killed the heads of the Turkestan and Tashkent soviets, V. D. Votintsev and N. V. Shumilov, local Communist Party leader I. Ia. Pershin, and other leading figures in regional and city governments, who became martyred in soviet lore as the "fourteen commissars." Confused accounts of the mutiny credit Hungarian prisoners of war for overcoming the mutineers. The failed coup's suppression included a search for "disloyal" and "bourgeois" elements in Russian Tashkent that led to four thousand deaths, with thousands more imprisoned and exiled.[47]

P. A. Kobozev, then still head of the Turkestan Autonomous Soviet Republic, had moved quickly to exploit the deaths of the "fourteen commissars," who had been leading opponents to greater Central Asian government representation. Kobozev created a "Muslim National Section" of the Communist Party. Munawwar Qari, Tursun Khojaev, and Turar Rysqulov created parallel organizations to encourage Central Asian participation in soviet power. Of the delegates to the Seventh Congress of Soviets in February 1919, half were of local origin.[48] This proportion aroused the ire of Russian representatives. Opposition, calling itself the "Old Communists," called for Kobozev's resignation. By August, Kobozev had fled Tashkent upon news of his planned arrest.[49] Kobozev's supporters battled the Old Communists at various congresses in the fall; both sides looked to the Turkkomissiia to break the deadlock.[50]

Kobozev, however, had done little to equalize social privileges. Russians and European prisoners of war still dominated the Red Guard, militias, and police. Russian Tashkent and other colonial enclaves continued inequitable ration policies. Central Asians faced requisitions even as they suffered from drought conditions. Kobozev recognized that violence and chaos in the countryside destroyed Turkestan's productivity, but had failed to find effective ways to address these issues.[51]

In this climate the Turkkomissiia set out to realize its mission. Two goals dominated its agenda. First, the commission planned to continue Kobozev's work to increase local participation in the soviet state and Communist Party. Aspirations of the region as a model postcolonial state persisted in Moscow, where it was hoped that Turkestan would become "a flower garden, wherein the bees of the neighboring lands of the Orient should take nourishment."[52] Circles of Indian communists, including Lenin's close associate M. N. Roy, arrived in Tashkent to plot a revolution to the east.[53] Second, the commission aspired to coordinate the regional economy with the center. Communist Party and soviet state leaders in Moscow were insistent on the need to restore cotton production to return to operation the textile factories of central Russia.[54] The Turkkomissiia, however, was not given any promise of food imports in order to entice farmers to return to producing cotton.

Turkkomissiia members moved quickly to abolish, in the words of V. I. Lenin, "privileges of one group over another." "Old Communists" were expelled from the party. These expulsions provoked a strong reaction. Turkkomissiia member Giorgii Safarov reported that "among the Russian population, not excluding workers, and even among communists, the attitude toward this new political course was semi-hostile." The Tashkent soviet resented losing political primacy, as well as prime office space, to the Turkkomissiia.[55] The Tashkent party organization declared that the commission "did not understand" the region.[56] Railway workers also attacked Moscow representatives, who had become known as the "centralizers." As the TurkTsIK sent a delegation to Moscow to protest the "conquest of Turkestan by soviet troops," stories of "soviet imperialism" circulated widely among Tashkent Russian socialists, who grumbled about a return of the "old regime." Rumors of railway worker plans to overthrow the commission in a "final October" proliferated.[57]

Tashkent Russian workers condemned any threat to their privileged status. They continued to portray the Central Asian population as "class enemies." The Turkkomissiia, for its part, decried the fracturing of the region, where local control (*vlast' na mestakh*) by Russian workers, soldiers, and prisoners of war dominated. The commission used class rhetoric to portray these actions as "petty bourgeois" and to decry the continued following of regional "demagogues."[58] Turkkomissiia members used central Red Army forces that had arrived after Dutov's defeat, as well as Moscow's authority, to begin a purge of the Communist Party and soviet state in Turkestan. Officials, officers, and soldiers accused of denying power to the Central Asian majority became prime targets. Over one thousand Russians were purged, ostensibly for "colonial" acts. Many of their crimes were mundane ones of abuse of power and corruption, and it is unclear from the records how many specifically involved an ethnic element.[59]

Turkkomissiia leaders consistently restated their view that Russian colonizers had brutally exploited the local population, who, as the oppressed, deserved to ascend to leadership posts within the party and state. Yet the commission retained a belief that the Russian proletariat, issuing from a more advanced society, needed to lead Central Asian lower classes, under the "yoke of bais, manaps [Kazakh tribal leaders], beks, and khans," to emancipation.[60] Its desire to initiate this transformation revealed a new vision of the "civilizing mission." This vision saw Central Asians as exploited by imperialists and capitalists and deserving, as oppressed peoples, emancipation and participation in a new socialist society. Yet in the end, racist beliefs in European superiority underpinned the Bolshevik civilizing mission. The local population was still considered behind according to Marxist stages of development. Commission leaders believed in their power to guide formerly colonized peoples toward civilization and an eventual equality, but would not tolerate any independent views or actions that compromised their primary mission of incorporating Turkestan into socialist Russia.

Central Asian activists nonetheless exploited the Turkkomissiia's arrival to advance their own goals. They used posts in party and state organs to unleash their own revolution, which, for the Jadids, was "comprehensible . . . only as national salvation."[61] Turar Rysqulov had built a regional organization through cells of the Muslim bureau (*Musbiuro*) of the Communist Party in 1919. These cells played an important administrative role in regions lacking a large Russian community, and were viewed with suspicion by the Old Communists.[62] Musbiuro delegates to the Fifth Party Congress in January 1920 seized upon the absence of purged Russian communists to pass resolutions liquidating all national inequities and "eliminating colonizers" in the party. Communist members in Asian Tashkent declared the intention not to take party orders unless approved by the Musbiuro.[63] Congress members voted to rename the party the "Communist Party of Turkic Peoples" to rule over a unified Turkestan republic. The use of the name "Turkic" instead of "Muslim" appeared to indicate not only a secular orientation for these local Communists, but a desire to express superiority over Persian-speaking members of the local population, who themselves were agitating for separate national rights as Tajiks. The congress elected Tursun Khojaev as party head, and Rysqulov prepared to call for the Turkkomissiia's expulsion, on the grounds it violated territorial integrity of an "autonomous" Turkestan.[64]

Tursun Khojaev's reign was short. Policies limiting the grain monopoly to Europeans, taxing Muslims according to the sharia, and most notably, forming a Turkic Red Army, proved excessive to Turkkomissiia member M. V. Frunze. Frunze declared that new party leaders were damaging commission goals of restoring order, reorganizing economic life, and ending the most egregious injustices against Central Asians. Nothing was said about political or social equality as an aim.[65] Turkkomissiia members retreated to a language of class similar to that of local Russians. One report to Moscow stated that "the type of Muslims that succeed in this regime are not workers, but corrupt mediators and traders"[66] Autonomist initiatives only sowed distrust between the proletariats of exploited and exploiting nations. The Turkkomissiia declared it would keep control until the Muslim masses were ready to assume power.[67]

Commission purges in spring 1920 attacked "pan-Turkic nationalists" as well as "Great Russian chauvinists."[68] Rysqulov and other Jadids, followed by Eliava and Rudzutak, made the trek to Moscow in May to press their respective cases to central authorities. Lenin, after debates within the central party, supported the Turkkomissiia, despite the damage this caused to his dream of "setting the east ablaze" via anticolonial revolutions. He demanded, however, an increase in expulsions of Russian "colonizers."[69] Nizametdin Khojaev, deputy head of TurkTsIK, resigned in protest in July 1920. His letter to Moscow regretted the "very difficult" situation in Turkestan due to the "incorrect role of the Turkkomissiia in soliciting support of the local colonizers," and the "state of soviet, civil, and military apparatuses . . . open only to the European population." "All of this," wrote Khojaev, "offers no possibility for full participation of the native poor in the construction of a soviet society, which increasingly leaves colonizing elements in roles of soviet builders, stifling the tasks of the Russian Communist Party in Turkestan."[70]

Khojaev's letter highlighted the growing links between central and local Russians in mid-1920. The Central Committee of the Russian Communist Party had begun to refer to the "vanguard" role of workers in guiding Central Asian society toward socialist goals, even as it recognized they had so far failed miserably in this task.[71] The party reflected language used by Lenin himself in his November 1917 address, when he characterized Muslim lower classes as "toilers" (*trudiashchiisia*) instead of "workers" (*rabochie*), indicating his own belief of these peoples as lower on the Communist evolutionary scale. Lenin and party members in Moscow appeared convinced by Turkkomissiia arguments that Turks and Muslims in the Communist Party, in large part intellectuals, were hostile to the working class. The declining importance of revolutionary internationalism in the early 1920s helped to seal the fate of the Turkic Communists. Purges affected Central Asians and Russians alike, as the Turkkomissiia sought to subject Turkestan to central authority. The commission hoped to realize on the ground what Moscow had done administratively in May 1922, when the Turkestan Autonomous Soviet Socialist Republic (Turkestan ASSR) was declared on the basis of, and subject to, the constitution of the Russian Soviet Federated Socialist Republic (RSFSR). Administrative control, however, meant little as long as social and economic crises festered.

At an open meeting at Tashkent's Coliseum theater at the beginning of December 1919, Ia. E. Rudzutak had outlined the Turkkomissiia's plan to centralize food supplies as part of an overall plan of economic development for Turkestan. Critical to this vision was overcoming the "separatism" of collection agents and organizations in a region where "states exist within states."[72] He castigated railway workers, miners, and leather workers for operating their own food organs, factories, and other enterprises to produce goods for sale and for barter. Ruduztak also sought to curb inequalities between Russians and Central Asians that had produced so much violence. The Turkkomissiia member, however, did not mention the main goal guiding these aims: the ultimate restoration of cotton exports to central Russia.[73] Small-scale agreements between peasants and workers, combined with ethnic and social tensions and the continuing inability of the center to bring food to Turkestan, posed potent challenges to this vision from 1920 to 1923.

The Tashkent soviet resisted pressure from Rudzutak to cease requisitions from Asian Tashkent and local villagers on the outskirts of the city, as well as include Central Asians in a rationing plan.[74] Fearing a Russian revolt, the Turkkomissiia did not press the issue. Instead, it established a bureau of complaints to investigate individual cases of ethnic abuse. Bureau investigations, however, focused not on Tashkent Russian workers, but on settler peasants. Following 1917, Russian peasants had seized lands from settled and nomadic Central Asians, ostensibly to establish artels or communes in line with socialist goals. The Bureau of Complaints portrayed these peasants as far from ideal Communists, lacking the knowledge and discipline to work the land and falling into laziness and drunkenness.[75] Carrying with them, as did many urban Bolsheviks, deep suspicions of peasant loyalty to socialism, the Turkkomissiia used anti-rural rhetoric and policies to gain the support of local Russian workers and soldiers, whom they did not feel powerful enough to confront.[76]

Russian peasants were chosen as an enemy also because their persecution avoided an awkward confrontation with the Central Asian majority, which would risk inflaming the Basmachi rebellion and contradict the Turkkomissiia's claims to eliminate colonialist legacies. In October, food supply director T. Shevchenko wrote in the official newspaper of the TurkTsIK, *Izvestiia*, that Russian peasants had proven more hostile to outside authority than their passive and poorer Central Asian counterparts.[77] Ignorant Muslim peasants, Shevchenko, argued, had at least the potential to awake to the bai's despotism; Russian farmers, however, manifested no empathy toward the workers of the city or the revolution.[78] Decrying ostensibly wealthy Russian peasants, *Izvestiia* complained that "grain must be torn from the hands of the countryside, for it is the source of everything!"[79] Lost in this rhetoric was the reality of a starving region. Economic and administrative chaos left many farmers without seeds for planting and little incentive to grow for more than basic needs. Turar Rysqulov, in his position as head of Komgolod, estimated that half of the population of Turkestan in the countryside was starving in 1919, as food production had declined by half from two years earlier.[80]

Rudzutak's words did nothing to even ethnic inequality at the administrative level. No Central Asians were placed on the Turkkomissiia or regional soviet food supply boards, which continued to divert grain to Russian cities in Turkestan.[81] Even as starvation returned to Asian Tashkent in 1919–20, the Tashkent soviet dissolved the "Old City" soviet provision committee and banned non-Russians from seeking food from any state organ. The Turkestan soviet replicated this latter policy, which continued throughout the early postrevolutionary years. Rudzutak himself turned to "vanguard" Russian workers to execute the next phase of his plan to deliver control of the food supply, and the economy, to central hands.

## Compulsion, Chaos, and Withdrawal: Delivering Food to the City, 1920–1922

In February 1920, squads of Russian workers gathered at the Tashkent railway station. Turkkomissiia members, soviet delegates, union heads, and other representatives of worker organizations met them with flags and music.[82] Soviet leaders had delegated several crucial responsibilities to new provision brigades (*prodovol'stvennyi otriady,* or *prodotriady*) composed of these workers from factories, enterprises, and ministries of Tashkent. Brigades were to obtain food from the countryside, through purchase, trade, or confiscation; convince peasants to increase their yields for the following year; carry out agitational work; and assure the loyalty of local officials. Brigade members, however, rapidly discovered the complexity of the countryside, where alliances between collection agents, local bureaucrats, and peasants formed and dissolved against a backdrop of hardship and starvation. In the end, efforts to use exhortation and force to establish a planned economy yielded to micro-relations driven by market exchanges in rural Turkestan.

Rudzutak and Communist Party members in Tashkent saw the brigades as a way to introduce class relations into the countryside and reduce the power of the market. Borrowing discourse from central Russia, members charged brigade leaders with assembling committees of poor peasants to crush the power of "village kulaks and speculators." Workers would be able, it was thought, to convince peasants of their shared legacy of exploitation. Brigade members had the right to appropriate all food beyond peasants' personal needs without compensation. Turar Rysqulov offered the only cautionary words at the January 1920 conference that debated this policy. Rysqulov approved of brigades for Russian villages, but argued that "the city must understand the Muslim mass has a different psychology than the Russian peasants. . . . [W]e need to keep in mind the fanaticism of the population and the danger of approaching them."[83] Rysqulov mobilized the image of the "fanatic Muslim" to shelter local villages from the brigades and prevent a resurgence in the rebel Basmachi movement. Conference leaders voted to send, when possible, local Muslims as mediators for brigades operating in the Central Asian countryside, but otherwise dismissed Rysqulov's warnings.[84]

As the music played to send off these brigades, leaders sensed their charges, including railway workers, carpenters, teachers, and tailors, were not the ideal messengers of soviet power and communist equality in the countryside.[85] Many brigade members reported to the station drunk.[86] Unions, enterprises, and ministries had dispatched not the "most dedicated" workers sought by the TurkTsIK Provision Bureau, but those they desired to shed. These workers displayed shifting loyalties toward their mission, which presented them with the contradictory roles of extracting food from the countryside while attracting the peasantry toward soviet power.[87] Initial encounters between brigades and indigenous villagers immediately soured once the former's task became clear. When available, Central Asian mediators made initial approaches, but violent searches unfailingly accompanied words of class solidarity and the need to feed the revolutionary cities. Anyone deemed an "exploiter" or "speculator" had their food and goods seized without compensation. In Russian settlements, efforts to establish class categories ignored the general economic equilibrium of the former migrants, who had barely established their farms before drought, a great equalizer, wiped them out.[88] To Central Asians, the language of class was completely alien.

Brigade members' behavior increased villagers' antipathy. A local militia member in Buka, near Tashkent, witnessed "impertinent" acts from the ninth provision brigade as it confiscated material, including valuable carpets, from traders. Squad commanders did not discourage "dark work," including beatings, assaults, robberies, and various other "scandals." Small bands roamed the countryside in search of personal gain, robbing nomads and peasants of food, goods, and animals.[89] In other brigades, apathy prevailed. Some workers, fearing retribution from peasants, remained in their dormitories. Up to half of the brigades returned to Tashkent long before their appointed tasks were complete. In some cases, members robbed supplies from their own brigades and disappeared.[90] The Turkkomissiia purged the provision brigades in October, but replacing these purged elements was not a simple task.[91] Accompanying official reports of a Basmachi resurgence in response to these brigades were stories retold on the streets of Russian Tashkent, including one of five brigade members decapitated and left naked on display. Russian peasants also killed brigade members.[92]

Brigade members faced strong opposition as well from village party and state officials. Brigade leader E. Shevchenko, working in Pishpek, found local officials had already confiscated grain supplies, and would surrender them only for market prices; otherwise, they would sell the grain to "foreigners." Shevchenko condemned his superiors for sending his brigade into such a hostile environment:

> "You sent us from Tashkent. . . . [E]verybody told us to go quickly, for bread was lying there and rotting, and not being sent as peasants were not giving it, but now we see otherwise, we are convinced that the hindrance is not here, but there, from whence we came. Local power is to blame, and even more to blame is you, who sent us here, that is central power. . . .[93]

Shevchenko's censure of "central" power—the TurkTsIK and Turkkomissiia—extended to its failure to ensure transport so foodstuffs collected by provision brigades reached cities before spoiling. Railway workers diverted wagons to deliver goods from their own collection agents. Lack of control over village officials and railway workers, among others, defeated central efforts to control provisioning.

Barter goods—textiles, seed, and tools to tea, tobacco, and alcohol—proved the only way to gain food without violence. As across Russia, central authorities in Turkestan lacked such products.[94] But factory, enterprise, and union collection units—still operating alongside the state brigades—were able to provide these goods. Local soviets, including railway worker soviets, also had superior barter supplies to offer peasants.[95] Russian and Central Asian peasants traded with these bodies while resisting the state provision brigades. Resistance tactics ranged from requesting Basmachi protection to temporarily abandoning villages when provision brigades were operating in the region.[96] Other villagers agreed to brigade leaders' requests to establish committees of poor peasants to uncover speculators, only to disband them within hours of the brigades' departure.[97] Giorgii Safarov, on the agitational train "Red East," characterized Central Asian peasants as "terrorized" by the brigades and other urban invaders. Safarov arrested numerous Russian officials, militia, provision brigade, and other collection squad members in the summer of 1920. Yet he condemned Central Asian resistance as provoked by "Muslim nationalists" aligned with "bourgeois" elements.[98] Turkkomissiia leaders, seeking to halt the most egregious abuses of Russian power, did not challenge its foundations.

In Tashkent, workers were perceiving food brigades to be both an ineffective collection method and a dangerous assignment. State grain collections amounted to less than half of the targeted amount in 1920.[99]

The rationing system was collapsing. Finding work through a union or in an enterprise or ministry with its own provision apparatus became critical. Neighborhood committees also coordinated food deliveries.[100] A regional food supply conference held in early summer recognized in this atmosphere the growing reliance of urban residents on the market.[101]

## Playing the Market in Soviet Tashkent

Most Tashkent residents depended on the market to bring needed food-stuffs. Unrestrained inflation and the spread of communist ideology nonetheless reinvigorated frustration with market mechanisms. Once more, the market became linked in the press and popular imagination to Central Asian "speculators," eliding images of race and class. At the same time, Russian workers themselves were criticized for supporting unofficial methods of food collection. Communist commentators grudgingly recognized that Central Asian traders played vital roles in local society. Unease over the market in Tashkent combined with uncertainty over the effectiveness of existing provision policies.

*Izvestiia* wrote in the spring of 1920 that Russians had fallen prey to the evil charms of the market. A "wild dance" of prices on products was negatively affecting the psychology of the masses. The newspaper pointed its finger toward Bukhara, where a successful Red Army invasion had deposed the emir and installed in power Jadidist "Young Bukharans." Largely ignored by provision agents and requisition squads, Bukhara reaped a good harvest.[102] *Izvestiia* condemned the former emirate as the "nest of all speculatory operations in Turkestan." Evil price-fixers manipulated supplies.[103] The article also sought to combat increased frustration with Moscow, which, despite the end of Dutov's blockade, had still not supplied food to the region. Lenin had written to the Young Bukharans, asking them to send grain not to Turkestan, but to hungry regions of the RSFSR.[104] *Izvestiia* argued that popular discontent against the central Communists was misdirected. Food supply difficulties were the product of "internal republics"—unions, enterprises, and ministries—who were ignoring the TurkTsIK and producing a system that could only be described as "economic anarchy." As a result, Central Asian speculator "parasites" maintained control over the proletariat.[105]

Fears in Russian Tashkent of local control over the food supply produced rumors of insidious plots. One 1920 feuilleton by the author "Lucifer" in *Izvestiia* linked shortages of specific foods to a Central Asian design to attack Russian culture. According to "Lucifer," "There is no bread! We are being fed with rice. How offensive!"[106] Central Asian villagers were concentrating price rises on goods, such as potatoes, preferred by Russians. A later feuilleton, entitled "Who Is Eating Whom," satirized rumors, which had led to several complaints to the police, of evil Muslim traders, or "swallowers," mixing human flesh in beef or forcing mutton on Russian consumers.[107] Russians faced losing their Russianness by consuming local foods or losing their humanity by becoming unwitting cannibals. Tashkent commentators condemned Russian futurist intellectuals, recently expelled from Moscow, who were not only proudly partaking in Muslim food, but wearing Muslim clothing. In culture as in politics, Moscow seemed to be promoting, if not Central Asian supremacy, a dangerous hybridity that threatened Russian Tashkent's future.[108]

Unlike the situation in the imperial era, protests over food supplies and high prices did not escalate into protests or riots in the bazaars in 1919–21. Privileged Russian workers used the bazaars to supplement goods they obtained through their provision organs.[109] We have no record of the likely struggles or behavior of other Russians, particularly women, during this period. By late spring 1921, a good harvest, a decline in Basmachi operations near Tashkent, and a reduction in violent methods used by food brigades improved food supplies to the cities. Lenin's introduction of the New Economic Policy (NEP) in March 1921 throughout soviet territory only confirmed the primacy of market relations in Turkestan.[110] NEP nonetheless sounded the death knell for the already discredited state provision organs. Well-publicized trials of personnel accused of corruption and criminal activity ended the era of these bodies by September 1921.[111] Bazaars remained the primary site of food exchanges throughout Tashkent, although unions, enterprises, and ministries continued to cultivate barter arrangements with local villages.

Tashkent suddenly gained a mythical status throughout the Russian empire for abundance, and became the preferred destination for residents fleeing the famine-stricken Volga region. Aleksandr Skoblev detailed the myths in a novel based on his own desperate journey to find food for his family: "Again the men in the streets [of Samara] were talking about Tashkent, letting their thoughts play about the city that none had ever seen, picturing its vineyards, teasing their fancy with stories of two kinds of wheat growing at once. Prices were low. A paradise!"[112] Thousands of Volga refugees waited for weeks for Tashkent-bound trains.[113] Soviet officials first welcomed these refugees, seeing hosting them as a symbol of renewed prosperity. Private spectacles and concerts raised funds for orphanages and canteens. But, as in the tsarist era, fears of a city overrun supplanted desires to gain repute in the metropole through accommodating outsiders from elsewhere in central Russia. Russian Tashkent, unlike most cities in the Russian civil war, had gained population. Slavic farmers fearing ethnic violence or requisition squads flooded the city, whose population was estimated in 1920 at 110,000, more than 30,000 more than during the war years.[114] The 7,000 new migrants risked returning disease and malnutrition to Russian Tashkent. One commentator in *Izvestiia*, echoing tsarist-era language, complained that the arrival of poor migrants blurred the boundaries between Russian colonizers and the Central Asian colonized, providing easy targets for "speculators indulging in a bloody orgy over desperate, hungry citizens."[115]

The Tashkent soviet worried that such rhetoric against speculators would lead to attacks on the market. Hostile toward Central Asian traders since its inception, the soviet now saw the market as its preferred food supply mechanism, as it undercut the power of "independent" provision agents tied to individual workplaces or organizations. Central Asian traders, for the first time in the Tashkent Russian press, gained plaudits for resistance to "colonialist" behaviors. Traders were praised for fighting back with fists or sticks against Russian workers and soldiers perpetrating "all types of evil acts."[116] The soviet cooperated with the Turkkomissiia to punish railway workers accused of stealing food and animals from Central Asian peasants as part of a new "Campaign against Colonizers" in 1920–21. Tashkent soviet leaders also decried roving bands of soldiers in the countryside as "a circle of scoundrels bringing shame on the entire Red Army."[117] Railway workers continued to defy TurkTsIK orders and maintained independent provision organs, exporting surplus food to central Russia beginning in 1921–22.[118]

The Tashkent soviet, TurkTsIK, and Turkkomissiia all used campaigns against "colonizers" to consolidate control in 1921. The Turkkomissiia used new powers of taxation to attack independent supply organs.[119] Food obtained through taxation went primarily to central Russia, where famine continued to threaten. Renowned author Maksim Gorkii pleaded to the commission to save the "representatives of Russian sciences, people who are famous throughout the world . . . who now resemble starving Hindus [*sic*]."[120] Exports continued even as drought hit the Fergana valley, causing tens of thousands of Central Asians to starve. This famine, combined with Red Army strength, an end to requisition squads, and internal Central Asian dissent, sapped much of the strength of the Basmachi movement. By October 1922 many of the major leaders of the movement had surrendered.[121] Only in winter 1923 did Fergana valley residents see assistance from the Turkestan government.

Ambivalence toward the market marked the early NEP years. An April 1922 TurkTsIK decree allowed free trade in agricultural, artisanal, and factory goods not specifically designated to the state. As across the Soviet Union, Tashkent communists saw in the reinvigorated market a failure of a rational socialist regime to defeat a chaotic system controlled by class, and, in their case, ethnic enemies.[122] The day after the decree was released, *Izvestiia* published a poem by the renowned Russian worker-poet Pavel Druzhinin, entitled "Bazaar":

> Like a strange greedy beast, with a cruel horrible cry
> The foul bazaar opens its mouth wide
> These are our days of shame, of unspoken words
> These are our days—of ignorance and nightmares[123]

The use of the term "bazaar" instead of the Russian word for market (*rynok*) had special resonance in Tashkent, where Russians linked trade to the Central Asian population. As inflation rose rapidly in 1921–22, small-scale confrontations between Russian consumers and Central Asian merchants occurred in bazaars citywide.[124] A return to the market, which had brought food, had reduced the Basmachi threat, and had saved Russian workers from dangerous ventures into the countryside, nonetheless underwent no serious challenges until Stalin's rise to power in the late 1920s.

## Cotton, the Central Asian Economic Council, and the New/Old Colony

An improving food situation, alternating purges of "bourgeois nationalist" Central Asians and "chauvinist" or "colonizer" Russians, and a solid Red Army presence had brought a degree of government stability and control to Soviet Turkestan. The Turkkomissiia's key remaining task involved the linking of the region's economy to the RSFSR. Lenin and central Bolsheviks remained determined to restore the region as a cotton producer and restart textile factories throughout Russia. Voices in Turkestan opposed this continuation of tsarist colonial policy. Rudzutak had written on behalf of the Turkkomissiia to party and state leaders in June 1920 that a renewed cotton monoculture threatened to enslave the population once more to bais and kulaks waiting to reassert themselves. Turkestan needed to be industrialized.[125] Rudzutak's words were ignored. The Turkkomissiia dutifully continued work on cotton development, announcing numerous initiatives to encourage production, including assistance with labor and supplies, as well as establishing a congress of cotton-growers to discuss issues such as fixed prices for the plant. Requests by Lenin and Gorkii for Turkestan grain to feed starving areas of Russia in 1921 only temporarily halted central plans.[126] Representatives of ministries in Moscow dictated a firm policy of returning the land to cotton production as soon as possible. A Main Cotton Committee of Turkestan established purchase prices of cotton at 2.5 times those of grain and eliminated taxes on cotton.[127] No immediate increase was seen, however, in lands devoted to cotton, which had declined by 80 percent since the war years. Central planners and Turkestan residents both declared that only the delivery of food to the region would lead to growers shifting crops to cotton.[128]

Plans nonetheless began to integrate Central Asia fully into the polity and the economy of the RSFSR. In spring 1922, the Central Committee of the Communist Party created a new Central Asian Bureau to act as the leading organ in the region. The bureau was to coordinate economic and administrative plans to design a formal union of Turkestan with the semi-independent protectorates of Bukhara and Khiva as a first step to integration with the newly created Union of Soviet Socialist Republics. A March 1–5, 1923, conference in Tashkent created the Central Asian Economic Council, a permanent executive organ to regulate, supervise, and coordinate all aspects of the regional economy. Rudzutak, despite earlier misgivings, took the lead in this conference.[129] Including leading Central Asian Communists such as Rysqulov and Bukharan leader Faizulla Khojaev, the conference declared the council to be about much more than the reinstitution of a tsarist economic policy. A telegram sent to V. I. Lenin hailed the first steps toward "full freedom of the toiling masses of the east."[130] Other telegrams sent to Stalin and head of the Central Executive Committee of the Union of Soviet Socialist Republics Kalinin saluted the great significance for national relations and economic growth of a Central Asia now comfortably under a soviet roof.

Many Tashkent Russians maintained their distrust of these initiatives. Imports of grain recommenced to Turkestan in March 1923.[131] Even as Tashkent Russian Communists argued that these supplies would restore Russian prominence by "finishing the speculators," the TurkTsIK was planning to move "lazy" Russian peasants back to Ukraine and reduce the lots of other settlers, ostensibly in the name of national equality but likely in recognition that Russians were less likely than Central Asian peasants to grow cotton.[132] In the cities, meanwhile, according to police reports, Russians were already highly agitated about transfers of some factories to private hands, which they felt was a precursor to "eliminating industry completely" in Tashkent. Commerce, identified with the Central Asians, had returned as part of an ostensibly socialist order while industrial progress was once more deemed more suitable for central Russia. Was this a renewed colonial status, where the economic interests of the metropole predominated and, as before the arrival of Governor-General Kaufman, where the colonized population was seen as more important than local Russians?[133]

Tashkent Russian workers retained a significant degree of power even as Bolshevik central authorities tightened their grip over the city and region. Languages of class and legacies of colonialism combined to privilege the Russian "proletariat" as the leading force of progress, destined to civilize the local population and modernize Central Asia. Words and actions of central Bolshevik representatives nonetheless threatened the power that had accrued to the Tashkent soviet and local Russian workers following the 1917 revolutions. For the first time, the metropole was determined to give Central Asians prominent political roles and a share of executive power. Even as the Turkkomissiia beat back a bid for an independent "Turkic republic," it continued arrests and purges of Russian "chauvinists" and "colonizers." By 1923, Moscow had allowed private commerce, inextricably connected to local Central Asians, to prevail. Tashkent's, and Turkestan's, economies were tightly subjected to the center, with the city and region earmarked to feed industrial Russia with primary goods. Dreams of the latest generation of Russian leaders in Tashkent for progress were lost.

Early postrevolutionary Tashkent once more exposed interdependencies in colonial society, this time between city and village as well as between colonizer and colonized. Russian workers cooperated as well as struggled with Central Asian peasants to gain food at a time of great need. Barter and various exchange arrangements proved far more effective than violence, which threatened at points to bring open rebellion into Tashkent. Yet even in these exchanges, the balance of power clearly favored the colonizer. Russians possessed the political, administrative, and, most importantly, military strength. The central Red Army only confirmed the primacy of Europeanized military forces made clear post-1917 by the liquidation of the Kokand Autonomy. Turar Rysqulov and other Jadids could use their positions to publicize inequalities on the basis of race, but in the end had to rely upon Russian executive power to rectify the situation. Central Bolsheviks, for the most part, sincerely believed in minimizing differences between Russians and Central Asians, but only on their terms, at their pace. In the meantime, thousands in Asian Tashkent, and hundreds of thousands across Turkestan, died while food supplies were being inequitably distributed to Russians within, or even beyond, Turkestan. Ideas and practices of European, white, colonial superiority trumped socialist internationalism and liberation.

# Conclusion

Governor-General K. P. fon Kaufman and the first generation of tsarist administrators in Tashkent began their mission with confidence. Imperial rule in Central Asia could bear witness to a state now ready, in the wake of the Great Reforms, to assume its place among modern Western empires, and perhaps score a victory against Great Britain, Russia's main rival in Europe and Asia. Administrators, scholars, and businessmen arrived from central Russia, to seek promotions, knowledge, or wealth, as well as advance the fortunes of this new imperial possession and the empire as a whole. Kaufman sought to establish a colonial administration that would ensure peace and stability, and gradually attract Central Asians to "civilization." Russian Tashkent, designed to resemble the most modern of tsarist and European cities, St. Petersburg and post-1848 Paris, was at the center of Kaufman's plan to showcase the power and culture of the colonizer. N. A. Maev and other intellectuals who occupied leading posts in the tsarist administration expressed even loftier goals. They, along with some commentators from the central press, saw Russian Tashkent as a city of the future, freed from deadening national traditions that had so delayed modern reforms in the metropole. Russians could combine their history of interethnic contact with new, progressive methods of rule to demonstrate their superiority to Western nations in matters of empire.

Central Russian Tashkent's stately architecture, gardens, and broad, tree-lined boulevards impressed Western visitors, remained a point of pride for tsarist elites, and attracted many wealthy Central Asians to reside as well as work. Empire offered opportunities as well as challenges to indigenous Tashkent residents, who had grown accustomed to control from outside forces. Tsarist administrators needed the cooperation of important sections of the Central Asian population to rule the region in a cost-efficient manner. Notables in Tashkent pledged outward allegiance to the tsar in exchange for assurances of political and cultural autonomy. As we have seen, tsarist elites saw fit to violate written and tacit agreements with Central Asian notables during times of crisis. Yet imperial administrators, some fearing rebellion and others seeking financial opportunities, patronized these notables. Central Asian mercantile elites, who benefited following the conquest from new markets, in both Russian Tashkent and European Russia, joined notables in gaining access to the halls of power. They spoke at tsarist ceremonies, dined in the mansion of the governor-general, and visited with other leading imperial officials. Many, from Sattar Khan to Arif Khoja, circulated among the intellectual as well as political elites of Russian Tashkent. Central Asian Jadids joined these circles even as they condemned colonial rule. Central Asians below the rungs of the elite, from water managers to healers and petty traders, sought to profit from an expanded population and economy. Many established social and economic contacts with the Russians living across the Ankhor canal. Intercultural contacts were mutual and widespread: Russians and Central Asians used each other's court systems, and crossed the Ankhor canal to celebrate each other's holidays. Such relationships formed the backbone of a mediating mechanism between tsarist-era colonizers and the Central Asian population, and provided Tashkent with outward peace from the conquest to the First World War. During that period only, amid a cholera epidemic in 1892, did large-scale ethnic violence occur in the city.

Imperial rule, however, was neither benign nor stable. Tsarist, and later soviet, power flowed primarily from the military barracks outside the borders of city. Russian and European officers and soldiers continually displayed their vast superiority in arms and martial knowledge. Tsarist military personnel killed hundreds of Central Asians to suppress protests and acts deemed a threat to colonial rule, from the 1892 anti-cholera demonstration to the Kokand Autonomy of 1917–18. Equally importantly, frequent violence and compulsion occurred on an everyday level. Officers and soldiers used verbal and physical abuse to express their power over local Central Asians on the streets of Tashkent. Tsarist elites required that Central Asians—including notables—encountering them on the streets perform gestures of submission or face punishment. Notables gained privileges only if they delivered substantial taxation revenue to imperial authorities, who then focused their spending on Russian Tashkent. Many Central Asians used personal connections to imperial agents to triumph over their rivals, shifting relationships of power in the Asian city. Yet these connections did not allow the local population as a whole to gain greater rights. Russians across the social and political spectrum decried Central Asian efforts for a stronger political voice in the early twentieth century. Leaders of the Tashkent soviet raided the Asian city on several occasions in search of food and other goods. The violence of the postrevolutionary years, by severing links with local notables and traders, increased suffering on both sides of the Ankhor canal.

Divisions within the Russian community, as well as between colonizer and colonized, intensified even as Tashkent enjoyed economic growth. Intellectuals serving in the tsarist administration, who envisioned the city as a model of a new, open society, quickly came to realize that Kaufman and successive governors-general sought to replicate, instead of remake, tsarist mechanisms of state control. The clash between a strong state and a strong, progressive society, an obshchestvo, increased as St. Petersburg turned away from modernizing reform at the turn of the century. Yet progressive and conservative functionaries joined commercial and professional elites in Russian Tashkent to condemn a vital motor of early economic development: the "proletariat." Even as intellectuals and administrators in Russian Tashkent expressed perpetual concern over their community's vulnerability as a small minority in Central Asia, lower-class Slavic settlers were treated as unwelcome interlopers. The mud huts and dirt-filled streets of their settlements, established between the new city's radial boulevards, mocked Russian Tashkent's modern urban design. Characterized as dirty, drunk, and ragged, these lower-class Russians were uncomfortable reminders of a backward peasant Russia on the one hand, and the negative features of modern European urbanization on the other. Plebeian Russians dissolved boundaries that tsarist elites had set between privileged, modern, orderly European colonizers and lowly, backward and dirty Central Asians. Absent in Russian Tashkent were Eurasianist voices and Slavophile voices to promote the rural or Eastern aspects of Russia's identity. Boundaries of class, in some ways, proved less yielding than those of race; no poor Russians dined with the governor-general or could exploit the rhetoric of the "civilizing mission." Even poor Russians, however, found ways to benefit from their whiteness. Many took positions in the labor force above Central Asian counterparts and joined in the assaults and violence against the colonized population.

Russian skilled worker activists, frustrated by their isolation as the "proletariat," turned to open opposition against imperial authorities. Greater access to the benefits of colonial privilege following the 1905 revolution failed to forestall their drive for political power. Activist workers considered themselves forces of progress against a reactionary regime that denied rather than encouraged important aspects of European modernity, including democracy and civil rights. Despite condemning "uncivilized" tsarist treatment toward the colonized population, however, these workers neither demanded nor, later, extended such modern privileges to Central Asians. Rather, they sought to secure their own rights as colonizers. Perpetuating old and mobilizing new images of Central Asian otherness and backwardness, leaders of the Tashkent soviet claimed that the local poor lacked a sufficient "class consciousness" to participate in a modern, socialist society. Ironically, colonized Central Asians emerged primarily in soviet rhetoric as class enemies, dominated by wealthy capitalists as well as reactionary mullas.

In imperial Tashkent, racism became intertwined with languages of class. Racial and social stereotypes emerged early in Tashkent. Russians replicated European imperialist discourse that condemned the colonized as beholden to a backward cultural and religious system, as well as employed vocabulary used in St. Petersburg to condemn ignorant Russian peasants and workers. Languages of otherness intensified as Central Asians surpassed the Russians in domains, such as engineering and medicine, considered "modern." This frustration became an important factor in pushing Tashkent Russian elites to isolate themselves from Slavic newcomers who provided an uncomfortable reminder of the semi-Asiatic rural Russian as an archetype for the nation. Administrators and intellectuals in Russian Tashkent employed a peaceful Central Asian demonstration in 1892 to portray the local population as fanatics and demons, unwilling and unable to accept "civilizing" advances offered to them by the Russian population; at the same time, lower-class Russians also received blame for their willingness to abandon tenets of order and science. The strong rhetoric that characterized the tsarist reaction to the cholera riot of 1892 belied, or perhaps betrayed, self-doubt as to the potential of Russians as European colonizers. By the early twentieth century, as liberal Muslim thinkers adapted European ideas of modernity on the one hand, and poor Russian migrants flooded Tashkent and Turkestan while a conservative tsar ruled in St. Petersburg on the other, some Russian intellectuals in Tashkent wondered if civilization and backwardness had switched sides. Perhaps the civilizing mission needed to be applied to Russians themselves, elites as well as lower classes. In a sign of the extent of a fin-de-siècle confusion, as well as despondency, that swept across from Europe, both Central Asian and Russian modernist elements in Tashkent predicted decline for their own, backward, societies and discussed progress as best exemplified in their neighbors.

The use of the concept of race (*rasa*) itself reflected the confused nature of Russian colonialism. Russian intellectuals used the term very rarely, perhaps unsure of its scientific validity, or perhaps uncomfortable with many racial schema that placed a Slavic race somewhere between Europeans and Asians. The use of such a definitive marker may also have proven damaging to Russian intellectuals' efforts to present themselves, and their nation, as "universal civilizers," capable of bridging gaps between East and West. Such uncertainties, as discussed above, had done little to prevent other devices to racialize the relationship between Russians and Central Asians, particularly the trope of dirtiness. The term "race" did make its appearance at crisis moments, when boundaries between colonizers and colonized appeared most threatened. It is significant to note that the Russian Orientalists who immersed themselves in local culture, living in Asian Tashkent or Central Asian villages, learning the local language, reading and translating oral and written poems and stories, appeared among the most hostile toward granting increased social opportunities or political rights to the local population. In 1903, N. P. Ostroumov concluded that "I have since 1877 observed the native inhabitants, and also on the basis of historical facts . . . I have come to the conviction that a full coming together [*sblizhenie*] of Muslims with Christian states cannot happen anywhere in the world."[1] Orientalist N. G. Mallitskii, the city head of Tashkent, was among the most vocal opponents of increased rights for the Central Asian majority. Whether their own personal anxieties or experiences made these figures fear some type of hybridity is unclear. These views, however, illustrate that those with the closest relations to Central Asians appeared among the least willing to dissolve the many boundaries that upheld colonial rule and Russian superiority.

Race and class mixed with other hierarchies in imperial and early soviet Tashkent. Russian and Central Asian women expressed their own power on the city's streets in 1916. Gender had played an important role in the imperial elites' self-perception as colonizers. As across Europe, tsarist administrators and intellectuals saw "their" women as reminders of home and guardians of culture on the wild frontier. Central Asian women, meanwhile, apparently isolated and sometimes veiled, represented the primitive nature of local society. Yet praise from male elites concerning the importance of Russian women did not overcome patriarchal hierarchies of gender. Wives of leading tsarist administrators chafed at their isolation in Russian Tashkent. Lower-class Russian women were forced into dependent relationships with Central Asian merchants. In the 1916 food riots, Russian women expressed anger alternately at traders, the local population, imperial administrators, and men in general. Central Asian women protesting the draft of local labor in 1916 expressed their own frustration at the ability of the colonial state to disrupt their everyday lives. Wartime demands strained the multiple, interconnected hierarchies in imperial Tashkent, and set the stage for the widespread violence that followed.

The war also confirmed and heightened tensions between center and periphery in Tashkent. In many ways, this relationship was as critical to colonial rule as the one between colonizer and colonized. Central power provided the soldiers and the support for the imperial venture. St. Petersburg, however, remained divided over the vision of Kaufman, Maev, and others in Tashkent as a city of the future. M. E. Saltykov-Shchedrin's blistering condemnation of "Tashkent gentlemen" in 1869 opened avenues for central elites across the political spectrum to attack imperial rule as wasteful or venal. At the same time, military and strategic considerations revolving around the British presence in Central Asia pushed tsarist planners to continue their military presence and expand rail links to the region. A long-held dream of administrators in Tashkent, the railway triggered economic growth, but opened a terse debate between center and periphery on the nature of further economic development. St. Petersburg's policies favoring cotton angered local administrators, from governors-general to statisticians and geographers, who decried their region's being reduced to a pool of raw materials for the needs of the metropole. As businessmen and farmers, spurred by tsarist incentives, turned to cotton production, Turkestan lost self-sufficiency in food. The railway also facilitated the center's use of Tashkent and Turkestan as a place for political exiles and surplus peasants. These strains heightened pessimism toward the future among Russian Tashkent's elites, even as the urban economy and population enjoyed sustained growth in the early years of the twentieth century. When the war struck, the railway stopped delivering then-needed food, and central demands for taxes, goods, and labor prompted unrest on the streets.

The transition from tsarist to soviet rule in Tashkent reflected the instabilities and imbalances of empire. Multiple subject groups now competed for imperial privileges that had eroded as the center reduced its support to the periphery. Tensions and violence emerged along the interconnected hierarchies of race, class, gender, and nationality. The Tashkent soviet seized power; its main supporters, railway workers and former tsarist troops, conceived of the revolution as a chance to rule simultaneously as a political and a colonial elite. Through the soviet, they sought to extract goods from the local population, even if this led to the latter's starvation. Yet the soviet lacked internal as well as central backing. Seeing the 1917 revolution as an opportunity to end inequalities on the basis of race, Central Asians formed alternate political units, some of which sought alliances with Russian conservatives and liberals. Even followers of the soviet robbed vital state stocks and sent unauthorized requisition squads throughout the city and countryside. Workers, soldiers, peasants, and other Russians cooperated as well as clashed with local Central Asians. The soviet's discourse and practices of exclusion failed to alleviate food shortages or promote internal cohesion among the Russian population.

Bolshevik emissaries from Moscow, who portrayed themselves as promoters of order and socialist harmony among peoples to the frontier, faced great hostility from local Russians. In the end, however, although Central Asians were encouraged to fill administrative posts, the initial Bolshevik presence did little to alter relationships of power. Emissaries from Moscow shared Russian Tashkent's skilled workers' views of Central Asians as below Russians on the Marxist schema of historical progress. Quickly abandoning their dream of using Tashkent as a model for a future postcolonial city and spreading revolution to the east, central commissions focused primarily on subjecting Turkestan to the metropole. A primary goal of the Turkestan Commission involved restarting the cotton economy in the region, to put textile workers in Moscow back to work. By 1923, Turkestan, once considered by central and local Russian elites as a laboratory for national and international progress, was subjected tightly to the center.

Russian Tashkent's builders of empire, while placing themselves within national and global contexts, presided over a unique colonial society. Cultural and economic vigor among the local Central Asians belied myths of backwardness and defeated Russian efforts to guide them, ostensibly, in a slow and peaceful march toward "civilization." Russians' own anxieties over their marginal status in Europe contributed to internal divisions among the colonizer. For reasons we have discussed, the railway, capitalism, and Christianity, anchors of civilization in other European empires, proved difficult for Russian Tashkent's elites to accept as features of a progressive Russian province. Fear of Central Asian economic dominance and the power of lower-class Russian women further unsettled visions and practices of rule. Through all this confusion, however, the basic inequalities of empire remained. When Tashkent soviet leaders claimed the right to self-determination within a new socialist Russia, based on the argument that a unique society had evolved in the city and region, they were concerned primarily with their ability to continue the suppression of the Central Asian population. Central Asians who gained benefits from imperial rule ultimately never received treatments as equals; Arif Khoja, considered the most powerful and wealthy man in Asian Tashkent, and Turar Rysqulov, the most powerful Central Asian administrator in the soviet era, watched hopelessly as Russian-dominated soviet and communist bodies enacted policies that led to thousands of deaths. The story of imperial and early soviet Tashkent is one of complex relationships, interdependencies, and unforeseen results that contradicted core principles and challenged hierarchies of empire. But also, as the violence of the war and revolutionary eras showed, it is also a story of racism and other disparities that flowed from fundamental inequalities underpinning Russian and European methods of imperial control.

# Glossary

*aksakal:* respected Central Asian elder; literally "white beard"

*bai:* a wealthy Uzbek, often a member of the landholding elite; used by Russians as a pejorative term after 1917

*Basmachi:* literally "bandits;" term used by Russians to designate Central Asian opponents to Soviet rule (in Uzbek, known as *qorboshi*)

*desiatina:* 2.7 acres

*funt:* approximately 0.9 pounds

*Jadid:* member of a group of Muslim modernist thinkers that emerged in Central Asia at the turn of the twentieth century

*madrasa:* an institute of higher learning, focusing on Islamic religion and culture

*mahalla:* a neighborhood in Muslim cities

*mulla:* an Islamic cleric

*obshchestvo:* a Russian term generally equated to "educated society"

*Okhrana:* Tsarist secret police

*pud:* approximately 36 pounds

*qazi:* Islamic religious judge

*qazi-kalan:* chief religious judge among Tashkent Muslims

*Sart:* a term used by Central Asian locals before the Russian conquest to designate the sedentary population of the region. Tsarist authorities employed the moniker to designate Turkic-speaking urban-dwellers, and it eventually gained a pejorative connotation.

*sharia:* Islamic law

*tuzemtsy:* Russian term meaning "natives;" applied to the local population of Turkestan

*ulama:* carriers of Islamic legal and religious knowledge, including mullas and other learned individuals

# Notes

## Introduction

1. I use the term "Central Asian" to designate the local, non-Russian, non-European population. Before the conquest, Turkic, Muslim peoples dominated the area around Tashkent, though the city held significant Persian and Jewish minorities, as well as several other groups. Residents used a number of designations to refer to themselves and each other, including affiliation with their village or city, such as "Tashkenters," "Sarts" (urban-dwellers), and Muslims. Though not employed by people of the era, I have chosen the term "Central Asian" for several reasons. "Central Asians" allows the most neutral and inclusive designation for the local peoples, excluding not only Europeans and Slavs that came with the conquest, but also Tatars, who were Muslims, but lived apart from the local population. The term "Muslim" has gained a charged significance in current Western discourse, and I want to avoid the implications that come with calling the local population "Muslim" and the conquerors and settlers "Russians," "Europeans," and "Slavs" instead of "Christians."

2. Cathy A. Frierson has called this a "transitional epoch" and a period of "broad cultural self-definition" in the Russian empire. Frierson, *Peasant Icons: Representations of Rural People in Late Nineteenth-Century Russia* (New York: Oxford University Press, 1993), 6. On the conflicts facing the imperial world, see Frederick Cooper and Ann Laura Stoler, eds., *Tensions of Empire: Colonial Cultures in a Bourgeois World* (Berkeley: University of California Press, 1997).

3. Mark Bassin, *Imperial Visions: Nationalist Imagination and Geographical Expansion in the Russian Far East, 1840–1865* (Cambridge: Cambridge University Press, 1999), 177.

4. Seymour Becker, "Russia between East and West: The Intelligentsia, Russian National Identity, and the Asian Borderlands," *Central Asian Survey* 10, no. 4 (1991): 47–64.

5. Daniel Brower, *Turkestan and the Fate of the Russian Empire* (London: RoutledgeCurzon, 2003).

6. Brower, 1–25.

7. Douglas Northrop, *Veiled Empire: Gender and Power in Stalinist Central Asia* (Ithaca, N.Y.: Cornell University Press, 2004), 7.

8. On this void, see Andreas Kappeler, *The Russian Empire, A Multiethnic History*, trans. Alfred Clayton (London: Longman, 2001), 2.

9. For previous studies on Central Asia, see Richard Pierce, *Russian Central Asia, 1867–1917: A Study in Colonial Rule* (Berkeley: University of California Press, 1960); More recent works on other regions include Robert Geraci, *Window on the East: National and Imperial Identities in Late Tsarist Russia* (Ithaca, N.Y.: Cornell University Press, 2001); David Wolff, *To the Harbin Station: The Liberal Alternative in Russian Manchuria, 1898–1914* (Stanford, Calif.: Stanford University Press, 1999); and Paul Werth, *At the Margins of Orthodoxy: Mission, Governance, and Confessional Politics in Russia's Volga-Kama Region, 1827–1905* (Ithaca, N.Y.: Cornell University Press, 2002).

10. Adeeb Khalid, *The Politics of Muslim Cultural Reform: Jadidism in Central Asia* (Berkeley: University of California Press, 1998), 56; Virginia Martin, *Law and Custom in the Steppe: The Kazakhs of the Middle Horde and Russian Colonialism in the Nineteenth Century* (London: Curzon Press, 2001).

11. Yuri Slezkine, *Arctic Mirrors: Russia and the Small Peoples of the North* (Ithaca, N.Y.: Cornell University Press, 1994); Michael Khodarkovsky, *Russia's Steppe Frontier: The Making of a Colonial Empire, 1500–1800* (Bloomington: Indiana University Press, 2002).

12. Martin, 113.

13. *Okraina*, Jan. 15, 1894.

14. Geraci, 2.

15. Nathaniel Knight, "Grigor'ev in Orenburg, 1851–1862: Russian Orientalism in Service of Empire?" *Slavic Review* 59, no. 1 (2000): 74–100; Edward Said, *Orientalism* (New York: Vintage, 1979).

16. Adeeb Khalid, "Russian History and the Debate over Orientalism," *Kritika: Explorations in Russian and Eurasian History* 1, no. 4 (2000): 691–700.

17. Nezar Alsayyad, *Forms of Dominance: On the Architecture and Urbanism of the Colonial Enterprise* (Aldershot: Avebury Press, 1991), 8.

18. Ann Laura Stoler, "Rethinking Colonial Categories: European Communities and the Boundaries of Rule," *Comparative Studies in Society and History* 31, no. 1 (1989): 134–61; David Prochaska, *Making Algeria French; Colonialism in Bone, 1870–1920* (Cambridge: Cambridge University Press, 1990); Dane Kennedy, *The Magic Mountains: Hill Stations and the British Raj* (Berkeley: University of California Press, 1996). On plural societies, see Anthony D. King, *Colonial Urban Development: Culture, Social Power, and Environment* (London: Routledge and Kegan Paul, 1976).

19. On the "contact zone" of empire, see Mary Louise Pratt, *Imperial Eyes: Travel Writing and Transculturation* (London: Routledge, 1992).

20. On "poor Whites" in India, see David Arnold, "White Colonization and Labour in 19th Century India," *Journal of Imperial and Commonwealth History* 9, no. 2 (1983): 133–58.

21. Ania Loomba, *Colonialism/ Postcolonialism* (London: Routledge, 1998); Robert Young, *Postcolonialism: A Historical Introduction* (New York: Blackwell, 2001).

22. A. I. Dobrosmyslov, *Tashkent v proshlom i nastoiashchem: Istoricheskii ocherk'* (Tashkent: Tipo-litografiia A. O. Portseva, 1912), 374.

23. Khalid, *Politics of Muslim Cultural Reform*, 5–6.

24. Ronald Robinson, "Non-European Foundations of European Imperialism: Sketch for a Theory of Collaboration," in *Studies in the Theory of Imperialism*, ed. Roger Owen and Bob Sutcliffe (London: Longman, 1972), 120.

25. Edward J. Lazzerini, "Local Accommodation and Resistance to Colonialism in Nineteenth-Century Crimea," in *Russia's Orient: Imperial Borderlands and Peoples, 1700–1917*, ed. Lazzerini and Daniel Brower (Bloomington: Indiana University Press, 1997), 175.

26. James C. Scott, *Weapons of the Weak: Everyday Forms of Peasant Resistance* (New Haven, Conn.: Yale University Press, 1985).

27. Laura Engelstein, "Holy Russia in Modern Times: An Essay on Orthodoxy and Cultural Change," *Past and Present*, no. 173 (Nov. 2001): 129–56.

28. Michael Adas, *Machines as the Measure of Man: Science, Technology, and the Ideologies of Western Dominance* (Ithaca, N.Y.: Cornell University Press, 1989).

29. Zygmont Bauman, *Modernity and Ambivalence* (Cambridge: Polity Press, 1991), 10.

30. Alice J. Conklin, *A Mission to Civilize: The Republican Idea of Empire in France and West Africa, 1895–1930* (Stanford, Calif.: Stanford University Press, 1997).

31. Thomas C. Owen, "Impediments to a Bourgeois Consciousness in Russia, 1880–1905: The Estate Structure, Ethnic Diversity, and Economic Regionalism," in *Between Tsar and People: Educated Society and the Quest for Public Identity in Late Imperial Russia*, ed. Edith W. Clowes, Samuel D. Kassow, and James L. West (Princeton, N.J.: Princeton University Press, 1991), 76–89. On this phenomenon in Europe, see Carl E. Schorske, *Fin-de-siècle Vienna: Politics and Culture* (New York: Knopf, 1979).

32. On multiple axes of domination and subordination, see Mrinalini Sinha, *Colonial Masculinity: the "Manly Englishman" and the "Effeminate Bengali" in the Late Nineteenth Century* (Manchester, U.K.: Manchester University Press, 1995), 11.

## Prologue

1. For a discussion of these sources, see *Istoriia Tashkenta s drevneishikh vremen do pobedy fevralskoi burzhuazno-demokraticheskoi revoliutsii* (Tashkent: Izdatel'stvo "Fan" UzSSR, 1988). Most prominent of the primary accounts employed by historians of the city is a volume written by Muhammad Salih Tashkandi, *Tarikh i jadida-yi Tashkand* (A New History of Tashkent). Institute of Oriental Studies, Academy of Sciences of the Republic of Uzbekistan, no. 7791.

2. The most renowned author of the era remains V. V. Bartol'd, *Sochineniia*, 9 vols. in 10. (Moscow: Izdatel'stvo Vostochnoi Literatury, 1963–1977). For pre-revolutionary Russian sources on Tashkent before the conquest, see O. D. Chekovich, "Gorodskie samoupravlenie v Tashkente XVIII v," in *Istoriia i kul'tura narodov Srednei Azii* (Moscow: Izdatel'stvo "Nauka," 1976), 149–60. On the early nineteenth century, see R. N. Nabiev, *Tashkentskoe vosstanie 1847 g. i ego sotsial'no-ekonomicheskie predposylki* (Tashkent: Izdatel'stvo "Fan," 1966).

3. For the intricacies of Soviet historiography on Central Asia, see Lowell Tillett, *The Great Friendship: Soviet Historians on the Non-Russian Nationalities* (Chapel Hill: University of North Carolina Press, 1969).

4. On the geography of the region, see Peter Sinnott, "The Physical Geography of Soviet Central Asia and the Problem of the Aral Sea," in *Geographic Perspectives on Soviet Central Asia,* ed. Robert A Lewis (London: Routledge, 1992), 74–84.

5. Dobrosmyslov, *Tashkent v proshlom i nastoiashchem,* 4. Soviet policies have drastically the environment of the region. See Sinnott, 84–96.

6. On the land and harvests, see Elizabeth E. Bacon, *Central Asia under Russian Rule: A Study in Culture Change* (Ithaca, N.Y.: Cornell University Press, 1966), 8–13.

7. On the Arab invasion, see Bartol'd, vol. 2, part 1, 118–26.

8. N. A. Maev, "Aziatskii Tashkent," in *Materialy dlia Statistiki Turkestanskogo Kraia* (St. Petersburg, 1877), 4:269.

9. On the Mongol invasion of Turkestan and its consequences, see Bartol'd, II: 1, 137–62.

10. Dobrosmyslov, *Tashkent v proshlom i nastoiashchem,* 16.

11. Rozia Mukminova, cited in Scott C. Levi, *The Indian Diaspora in Central Asia and Its Trade, 1550–1900* (Leiden: E. J. Brill, 2002), 72. Levi's study provides an excellent introduction to the dynamics of trade in the region.

12. Nurmuhammed Mulla Alim Khan described the city to a Russian delegation while in Ufa in 1735. His report is held in the State Archive of the Orenburg Oblast. On his account and on the politics in the city in the eighteenth century, see Chekovich, 149–56. Tashkent's political administration has evoked comparisons by Soviet historians to the city-state of Novgorod. See Iu. A. Sokolov, *Tashkent, Tashkenttsy, i Rossiia* (Tashkent: Izdatel'stvo "Uzbekistan," 1965), 31.

13. Khalid, *The Politics of Muslim Cultural Reform,* 37.

14. *Istoriia Tashkenta,* 77–78.

15. Sokolov, 63–92.

16. Dobrosmyslov, *Tashkent v proshlom i nastoiashchem,* 26.

17. On the controversy over the term, see Ingeborg Baldauf, "Some Thoughts on the Making of the Uzbek Nation," *Cahiers du monde russe et soviétique* 23, no. 1 (1991): 79–96.

18. *Istoriia Tashkenta,* 79; Maev, "Aziatskii Tashkent," 261–66; F. Azadaev, *Tashkent vo vtoroi polovine XIX veka: Ocherki Sotsial'no-Ekonomicheskoi i Politicheskoi Istorii* (Tashkent: Izdatel'stvo Akademii Nauk Uzbekskoi SSR, 1959), 24–25.

19. M. K. Rozhkova, *Ekonomicheskie sviazi Rossii so Srednei Aziei (40–60 gody XIX veka)* (Moscow: Izdatel'stvo Akademii Nauk SSSR, 1963).

20. Azadaev, 41.

21. N. G. Mallitskii, "Tashkentskie makhallia i mauza," in *V. V. Bartol'du Turkestanskie druz'ia ucheniki i pochiteteli* (Tashkent, 1927), 119–21.

22. Janet L. Abu-Lughod, "The Islamic City—Historic Myth, Islamic Essence, and Contemporary Relevance," *International Journal of Middle East Studies* 19, no. 1 (1987): 155–76.

23. Mallitskii, 108–21.

24. I have chosen this transliteration (from the Cyrillic) for simplicity; transliterations from various styles of Uzbek render the word as *aqsaqqal* or *oqsaqqol.*

25. Maev, "Aziatskii Tashkent," 271.

26. These districts apparently had existed since the foundation of the city in the ninth century, but had reasserted themselves administratively in the 1700s–1800s. Sokolov, 26.

27. Chekovich, 157.

28. Maev, "Aziatskii Tashkent," 262.

29. On reports of the khojas in contemporary sources, see Chekovich, 149–56, and Nabiev, 23.

30. Khalid, *The Politics of Muslim Cultural Reform*, 36–40.

31. Stefano Bianca, *Urban Form in the Arab World: Past and Present* (London: Thames and Hudson, 2000), 38–39.

32. On the importance of private space in Uzbek culture, see Morgan Liu, "Recognizing the Khan: Authority, Space, and Political Imagination among Uzbek Men in the Post-Soviet Osh, Kyrgyzstan" (Ph.D. diss., University of Michigan, 2002).

33. Khalid, *The Politics of Muslim Cultural Reform*, 19–21.

34. Sokolov, 123.

35. Nabiev, 10; Sokolov, 127.

36. Maev, "Aziatskii Tashkent," 283; *Istoriia Tashkenta*, 91.

37. Khalid, *The Politics of Muslim Cultural Reform*, 35.

38. The date of this uprising remains in dispute. Nabiev, who has studied the rebellion most closely, places it in 1847, though Azadaev and Sokolov both give 1850 as the date. On the rebellion, see Nabiev, 62–80.

39. Khalid, *The Politics of Muslim Cultural Reform*, 43.

40. Studies of the "Great Game" (or the "Tournament of Shadows," as the Russians called it) remain in the realm of popular histories. See Peter Hopkirk, *The Great Game: The Struggle for Empire in Central Asia* (New York: Kodansha, 1992), and David Gillard, *The Struggle for Asia, 1828–1914: A Study in British and Russian Imperialism* (London: Methuen, 1977).

41. See N. V. Khanykov, *Opisanie Bukharskogo Khanstva* (St. Petersburg: Tipografii Imperatorskoi Akademii Nauk, 1843); Joseph Wolff, *Narrative of a Mission to Bokhara in the Years 1843–1845 to Ascertain the Fate of Captain Stoddard and Colonel Connolly* (London: J. W. Parker, 1846); Arminius Vambery, *History of Bokhara* (London: Henry S. King, 1873).

42. David MacKenzie, *The Lion of Tashkent: The Career of General M. G. Cherniaev* (Athens: University of Georgia Press, 1974), 21.

43. On the Perovskii mission, see Hélène Carrère d'Encausse, "Encounter," in *Central Asia: 130 Years of Russian Dominance*, ed. Edward Allworth (Durham, N.C.: Duke University Press, 1998), 13.

44. On Russian embassies to Central Asia, see John Wentworth Strong, *Russian Relations with Khiva, Bukhara, and Kokand 1800–1858* (Ph.D. diss., Harvard University, 1964).

45. On the Russian conquest of Central Asia, see Pierce, *Russian Central Asia*; N. A. Khalfin, *Prisoedinenie Srednei Azii k Rossii (60–90-e gody XIX v.)* (Moscow: Izdatel'stvo "Nauka," 1965). On the role of frontier generals, see David MacKenzie, "Expansion in Central Asia: St. Petersburg vs. the Turkestan Generals, 1863–1866," *Canadian Slavic Studies* 3, no. 2 (1969): 286–311.

46. Such a tactic was seen as particularly effective given the British obsession with protecting India. See Fitzroy McLean, *A Person from England and Other Travelers to Turkestan* (London: Jonathan Cape, 1958).

47. N. V. Riasanovsky, "Asia through Russian Eyes," *Russia and Asia: Essays on the Influence of Russia on the Asian Peoples,* ed. W. S. Vucinich (Stanford, Calif.: Stanford University Press, 1972), 3–29.

48. Soviet historians have tended to present economic factors as decisive in driving the decision to conquer Central Asia, but no direct evidence exists to conclude that economic considerations decisively influenced policy makers within tsarist administrative circles. See Dietrich Geyer, *Russian Imperialism: The Interaction of Domestic and Foreign Policy 1860–1914,* trans. Bruce Little (New York: Berg, 1987), 92.

49. Alfred J. Rieber, ed., *The Politics of Autocracy: Letters of Alexander II to Prince A. I. Bariatinskii 1857–1864* (Paris: Mouton, 1966), 23; see also Richard Wortman, *Scenarios of Power: Myth and Ceremony in Russian Monarchy,* vol. 2: *From Alexander II to the Abdication of Nicholas II* (Princeton, N.J.: Princeton University Press, 2000): 129–133.

50. MacKenzie, *Lion of Tashkent,* 30–33.

51. Sokolov, 133–43. On the rebellions, see Khalfin, *Prisoedinenie Srednei Azii k Rossii,* 192, 197; on Cherniaev's reaction, see MacKenzie, *Lion of Tashkent,* 49.

52. Sokolov, 153–56, based on Salih's account.

53. Sokolov, 161–66.

54. A translated copy of the proclamation, issued in Persian and publicly distributed, can be found in Eugene Schuyler, *Turkistan: Notes of a Journey in Russian Turkistan, Khokand, Bukhara, and Kuldja,* vol. 1 (New York: Scribner, Armstrong, 1877), 115–16.

55. David MacKenzie, "The Conquest and Administration of Turkestan, 1860–85," in *Russian Colonial Expansion to 1917,* ed. Michael Rywkin (New York: Mausell, 1988), 216; *Istoriia Uzbekskoi SSR,* vol. 1 (Tashkent: Izdatel'stvo Akademii Nauk UzSSR, 1956), pt. 2, 89.

56. On the reaction of the British to the capture, see Mohammad Anwar Khan *England, Russia, and Central Asia: A Study In Diplomacy, 1857–1879* (Peshawar, Pakistan: University Book Agency, 1969), 57–59.

57. Khalfin, *Prisoedinenie Srednei Azii k Rossii,* 206–208.

58. P. I. Pashino, who arrived in Tashkent in 1866, noted the number of social visits between Cherniaev and local Muslim notables. Pashino, *Turkestanskii Krai v 1866 godu. Putevye zametki P. I. Pashino.* (St. Petersburg, 1866), 96–97, 123.

59. Nabiev, 38.

60. Many other merchants followed the pattern of Seid Azim. Sokolov, 170–74.

61. Sokolov, 170–71; Pashino, 95.

62. I. I. Popov, *Minuvshee i perezhitoe: vospominaniia za 50 let: Sibir i emigratsiia* (Leningrad: Kolos, 1924), 220.

# 1. Ceremonies, Construction, and Commemoration

1. Tsentral'nyi Gosudarstvennyi Arkhiv Respubliki Uzbekistan (hereafter TsGARUz)/Ozbekistan respublikasi markaziy daviat arkhivi (Central State Ar-

chive of the Republic of Uzbekistan) f. I [Istoricheskiiaia Chast']-1 (Office of the Governor-General), op. 32, d. 11, l. 31.

2. *Moskovskiia Viedomosti*, no. 15 (1868).

3. Catherine Bell, *Ritual Theory, Ritual Practice* (Oxford: Oxford University Press, 1992), 90.

4. Richard Wortman, *Scenarios of Power: Myth and Ceremony in Russian Monarchy*, 2 vols. (Princeton, N.J.: Princeton University Press, 1995–2000).

5. TsGARUz, f. I-36, op. 1, d. 54, l. 5.

6. TsGARUz, f. I-36, op. 1, d. 54, l. 3.

7. *Golos*, no. 32 (1868).

8. *Russkii Invalid*, no. 94 (1867).

9. One thousand peach trees, in the local language. The gardens had existed before the Russian conquest, but were "incorporated" into the Russian city in 1866.

10. Pashino, 43.

11. On battles between Russia and Bukhara, see N. A. Khalfin, *Politika Rossii v Srednei Azii* (Moscow: Izdatel'stvo Vostochnoi Literatury, 1960), 223–35.

12. *Golos*, no. 32 (1868).

13. E. M—skii, "Rasskazy soldata o Turkestanskom Krae," *Mirskoi Viestnik*, no. 11 (1866): 54.

14. *Russkii Invalid*, no. 119 (1868).

15. *St. Petersburgskiia Viedomosti*, no. 16 (1868).

16. *Moskovskiia Viedomosti*, no. 37 (1867).

17. Tashkent Russians were aware of greeting ceremonies offered to the tsar or tsarina and their families during their travels, a process that had endured for centuries. See, for example, Nancy Shields Kollmann, "Pilgrimage, Procession, and Symbolic Space in Sixteenth Century Russian Politics," in *Medieval Russian Culture*, vol. 2, ed. Michael Flier and Daniel Rowland, California Slavic Studies 19 (Berkeley: University of California Press, 1994), 163–81; Richard Wortman, "Rule by Sentiment: Alexander II's Journeys through the Russian Empire," *American Historical Review* 95, no. 3 (1990): 745–71.

18. TsGARUz, f I-36, op. 1, d. 525, l. 25.

19. *Vsemirnaia Illiustratsiia*, no. 349 (1875): 191.

20. V. A. Poltoratskii, "Vospominaniia V. A. Poltoratskago," *Istoricheskii Viestnik* 16, no. 4 (1875): 106.

21. First-level merchants were the elite among the merchant estate (*soslovie*). See Alfred J. Rieber, *Merchants and Entrepeneurs in Imperial Russia* (Chapel Hill: University of North Carolina Press, 1982). On the ceremony, see *Vsemirnaia Illiustratsiia*, no. 349 (1875): 191; N. P. Ostroumov, *Konstantin Petrovich fon-Kaufman. Ustroitel' Turkestanskogo Kraia. Lichnaia Vospominaniia N. Ostroumova (1877–1881)* (Tashkent: G. Kaminskii, 1899), 77; *Turkestanskiia Viedomosti* (hereafter *TV*), no. 8 (1873).

22. On the opposition, see Azadaev, 96–7, 102; K. P. fon Kaufman, *Proekt vsepoddanneishago otcheta po grazhdanskomu upravleniiu i ustroistvu v' oblastiakh Turkestankago general-gubernatorstva 7 noiabria 1867–25 marta 1881g.* (St. Petersburg, 1885), 50.

23. Kaufman's tactics bear a striking resemblance to those developed by the

British following the 1857 rebellion in India. See Bernard S. Cohn, "Representing Authority in Victorian India," in *The Invention of Tradition,* ed. Eric Hobsbawm and Terence Ranger (Cambridge: Cambridge University Press, 1983), 165–209.

24. N. N. Karazin, *Na dalekikh okrainakh* (St. Petersburg: Izdanie P. P. Soikina, 1877), 7.

25. Schuyler, *Turkistan,* 1:19.

26. TsGARUz, f. I-1, op. 16, d. 129, l. 7ob.

27. Fred Richard Belk, *The Great Trek of the Russian Mennonites to Central Asia 1880–1884* (Scottsdale, Pa.: Herald Press, 1976), 89.

28. *St. Petersburgskiia Viedomosti,* no. 16 (1868).

29. *Golos,* no. 69 (1866).

30. Ibid.; Pashino, 91.

31. Karazin, 1–13.

32. *TV,* no. 3 (1876).

33. *TV,* no. 27 (1875).

34. Schuyler, 1:82. For panegyrics showered upon Kaufman by his contemporaries, see G. P. Fedorov, "Moia sluzhba v Turkestanskom Krae (1870–1906 goda)," *Istoricheskii Viestnik,* no. 10 (1913): 35–55; *Kaufmanskii Sbornik: Izdannyi v pamiat' 25 let istekshikh so dnia smerti pokoritelia i ustroitel'ia Turkestanskogo Kraia, General-Ad"iutanta K. P. fon-Kaufman I-go* (Moscow: Tipo-lit T-va I. N. Kushnerev, 1910); Ostroumov, *Konstantin Petrovich fon-Kaufman.*

35. Ostroumov, *Konstantin Petrovich fon-Kaufman,* 108.

36. Ibid., 31, 180; Schuyler, 1:80.

37. *Russkii Invalid,* no. 97 (1869); M. A. Terent'ev, *Istoriia zavoevaniia Srednei Azii* (St. Petersburg: Tipo-litografiia V. V. Komarova, 1906) 1:472–75; *Kaufmanskii Sbornik,* xxvii.

38. Dane Kennedy, *Islands of White: Settler Society and Culture in Kenya and Southern Rhodesia, 1890–1939* (Durham, N.C.: Duke University Press, 1987), 128.

39. TsGARUz, f. I-17, op. 1, d. 9716, l. 1–1ob.

40. *TV,* nos. 25 and 39 (1873).

41. TsGARUz, f. I-36, op. 1, d. 2418, ll. 4–5.

42. N. A. fon Rozenbakh, "Zapiski N. A. fon-Rozenbakha," *Russkaia Starina,* no. 4 (1916): 112.

43. Varvara Dukhovskaia, *Turkestanskiia Vospominaniia* (St. Petersburg: R. Golke i A. Vil'borg, 1913), 17.

44. *TV,* no. 23 (1884).

45. *TV,* no. 10 (1890).

46. *TV,* no. 8 (1873).

47. Ibid.

48. Kaufman, 8. See similar views in TsGARUz, f. I-1 op. 16, d. 243, l. 1.

49. Kaufman, 6.

50. A. A. Semenov, "Pokoritel' i ustroitel' Turkestanskogo Kraia, general-ad"iutant K. P. fon-Kaufman 1-i (materialy dlia biograficheskago ocherka)," in *Kaufmanskii Sbornik,* iii–lxxxiv; early drafts of this work are held in TsGARUz f. I-1, op. 32, d. 11.

51. On the briefness of Kaufman's stay in Vilna, see David MacKenzie, "Kaufman of Turkestan: An Assessment of His Administration 1867–1881,"

*Slavic Review* 26, no. 2 (1967): 265. On his impressions of Vilna, see A. I. Maksheev, "Prebyvanie v Vernom' i vstrecha Kaufmana," *Russkaia Starina*, no. 3 (1913): 644–49; A. V. Eval'd, "Vospominaniia o K. P. fon-Kaufman," *Istoricheskii Viestnik*, no. 10 (1897): 184–99.

52. Eval'd, 188.

53. Maksheev, "Prebyvanie v Vernom' i vstrecha Kaufmana," 648–49.

54. Azadaev, 100.

55. On the policy of disinterest, see Daniel Brower, *Turkestan and the Fate of the Russian Empire*, 35–55.

56. Ostroumov, *Konstantin Petrovich fon-Kaufman*, 31–32.

57. Kaufman, 8.

58. TsGARUz, f. I-1 op. 16, d. 243, l. 1.

59. TsGARUz, f. I-1, op. 16, d. 224, l. 5, 28.

60. TsGARUz, f. I-36, op. 1, d. 469 l. 11ob.

61. Other members of the committee included City Commandant Meditskii, military officers, one merchant, and M. N. Kolesnikov, who had designed the first street plan of the Russian section of Tashkent. TsGARUz, f. I-1 op. 16, d. 243, l. 8.

62. TsGARUz, f. I-1 op. 16, d. 243, l. 8.

63. On Makarov's background and education, see TsGARUz, f. I-17, op. 1 d. 38458, l. 1.

64. Iu. F. Buriakov, *Po ulitsam Tashkenta* (Tashkent: Izdatel'stvo "Uzbekistan," 1971), 57–58.

65. Wortman, *Scenarios of Power*, 1:53.

66. On Western urban planning, see Anthony Sutcliffe, *Towards the Planned City: Germany, Britain, the United States and France, 1780–1914* (New York: St. Martin's Press, 1981).

67. Buriakov, 34.

68. N. G. Chabrov, "Russkie arkhitektory dorevoliutsionnogo Turkestana (1865–1916gg.)," *Arkhitekturnoe Nasledie Uzbekistana* (Tashkent: Izdatel'stvo Akademii Nauk Uzbek SSR, 1960), 226; see also V. A. Nil'sen and A. Ziaev, "Pervye Proekt Planirovok Tashkenta," *Stroitel'stvo i Arkhitektura Uzbekistana*, no. 2 (1981): 37–38.

69. *Russkii Invalid*, no. 95 (1869).

70. TsGARUz, f. I-1, op. 16, d. 222, l. 57, 57ob. On the collapse of the trade fairs, one of Kaufman's most infamous failures, see Fedorov, 35; Schuyler, 1:208–11.

71. Some of these "Muslims" were likely Tatars serving in the administration. L. F. Kostenko, *Turkestanskii Krai. Opyt Voenno-Statisticheskago Obozrenie* (St. Petersburg: Tipografii A. Transhelia, 1880), 1:412–13.

72. TsGARUz, f. I-36, op. 1, d. 525, ll. 20–21.

73. TsGARUz, f. I-1, op. 16, d. 224, l. 5.

74. N. N. Karazin, "Iz Turkestanskoi Boevoi Zhizn'," *Vsemiranaia Illiustratsiia*, no. 59 (1872): 46. Karazin's phrase "a city growing literally out of the ground," most likely refers to the clay settlers extracted from the ground to build their houses.

75. *TV*, no. 1 (1876).

76. Bauman, 20–36.

77. The role of gardens in colonial situations has been examined in Kennedy, *The Magic Mountains*, 39–47.

78. *Russkii Invalid*, no. 97 (1869).

79. Karazin, *Na dalekikh okrainakh*, 23.

80. N. A. Maev, "Ot Tashkenta do Katy-Kurgan," *Russkii Viestnik* 86, no. 3 (1870): 243.

81. Ibid.

82. *TV*, no. 33 (1876).

83. Dukhovskaia, 24.

84. Schuyler, 1:112.

85. *Russkii Invalid*, no. 94 (1867).

86. *Golos*, no. 32 (1868).

87. William Craft Brumfield, *A History of Russian Architecture* (Cambridge: Cambridge University Press, 1993), 411.

88. V. A. Nil'sen, "Iz istorii zastroiki Tashkenta," *Arkhitektura i Stroitel'stvo Uzbekistana*, no. 9 (1983): 4.

89. Thomas Metcalf, *An Imperial Vision: Indian Architecture and Britain's Raj* (Berkeley: University of California Press, 1989), 2.

90. Patrick Conner, *Oriental Architecture in the West* (London: Thames and Hudson, 1979).

91. Schuyler, 1:76.

92. *Russkaia Gazeta*, no. 31 (1878).

93. Henri Moser, *A travers l'Asie Centrale* (Paris: Librarie Plon, 1885), 82.

94. Ibid.

95. N. A. Burov, "Istoricheskaia spravka o vremeni osnovaniia Tashkentskoi Publichnoi (Nyne Sredne-Aziatskoi Gosudarstvennoi) Biblioteki," *V. V. Bartol'du. Turkestanskie druz'ia ucheniki i pochiteteli* (Tashkent, 1927), 123.

96. Colonial states employed "investigative modalities" to create their own "modern" culture as well as to "classify, categorize, and [bind]" the vast worlds that surrounded them. Cohn, *Colonialism and Its Forms of Knowledge: The British in India* (Princeton, N.J.: Princeton University Press, 1996), 3–15.

97. A. I. Dobrosmyslov, "Tashkentskaia publichnaia biblioteka i muzei: Istoricheskii ocherk," *Sredniaia Aziia*, no. 2 (1910): 106.

98. Kostenko, *Turkestanskii Krai*, 1:411. The observation on the content of the collection follows my viewings (in 1996–98) of the rare book collection then held in the Alisher Navoi State Library of Uzbekistan.

99. This version of events is the one recited by Mezhov in a letter to one of Kaufman's successors, Governor-General Rozenbakh. TsGARUz, f I-1, op. 11, d. 47, l. 221.

100. TsGARUz f. I-1, op. 20, d. 2157, ll. 1–7.

101. V. I. Mezhov, *Recueil du Turkestan comprenant des livres et articles sur l'Asie Centrale en générale et la province du Turkestan en particulier: composé sous les auspices du Gouverneur Générale du Turkestan Konstantin Petrovich fon-Kaufman*, tome 1–150 (St. Petersburg, 1878).

102. A. G. Kasymova, "Turkestanskii Sbornik," *Sovetskaia Bibliografiia* 57, no. 5 (1969): 72–73.

103. Ibid., 73.

104. Dobrosmyslov, *Tashkent v proshlom i nastoiashchem*, 286.

105. *TV*, no. 1 (1870).

106. Ibid.

107. *TV*, no. 46 (1888); on the Indian collections, see Radhkia Singha, "Settle, Mobilize, Verify: Identification Practices in Colonial India," *Studies in History* 16, no. 2 (2000): 153–98.

108. "O Turkestanskom fotograficheskom al'bome," *Izvestiia Imperatorskago Geograficheskago Obshchestva* 10, no. 3 (1874): 97.

109. P. K., "Russkoe Znamia v Srednei Azii," *Istoricheskii Viestnik*, no. 4 (1899): 96–7.

110. The Russian Geographical Society zealously pursued this goal. "O Turkestanskom fotograficheskom al'bome," 97.

111. N. A. Maev, "Russkii Tashkent," *Niva: Literaturnoe Prilozheniia* (1894), 144.

112. This figure represents a sixfold increase over the population of 1870 (2,073). See *Materialy dlia Statistiki Turkestanskogo Kraia*, vol. 1 (St. Petersburg, 1872); for the 1890 statistics, see *TV*, no. 10 (1890).

113. An 1879 municipal survey of Russian Tashkent lists 1,195 reserve or former soldiers, and 617 soldiers' wives out of a Russian population (excluding active military) of 5,610. TsGARUz, f. I-17, op. 1, d. 3686, l. 17ob.. See also N. A. Maev, *Putevoditel' ot S-Petersburga do Tashkenta* (St. Petersburg: Voennaia Tipografiia, 1870), 53. Karazin's novel tells the story of former officers who exploited military campaigns to sell goods and services to tsarist forces. Karazin, *Na Dalekikh Okrainakh*, 1–88.

114. *Vsemirnaia Illiustratsiia*, no. 47 (1886): 382–83.

115. Malov solicited donations from leading military administrators and civilians throughout Turkestan, raising 2,410 rubles. *TV*, no. 23 (1886).

116. See MacKenzie, *The Lion of Tashkent*, 99–116.

117. Ostroumov, 51, 81.

118. Ibid., 32.

119. *TV*, no. 24 (1879).

120. *TV*, no. 24 (1883).

121. *Vsemirnaia Illiustratsiia*, no. 47 (1886): 382–83; *TV*, no. 23 (1886).

122. For Rozenbakh's background and actions as governor-general, see fon Rozenbakh, no. 4:100–113; no. 5: 72–241.

123. *TV*, no. 23 (1886).

124. *Vsemirnaia Illiustratsiia*, no. 47 (1886): 382–83.

125. Dobrosmyslov, "Uchebnyia zavedeniia v g. Tashkente," *Sredniaia Aziia*, no. 4 (1910): 114.

126. Ostroumov, 90–110.

127. Fedorov, no. 10 (1913): 38.

128. Penny Edwards, "Womanizing Indochina: Fiction, Nation, and Cohabitation in Colonial Cambodia, 1890–1930," in *Domesticating the Empire: Race, Gender, and Family Life in French and Dutch Colonialism*, ed. Julia Clancy-Smith and Frances Gouda (Charlottesville: University Press of Virginia, 1998), 113.

129. Pashino, 121–22; Karazin, *Na daleikikh okrainakh*, 26.

130. *TV*, no. 48 (1893).

131. *TV*, no. 25 (1887).

132. *TV*, nos. 29, 32 (1886).

133. All official personnel not stricken by illness were required to report. *TV*, no. 25 (1889).

134. Ibid.

135. N. P. Ostroumov, *Sarty. Ethnograficheskie Materialy (Obshchii Ocherk)*, 3rd. ed. (Tashkent, 1908).

136. TsGARUz, f. I-36, op. 1, d. 2418, ll. 4, 4ob.

137. *TV*, no. 24 (1886).

138. Ostroumov, *Sarty*, 94–97.

139. Theodore R. Weeks, *Nation and State in Imperial Russia: Nationalism and Russification on the Western Frontier* (De Kalb: Northern Illinois University Press, 1996), 68.

140. Dobrosmyslov, *Tashkent v proshlom i nastoiashchem*, 319.

141. Ibid.

142. Eric Hobsbawm and Terence Ranger, eds. *The Invention of Tradition* (Cambridge: Cambridge University Press, 1983).

143. *TV*, no. 48 (1893); TsGARUz, f. I-1, op. 11, d. 1353.

144. On the reporting of Kaufman's illness and death, see *TV*, nos. 13–18 (1882).

145. For the text of these speeches, see *TV*, no. 21 (1882), and Ostroumov, *Konstantin Petrovich fon-Kaufman*, 190–94.

146. On the background to the construction of the cathedral, see TsGARUz, f. I-17, op. 1, d. 1203, l. 6; *TV*, nos. 15, 28 (1888). On Rozenbakh's views, see TsGARUz, f. I-17, op. 1, d. 1203, l. 6

147. *TV*, no. 19 (1889).

148. The procession separated the civil institutions of the education, communications, customs, and excise departments; state and control bureaus; the district court; district administration; and representatives of the administrative-police management in Tashkent. Military representation was led by the intendant, medical, artillery, and engineering management, the regional courts and staff, together with the military-topographical division. See the procession orders in TsGARUz, f. I-17, op. 1, d. 1203, l. 2.

149. *TV*, no. 19 (1889).

150. Ibid.

151. On the continuing local memories of Kaufman, including a statue built to him in 1910 on the central square of Russian Tashkent, see Jeff Sahadeo, "Empire of Memories: Conquest and Civilization in Imperial Russian Tashkent," *Canadian Slavonic Papers* 46, no. 1–2 (2004): 395–417.

152. Maev, "Russkii Tashkent," 158.

## 2. Educated Society, Identity, and Nationality

1. Brower, *Turkestan and the Fate of the Russian Empire*, ix-xii, 4, 58 ff.

2. On the reforms, see *Russia's Great Reforms, 1855–1881*, ed. Ben Eklof, John Bushnell, and Larissa Zakharova (Bloomington: Indiana University Press, 1994).

3. For the excitement surrounding these reforms with particular emphasis on the role of the independent urban community, see Daniel Brower, *The Russian City between Tradition and Modernity, 1850–1900* (Berkeley: University of California Press, 1990), 92–104.

4. On the term "new Tashkent men," see *Birzhevyia Viedomosti*, no. 120 (1870).

5. B. V. Lunin, *Nauchnye obshchestva Turkestana i ikh progressivnaia deiatel'nost' (konets XIX–nachalo XX v.)* (Tashkent: Izdatel'stvo Akademii Nauk Uzbekskoi SSR, 1962), 49.

6. See Lunin, *Nauchnye obshchestva Turkestana*, 11–32, and A. I. Dobrosmyslov, *Tashkent v proshlom i nastoiashchem*, 96–98, 444–48.

7. Ostroumov in Lunin, 24.

8. Dobrosmyslov, *Tashkent v proshlom i nastoiashchem*, 287.

9. Samuel D. Kassow, "The University Statute of 1863: A Reconsideration," in *Russia's Great Reforms, 1855–1881*, ed. Ben Eklof, John Bushnell, and Larissa Zakharova (Bloomington: Indiana University Press, 1994), 248.

10. On the multiple definitions of *obshchestvo* in Russia, see Edith Clowes, Samuel D. Kassow, and James L. West, eds., *Between Tsar and People: Educated Society and the Quest for a Public Identity in Imperial Russia* (Princeton, N.J.: Princeton University Press, 1991); Elise Kimerling Wirtschafter, *Social Identity in Imperial Russia* (De Kalb: Northern Illinois University Press, 1997); Harley D. Balzer, ed., *Russia's Missing Middle Class: The Professions in Russian History* (Armonk, N.Y.: M. E. Sharpe, 1996).

11. On the importance of these features to definitions of civil society, see Charles Taylor, *Philosophical Arguments* (Cambridge: Cambridge University Press, 1995), 204–24; See also John Ehrenberg, *Civil Society: The Critical History of an Idea* (New York: New York University Press, 1999). Jurgen Habermas has expressed similar criteria in the efforts of European non-state actors to develop a "public sphere" of activity. Jürgen Habermas, "The Public Sphere," *New German Critique* 3 (1974): 49.

12. Balzer, "Introduction," *Russia's Missing Middle Class*, 3–38.

13. This perception of the tsarist state was not unique to Turkestan. See Laura Engelstein, *The Keys to Happiness: Sex and the Search for Modernity in Fin-de-siecle Russia* (Ithaca, N.Y.: Cornell University Press, 1992).

14. Lunin, 38.

15. Bassin, *Imperial Vision*, 2–14.

16. *Russkii Invalid*, no. 119 (1868).

17. *Birzhevyia Viedomosti*, no. 49 (1869).

18. *Russkiia Viedomosti*, no. 38 (1869).

19. *Birzhevyia Viedomosti*, no. 120 (1870).

20. See, for example, *Golos*, no. 88 (1870).

21. M. E. Saltykov-Shchedrin was a central figure in the radical literary politics of the mid-nineteenth century, and his popularity made the journal *Otechestvennye Zapiski* one of the most popular of the tsarist era. See A. S. Bushmin, *Satira Saltykova-Shchedrina* (Moscow: Izdatel'stvo Akademii Nauk SSSR, 1959).

22. S. A. Makashin, *Saltykov-Shchedrin Seredina Puti 1860-e–1870-e gody: Biografiia* (Moscow: Khudozhestvennaia Literatura, 1984), 447.

23. M. E. Saltykov-Shchedrin, "Chto takoe 'Tashkenttsy'?" *Otechestvennye Zapiski*, no. 5 (Oct. 1869): 187–207.

24. Ibid., 189ff.

25. Ibid., 192.

26. Schuyler's account of his journey was issued by the American Department of State in 1874 and published as a monograph three years later. On Schuyler's background, see Frank G. Siscoe, "Eugene Schuyler, General Kaufman, and Central Asia," *Slavic Review* 27, no. 1 (Mar. 1968): 119–20.

27. Schuyler, 1:83.

28. Ibid., 1:79.

29. On the editorial position of the newspapers and their reactions to the conquest of Central Asia, see Louise McReynolds, *The News under Russia's Old Regime: The Development of a Mass Circulation Press* (Princeton, N.J.: Princeton University Press, 1991), 11–71.

30. *Golos*, no. 88 (1870).

31. Schuyler, 2:247.

32. Ibid., 2:213.

33. *St. Petersbugskiia Viedomosti*, no. 42 (1875).

34. *Russkii Mir*, Jan. 30 and Mar. 2, 1875; on Cherniaev and *Russkii Mir*, see David MacKenzie, *The Lion of Tashkent*, 108–116.

35. On the effects of the failure of the reforms, see Geyer, 17–32.

36. B. V. Lunin, *Istoriia Obshchestvennykh Nauk v Uzbekistane* (Tashkent: Izdatel'stvo "Fan," 1974), 223.

37. N. A. Maev, "Nashe Polozhenie v Srednei Azii," in *Materialy dlia Statistiki Turkestanskogo Kraia*, vol. 3 (1872), 446.

38. Ibid.

39. Ibid., 445.

40. Ibid., 439.

41. Maev, "Nashe Polozhenie v Srednei Azii," 436. Lunin, *Nauchnye obshchestva Turkestana*, 34.

42. Dobrosmyslov, *Tashkent v proshlom i nastoiashchem*, 301.

43. Lunin, *Nauchnye obshchestva Turkestana*, 73.

44. TsGARUz, f. I-591, op. 1, d. 1, ll. 1–14.

45. TsGARUz, f. I-591, op. 1, d. 1, ll. 1, 6.

46. Lunin, *Nauchnye obshchestva Turkestana*, 80.

47. Dobrosmyslov, *Tashkent v proshlom i nastoiashchem*, 301.

48. TsGARUz, f. I-591, op. 1, d. 1, l. 112.

49. *TV*, no. 29 (1872).

50. Dobrosmyslov, *Tashkent v proshlom i nastoiashchem*, 419.

51. *Birzhevyia Viedomosti*, no. 120 (1870); see also *TV*, no. 46 (1876).

52. On the use of gendered hierarchies to establish values and identities in nineteenth-century Europe, see Mary Poovey, *Uneven Developments: The Ideological Work of Gender in Mid-Victorian England* (Chicago: University of Chicago Press, 1998). On idea of alternative masculinities, see Sinha, *Colonial Masculinity*, and Adele Perry, *On the Edge of Empire: Gender, Race, and the Making of British Columbia, 1849–1871* (Toronto: University of Toronto Press, 2001).

53. Harriet Ritvo, *The Animal Estate: The English and Other Creatures in the Victorian Age* (Cambridge, Mass.: Harvard University Press, 1987); cited in Richard Wortman, *Scenarios of Power*, 2:55.

54. John M. MacKenzie, *The Empire of Nature: Hunting, Conservation, and British Imperialism* (Manchester, U.K.: Manchester University Press, 1988), 176–77.

55. *TV*, no. 10 (1876).

56. Ibid.

57. On the details of the electoral body, see Dobrosmyslov, *Tashkent v proshlom i nastoiashchem*, 114–20.

58. *TV*, no. 24 (1877); *TV*, no. 44 (1879).

59. The responsibilities of municipal government are outlined in TsGARUz, f. I-37, opis 1.

60. For details on Cherniaev's appointment, see David MacKenzie, *The Lion of Tashkent*, 207–15.

61. A. I. Dobrosmyslov, "Tashkentskaia publichnaia biblioteka i muzei," 108–109.

62. Ibid., 110.

63. Books of "scientific importance" were sent to the local museum, and works with military value to the Turkestan Military Staff. Some were donated to local schools.

64. Dobrosmyslov, "Tashkentskaia publichnaia biblioteka i muzei," 110.

65. *TV*, no. 23 (1884); on the memory of the event, see Dobrosmyslov, "Tashkentskaia publichnaia biblioteka i muzei," 106–135.

66. Lunin, *Nauchnye obshchestva Turkestana*, 128.

67. I. I. Popov, *Minuvshee i perezhitoe: vospominaniia za 50 let: Sibir i emigratsiia* (Leningrad: Kolos, 1924), 193.

68. Evgenii Markov, *Rossiia v Srednei Azii. Ocherk Puteshestviia* (St. Petersburg: Tipografiia M. M. Stasliuvich, 1901), 1, 1:63.

69. Fedorov, no. 10 (1913), 35–55.

70. *TV*, no. 60 (1898). Records on the influence of the Geographic Society are located in TsGARUz, f. I-69, op. 1, d. 1, ll. 13–85.

71. TsGARUz, f. 69, op. 1, d. 5, l. 47.

72. *TV*, no. 43 (1886); *TV*, no. 3 (1889); *TV*, no. 21 (1890).

73. *TV*, no. 26 (1886); *TV*, no. 16 (1887).

74. See, for example, Ostroumov, *Sarty*, 128.

75. *Okraina*, May 28, 1894.

76. *TV*, no. 22 (1872).

77. *TV*, no 26 (1872). See also, for example, *TV*, nos. 19, 22, 33 (1872).

78. On the attitudes of the British toward Central Asia, see George Curzon, *Russia in Central Asia in 1889 and the Anglo-Russian Question* (London: Cass, 1889).

79. *TV*, no. 75 (1897).

80. *TV*, no. 90 (1897).

81. Ostroumov, *Sarty*, 94.

82. On the debate over Russians as more "gentle" colonizers, see the introduction to this volume.

83. On the Eurasianists and Asianists, see David Schimmelpennick Van Der Oye, *Towards the Rising Sun: Russian Ideologies of Empire and the Path to War with Japan* (De Kalb: Northern Illinois University Press, 2001), 43–51.

84. Geraci, 348.

85. This claim echoed those from elsewhere in the colonial world. See Kennedy, *Magic Mountains*, 19–38.

86. "Beglyi rasskaz o medlennom puteshestvii v Tashkente," *Voennyi Sbornik* 66, no. 4 (1869): 303.

87. E. Shlitter, "V Turkestane," *Voennyi Sbornik*, no. 3 (1902): 214.

88. Kostenko, *Turkestanskii Krai*, 3:244; *TV* no. 29 (1872).

89. *TV*, no. 48 (1888).

90. Dukhovskaia, 23.

91. Kennedy, *Magic Mountains*, 32–37.

92. *TV*, no. 28 (1879).

93. *TV*, no. 50 (1891).

94. Ibid.; *Russkii Turkestan*, no. 59 (1899).

95. *Russkii Turkestan*, no. 59 (1899).

96. *TV*, no. 29 (1882).

97. Ibid.

98. *Golos*, no. 253 (Nov. 13, 1866).

99. Laura Engelstein, "Holy Russia in Modern Times," 148.

100. On Kaufman and secularism, see Brower, *Turkestan and the Fate of the Russian Empire*, 37.

101. Schuyler, 1:78.

102. M. A. Terent'ev, "Turkestan i Turkestantsy," *Viestnik Evropy* 5, no. 10 (1875): 529.

103. *TV*, no. 20 (1904).

104. N. P. Ostroumov claimed that officers simply purchased alcohol with state moneys from military traders, not willing to deprive their troops of drink in times of war. Ostroumov, *Konstantin Petrovich fon Kaufman*, 18; on reaction in the metropole, see *Moskovskiia Viedomosti*, no. 99 (1876).

105. *TV*, no. 48 (1883).

106. See Syed Hussein Alatas, *The Myth of the Lazy Native: A Study of the Malays, Filipinos, and Javanese from the Sixteenth Century* (London: P. Cass, 1977).

107. *TV*, no. 15 (1870).

108. Maev, "Russkii Tashkent," 136.

109. Ibid., 138.

110. Robert Owen, *Russian Corporate Capitalism from Peter the Great to Perestroika* (New York: Oxford University Press, 1995), 8–9, 116–19.

111. N. N. Karazin, *Zhivopisnaia Rossiia*, vol. 20: *Russkaia Sredniaia Aziia* (St. Petersburg, 1885).

112. Ibid, 150.

113. Ibid.

114. TsGARUz, f. I-1 op. 27. d. 774, ll. 1, 149.

115. See *TV*, no. 32 (1884); *TV*, no. 51 (1904).

116. *Russkii Invalid*, no. 119 (1868).

117. Maev, "Russkii Tashkent," 133–34.

118. *Russkii Turkestan,* no. 28 (1904).

119. Shlitter, 206–210; Maev, "Russkii Tashkent," 131–33; E. M—skii, 52–56; Dobrosmyslov, *Tashkent v proshlom i nastoiashchem,* 80, 368.

120. On fears of hybridity elsewhere in the colonial world, see Ann Laura Stoler, "Sexual Affronts and Racial Frontiers: European Identities and the Cultural Politics of Exclusion in Colonial Southeast Asia," in *Tensions of Empire: Colonial Cultures in a Bourgeois World,* ed. Frederick Cooper and Ann Laura Stoler (Berkeley: University of California Press, 1997), 198–237.

121. *TV,* no. 8 (1888).

122. N. S. Lykoshin, *Pol zhizni v Turkestane: ocherki byta tuzenago naseleniia* (Petrograd, 1916), 323.

123. Popov, 195.

124. Dukhovskaia, 30.

125. On the backgrounds of Andreev and Nalivkin, see Lunin, *Istoriia Obshchestvennykh Nauk,* 88–95, 247–58. On the extent of "going native," see Brower, *Turkestan and the Fate of the Russian Empire,* 68.

126. On Alexander III's nationalism, see Wortman, *Scenarios of Power,* vol. 2; Rosamund Bartlett and Linda Edmondson, "Collapse and Creation: Issues of Identity and the Russian Fin de Siecle," in *Constructing Russian Culture in the Age of Revolution, 1881–1940,* ed. Catriona Kelly and David Shepherd (Oxford: Oxford University Press, 1998), 168.

127. Rozenbakh, 207.

128. TsGARUz, f. I-1, op. 4, d. 50, l. 3.

129. TsGARUz, f. I-462, op. 1, d. 181, l. 37; TsGARUz, f. I-36, op. 1, d. 4133, l. 14.

130. TsGARUz, f. I-1, op. 17, d. 96a, ll. 30, 67.

131. *TV,* no. 5 (1891).

132. Ibid.

133. Ibid.

## 3. Unstable Boundaries

1. A. Shvarts, *Sredniaia Aziia,* no. 8 (1911): 134.

2. On the statute, see Brower, *Turkestan and the Fate of the Russian Empire,* 27–31.

3. On the implementation of these new methods of rule, see Azadaev, 95–127.

4. TsGARUz, f. I-36, op. 1, d. 530. l. 10.

5. On the issue of tax revenue, *see Istoriia Tashkenta,* 153.

6. TsGARUz, f. 36, op. 1, d. 580, l. 7.

7. Brower, *Turkestan and the Fate of the Russian Empire,* 30.

8. Azadaev, 122.

9. Martin, 87–113.

10. TsGARUz, f. I-36, op. 1, d. 480, l. 7.

11. TsGARUz, f. I-36, op. 1, d. 1457, l. 81.

12. Dobrosmyslov, *Tashkent v proshlom i nastoiashchem,* 403.

13. *Istoriia Tashkenta*, 162.

14. Ostroumov, *Sarty*, 118; Markov, 1:517–18.

15. Khalid, *The Politics of Muslim Cultural Reform*, 82–89.

16. TsGARUz, f. I-36, op. 1, d. 480, l. 6.

17. *Turkestanskiia Viedomosti*, no. 3 (1884).

18. *Istoriia Tashkenta*, 171.

19. Azadaev, 195–96.

20. On Muhiddin Khoja, see Markov, 1:520–23; Ostroumov, *Sarty*, 121–32.

21. Markov, 1:523–24.

22. Ostroumov, *Sarty*, 132. On the veil in Asian Tashkent, see Northrop, 19.

23. Ostroumov, *Sarty*, 151–53.

24. Brower, *Turkestan and the Fate of the Russian Empire*, 67.

25. Edward Said, *Culture and Imperialism*, 2.

26. Vijay Prashad notes this tactic in British rule over India: "Native Dirt/Imperial Ordure: The Cholera of 1832 and the Morbid Resolutions of Modernity," *Journal of Historical Sociology*, 7, no. 3 (1994): 253.

27. On the cultural significance of dirt in European colonialism, see Anne McClintock, *Imperial Leather: Race, Gender and Sexuality in the Colonial Contest* (New York: Routledge, 1995), 152. On dirt in the Russian imperial context, see Slezkine, 115.

28. *Syn Otechestva*, no. 97 (1868).

29. Ibid.

30. Central Asian Muslims received far different treatment than, for example, Tatar Muslims conquered in the sixteenth century, who could ascend even to positions of nobility. Studies have argued that the time period in which peoples were conquered affected their status within the empire. See, for example, Slezkine. Kazakhs were praised by Russians for their martial skills, particularly in horsemanship.

31. *Russkii Invalid*, no. 119 (1868).

32. *Syn Otechestva*, no. 97 (1868).

33. Karazin, "Iz Turkestanskoi boevoi zhizni," *Vsemirnaia Illiustratsiia*, 1872, no. 161: 83.

34. Pashino, 90.

35. Ibid., 91.

36. *TV*, nos. 45–48 (1877).

37. *Russkii Invalid*, no. 119 (1869).

38. Dobrosmyslov, *Tashkent v proshlom i nastoiashchem*, 148.

39. *TV*, no. 1 (1875).

40. Dobrosmyslov, *Tashkent v proshlom i nastoiashchem*, 136.

41. TsGARUz, f. I-17, op. 1, d. 18005, ll. 4–5; F. K. Girs, *Otchet revizuiushchago, po Vysochaishemu poveleniiu, Turkestanskii krai, Tainogo sovetnika Girsa* (St. Petersburg, 1883), 50. The salary for a Russian police officer, by comparison, was 250 rubles in 1883.

42. *Khalatnik* is a derogatory term that refers to the wearer of a *khalat*, a robe used by the local population. M. A. Terent'ev, 3:292.

43. *TV*, no. 45 (1877).

44. Kostenko, *Turkestanskii Krai,* 1:310.

45. Schuyler, 1:147; Kostenko, "Turkestanskaia Voiska i usloviia ikh," *Voennyi Sbornik* 103, no. 5 (1875): 76; *Russkii Turkestan: Sbornik izdanno po povodu politekh-nicheskoi vystavki* (Moscow: Universitetskoi tipografii, 1872) 2:273–89.

46. Cassandra Marie Cavanaugh, *Backwardness and Biology: Medicine and Power in Russian and Soviet Central Asia, 1868–1934* (Ph.D. diss., Columbia University, 2001), 22–26, ff.

47. Cavanaugh, 72.

48. *TV,* no. 21 (1878).

49. Pashino, 94.

50. Ibid.

51. *Petersburgskaia Gazeta,* no. 57 (1868).

52. *Russkii Invalid,* no. 113 (1867).

53. *TV,* no. 3 (1890).

54. Dobrosmyslov, *Tashkent v proshlom i nastoiashchem,* 103; TsGARUz, f. I-36, op. 1, d. 530, l. 7.

55. See Pashino, 106.

56. Karazin, *Na Dalekikh Okrainakh;* M. E. Saltykov-Shchedrin, *Gospoda Tash-kenttsy. Kartina nravov'* (St. Petersburg: Tipografiia V. V. Pratts', 1873).

57. R. J. Morris, *Cholera 1832: The Social Response to an Epidemic* (London: Croon Helm, 1976), 17.

58. Richard J. Evans, "Epidemics and Revolutions: Cholera in Nineteenth-Cen-tury Europe," *Past and Present,* no. 120 (Aug. 1988): 124–25; Charles E. Rosenberg, "Cholera in Nineteenth-Century Europe: A Tool for Social and Economic Analy-sis," *Comparative Studies in Society and History* 8, no. 4 (1966): 452–63.

59. In the nineteenth century, approximately one-half of those who contracted cholera died from it. Roderick E. McGrew, *Encyclopedia of Medical History* (New York: McGraw-Hill, 1985), 59.

60. This description is paraphrased from McGrew, 59.

61. David Arnold, *Colonizing the Body: State Medicine and Epidemic Disease in Nineteenth-Century India* (Berkeley: University of California Press, 1993), 161.

62. Colonial officials in India referred to cholera as an "enemy force." Arnold, 169. On the importance of military considerations in epidemics in the colonial world, see Warwick Anderson, "Where Is the Postcolonial History of Medicine?" *Bulletin of the History of Medicine,* no. 72 (1998): 524.

63. Nancy Frieden, *Russian Physicians in an Era of Reform and Revolution, 1856–1905* (Princeton, N.J.: Princeton University Press, 1981), 135–36.

64. Ibid., 135.

65. TsGARUz, f. I-36, op. 1, d. 876, l. 3.

66. TsGARUz, f. I-36, op. 1, d. 876, l. 81.

67. TsGARUz, f. I-36, op. 1, d. 876, l. 3.

68. The figures for Asian Tashkent were all listed as "male." Whether this means tsarist officials only counted male deaths is unclear. As the 1892 epidemic made evident, Central Asians sought to conceal female deaths from the authori-ties. TsGARUz, f. I-36, op. 1, d. 876, l. 173.

69. TsGARUz f. I-36, op. 1, d. 876, l. 160.

70. See *TV*, no. 50 (1892).
71. Evans, 266.
72. K. K. Kazanskii, "V vidu slukhov o kholere," *Turkestanskiia Viedomosti*, no. 40 (Oct. 2, 1890).
73. Ibid.
74. Ibid.
75. *TV*, no. 20 (1891).
76. Rozenbakh, 113.
77. TsGARUz, f. I-1, op. 31, d. 33, l. 19.
78. Russian census figures, though highly unreliable given the propensity of the Muslims to avoid being counted for taxation purposes, placed the Muslim city at 100,255 persons in 1890, See *Obzor Syr-Dar'inskoi Oblasti za 1890g*, (Tashkent: Tipografiia brat'ev G. i O. Portsevykh, 1892), 260–61.
79. TsGARUz, f. I-718, op. 1, d. 12, l. 1.
80. *TV*, no. 22 (1892).
81. TsGARUz, f. I-36, op. 1, d. 3384, ll. 19–19ob.
82. The document was printed in *TV*, no. 20 (1892).
83. Ibid.
84. Ibid.
85. Central Asians of the period relied far more on oral than written transmissions. See Khalid, *The Politics of Muslim Cultural Reform*, 24–25, 126.
86. On the role of Tatars as mediators, see Marianne Kamp, *Unveiling Uzbek Women: Liberation, Representation, and Discourse, 1906–1929* (Ph.D. diss., University of Chicago, 1998), 54–58.
87. Cavanaugh, 32.
88. TsGARUz, f, I-718, op. 1, d. 21, l. 154.
89. TsGARUz, f. I-718, op. 1, d. 12, l. 158.
90. TsGARUz, f. I-36, op. 1, d. 3384, l. 16.
91. TsGARUz, f. I-36, op. 1, d. 3384, l. 58.
92. *TV*, no. 21 (1892).
93. For the broadsheet, see TsGARUz, f. I-36, op. 1, d. 3384, l. 14.
94. M. A. Terent'ev, *Istoriia Zavoevaniia Srednei Azii*, 3:371.
95. TsGARUz, f. I-36, op 1, d. 3384, ll. 30–4.
96. Alimov is identified simply as a "Sart from the Kokcha district of Tashkent." TsGARUz, f. I-723 op. 1, d. 3, l. 237.
97. A. A. Kadyrov, *Istorii Meditsiny Uzbekistana* (Tashkent: Ibn Siny, 1994), 139–42.
98. TsGARUz, f. I-36, op. 1, d. 3384, l. 136.
99. TsGARUz, f. I-723, op. 1, d. 3, l. 16ob.
100. Kadyrov, 141–42.
101. *TV*, no. 36 (1892).
102. TsGARUz, f. I-723, op. 1, d. 4.
103. Maulana Muhammad Ali, *The Religion of Islam: A Comprehensive Discussion of the Sources, Principles, and Practices of Islam* (New Delhi: S. Chand, 1968), 448–49.
104. TsGARUz, f. I-723, op. 1, d. 4, l. 76; On Muslim burial practices see Ali, 444–51; John A. Williams, ed. *Islam* (New York: G. Braziller, 1961), 104–108.

105. TsGARUz, f. I-723, op. 1, d. 3, l. 17.

106. TsGARUz, f. I-1, op. 31, d. 33, l. 19.

107. One scheme allowed Russian officials to purchase waqf land at advantageous prices. V. Zykin, "Pod Dvoinom Pressom: Vosstanie v Tashkente v 1892 t.n. 'Kholernyi Bunt,'" *Uchenye Zapiski Permskogo Gosudarstvennogo Universiteta (otdel Obshchestvennykh Nauk)* Vyp. II (Perm, 1931), 329–30.

108. Terent'ev, *Istoriia zavoevaniia Srednei Azii,* 3:372.

109. For figures on cholera deaths, see *TV,* no. 27 (1892).

110. TsGARUz, f. I-723, op. 1, d. 2, l. 76.

111. On this phenomenon elsewhere in Russia in 1892, see Frieden 150–51; Sylvain Bensidoun, "'A propos d'une centenaire': Le cholera et les émeutes de 1892 dans l'empire de Russie," *Revue Historique* 287 no. 2 (1992): 379–85. On rumors, see Donald L. Horowitz, *The Deadly Ethnic Riot* (Berkeley: University of California Press, 2001), 74–88.

112. These stories appears in several Central Asian witness accounts. Several refer to a deadly "white powder," likely lime, used as a disinfecting agent by Russian doctors during the 1892 epidemic. Cholera can furthermore cause confusion as afflicted bodies convulse after death. TsGARUz, f. I-723, op. 1, d. 3, ll. 17, 79, 224.

113. The Senate had been responsible for sending the Girs Commission, charged with investigating finances and local abuses of power in Turkestan, to the region in 1881.

114. TsGARUz, f. I-723, op. 1, d. 4, l. 36.

115. TsGARUz, f. I-723, op. 1, d. 3, l. 78ob.

116. *Turkestanskiia Viedomosti,* no. 25 (1892). For a discussion of how race and class worked together in the 1892 cholera riot, see Jeff Sahadeo, "Epidemic and Empire: Ethnicity, Class, and 'Civilization' in the 1892 Tashkent Cholera Riot," *Slavic Review* 64, no. 1 (2005): 117–139. *Slavic Review* is the official journal of the American Association for the Advancement of Slavic Studies, and material used in that article is republished here with permission.

117. One of the main cultural and religious holidays in the region, as across the Muslim world, Qurban-bayram (also known as *Qurban-Hayt*), marks the Feast of the Sacrifice.

118. TsGARUz, f. I-723, op. 1, d. 3, l. 13ob.

119. The origins and meanings of the term "white tsar" remain unclear. Richard Wortman has argued that the term originated with the local population, who used the term "white tsar" to parallel Russia to the power of the golden horde, known in the region as the "white horde." Wortman, *Scenarios of Power,* 2:63 n. 19. Other contemporary discussions attributed the term to the white uniforms of the Russian soldiers in Central Asia. Although no explicit mention of the label as a racial marker exists, it was used, as in this case, in terms that applied a clear sense of superiority of European over Asian.

120. TsGARUz, f. I-723, op. 1, d. 3, l. 79.

121. TsGARUz, f. I-723, op. 1, d. 3, l. 237.

122. TsGARUz, f. I-723, op. 1, d. 3, l. 80ob.

123. Zykin, 336.

124. Of the fifty-one Muslims arrested for participation in the crowd, Russian

statistics record nineteen of them as workers, twenty-two as artisans, eight as traders, and two as landowners. Zykin, 340.

125. TsGARUz, f. I-723, op. 1, d. 3, l. 16.

126. TsGARUz, f. I-723, op. 1, d. 3, l. 339.

127. Fedorov, no. 11 (1913): 459.

128. TsGARUz, f. I-723, op. 1, d. 3, l. 39.

129. TsGARUz, f. I-723, op. 1, d. 3, l. 37.

130. TsGARUz, f. I-723, op. 1, d. 3, l. 37.

131. TsGARUz, f. I-723, op. 1, d. 3, l. 14.

132. TsGARUz, f. I-723, op. 1, d. 3, l. 15ob.

133. TsGARUz, f. I-723, op. 1, d. 3, l. 25.

134. TsGARUz, f. I-723, op. 1, d. 3, l. 47ob.

135. TsGARUz, f. I-723, op. 1, d. 3, l. 3.

136. Fedorov, no. 11 (1913): 458.

137. Horowitz, 2.

138. Terent'ev, *Istoriia zavoevaniia Srednei Azii*, 3:377.

139. TsGARUz, f. I-723, op. 1, d. 3, l. 38.

140. TsGARUz, f. I-723, op. 1, d. 3, l. 18ob.

141. Grodekov vigorously denied making such a remark. TsGARUz, f. I-723, op. 1, d. 4, l. 76.

142. TsGARUz, f. I-723, op. 1, d. 3, l. 37.

143. The one Central Asian convicted for this incident was accused of yelling not to trust any promises the Russians might make regarding easing anti-cholera measures. TsGARUz, f. 723, op. 1, d. 2, l. 4.

144. Zykin, 348.

145. *TV*, no. 27 (1892).

146. Ibid.

147. The epidemic peaked from June 29 to July 12; official statistics record cholera striking an average of thirty people in the Russian city and one hundred and fifty people in the Asian city daily. *Turkestanskiia Viedomosti*, no. 28 (1892).

148. TsGARUz, f. I-36, op. 1, d. 3384, l. 155.

149. The military trial began on November 28, 1892. For the background to the trial, see Zykin, 347–50. The transcripts are held in TsGARUz, f. I-723, op. 1, d. 2.

150. Zykin, 333.

151. TsGARUz, f. I-723, op. 1, d. 4, l. 38.

152. TsGARUz, f. I-1, op. 31, d. 33, l. 1.

153. TsGARUz, f. I-1, op. 31, d. 33, l. 1ob.

154. TsGARUz, f. I-1, op. 31, d. 33, l. 364.

155. TsGARUz, f. I-1, op. 31, d. 33, l. 39.

156. Fedorov, 459.

157. Terent'ev, *Istoriia zavoevaniia Srednei Azii*, 3:374, 378.

158. Ibid., 373–74.

159. Fedorov, 458.

160. TV, no. 51 (1892).

161. TV, no. 50 (1892).

162. TsGARUz, f. I-1, op. 31, d. 33, l. 36.

163. Central Asians' visits to Russian doctors decreased by one-third in the wake of the cholera epidemic. Cavanaugh, 81.

164. Terent'ev, *Istoriia zavoevaniia Srednei Azii*, 3:378.

165. Shvarts, 128.

166. Ibid., 129.

167. Daniel Brower refers to the Central Asian demonstrators in 1892 as a "lynch mob." Brower, *Turkestan and the Fate of the Russian Empire*, 92.

## 4. Migration, Class, and Colonialism

1. *TV*, no. 49 (1884).

2. In so doing, they imagined class before, in the words of E. P. Thompson, "class happened." Thompson, *The Making of the English Working Class* (London: Penguin, 1963), 12.

3. Reginald Zelnik, *Labor and Society in Tsarist Russia: The Factory Workers of St. Petersburg, 1855–1870* (Stanford, Calif.: Stanford University Press, 1971).

4. Peasants were treated with more positive, albeit still ambivalent, imagery prior to the 1890s, as a wellspring of pure Russian culture against the degeneracy perceived in contemporary Russian cities. Frierson, *Peasant Icons*, 8.

5. These stories of early settler motives for arriving are largely anecdotal, though remarkably consistent. See Karazin, *Na Dalekikh Okrainakh*, 1–88.

6. The census was taken over one day by functionaries in the new city administration. *Materialy dlia Statistiki Turkestanskogo Kraia*, 1 (1872): prilozhenie, 7–12.

7. These censuses divided the population of Tashkent into nobles, clergy, honored citizens, traders, townspeople, soldiers, and various categories of "non-Russian" peoples.

8. On *sosloviia* and social realities, see Gregory Freeze, "The Sosloviia (Estate) Paradigm and Russian Social History," *American Historical Review* 91, no. 1 (1986): 11–36.

9. Maev, *Putevoditel' ot S-Peterburga do Tashkenta*, 53.

10. Karazin, *Russkaia Sredniaia Aziia*, 153.

11. Fedorov, no. 10 (1913): 35.

12. The Civil War in the United States had driven up the price of cotton and catalyzed a search in Russia for cheaper, more reliable sources of supply. See Rozhkova, *Ekonomicheskie sviazi Rossii so Srednei Aziei*, 48–92.

13. *Istoriia Uzbekskoi SSR*, 2:57.

14. Henri Moser, private letter to M. Bunau Varilla in an edition of Moser, *A travers l'Asie centrale*, at the library of the University of Illinois, Urbana-Champaign.

15. Rozenbakh, 114.

16. Azadaev, 149.

17. TsGARUz, f. I-1, op. 17, d. 96a, ll. 117–9.

18. *TV*, no. 47 (1883).

19. Ibid.

20. On the city commandant's worries over relations between Russian women and Muslim men, see TsGARUz, f. I-17, op. 1, d. 1132, l. 6.

21. Fedorov, no. 10 (1913): 35; Dobrosmyslov, *Tashkent v proshlom i nastoiashchem*, 81.

22. *Turkestanskii Kur'er* (hereafter *TK*), May 14, 1913.

23. TsGARUz, f. I-17, op. 1, d. 1132, l. 1.

24. On the figures, see Dobrosmyslov, *Tashkent v proshlom i nastoiashchem*, 325. On Central Asian prostitutes, see Kamp, 41, 55–57.

25. TsGARUz, f. I-17, op. 1, d. 1132, l. 42.

26. *TV*, no. 49 (1884).

27. Ibid.

28. See N. A. Maev, "Russkii Tashkent," 150, and Dobrosmyslov, *Tashkent v proshlom i nastoiashchem*, 98–99.

29. *TV*, no. 49 (1884).

30. *TV*, no. 50 (1884).

31. TsGARUz, f. I-36, op. 1, d. 2208, l. 5.

32. A. I. Ginzburg, *Russkoe Naselenie v Turkestane (konets XIX–nachalo XX veka)* (Moscow: Akademii Nauk SSSR, 1992), 31–32.

33. Pierce, *Russian Central Asia 1867–1917*, 116.

34. I. Geier, "Golod i kolonizatsiia Syr-Dar'inskoi oblasti v 1891 godu," *Sbornik Materialov dlia Statistiki Syr-Dar'inskoi oblasti* 3 (1894): 13.

35. *Obzor Syr-Dar'inskoi Oblasti za 1890 god*, 38.

36. Azadaev, 143.

37. *TV*, no. 2 (1890).

38. Ibid.

39. *TV*, no. 46 (1890); Dobrosmyslov, *Tashkent v proshlom i nastoiashchem*, 106–107.

40. K. K. Palen, *Otchet po revizii Turkestanskogo kraia, proizvedennoi po vysochaishchemu poveleniiu Senatorom Gofmeisterom Grafom K. K. Palenom* (St. Petersburg, 1910) 3:43–45.

41. Geier, "Golod i kolonizatsiia," 58.

42. Ibid., 25.

43. *TV*, nos. 44, 51 (1891).

44. Geier, "Golod i kolonizatsiia," 58.

45. TsGARUz, f. I-36, op. 1, d. 3339, l. 213.

46. TsGARUz, f. I-36, op. 1, d. 3339, l. 123.

47. TsGARUz, f. I-36, op. 1, d. 3339, l. 161.

48. Geier, "Golod i kolonizatsiia," 27, 58.

49. Ibid., 15.

50. *TV*, no. 1 (1893).

51. TsGARUz, f. I-36, op. 1, d. 876, l. 41.

52. *TV*, no. 33 (1892).

53. *TV*, no. 51 (1892).

54. TsGARUz, f. I-723, op. 1, d. 4, l. 78.

55. TsGARUz, f. I-723, op. 1, d. 4, l. 77.

56. TsGARUz, f. I-1, op. 31, d. 33, l. 25.

57. *Okraina,* Jan. 3, 1894.

58. Ibid.

59. *Okraina,* Mar. 19, 1894.

60. Ibid.

61. Stephen P. Frank, "Confronting the Domestic Other: Rural Popular Culture and Its Enemies in Fin-de-Siecle Russia," in *Cultures in Flux: Lower-class Values, Practices, and Resistance in Late Imperial Russia,* ed. Stephen P. Frank and Mark D. Steinberg (Princeton, N.J.: Princeton University Press, 1994), 77.

62. *Okraina,* Jan. 3, 1894.

63. Ginzburg, 31–32, 40.

64. *TV,* no. 20 (1893).

65. TsGARUz, f. I-1, op. 17, d. 96a, ll. 117–19.

66. TsGARUz, f. I-36, op. 1, d. 3442, l. 7.

67. TsGARUz, f. I-36, op. 1, d. 3442, l. 38.

68. *Russkii Turkestan* (hereafter *RT*), no. 66 (1898).

69. TsGARUz, f. I-1, op. 31, d. 33, l. 386.

70. Census tables can be found in Azadaev, 225.

71. Azadaev, 153–54, 159.

72. *RT,* no. 17 (1899).

73. A close associate wrote that the governor-general saw the building of a railway as the most important need for Turkestan. Eval'd, 192.

74. Brower, *Turkestan and the Fate of the Russian Empire,* 80.

75. *Putevoditel' po Turkestanu i Sredne-Aziatskoi Zheleznoi Dorogi,* ed. A. I. Dmitriev-Mamonov (St. Petersburg: Tipografiia I. Gol'dberga, 1903), 141.

76. Ibid.

77. *Istoriia Uzbekskoi SSR,* 2:62.

78. *Putevoditel' po Turkestanu,* 312.

79. *TV,* no. 1 (1901).

80. G. S. Kunavina, *Formirovanie Zheleznodorozhnogo Proletariata v Turkestane (1881–1914 gg)* (Tashkent: Izdatel'stvo "Fan," 1967), 20.

81. Henry Reichman, *Railwaymen and Revolution: Russia, 1905* (Berkeley: University of California Press, 1987), 71.

82. Kunavina, 57–58.

83. *Istoriia Uzbekskoi SSR,* 2:62.

84. Azadaev, 221.

85. *Putevoditel' po Turkestanu,* 312–15.

86. Five hundred and forty workers were employed in the main shops, with over one hundred more working elsewhere in the station.

87. Ginzburg, 136–37.

88. Kunavina, 46.

89. TsGARUz, f. I-1 op. 31, d. 212, l. 1.

90. Anatolii V. Piaskovskii, *Revoliutsiia 1905–1907 godov v Turkestane* (Moscow: Izdatel'stvo Akademii Nauk SSSR, 1958), 91.

91. TsGARUz, f. I-1, op. 31, d. 212, l. 1.

92. Exports of roughly processed cotton, fruits, rice, other foods, and leather totaled 1,631,016 *pudy* in 1900. Imports of manufactured goods, iron, tea, kero-

sene, foodstuffs, oil, sugar, and salt that year weighed in at 1,886,191 *pudy*. The Central Asian railway provided the largest source of employment in Tashkent. See *Putevoditel' po Turkestanu,* 348.

93. Jeffrey Richards and John MacKenzie, *The Railway Station: A Social History* (New York: Oxford University Press, 1986), 137.

94. *RT,* Oct. 1, 1905.

95. *RT,* July 3, 1904.

96. *RT,* Jan. 10, 1904.

97. *RT,* Jan. 23, 1904.

98. *RT,* Oct. 1, 1904.

99. On these efforts in the metropole, see Frank, 82–104.

100. Mark D. Steinberg, "Vanguard Workers and the Morality of Class," in *Making Workers Soviet: Class, Power, and Identity,* ed. Lewis H. Siegelbaum and Ronald Grigor Suny (Ithaca, N.Y.: Cornell University Press, 1994), 67.

101. On the tensions between inclusionary and exclusionary ideals and practices in modernist thought, see Uday S. Mehta, "Liberal Strategies of Exclusion," in *Tensions of Empire,* ed. Frederick Cooper and Ann Laura Stoler (Berkeley: University of California Press, 1997), 59–86.

102. On central policy, see Hans Rogger, *Russia in the Age of Modernization and Revolution 1881–1917* (London: Longman, 1983), 110–11.

103. Arnold, "White Colonization and Labor in 19th Century India," 152.

104. *RT,* Feb. 10 and Apr. 1, 1905.

105. *RT,* Feb. 25, 1904.

106. *RT,* Mar. 9, 1904.

107. On Bloody Sunday, see Gerald D. Surh, *1905 in St. Petersburg: Labor, Society, and Revolution* (Stanford, Calif.: Stanford University Press, 1989), 155–66.

108. For a list of worker demands, see *RT,* Feb. 19, 1905. The importance of the demand for the formal form of address has been recently argued by Jonathan Sanders, "Lessons from the Periphery: Saratov, January, 1905," *Slavic Review* 46, no. 2 (1987): 241.

109. *Samarkand,* Feb. 23, 1905; cited in Piaskovskii, 113.

110. *RT,* Feb. 22, 1905.

111. Ibid.

112. *Revoliutsiia 1905–1907 gg. v Uzbekistane. Dokumenty i Materialy* (Tashkent: Uzbekistan, 1984), 12.

113. *RT,* Mar. 25 and Apr. 14, 1905.

114. Management pressure may have played some role in this: Railway directors Ul'ianin and Ol'shevskii issued preemptive orders that any worker who joined the strike would be immediately sacked and replaced by a member of the railway battalions. *RT,* June 14 and July 14, 1905.

115. TsGARUz, f. I-129, op. 1, d. 769, l. 20. On the Bulygin duma, see Rogger, 211.

116. The editors of the liberal newspaper had begun to adopt a sympathetic viewpoint toward railway workers in 1904. Leaders of the railway strike in February 1905 became regular contributors to the publication, joining some of the leading exiles in the city, including G. I. Shavdiia. Aleksei Gol'bert and M. V. Morozov, once the leader of Samarkand's Social Democrats, had become

the leading forces on the newspaper by the end of 1905. G. S. Reiser, the liberal editor of the newspaper, wrote in November 1905, "I was no longer the editor of the newspaper *Russkii Turkestan;* my signature figured on the newspaper only when a certificate of permission was needed from St. Petersburg to continue operating the printshop." Writers used articles from metropolitan socialist newspapers *The Spark (Iskra)* and *The Proletarian (Proletarii)* for months, making clear the socialist orientation of the journal.

117. On hooliganism in the metropole, see Frank, 87–92; Joan Neuberger, *Hooliganism: Crime, Culture, and Power in St. Petersburg, 1900–1914* (Berkeley: University of California Press, 1993).

118. *RT,* June 17, 1905.

119. *RT,* Aug. 12, 1905.

120. *RT,* July 22, 1905.

121. For these attacks, see, for example, *RT,* Aug. 20 and Oct. 13, 1905.

122. *RT,* Dec. 4, 1905.

123. TsGARUz, f. I-133, op. 1, d. 344, l. 10–1.

124. TsGARUz, f. I-133, op. 1, d. 281, l. 31.

125. Piaskovskii, 23.

126. See, for example, *RT,* July 15, 1905.

127. *RT,* Oct. 15, 1905; V. D. Korniushin formed a "workers' militia" in October to protect the Jewish population of Russian Tashkent. Railway worker S. Anfinov wrote that "[militia] Groups were organized in the railway and central sections of town from railway and city workers. A duty roster was established for the most dangerous parts of the city and for apartments of some Jewish families." Anfinov, unpublished memoir, quoted in Piaskovskii, 23.

128. TsGARUz, f. I-129, op. 1, d. 774, l. 19.

129. *RT,* Mar. 27, 1905.

130. Ibid.

131. *RT,* Nov. 8, 1905.

132. Neuberger, 66.

133. *RT,* Apr. 24, 1905.

134. For a full list of demands, see Reichman, 217.

135. *RT,* Oct. 15–16, 1905.

136. *RT,* Oct. 30, 1905.

137. Piaskovskii, 230–31.

138. Sakharov was still requesting a copy from St. Petersburg on Oct 20. *Revoliutsiia 1905–1907 gg. v Uzbekistane. Dokumenty i Materialy* [hereafter R1905vUz], 78.

139. Piaskovskii, 215.

140. Fedorov, no. 12 (1913): 887.

141. TsGARUz, f. I-718, op. 1, d. 24, l. 385.

142. *R1905vUz,* 317.

143. Piaskovskii, 221.

144. *Sredneaziatskaia Zhizn'* (hereafter *SZ*), Nov. 13, 1905.

145. The motives for and organization and projected goals of the uprising remain hazy. See Piaskovskii, 273–76.

146. *RT,* Nov. 23, 1905.

147. Steinberg, "Vanguard Workers," 67.

148. *RT,* Dec. 8 and 10, 1905, and Feb. 8, 1906.

149. *RT,* June 1, 1906; Charters Wynn, *Workers, Strikes, and Pogroms: The Donbass-Dnepr Bend in Late Imperial Russia, 1870–1905* (Princeton, N.J.: Princeton University Press, 1992), 177.

150. William G. Rosenberg and Diane P. Koenker, "The Limits of Formal Protest: Worker Activism and Social Polarization in Petrograd and Moscow, March to October, 1917," *American Historical Review,* 92, no. 2 (1987): 307.

151. For the text of the order allowing workers to return, see Piaskovskii, 388.

152. *RT,* June 1,1906.

153. *RT,* June 27, 1906.

154. A. Rudyi, "Iul'skoe Vosstanie v Tashkente," *Istoricheskii Viestnik,* no. 6 (1909): 895.

155. TsGARUz, f. I-133, op. 1, d. 175, ll. 3–4.

156. *RT,* July 6, 1906.

157. *RT,* July 10, 1906.

158. *SZ,* no. 20 (1907).

159. *RT,* Aug. 24, 1906; *Turkestan,* Sept. 29, 1906.

160. Piaskovskii, 243.

161. *RT,* Jan. 9, 1906.

162. *Turkestan,* Sept. 24, 1906.

163. TsGARUz, f. I-133, op. 1, d. 477, l. 1.

164. *R1905vUz,* 278.

165. TsGARUz, f. I-213, op. 1, d. 259, ll. 3, 11.

166. *SZ,* Jan. 9, 1907; Piaskovskii, 512.

167. *Na Rubezhe,* Feb. 10, 1910.

## 5. The Predicaments of "Progress," 1905–1914

1. *SZ,* Nov. 24, 1905.

2. Ibid.

3. *RT,* Nov. 11, 1905.

4. *RT,* Nov. 3, 1905.

5. *SZ,* Nov. 2, 1905.

6. *Ibid.*

7. *TV,* Jan. 6, 1906.

8. *RT,* Nov. 1, 1905.

9. On these attacks, see *RT,* Nov. 15 and Dec. 16, 1905.

10. *RT,* Jan. 9, 1906.

11. Weeks, 21–43. As Weeks notes, however, these stances grew more ambiguous when discussed in practice.

12. *SZ,* Jan. 6, 1906.

13. Ibid.

14. Ibid.

15. *TV,* Jan. 6, 1906.

16. *SZ,* Jan. 6, 1906.

17. This trend became evident in central Russia as well. See Robert J. Edelman,

*Gentry Politics on the Eve of the Russian Revolution: The Nationalist Party, 1907–1917* (New Brunswick, N.J.: Rutgers University Press, 1980): 9, 24–26.

18. *TV*, no. 20 (1904).

19. *SZ*, Jan. 14, 1907.

20. *RT*, Nov. 3, 1905.

21. *SZ*, Nov. 4, 1905.

22. *SZ*, Feb. 2, 1906.

23. Fedorov, no. 12 (1913): 888; Piaskovskii, 256.

24. See Pierce, *Russian Central Asia*, 212–27.

25. Khalid, *The Politics of Muslim Cultural Reform*, 122–23.

26. Ibid.

27. Ibid., 93.

28. On the "mentality of modernism" see Edward Lazzerini, "Ismail Bey Gasparinskii (Gasparali): The Discourse of Modernism and the Russians," in *The Tatars of the Crimea: Return to the Homeland*, ed. Edward A. Allworth, 2nd ed. (Durham, N.C.: Duke University Press, 1998), 50.

29. On the development of these schools in the tsarist empire, beginning in Tatar regions, and the spread of Jadidist ideas to Central Asia, see Serge Zenkovsky, *Pan-Turkism and Islam in Russia 1905–1920* (Cambridge, Mass.: Harvard University Press, 1960).

30. *Taraqqi*, Jan. 29, 1906.

31. Khalid, *The Politics of Muslim Cultural Reform*, 100–101.

32. *Taraqqi*, Jan. 14, 1906; on *Khurshid*, see Khalid, *The Politics of Muslim Cultural Reform*, 108.

33. Khalid, *The Politics of Muslim Cultural Reform*, 122.

34. *Turkestan*, Sept. 23, 1906.

35. Zenkovsky, 42.

36. Khalid, *The Politics of Muslim Cultural Reform*, 91–2.

37. Ibid., 233.

38. *SZ*, May 11, 1906.

39. *Revoliutsiia 1905–1907 gg. v Uzbekistane. Dokumenty i Materialy*, 265.

40. Ibid., 267.

41. Khalid, *The Politics of Muslim Cultural Reform*, 234.

42. On Stolypin's actions, see Rogger, 225–26.

43. Russian moderate socialist I. I. Geier backed the publication of *Taraqqi* in 1905–1906. See Khalid, *The Politics of Muslim Cultural Reform*, 121–22.

44. *Taraqqi*, Jan. 29 and Mar. 17, 1906.

45. *Tujjor*, Nov. 21, 1907.

46. TsGARUz, f. I-36, op. 1, d. 4204, l. 7.

47. Ostroumov, *Sarty*, 102.

48. TsGARUz, f. I-718, op. 1, d. 37, l. 26.

49. Ibid.

50. Khalid, *The Politics of Muslim Cultural Reform*, 123.

51. *SZ*, Mar. 17, 1906.

52. P. G. Galuzo, *Turkestan-Koloniia. (Ocherk istorii Turkestana ot zavoevaniia russkimi do revoliutsii 1917 goda)* (Moscow, 1929), 74.

53. *Turkestanskiia Viedomosti*, no 4 (1908).,

54. N. Gavrilov, *Pereselencheskoe delo v Turkestanskom krae (oblasti Syr-Dar'inskaia, Samarkandskaia, i Ferganskaia)* (St. Petersburg, 1911), 4.

55. On these decrees, see Ginzburg, 31–32, and Gavrilov, 4.

56. TsGARUz, f. I-16, op. 1, d. 29a, ll. 30, 180.

57. Kunavina, 57–58.

58. The Resettlement Administration published information on the advantages of settlement, provided reduced rail fares to migrants, and built shelters for them at various transit points, along with other initiatives to enable a large flow to Asiatic Russia. See Pierce, *Russian Central Asia*, 130–32.

59. On Stolypin's policies, see Donald W. Treadgold, *The Great Siberian Migration: Government and Peasant in Resettlement from Emancipation to the First World War* (Princeton, N.J.: Princeton University Press, 1957).

60. Treadgold, 184–204.

61. Dov B. Yaroshevski, "Russian Regionalism in Turkestan," *Slavonic and East European Review* 65, no. 1 (1987): 81–82.

62. *SZ*, Feb. 18, 1906, and Jan. 11, 1907.

63. *Na Rubezhe*, Oct. 9, 1910.

64. See Anatole Maria Bariatinsky, *My Russian Life* (London: Hutchinson, 1923), 176–83; *SZ*, Jan. 11, 1907.

65. *SZ*, Jan. 24, 1907.

66. TsGARUz, f. 69, op. 1, d. 1, l. 26.

67. Ginzburg, 66.

68. *SZ*, Jan. 11, 1907.

69. *Obzor Syr-Dar'inskoi Oblasti za 1912 god* (Tashkent: Tipo-litografiia V. M. Il'ina, 1914): 38.

70. Ginzburg, 51, 122; Galuzo, 195–208.

71. Ginzburg, 51, 122; Galuzo, 195–208.

72. *SZ*, Jan. 11, 1907; Ginzburg, 87, 95.

73. Pierce, 136.

74. *Obzor Syr-Dar'inskoi Oblasti za 1912 god*, 163.

75. *Na Rubezhe*, nos. 95, 109 (1909).

76. *TV*, no. 250 (1911); on hostility to migrants, see also *Na Rubezhe*, nos. 95, 109 (1909).

77. TsGARUz, f. I-16, op. 1, d. 29a, l. 129.

78. Palen, 1:378–79.

79. Muriel Joffe, "Autocracy, Capitalism, and Empire: The Politics of Irrigation," *Russian Review* 54, no. 3 (1995): 370–73.

80. Galuzo, 110.

81. Gavrilov, 99–100.

82. Galuzo, 113.

83. Masal'skii published an article on the subject in *Moskovskiia Viedomosti* on May 18, 1912. See Joffe, 372.

84. A. P. Demidov, *Ekonomicheskii Ocherk khlopkovodstva, khlopkotorgovli i khlopkovoi promyshlennosti Turkestana* (Moscow, 1922), 36.

85. *Obzor Syr-Dar'inskoi Oblasti za 1912 god*, 125.

86. Ibid., 126.

87. The most renowned example of this was N. M. Iadrintsev's *Sibir kak kolo-niia: k iubileiu trekhsotletiia* (St. Petersburg: Tipografii M. M. Stasiulevicha, 1882). See his arguments on 258–62, 295.

88. Yaroshevski, 81.

89. On the definition of *koloniia*, see *Entsiklopedicheskii slovar' Russkogo biblio-graficheskago instituta Granat* (Moscow, 1912), 24:518.

90. *Tashkentskii Kur'er,* Feb. 13, 1906.

91. *Obzor Syr-Dar'inskoi Oblasti za 1912 god,* 125.

92. *SZ,* Nov. 24, 1905.

93. See, for example, *SZ,* Feb. 26, 1906; *TV,* no. 3 (1912).

94. *SZ,* Feb. 26, 1906.

95. Markov, 1:528.

96. *SZ,* Mar. 17, 1906.

97. *Tashkentskii Kur'er,* Jan. 17, 1908.

98. Ibid.

99. *SZ,* July 25, 1906.

100. Dobrosmyslov, *Tashkent v proshlom i nastoiashchem,* 99.

101. Ginzburg, 72, 95, 115.

102. Karazin, *Russkaia Sredniaia Aziia,* 150.

103. *TV,* no. 74 (1903).

104. The term emerged from the Russian *chistit'* (to clean), reflecting their posi-tion as agents of cotton cleaning factories. See *Istoriia Tashkenta,* 184; Galuzo, 118; Khalid, *The Politics of Muslim Cultural Reform,* 65.

105. In 1914, 159 cotton-processing plants were operating in Fergana, compared to 28 in the Syr-Dar'ia oblast. V. Suvorov, *Istoriko-Ekonomicheskii ocherk razvitiia Turkestana* (Tashkent: Gosizdat Uzbekskaia SSR, 1962), 35–36.

106. Dobrosmyslov, *Tashkent v proshlom i nastoiashchem,* 374.

107. *SZ,* June 13, 1906; *Istoriia Tashkenta,* 185.

108. *SZ,* Jan. 1, 1907.

109. Such a trend was present in central Russia. For explorations of this topic, see Clowes, Kassow, and West, 41–130.

110. *Na Rubezhe,* Oct. 6, 1909.

111. TsGARUz, f. I-36, op. 1, d. 4699 ll. 28–32.

112. *Na Rubezhe,* Sept. 12, 1909.

113. *Turkestanskii Kara-Kurt,* no. 1–4, 6, 8 (1911).

114. Joffe, 378–85.

115. Dobrosmyslov, *Tashkent v proshlom i nastoiashchem,* 374. On Russian capital in Tashkent at this period, see also *Istoriia Tashkenta,* 178–88.

116. *Obzor Syr-Dar'inskoi Oblasti za 1912 god,* 136; Marco Buttino, "Turkestan 1917: La révolution des russes," *Cahiers du monde russe et soviétique* 32, no. 1 (1991): 63.

117. Steven G. Marks, *Road to Power: The Trans-Siberian Railroad and the Coloniza-tion of Asian Russia* (Ithaca, N.Y.: Cornell University Press, 1991), 222.

118. *TK,* May 17, 1913.

119. *Turkestanskii Sbornik,* 502:221.

120. *Na Rubezhe,* Sept. 24, 1909.

121. Alice J. Conklin, "Colonialism and Human Rights: A Contradiction in Terms?" *American Historical Review* 103, no. 2 (1998): 419–42.

122. Slezkine, 390.

123. Bernard Semmel, *The Liberal Ideal and the Demons of Empire* (Baltimore: Johns Hopkins University Press, 1993).

124. On the impact of the Russo-Japanese war in Russia, see Geraci, 266.

125. See *Obzor Syr-Dar'inskoi Oblasti za 1912 god,:* 131; *Istoriia Tashkenta,* 168; *Istoriia Uzbekskoi SSR,* 2:176–77.

126. Dobrosmyslov, *Tashkent v proshlom i nastoiashchem,* 79–80.

127. Ibid., 79.

128. Mallitskii, 108–109.

129. Muslim workers earned an estimated 37 percent less than Russian workers in Tashkent. *Istoriia Uzbekskoi SSR* (1968), 2:202–203, 336–37.

130. Palen, 3:50–52.

131. *Sada-yi Turkistan,* Dec. 4, 1914.

132. TsGARUz, f. I-718, op. 1, d. 55, l. 341.

133. On these methods, see Khalid, *The Politics of Muslim Cultural Reform,* 127–54.

134. *Sada-yi Turkestan,* Apr. 17, 1914.

135. Zenkovsky, 85.

136. Adeeb Khalid, "Representations of Russia in Central Asian Jadid Discourse," in *Russia's Orient: Imperial Borderlands and Peoples, 1700–1917,* ed. Daniel R. Brower and Edward J. Lazzerini (Bloomington: Indiana University Press, 1997), 194.

137. *Sada-yi Turkestan,* July 25 and Aug. 14, 1914.

138. *Sada-yi Turkestan,* May 2, 1914.

139. Behbudi, quoted in Khalid, *The Politics of Muslim Cultural Reform,* 219.

140. *Sada-yi Turkestan,* Apr. 4 and May 17, 1914.

141. *Na Rubezhe,* Jan. 24, 1910.

142. *TV,* no. 83 (1903); on the activities of these women's clinics, see Cavanaugh, 56–61.

143. *TK,* June 15, 1914.

144. Bariatinsky, 175.

145. *Sada-yi Turkestan,* May 30, 1914; see also Khalid, *The Politics of Muslim Cultural Reform,* 223–26.

146. On the phenomenon of Panislamism, see Zenkovsky.

147. TsGARUz, f. I-36, op. 1, d. 6100, l. 8.

148. TsGARUz, f. I-36, op. 1, d. 4699, ll. 30, 30ob.

149. Khalid, *The Politics of Muslim Cultural Reform,* 183.

150. *Sada-yi Turkestan,* Dec. 3, 1914.

151. On the court case, see TsGARUz, f. I-133, op. 1, d. 174, l. 2. On reports of beatings in the Russian press, see *Russkii Turkestan,* Mar. 11, 1898; *Na Rubezhe,* July 22 ,1910. On other forms of extortion, see V. P. Nalivkin, *Tuzemtsy ran'she i teper'* (Tashkent, 1913), 129–34; Galuzo, 119.

152. *Turkistan Wilayatining Gazeti,* Feb. 14, 1910.

153. Frierson, 182.

## 6. War, Empire, and Society, 1914–1916

1. TsGARUz, f. I-461, op. 1, d. 1840, l. 24.

2. Sinha, 11.

3. As G. C. Spivak argues, the voices of the underprivileged and oppressed are almost always heavily mediated in imperial situations, recorded within a context of, and often in direct response to, the oppressive mechanisms of colonialism. G. C. Spivak, "Can the Subaltern Speak?," in *Marxism and the Interpretation of Culture*, ed. C. Nelson and L. Grossberg (Basingstoke, U.K.: MacMillan Education, 1988), 272–313.

4. *TK*, July 22, 1916.

5. *TK*, Aug. 22, 1916.

6. *Obzor Syr-Dar'inskoi oblasti za 1912 god*, prilozheniia, ii–iii.

7. *TV*, July 1, 1916; *Nasha Gazeta*, June 15, 1917.

8. Peter Gatrell, *A Whole Empire Walking: Refugees in Russia in World War I* (Bloomington: Indiana University Press, 1999), 36–47.

9. On reactions across Russia, see Gatrell, 49–72; on Tashkent, see TsGARUz, f. I-37, op. 1, d. 546, l. 58.

10. Members included the wives of the mayor and police chiefs of Tashkent, as well as other prominent local officials. On press coverage, *TV*, Jan. 27, Mar. 13 and 25, and July 7, 1916.

11. The committee took its name from the second daughter of the tsar.

12. Gatrell, 40–42.

13. *TK*, Jan. 1, 1916.

14. Gosudarstvennyi Arkhiv Goroda Tashkenta (Toshkent Shahar Davlat Arkhivi) (State Archive of the City of Tashkent) (hereafter GAGT), f. 10, op. 1, d. 33, ll. 1–6.; TsGARUz, f. 37, op. 1, d. 633, ll. 1–2.

15. *TK*, Jan. 9, 1916. See also *TV*, July 27, 1916.

16. *TK*, July 1, 1916.

17. *TK*, Sept. 30, 1914.

18. *TK*, Mar. 7, 1916.

19. TsGARUz, f. I-461, op. 1, d. 1830, l. 1.

20. *TV*, no. 125 (1915).

21. *TK*, Nov. 23, 1916.

22. See, for example, *TV*, Aug. 12 and Nov. 10, 1916.

23. TsGARUz, f. I-461, op. 1, d. 1830, l. 655.

24. *TK*, Apr. 2, 1916.

25. Davis visited the camp as a representative of the YMCA. Jerome Davis, "The Death Camp in Turkestan," *Unpartizan Review* 13, no. 1 (1920): 60–70.

26. Alf H. Brun, *Troublous Times: Experiences in Bolshevik Russia and Turkestan* (London: Constable, 1931), 55, 95–100.

27. TsGARUz, f. I-16, op. 1, d. 1867, l. 110, 186.

28. *Istoriia Uzbekskoi SSR*, 2:520.

29. P. A. Kovalev, "Zhenkii 'babii' bunt v Tashkente," *Nauchnye Trudy Tashkentskogo gosudarstvennogo universiteta imeni V. I. Lenina* 233 (1964): 18. The land use for cotton increased from 643,568 to 724,997 hectares.

30. Kovalev, 19.

31. Buttino, "Turkestan 1917: La révolution des russes," 65.

32. Ibid., 63.

33. Gatrell, 28.

34. *TK*, Apr. 11 and 22, 1915.

35. *TK*, Apr. 11, 1915.

36. Complaints of these practices are ubiquitous in the Russian press as well as in archival reports about market activity in Tashkent. See *TV*, no. 25 (1901), no. 89 (1905), no. 4 (1912), as well as *Na Rubezhe*, Apr. 22, 1910. *Turkestanskii Skorpion*, no. 2 (1907), and TsGARUz, f. I-37, op. 1, d. 569, l. 182.

37. Turkestanskii Sbornik, 515:88.

38. *TK*, Mar. 20, 1915.

39. *TV*, no. 3 (1912).

40. *TV*, no. 89 (1905).

41. *TV*, no. 74 (1903); no. 2 (1912).

42. Palen, 3:48–51.

43. *TK*, July 12, 1915.

44. *TK*, May 27, 1915.

45. TsGARUz, f. I-37, op. 1, d, 569, l. 83; *TK*, Jan. 13, 1916.

46. TsGARUz, f. I-37, op. 1, d. 569. l. 30.

47. *TK*, Jan. 5, 1916.

48. Many refugees feared that if they took a job and were subsequently released from employment, they would lose all claims to state assistance. TsGARUz, f. I-37, op. 1, d. 546, l. 72. On prisoners of war, see TsGARUz, f. I-461, op. 1, d. 1840, l. 24.

49. *TK*, Jan. 23 and Feb. 14, 1916.

50. Engel acknowledges her debt to E. P. Thompson in making this argument. See Engel, 701.

51. Ibid., 713.

52. John Bohstedt, "The Myth of the Feminine Food Riot: Women as Proto-Citizens in English Community Politics, 1790–1810," in *Women and Politics in the Age of Democratic Revolution*, ed. Harriet Applewhite and Darlene Levy (Ann Arbor: University of Michigan Press, 1990), 38.

53. TsGARUz, f. I-1011, op. 1, d. 164a, l. 28.

54. *Turkestanskii Kara-Kurt*, 1911, no. 3.

55. TsGARUz, f. I-1011, op. 1, d. 164, l. 22.

56. TsGARUz, f. I-1011, op. 1, d. 164, l. 9.

57. TsGARUz, f. I-1011, op. 1, d. 164, l. 135.

58. TsGARUz, f. I-1011, op. 1, d. 164b, l. 105.

59. TsGARUz, f. I-1011, op. 1, d. 164a, l. 27.

60. TsGARUz, f. I-1011, op. 1, d. 164b, l. 69.

61. TsGARUz, f. I-1011, op. 1, d. 164a, l. 125.

62. TsGARUz, f. I-1, op. 31, d. 315, l. 3.

63. TsGARUz, f. I-1011, op. 1, d. 164b, l. 104.

64. TsGARUz, f. I-1011, op. 1, d. 164a, l. 28ob.

65. TsGARUz, f. I-1011, op. 1, d. 164a, l. 111.

66. TsGARUz, f. I-1011, op. 1, d. 164, l. 111.

67. TsGARUz, f. I-1011, op. 1, d. 164a, l. 222.

68. TsGARUz, f. I-1011, op. 1, d 164 l. 114; d. 164v, ll. 120–22.

69. *TV,* Jan. 16, 1916.

70. TsGARUz, f. I-1011, op. 1, d. 164a, l. 111.

71. TsGARUz, f. I-1011, op. 1, d. 164, l. 75.

72. TsGARUz, f. I-1011, op. 1, d. 164b, l. 141.

73. See Hubertus Jahn, *Patriotic Culture in Russia during World War I* (Ithaca, N.Y.: Cornell University Press, 1995).

74. On the Baku riots, see Ronald Grigor Suny, *The Baku Commune 1917–1918: Class and Nationality in the Russian Revolution* (Princeton, N.J.: Princeton University Press, 1972), 64; for Kliutko's testimony, see TsGARUz, f. I-1011, op. 1, d, 164a, l. 112.

75. TsGARUz, f. I-1, op. 32, d. 315, l. 1.

76. TsGARUz, f. I-718, op. 1, d. 54, ll. 558–62; see also *TK,* Mar. 5, 1916.

77. *TK,* Mar. 9 and 11, 1916.

78. *TV,* Mar. 30, 1916.

79. *TV,* Mar. 6 and 8, 1916.

80. Ibid.

81. Kovalev, 26.

82. *TV,* Mar. 4, 1916.

83. *TK,* Sept. 29, 1916.

84. *TK,* Mar. 7, 1916.

85. TsGARUz, f. I-1, op. 32, d. 315, l. 19ob.

86. Khalid, *Politics of Muslim Cultural Reform,* 237.

87. Adeeb Khalid argues that Khojaev and other Russian-educated Central Asian professionals should be viewed separately from the Jadids. The former rose from aristocratic status instead of from cultural elites from middle strata. In this case, however, the two groups worked together. Khalid, *Politics of Muslim Cultural Reform,* 105.

88. *Sada-yi Turkestan,* Aug. 28, 1914.

89. Ibid.

90. Buttino, 65. See also Edward Dennis Sokol, *The Revolt of 1916 in Russian Central Asia* (Baltimore, Md.: Johns Hopkins University Press, 1954), 72–73.

91. *TV,* Mar. 24, 1916.

92. Sokol, 76–77.

93. *Vosstanie 1916 g. v Kirgizstane. Dokumenty i Materialy* (Moscow: Sotsial'no-Ekonomicheskoe Izdatel'stvo, 1937), 18.

94. Demonstrators possibly heard of the order through telegraphists who had transmitted it from Petrograd.

95. *Vosstanie 1916 goda v Srednei Azii i Kazakhstane. Sbornik Dokumentov.* (Moscow: Izdatel'stvo Akademii Nauk SSSR, 1960), 261–320.

96. TsGARUz, f. I-1, op. 31, d. 1100, l. 232.

97. Turar Rysqulov, *Revoliutsiia i korennoe naselenie Turkestana* (Tashkent: Uzbekskoe Gosudarstvennoe Izdatel'stvo, 1925), 96.

98. TsGARUz, f. I-1, op. 31, d. 1100, l. 230.

99. TsGARUz, f. I-1, op. 31, d. 1100, l. 232.

100. TsGARUz, f. I-132, op. 1, d. 472, l. 18.

101. TsGARUz, f. I-1, op. 31, d. 1100, ll. 231, 250.

102. Rysqulov, 96.

103. TsGARUz, f. I-1, op. 31, d. 1100, l. 232.

104. Kamp, 103–106.

105. *TV*, July 15 and 18, 1916.

106. "Gubernator v roli propovednika korana," *Krasnyi Arkhiv* 75 (1936): 187–90.

107. D. I. Manzhara, *Revoliutsionnoe Dvizhenie v Srednei Azii 1905–1920 gg. (Vospominaniia)* (Tashkent: Sredpartizdat, 1934), 32.

108. *TK*, Aug. 9, 1916.

109. *TV*, Sept. 14, 1916; for Kuropatkin's recounting of the tours, see his diary in "Vosstanie 1916 g. v Srednei Azii," *Krasnyi Arkhiv* 34 (1929): 50–62.

110. *TK*, Aug. 24 and Sept. 7, 1916; *TV*, Sept. 1, 1916.

111. *TV*, Nov. 5, 1916.

112. Khalid, *The Politics of Muslim Cultural Reform*, 241.

113. Galuzo, 157.

114. *TV*, Sept. 29, 1916.

115. *TK*, Nov. 5 and 11, 1916.

116. *TK*, Nov. 23, 1916.

117. *TV*, Nov. 27, 1916.

118. *TV*, Sept. 23, 1916.

119. *TV*, Aug. 21, 1916.

120. *TV*, July 26, 1916; *TK*, Nov. 11, 1916.

121. *TV*, Aug. 14, 1916.

122. *TV*, June 8, 1916.

123. *TV*, June 22, and July 15, 1916.

124. Buttino, 63.

125. *Istoriia Uzbekskoi SSR*, 2:524.

126. TsGARUz, f. I-461, op. 1, d. 1840, ll. 27–31.

127. *TV*, Nov. 11, 1916.

128. *TV*, Nov. 11, 1916.

129. *TV*, Sept. 18, 1916.

130. Ibid.

131. *TK*, Oct. 28, 1916.

132. *TV*, Nov. 10, 1916.

133. *TK*, Sept. 8, 1916.

134. TsGARUz, f. I-37, op. 1, d. 569, l. 438.

135. *TV*, Nov. 11, 1916.

136. *TV*, Dec. 16, 1916.

137. *TV*, Dec. 23, 1916.

138. TsGARUz, f. I-37, op. 1, d. 569, ll. 377, 438.

## 7. Exploiters or Exploited?

1. For a recent study of "dual power" at the center and on the periphery, see Peter Holquist, *Making War, Forging Revolution: Russia's Continuum of Crisis, 1914–1921* (Cambridge, Mass.: Harvard University Press, 2002). Holquist

describes a "dual power" in the Don region split along ethnic rather than class lines, but still uses traditional historiographical terms to simplify a chaotic situation.

2. Orlando Figes and Boris Kolonitskii, *Interpreting the Russian Revolution: The Languages and Symbols of 1917* (New Haven, Conn.: Yale University Press, 1999), 126.

3. R. G. Suny has examined the complex relationship between class and nationality in the Russian revolutionary era, but regards the issue primarily from the perspective of minority nationalities within the empire. See Suny, *The Baku Commune 1917–1918*, and "Nationalism and Class in the Russian Revolution: a Comparative Discussion," in *Revolution in Russia: Reassessments of 1917*, ed. Edith Rogovin Frankel, Jonathan Frankel, and Baruch Knei-Paz (Cambridge: Cambridge University Press, 1992), 219–46.

4. Lars T. Lih, *Bread and Authority in Russia, 1914–1921* (Berkeley: University of California Press, 1990), 156.

5. Such a parting of ways between workers and soviets over the politics of provisioning has been noted elsewhere in revolutionary Russia. See, for example, Lih; Alexander Rabinowitch, "The Petrograd First City Soviet during the Civil War," and Mary McAuley, "Bread without the Bourgeoisie," in *Party, State, and Society in the Russian Civil War: Explorations in Social History*, ed. Diane P. Koenker, William G. Rosenberg, and Ronald G. Suny (Bloomington: Indiana University Press, 1989), 133–57, 158–79; and Donald J. Raleigh, "Languages of Power: How the Saratov Bolsheviks Imagined their Enemies," *Slavic Review* 57, no. 2 (1998): 320–49.

6. These concessions included short working days, the right to "rest" before as well as during holidays, medical assistance at the cost of the employer, severance pay in case of terminations without warning, and "etc." K. K. Palen, *Otchet po revizii Turkestanskogo kraia*, quoted in G. Safarov, *Kolonial'naia Revoliutsiia. Opyt Turkestana* (Moscow: Gosudarstvennoe Izdatel'stvo, 1921), 39.

7. For this and other schemes, see Manzhara, 6–7.

8. Ibid., 10.

9. Ibid., 8.

10. *TV*, July 26, 1916; TsGARUz, f. I-1044, op. 1, d. 164a, l. 148.

11. Manzhara, 31.

12. Ibid.

13. *Nasha Gazeta* (hereafter *NG*), June 15, 1917.

14. Manzhara, 36.

15. Khalid, *The Politics of Muslim Cultural Reform*, 247.

16. GAGT, f. 10, op. 13, d. 2, ll. 1–2; *NG*, Apr. 23, 1917.

17. Khalid, *The Politics of Muslim Cultural Reform*, 248.

18. Joseph Castagné, "Le Turkestan depuis la révolution russe," *Revue du monde musulman* 50 (1922): 33.

19. Castagné, 35.

20. *TV*, Apr. 20, 1917.

21. *TV*, Apr. 28, 1917.

22. TsGARUz, f. I-1044, op. 1, d. 16, l. 1; *TV*, Jan. 4, 5, and 14, 1917.

23. See Manzhara, 58–73; V. Bauman, *Bor'ba za vlast sovetov v Tashkente* (Tash-

kent, 1922), 1–2; *TV*, Feb. 23 and Apr. 28, 1917; *Turkestanskoe Slovo*, Aug. 30, 1917.

24. TsGARUz, f. I-37, op. 1, d. 661, ll. 18–19.

25. *TV*, Jan. 11 and Feb. 23, 1917.

26. *Pobeda Oktiabr'skoi Revoliutsii v Uzbekistane: Sbornik Dokumentov* (hereafter *PORvUz*) (Tashkent: Izdatel'stvo Akademii Nauk UzSSR, 1963) 1:84–85.

27. Manzhara, 40.

28. GAGT, f. 10. op. 13, d. 2, l. 3.

29. *TK*, Apr. 2, 1917.

30. *Revoliutsiia i natsional'nyi vopros. Dokumenty i materialy po istorii natsional'nogo voprosa v Rossii i SSSR v XX veke* (Moscow: Izdatel'stvo Kommunisticheskoi akademii, 1930), 3:71–2.

31. Tensions between Russian farmers and the local population in the region continued following the mass violence there in 1916. *Istoriia Uzbekskoi SSR* (1968), 2:579.

32. "Iz dnevnika A. N. Kuropatkina," *Krasnyi Arkhiv* 20 (1927): 64.

33. Eight of the members were from the state duma; in addition, there was a Tatar officer, Abdel Azis Azisov Davletshin. TsGARUz, f. I-1044, op. 1, d. 37, l. 2.

34. *PORvUz* 1: 89–90.

35. For details on Nalivkin's career, see B. V. Lunin, *Istoriia Obshchestvennykh nauk v Uzbekistane*, 247–58.

36. *Utro Rossii*, June 15, 1917; quoted in Castagné, 36.

37. On soviet activities, see *NG*, Apr. 23, 1917; GAGT, f. 10, op. 13, d. 1. By early August, the Procurator of the Tashkent Okrug Court, I. D. Baranovskii, reported that urban soviets in Turkestan appeared "as the unique organizations holding power connected to the population, and which, not only in words, but in deeds, can support its demands." *PORvUz*, 1: 212–13. Other studies of the Russian periphery have reached similar conclusions; see Donald Raleigh, *Revolution on the Volga: 1917 in Saratov* (Ithaca, N.Y.: Cornell University Press, 1986), and Suny, *The Baku Commune 1917–1918*, 120–24.

38. *NG*, Aug. 19, 1917.

39. *TK*, Apr. 7, 1917.

40. *TV*, Apr. 28, 1917.

41. *NG*, May 3, 1917.

42. *TK*, June 11, 1916.

43. Protokol No. 8, First Turkestan Regional Assembly of Soviets and Workers and Soldiers Deputies, in *PORvUz*, 1:64.

44. *TK*, July 5, 1917.

45. In June, the soviet announced that, to support the war effort, it favored the revocation of the ability of those born or having moved to Turkestan as children to decline military service. *NG*, June 4 and 15, 1917.

46. *TK*, July 8, 1917.

47. *TK*, July 7, 1917.

48. *TK*, July 18, 1917.

49. *NG*, June 20, 1917.

50. Khalid, *The Politics of Muslim Cultural Reform*, 264.

51. Ibid., 258–60.

52. Ibid., 252–69.

53. *TV*, Apr. 25, 1917; *TK*, May 14, 1917.

54. *TK*, Aug. 2, 1917.

55. Receiving two seats each were the Radical Democrats (a moderate Russian liberal organization), the Union of Houseowners, and the Committee of Public Organizations. Single seats were obtained by the Russian Jewish party, the Union of Cossacks, the Party of People's Freedom, the Society of Native Jews and the Muslim Union of Construction Workers. Neither the "Progressive Women" or the "Union of Soldier's Wives," received seats. For complete results, see *TV*, Aug. 3, 1917.

56. *TV*, Aug. 5, 1917.

57. On these fears, see *NG*, Aug. 5, 1917. The ulama majority had nominated in turn two Russian conservatives, the Orientalist-turned-tsarist functionary-turned-politician N. S. Lykoshin and Iakomovich. Both times, the Socialist Revolutionaries, calling Lykoshin a "tsarist lackey," protested by leaving the chamber, followed by the Social Democrats. The Muslim council also opposed the election of these conservatives. The duma, becoming absorbed in these conflicts, never wielded significant power. See *NG*, Aug. 20 and 25, 1917; *TV*, Sept. 8, 1917.

58. Jadids pressed for women to vote (they had the formal right to do so) but the ulama largely prevented this. *TK*, Aug. 3, 1917.

59. *NG*, Sept. 5, 1917.

60. *Sovetskii Turkestan*, Jan. 19, 1918.

61. *NG*, Aug. 23, 1917.

62. *TV*, July 15, 1917; see also *TV*, Aug. 5 and 6, 1917, and *NG*, Aug. 5, 1917.

63. *NG*, Aug. 5, 1917.

64. Hostilities in the Semirechie, the scene of some of the heaviest fighting during the rebellion of 1916, began once more following the return of thousands of Kazakhs who had fled to China. Kuropatkin had distributed arms to Russian settlers in March 1917. Settlers and some Russian soldiers released to work on agricultural lands initiated a series of "hunts" against the Kazakhs as well as slaughtering their livestock. See Marco Buttino, "Study of the Economic Crisis and Depopulation in Turkestan, 1917–1920," *Central Asian Survey* 9, no. 4 (1990): 69–70.

65. *Ulugh Turkestan*, Aug. 23, 1917, quoted in Khalid, *The Politics of Muslim Cultural Reform*, 272.

66. *NG*, Aug. 20, 1917.

67. *TV*, July 20, 1917.

68. *NG*, Aug. 9, 1917.

69. Bauman, 2; TsGARUz, f. I-1044, op. 1, d. 8, l. 176ob.

70. *TV*, Sept. 10, 1917.

71. Bauman, 3; *Turkestanskoe Slovo*, Sept. 3, 1917.

72. GAGT, f. 10, op. 13, d. 4, l. 18; *TV*, Sept. 20, 1917.

73. Manzhara, 59.

74. On the meeting, see Bauman, 3–4. The soviet had split in August into radical and moderate factions, with the radicals, calling themselves Social Demo-

crats, intent on overthrowing the duma and the Turkkom, and the moderates, under the Soviet Revolutionary banner, willing to adhere to the status quo. See *NG*, Aug. 10, 1917; Manzhara, 57.

75. *NG*, Sept. 14, 1917.

76. Manzhara, 60.

77. *PORvUz*, 1:330.

78. *TV*, Oct. 19, 1917.

79. GAGT, f. 10, op. 13, d. 8, l. 76.

80. For a firsthand account of the fighting, see A. Baratov, "Oktiabr' i Grazhdanskaia voina v Srednei Azii," *Istoriia Proletariata SSR* no. 1 (1934): 149–51.

81. *PORvUz*, 1:326, 384.

82. Ibid., 274.

83. *TV*, Nov. 19, 1917.

84. *TV*, Nov. 21, 1917.

85. *NG*, Nov. 23, 1917; see also Safarov, 70, and Manzhara, 80.

86. *NG*, Dec. 9, 1917.

87. A. H. Brun, 55, and Castagné, 43–44.

88. GAGT, f. 10, op. 13, d. 2, l. 180.

89. TsGARUz, f. R-[Revoliutsionnaia chast'] 25, op. 1, d. 4, l. 46.

90. GAGT, f. 10, op. 1, d. 62, l. 56.

91. GAGT, f. 10, op. 13, d. 4, l. 125.

92. GAGT, f. 10, op. 13, d. 4, l. 129.

93. Several sources mention the presence of Russians at these deliberations, but none offer any specific details. See, for example, Safarov, 73. On the rally, see GAGT, f. 10, op. 1, 32, l. 327.

94. Mustafa Chokayev, "Turkestan and the Soviet Regime," *Journal of the Royal Central Asian Society* 18 (1931): 407–408.

95. Turkestan's Russian population was estimated between 5 and 7 percent. Ibid.

96. GAGT, f. 10, op. 13, d. 4, l. 184.

97. See *Turkestanskoe Slovo*, Sept. 16, 1917, and *Svobodnyi Turkestan*, Jan. 6, 1918.

98. GAGT, f. 10, op. 13, d. 2, l. 188.

99. Ibid.

100. Manzhara, 83; Brun, 61–62.

101. GAGT, f. 10, op. 1, d. 25, l. 28.

102. *NG*, Dec. 21, 1917, and Jan. 3 and 4, 1918.

103. *TV*, Nov. 15, 1917.

104. Miserable conditions in the prison camps also facilitated recruitment. Brun, 74–111.

105. Gustav Krist, *Prisoner in the Forbidden Land*, trans. E. O. Lorimer (London: Faber and Faber, 1938); F. M. Bailey, *Mission to Tashkent* (London: Jonathan Cape, 1946), 42.

106. Safarov, 80; on the assault, see GAGT, f. 10, op. 13, d. 35, l. 19, and Alexander G. Park, *Bolshevism in Turkestan, 1917–27* (New York: Columbia University Press, 1957), 21.

107. GAGT, f. 10, op. 13, d. 35, l. 19.

108. Brun, 79.

109. A. Rakhimov, "K voprosu o kharaktere prodovol'stvennoi politiki sovets-koi vlasti v Turkestane v gody grazhdanskoi voiny (1918–1921 gg.)," *Nauchnye Raboty i Soobshcheniia* (Akademii nauk Uzbekskoi SSR, Otdel Obshchestvennykh nauk) 2 (1961): 63.

110. *Novyi Turkestan*, Feb. 11, 1918; for the recent study, see V. Semeniuta, "Golod v Turkestane v 1917–1920 godakh," *Chelovek i Politika* (Dec. 1991): 74.

111. Castagné, 55.

112. For biographical portrait of many of these figures over the revolutionary years, see Lunin, *Istoriia Obshchestvennykh Nauk v Uzbekistane.*

113. *NG,* Jan. 22, 1918.

114. *Novyi Turkestan,* Feb. 28, 1918.

115. *Novyi Turkestan,* Mar. 6, 1918; *Sovetskii Turkestan,* July 26, 1918.

116. See *Svobodnyi Turkestan,* Feb. 4, 1918, and *Novyi Turkestan,* Feb. 11, 1918.

117. Brun, 54–55; Bailey, 48–55.

118. *NG,* Apr. 18, 1918.

119. GAGT, f. 10, op. 1, d. 36, l. 125; the Red Guard was renamed the Red Army in mid-1918.

120. GAGT, f. 10, op. 1, d. 48, l. 23.

121. GAGT, f. 10, op. 1, d. 48, ll. 94–96.

122. GAGT, f. 10, op. 1, d. 148, l. 139; *Sovetskii Turkestan,* July 30, 1918.

123. *Sovetskii Turkestan,* June 26 and Sept. 25, 1918.

124. Park, 257.

125. Although the struggle between the soviet and worker collections of food was not unique to Tashkent, previous works have not explored the extent of organized worker efforts to compete with the soviet for food. McAuley, "Bread without the Bourgeoisie," 167–69; Suny, *The Baku Commune,* 303–304.

126. Ibid.

127. GAGT, f. 10, op. 1, d. 62, l. 531.

128. *NG,* Jan. 19, 1918. Unfortunately, no records of the dissolved duma appear to have survived. See also *Novyi Turkestan,* Mar. 14 and 21, 1918.

129. *Svobodnyi Turkestan,* Feb. 2 and 4, 1918.

130. *Novyi Turkestan,* Feb. 26, 1918.

131. On the failed invasion of Bukhara, see Park, 24–26; on the refugees see *Novyi Turkestan,* Apr. 5, 1918.

132. See, for example, GAGT, f. 10, op. 1, d. 62, l. 443; GAGT, f. 10, op. 1, 210, l. 11.

133. R. Vaidyanath, *The Formation of the Soviet Central Asian Republics* (New Delhi: People's Publishing House: 1967), 97.

134. GAGT, f. 10, op. 1, d. 44, l. 75.

135. GAGT, f. 10, op. 1, d. 44, l. 203.

136. *Sovetskii Turkestan,* June 19, 1918.

# 8. "Under a Soviet Roof"

1. Rossiskii Gosudarstvennyi Arkhiv Sotsial no-Politicheskoi Istorii (Russian State Archive of Social and Political History) (hereafter RGASPI), f. 122, op. 1, d. 31, l. 64ob.

2. G. Safarov, *Kolonial'naia Revoliutsiia: Opyt Turkestana* (Moscow: Gosudarst-vennoe Izdatel'stvo, 1921), 81–2. On other works, see I. Trainin, "Postanovka natsional'nogo voprosa," *Vlast' sovetov,* no. 5 (1923): 48–62, and Rysqulov.

3. On such views, based largely on the writings of central Bolsheviks of the era, see Yaroshevski; Vaidyanath; Alexandre Bennigsen and S. Enders Wimbush, *Muslim National Communism in the Soviet Union* (Chicago: University of Chicago Press, 1979); and Hélène Carrère d'Encausse, "Civil War and New Govern-ments," in *Central Asia: 130 Years of Russian Dominance,* ed. Edward A. Allworth (Durham, N.C.: Duke University Press, 1998), 224–53.

4. TsGARUz, f. I-1044, op. 1, d. 16, l. 1; *Turkestanskiia Viedomosti,* Jan. 4, 5, and 14, 1917.

5. The provisional government determined it lacked the administrative au-thority and the capacity to enforce the monopoly; on the grain monopoly, see Lih, 57.

6. Buttino, "Turkestan 1917: la révolution des russes," 69.

7. TsGARUz, f. I-1044, op. 1, d. 17, l. 20, l. 52.

8. For the text of the decree, see *PORvUz,* 1:570–72.

9. Chokayev, 408.

10. *PORvUz,* 2: 66–67.

11. Brun, 78.

12. *NG,* Jan. 25, 1918.

13. Ibid.

14. *Svobodnyi Turkestan,* Jan. 24, 1918.

15. Gosudarstvennyi Arkhiv Rossitskii Federatsii (State Archive of the Russian Federation) (hereafter GARF), f. 1235, op. 93, d. 581, l. 147.

16. Lenin and Stalin supported regional autonomy along cultural and educa-tional lines as an intermediate step to allow the proletariat of diverse regions and nationalities to cooperate before entering into a larger union. See Hélène Carrère d'Encausse, *The Great Challenge: Nationalities and the Bolshevik State, 1917–1930,* trans. Nancy Festinger (New York: Holmes and Meier, 1972), 31–43. On Lenin's letter, see Vaidyanath, 86.

17. Park, 66.

18. TsGARUz, f. R-25, op. 1, d. 107, l. 45.

19. GARF, f. 1318, op. 1, d. 420, ll. 33, 52.

20. GARF, f. 1318, op. 1, d. 441.

21. Adeeb Khalid, "Nationalizing the Revolution in Central Asia: The Transfor-mation of Jadidism, 1917–1920," in *A State of Nations: Empire and Nation-Making in the Age of Lenin and Stalin,* ed. Ronald Grigor Suny and Terry Martin (Oxford: Oxford University Press, 2001), 146; For Lenin's views on nation-building, see Carrère d'Encausse, *The Great Challenge,* 41–3.

22. "Soviet Central Asia: The Turkestan Commission, 1919–1920," *Central Asian Review* 12, no. 1 (1964): 6; see also Khalid, "Nationalizing the Revolution," 153.

23. For records of debates of the Central Asian Communists, see GARF, f. 1318, op. 1, d. 441.

24. *NG,* July 14, 1918.

25. GARF, f. 1318, op. 1, d. 441, l. 21.

26. G. Skalov, "Sotsial'naia priroda basmachestva v Turkestane," *Zhizn' natsional'nostei* 3–4 (1923): 56.

27. Park, 31, 41.

28. TsGARUz, f. R-25, op. 1, d. 107, l. 240.

29. Official figures placed the number of hungry in Turkestan in summer of 1919 at 103,320 people, though the actual total was most likely far higher; TsGA-RUz, f. R-25, op. 1, d. 194, ll. 2–3.

30. *NG*, Apr. 4 and July 4, 1919.

31. TsGARUz, f. R-17, op. 1, d. 909, l. 165.

32. *NG*, Jan. 18, 1919.

33. *Sovetskii Turkestan*, Oct. 6, 1918. City and regional food committees had found success in procuring rice and grain from southern steppe regions. See *NG*, Nov. 9, 11, and 26, 1918, and Jan. 17, 1919, and R. A. Nurullin, "Osushchestvlenie leninskikh printsipov prodovol'stvennoi politiki v Turkestane (1918–1921)," *Obshchestvennye nauki v Uzbekistane*, no. 4 (1968): 14–6.

34. Rakhimov, *Mobilizatsiia prodovol'stvennykh resursov v Turkestane v periode voennoi interventsii i grazhanskoi voiny (1918–21 gg.)* (Ph.D. diss., Akademii Nauk UzSSR, Tashkent, 1962), ch. 2.

35. *NG*, Mar. 14, 1919.

36. *Sovetskii Turkestan* Sept. 20, 1919.

37. Safarov, 106.

38. TsGARUz, f. R-31, op. 1, d. 39, l. 661.

39. TsGARUz, f. R-25, op. 1, d. 214, l. 119.

40. *Izvestiia Tsentral'nago ispolnitel'nago komiteta Turkestanskoi Respubliki i Rossiskoi Sovetskoi Federatsii i Tashkentskago soveta rabochikh, soldatskikh i dekhanskikh deputatov* (hereafter *ITTs*), July 12, 1919.

41. *ITTs*, July 4, 1919; *Turkestanskii Kommunist*, Sept. 18, 1919.

42. R. Nurullin, *Bor'ba Kompartii Turkestana za osushchestvlennie politiki "Voennago Kommunizma"* (Tashkent: Izdatel'stvo "Uzbekistan," 1975), 82.

43. TsGARUz, f. R-31, op. 1, d. 39, l. 662ob.

44. The official name of the commission was the Komissiia VTsIK po delam Turkestana; on the welcome, see RGASPI, f. 122, op. 1, d. 31, l. 201.

45. On the Osipov mutiny, see D. Salikov and S. Bolotov, "Iz istorii Osipovskogo miatezhe v Turkestane," *Proletarskaia revoliutsiia* 53, no. 6 (1926); see also memoir accounts from Brun and Bailey.

46. On the possible alliance with forces in Asian Tashkent, see GARF, f. 1318, op. 1, d. 420, l. 68. For the suggested link between Agapov and Osipov, see the memoirs of D. Salikov, "Osipovskii Miatezh v Tashkente (18–22 ianvaria 1919 goda) (Vospominaniia)," *Istorik-Marksist* 92, no. 4 (1941): 62.

47. GARF, f. 1318, op. 1, d. 420, l. 68.

48. Safarov, 96.

49. RGASPI, f. 122, op. 1, d. 8, l. 72; Vaidyanath, 96.

50. *Rezoliutsiia i postanovleniia s"ezdov Kommunisticheskoi partii Turkestana (1918–1924 gg.)* (Tashkent: Izdatel'stvo "Uzbekistan," 1968), 56–68; RGASPI, f. 122, op. 1, d. 50, l. 22.

51. RGASPI, f. 122, op. 1, d. 8, l. 36; GARF, f. 1235, op. 93, d. 583a, l. 36.

52. "Soviet Central Asia: The Turkestan Commission," 6.

53. Hubert Evans, "Indian Revolutionary Organizations in Central Asia," *Central Asian Review* 16, no. 4 (1968): 322–27.

54. GARF, f. 3969, op. 1, d. 5, ll. 1, 238.

55. RGASPI, f. 122, op. 1, d. 89, l. 154.

56. RGASPI, f. 122, op. 1, d. 50, l. 72.

57. Safarov, 107.

58. RGASPI, f. 122, op. 1, d. 29, l. 41.

59. Official figures of the 1919 purge were stated as: 175 former police officials, 443 "white guardists," 340 bribe-takers, 92 recognized guilty of extortion, 231 for abuse of their office, 153 work-deserters, and 192 "chauvinists." Vaidyanath, 105.

60. RGASPI, f. 122, op. 1, d. 31, l. 64ob.

61. Khalid, "Nationalizing the Revolution in Central Asia," 153.

62. These included I. I. Tobolin and A. A. Kazakov. See *Rezoliutsiia i postanovleniia*, 22–23.

63. RGASPI, f. 122, op. 1, d. 50, l. 98.

64. Vaidyanath, 108.

65. M. V. Frunze, *Sobranie sochinenii* (Moscow, 1929), 1: 119–20; see also "Soviet Central Asia: The Turkestan Commission," 9.   ·

66. RGASPI, f. 122, op. 1, d. 29, ll. 41–43.

67. RGASPI, f. 122, op. 1, d. 50, ll. 256–57; f. 122, op. 1, d. 29, l. 43.

68. In addition to these purges, the Turkkomissiia in September 1920 at the Seventh Congress of Soviets rewrote the constitution of the Turkestan Autonomous Soviet Socialist Republic that clearly subordinated the region to the RSFSR, giving the latter control over communications, transport, foreign affairs, trade, and the military. See Park, 69.

69. See Vaidyanath, 111–12.

70. RGASPI, f. 122, op. 1, d. 50, l. 252.

71. RGASPI, f. 122, op. 1. d. 47, l. 7.

72. *Izvestiia Turkestanskago Komiteta Rossisskoi Kommunisticheskoi Partii (Kraikom) i Turkestanskago Tsentral'nogo Ispol'nitelnago Komiteta (TurkTsika) sovetov rabochikh, dekhanskikh, krest'ianskikh, i kazachikh deputatov RSFSR* (hereafter *ITK*), Dec. 4, 1919; see also Safarov, 105.

73. RGASPI, f. 122, op. 1, d. 50, l. 195.

74. A ration system started by the provision committee of Asian Tashkent's soviet in 1918–19 included only 48,000 of the more than 200,000 population, and received supplies only sporadically. See *ITTs*, Sept. 4, 1919, and *ITK*, Dec. 4, 1919.

75. RGASPI, f. 122, op. 1, d. 121, l. 1; f. 122, op. 1, d. 158, ll. 8–9.

76. See Lewis Siegelbaum, *Soviet State and Society between Revolutions, 1918–1929* (Cambridge: Cambridge University Press, 1992), 41–43.

77. *ITTs*, Oct. 28, 1919.

78. Russian peasants in Turkestan, especially those arriving as part of the Stolypin reforms, did not form the peasant communes common in the metropole.

79. *ITTs*, Oct. 26, 1919.

80. Rysqulov, 212.

81. GAGT, f. 10, op. 1, d. 226, l. 10.

82. On the ceremony, see the interview with prodotriady member N. P. Iakovlev in Rakhimov, *Mobilizatsiia*, 232.

83. *ITK*, 8 Feb. 1920.

84. Rakhimov, *Mobilizatsiia*, 245.

85. Five brigades, each with between sixty and eighty-four workers, originally left Tashkent for work in the surrounding regions of Pishpek, Tokmakskii, Aulie-Ata, and Cherniaev districts. In total Tashkent supplied fifteen squads consisting of approximately one thousand of the total four thousand workers in 1920–21. TsGARUz f. R-805, op. 1, d. 99, l. 56.

86. TsGARUz, f. R-805, op. 1, d. 23, l. 94.

87. A copy of TurkTsIK instructions to these brigades can be found in *Inostrannaia voennaia interventsiia i grazhanskaia voina v Srednei Azii i Kazakhstane* (Alma-Ata, Kazakhstan: Izdatel'stvo "Nauka," 1964) 2:576–77.

88. TsGARUz, f. R-805, op. 1, d. 17, l. 2.

89. TsGARUz, f. R-805, op. 1, d. 23, l. 76.

90. TsGARUz, f. R-805, op. 1, d. 17, l. 63.

91. Nurullin, *Bor'ba kompartii Turkestana*, 103.

92. TsGARUz, f. R-805, op. 1, d. 17, ll. 9–10, 81.

93. TsGARUz, f. R-805, op. 1, d. 20, l. 28ob.

94. Holquist, 243–51.

95. TsGARUz, f. R-805, op. 1, d. 20, l. 14; TsGARUz, f. R-735, op. 1, d. 53, l. 120.

96. TsGARUz, f. R-805, op. 1, d. 23, l. 6.

97. TsGARUz, f. R-805, op. 1, d. 23, l. 89.

98. RGASPI f. 122, op. 1, d. 66, ll 54, 90.

99. *ITK*, Feb. 5, 1920; Nurullin, *Bor'ba kompartii Turkestana*, 105.

100. GAGT, f. 344, op. 1, d. 9, l. 2.

101. *ITK*, June 25, 1920.

102. After a failed 1918 invasion, soviet leaders had established relations with Bukharan Jadids in an alliance against the emir. In 1920, unwilling to take direct control of the state, Turkkomissiia leaders sanctioned a Jadidist government led by Faizulla Khojaev. Becker, 265–95.

103. *ITK*, May 4, 1920.

104. On the shipments, see RGASPI, f. 122, op. 1, d. 39, l. 15.

105. *ITK*, May 4, 1920.

106. *ITK* Feb. 25, 1920.

107. On the rumors, see TsGARUz, f. R-17, op. 1, d. 932, l. 29.

108. *ITK*, Oct. 20, 1920.

109. *ITK*, Jan. 1, 1922.

110. On the introduction of the New Economic Policy, see Siegelbaum, 67–134.

111. On April 9, the head of the Voenprodbiuro, Ukhora, and several of his associates received sentences for embezzlement.

112. Alexander Neweroff (Aleksandr Skobolev), *City of Bread* (Westport, Conn.: Hyperion, 1973), 33.

113. For a poignant account of the journey, see Neweroff (Skobolev), 36–236; estimates of refugees in Turkestan in 1921 range from 200,000 to 400,000. GARF, f. 1318, op. 1, d. 420, l. 186.

114. *ITTs*, Sept. 4, 1919; *ITK*, Feb. 18 and July 25, 1920.

115. *ITK*, Oct. 25, 1921; *ITK*, Dec. 4, 1921.

116. *ITK*, Feb. 10, 1922.

117. GAGT, f. 10, op. 1, d. 226, l. 37.

118. *ITK*, Jan. 6, 1921.

119. RGASPI, f. 122, op. 2, d. 86, l. 101.

120. RGASPI, f. 122, op. 1, d. 158, l. 191.

121. RGASPI, f. 62, op. 2, d. 11, l. 177; on the decline of the Basmachi, see I. I. Mintsa, ed., *Basmachestvo: vozniknovenie, sushchnost, krakh* (Moscow: Izdatel'stvo "Nauka," 1981).

122. Such frustration, of course, was commonplace throughout the soviet state, where the New Economic Policy, with its reliance on market economics, was treated as an unconscionable retreat from the politics of communism. See Siegelbaum, 86–87.

123. *ITK*, Apr. 22, 1922.

124. RGASPI, f. 122, op. 2, d. 86, l. 64.

125. GARF, f. 1318, op. 1, d. 441, l. 18.

126. In January 1922, 1,000,000 *pudy* of grain and 200,000 *pudy* of wheat left the region for central Russia. TsGARUz, f. R-25, op. 1, d. 663, ll. 23–30ob.; *ITK*, Jan. 1 and 15, 1922.

127. RGASPI, f. 62, op. 2, d. 25, l. 156.

128. RGASPI, f. 122, op. 1, d. 8, l. 36.

129. RGASPI, f. 62, op. 1, d. 6, l. 50ob.

130. RGASPI, f. 62, op. 2, d. 45, l. 4.

131. Park, 301.

132. RGASPI, f. 122, op. 1, d. 243, l. 18; TsGARUz, f. R-25, op. 1, d. 732, l. 2.

133. RGASPI, f. 62, op. 2, d. 25, l. 48.

## Conclusion

1. TsGARUz, f. I-361, op. 1, d. 1, l. 4.

# Bibliography

## Archival Sources

Gosudarstvennyi Arkhiv Goroda Tashkent (GAGT)/Toshkent shahar davlat arkhivi (State Archive of the City of Tashkent)

f. 10    Ispolkom Tashkentskogo gorodskogo soveta rabochikh, krestianskikh, dekhanskikh, i krasnoarmeiskikh deputatov

f. 344   Tashkentskii gorodskoi prodovol'stvennyi otdel

Gosudarstvennyi Arkhiv Tashkentskoi Oblasti/Toshkent viloyat davlat arkhivi (State Archive of Tashkent Oblast, Tashkent)

f. 3     Tashkentskii uezdnyi ispolnitel'nyi komitet

f. 5     Tashkentskii okruzhnoi ispolnitel'nyi komitet

Tsentral'nyi Gosudarstvennyi Arkhiv Respubliki Uzbekistan (TsGARUz)/Ozbekistan respublikasi markaziy daviat arkhivi (Central State Archive of the Republic of Uzbekistan, Tashkent). Istoricheskaia Chast' (Historical Section)

f. 1     Kantselliariia Turkestanskogo General-Gubernatora

f. 16    Upravlenie pereselencheskoi delom Syr-Dar'inskago raion

f. 17    Syr-Dar'inskoe oblastnoe upravlenie

f. 36    Upravlenie nachal'nika gorod Tashkenta

f. 37    Tashkentskaia gordoskaia uprava

f. 69    Turkestanskii otdel "Imperatorskago Russkago Geograficheskago obshchestva"

f. 129   Tashkentskaia sudebnaia palata

f. 132   Prokuror Tashkentskago okruzhnago suda

f. 133   Prokuror Tashkentskoi sudebnoi palati

f. 461   Turkestanskoe raionnoe okhrannoe otdelenie

f. 462   Poleitskoe upravlenie Russkoi chasti gorod Tashkenta

f. 591   Sredne-Aziatskoe nauchnoe obshchestvo

f. 718   Zhurnal zasedanii Tashkentskoi gorodskoi dumy

f. 723   Turkestanskii voennyi orkug sud. Kholernyi Bunt' 24 iiunia 1892

f. 1011  O pogrome lavok v gorode Tashkent 29 fevralia i 1 marta 1916

f. 1044  Turkestanskii Komitet Vremennogo Pravitel'stvo

Revoliutsionnaia Chast' (Revolutionary Section)
f. 17    Tsentral'nyi ispolnitel'nyi komitet sovetov rabochikh, dekhanskikh, i
         krasnoarmeiskikh deputatov TASSR
f. 25    Sovet narodnykh kommissarov TASSR
f. 31    Narkom Prodovol'stviia Turkrespubliki
f. 735   Turkestanskoe biuro Vesrossitskogo Tsentral'nogo Soveta Profsoiuzov
f. 805   Kraevoe voenno-prodovol'stvennoe biuro pri Turkbiuro VTsSPS

Rossiskii Gosudarstvennyi Arkhiv Sotsial'no-Politicheskoi Istorii (RGASPI)
    (Russian State Archive of Social and Political History, Moscow)
f. 61    Turkestanskoe Biuro TsK RKP (b)
f. 62    Sredne Aziatskoi Biuro TsK VKP (b)
f. 122   Komissiia VtSIK i SNK po delam Turkestana

Gosudarstvennyi Arkhiv Rossiskoi Federatsii (GARF) (State Archive of the Rus-
    sian Federation, Moscow)
f. 1318  Narodnyi Komissariat po delam Natsional'nostei
f. 3969  Moskovskoe Biuro Komissii VtSIK i Soveta Narodnykh Komisssarov
         RSFSR po delam Turkestana

Tsentral'nyi Gosudarstvennyi arkhiv kinofotofonodokumentov Uzbekistana/
Ozbekiston respublikasi kinofotofonohujjatlar markaziy davlat arkhivi (Central State Archive of Film, Photography, and Sound of Uzbekistan, Tashkent)

# Newspapers

*Birzhevyia Viedomosti* (St. Petersburg)
*Golos* (St. Petersburg)
*Izvestiia Tsentral'nago ispolnitel'nago komiteta Turkestanskoi Respubliki i Rossiskoi
    Sovetskoi Federatsii i Tashkentskago soveta rabochikh, soldatskikh i dekhanskikh
    deputatov* (Tashkent) (*ITTs*)
*Izvestiia Turkestanskago Komiteta Rossisskoi Kommunisticheskoi Partii (Kraikom) i
    Turkestanskago Tsentral'nogo Ispol'nitelnago Komiteta (TurkTsika) sovetov rabo-
    chikh, dekhanskikh, krest'ianskikh, i kazachikh deputatov RSFSR* (Tashkent) (*ITK*)
*Moskovskiia Viedomosti* (Moscow)
*Na Rubezhe* (Tashkent)
*Nasha Gazeta* (*NG*) (Tashkent)
*Novyi Put'* (Tashkent)
*Novyi Turkestan* (Tashkent)
*Okraina* (Tashkent)
*Petersburgskaia Gazeta* (St. Petersburg)
*Russkaia Gazeta* (St. Petersburg)
*Russkii Invalid* (St. Petersburg)
*Russkii Mir* (St. Petersburg)
*Russkii Turkestan* (*RT*) (Tashkent)
*Russkiia Viedomosti* (Moscow)
*Sada-yi Turkestan* (Tashkent)
*St. Peterburgskiia Viedomosti* (St. Petersburg)

*Sovietskii Turkestan* (Tashkent)
*Sredneaziatskaia Zhizn' (SZ)* (Tashkent)
*Svobodnyi Turkestan* (Tashkent)
*Syn Otechestva* (St. Petersburg)
*Taraqqi* (Tashkent)
*Tashkentskii Kur'er* (Tashkent)
*Tujjor* (Tashkent)
*Turkestan* (Tashkent)
*Turkestanskii Kara-Kurt* (Tashkent)
*Turkestanskii Kommunist* (Tashkent)
*Turkestanskii Kur'er (TK)* (Tashkent)
*Turkestanskii Skorpion* (Tashkent)
*Turkestanskiia Viedomosti (TV)* (Tashkent)
*Turkestanskoe Slovo* (Tashkent)

## Unpublished Documentary Collections

*Turkestanskii Al'bom.* 4 vols.
*Turkestanskii Sbornik.* Sobranie statei o stranakh Srednei Azii voobshche i Turke-
    stanskoi oblasti v osobennosti. 591 vols.

## Published Primary Sources

*Aziatskaia Rossiia.* 3 vols. St. Petersburg: Izdanie Pereselencheskogo Upravlenie,
    1914.
Bailey, F. M. *Mission to Tashkent.* London: Jonathan Cape, 1946.
Bariatinsky, Anatole Maria. *My Russian Life.* London: Hutchinson, 1923.
Bauman, V. *Bor'ba za vlast sovetov v Tashkente.* Tashkent, 1922.
"Beglyi rasskaz o medlennom puteshestvii v Tashkente." *Voennyi Sbornik* 66, no.
    4 (1869): 263–309.
Brun, Alf H. *Troublous Times: Experiences in Bolshevik Russia and Turkestan.* Lon-
    don: Constable, 1931.
Castagné, Joseph. "Le Turkestan depuis la révolution russe." *Revue du monde
    musulman* 50 (1922): 28–74.
Curzon, George. *Russia in Central Asia in 1889 and the Anglo-Russian Question.*
    London: Cass, 1889.
"Das neue Taschkent, die russische Metropole in Zentralasien." *Globus* (Sept.
    25, 1902): 181–86.
Davis, Jerome. "The Death Camp in Turkestan." *Unpartizan Review* 13, no. 1
    (1920): 60–70.
Dmitriev-Mamonov, A. I., ed. *Putevoditel' po Turkestanu i Sredne-Aziatskoi Zhe-
    leznoi Dorogi.* St. Petersburg: Tipografiia I. Gol'dberga, 1903.
Dobrosmyslov, A. I. "Tashkentskaia publichnaia biblioteka i muzei: Istoricheskii
    ocherk'." *Sredniaia Aziia,* no. 2 (1910): 106–23.
———. *Tashkent v proshlom i nastoiashchem: Istoricheskii ocherk'.* Tashkent: Tipo-
    litografiia A. O. Portseva, 1912.

———. "Uchebnyia zavedeniia v g. Tashkente." *Sredniaia Aziia*, no. 4 (1910): 113–22.

Dukhovskaia, Varvara. *Turkestanskiia Vospominaniia*. St. Petersburg: R. Golike i A. Vil'borg, 1913.

Eval'd, A. V. "Vospominaniia o K. P. fon-Kaufman." *Istoricheskii Viestnik*, no. 10 (1897): 184–99.

Fedorov, G. P. "Moia sluzhba v Turkestanskom krae (1870–1906 goda)." *Istoricheskii Viestnik*, no. 6 (1912): 786–812; no. 10 (1913): 33–55; no. 11 (1913): 438–67; no. 12 (1913): 860–93.

Frunze, M. V. *Sobranie sochinenii*. Moscow, 1929.

Gavrilov, N. *Pereselencheskoe delo v Turkestanskom krae (oblasti Syr-Dar'inskaia, Samarkandskaia, i Ferganskaia)*. St. Petersburg, 1911.

Geier, I. "Golod i kolonizatsiia Syr-Dar'inskoi oblasti v 1891 godu." *Sbornik Materialov dlia Statistiki Syr-Dar'inskoi oblasti* 3 (1894): 14–15.

Girs, F. K. *Otchet revizuiushchago, po Vysochaishemu poveleniiu, Turkestanskii krai, Tainogo sovetnika Girsa*. St. Petersburg, 1883.

Gnesin, F. "Turkestan v dni revoliutsii i Bol'shevizma." *Belyi Arkhiv* no. 1 (1926): 81–94.

"Gubernator v roli propovednika korana." *Krasnyi Arkhiv* 75 (1936): 187–90.

Iadrintsev, N. M. *Sibir kak koloniia: k iubileiu trekhsotletiia*. St. Petersburg: Tipografii M. M. Stasiulevicha, 1882.

*Inostrannaia voennaia interventsiia i grazhanskaia voina v Srednei Azii i Kazakhstane*. Alma-Ata: Izdatel'stvo "Nauka," 1964.

"Iz dnevnika A. N. Kuropatkina." *Krasnyi Arkhiv* 20 (1927): 56–77.

Karazin, N. N. "Iz Turkestanskoi boevoi zhizn'." *Vsemirnaia Illiustratsiia*, no. 59 (1872): 45–47.

———. *Na dalekikh okrainakh*. St. Petersburg: Izdanie P. P. Soikina, 1877.

Kaufman, K. P. fon. *Proekt vsepoddaneishago otcheta general-ad'iutanta K. P. fon-Kaufman 1-go po grazhdanskomu upravleniiu i ustroistvu v oblastiakh Turkestanskogo general-gubernatorstva, 7 noiabria 1867–25 marta 1881 gg.* St. Petersburg, 1885.

*Kaufmanskii Sbornik: izdannyi v pamiat' 25ti let iztekshikh so dnia smerta pokoritelia i ustroitelia Turkestanskogo kraia, General'-adiutanta K. P. fon-Kaufmana 1-go*. Moscow: Tipo-lit T-va I. N. Kushnerev, 1910.

Khanykov, N. V. *Opisanie Bukharskogo Khanstva*. St. Petersburg: Tipografii Imperatorskoi Akademii Nauk, 1843.

Kostenko, L. *Sredniaia Aziia i vodvorenie v nei russkoi grazhdanstvennosti*. St. Petersburg, 1871.

———. "Turkestanskaia Voiska i usloviia ikh." *Voennyi Sbornik* 103, no. 5 (1875): 61–82.

———. *Turkestanskii Krai. Opyt' Voenno-Statisticheskago Obozreniia*. 3 vols. St. Petersburg: Tipografii A. Transhelia, 1880.

Krist, Gustav. *Prisoner in the Forbidden Land*. Trans. E. O. Lorimer. London: Faber and Faber, 1938.

Lerkh, N. "O Turkestanskom 'Fotograficheskom' Albome." *Izvestiia Imperatorskogo Geograficheskago Obshchestva* 10, no. 3 (1874): 97–99.

Lykoshin, N. S. *Pol zhizni v Turkestane: ocherki byta tuzenago naseleniia.* Petrograd, 1916.

M—skii, E. "Rasskazy soldata o Turkestanskom Krae." *Mirskoi Viestnik,* no. 11 (1866): 46–63.

Maev, N. A. "Aziatskii Tashkent." In *Materialy dlia Statistiki Turkestanskogo Kraia.* St. Petersburg, 1877.

———. "Nashe Polozhenie v Srednei Azii." In *Materialy dlia Statistiki Turkestanskogo Kraia,* vol. 3. St. Petersburg, 1872.

———. "Ot Tashkenta do Katy-Kurgana." *Russkii Viestnik* 86, no. 3 (1870): 243–71.

———. *Putevoditel' ot S-Petersburga do Tashkenta.* St. Petersburg: Voennaia Tipografiia, 1870.

———. "Russkii Tashkent." *Niva: Literaturnoe Prilozheniia,* supplement (1894): 126–62.

Maksheev, A. I. *Istoricheskii obzor Turkestana i nastupatel'nogo dvizhenia v nego russkikh.* St. Petersburg, 1880.

———. "Prebyvanie v Vernom' i vstrecha Kaufmana." *Russkaia Starina,* no. 3 (1913): 644–49.

Manzhara, D. I. *Revoliutsionnoe Dvizhenie v Srednei Azii 1905–1920 gg. (Vospominaniia).* Tashkent: Sredpartizdat, 1934.

Markov, Evgenii. *Rossiia v Srednei Azii. Ocherk Puteshestviia.* 2 vols. St. Petersburg: Tipografiia M. M. Stasliuvich, 1901.

*Materialy dlia Statistiki Turkestanskogo Kraia.* 5 vols. St. Petersburg, 1872–79.

Mezhov, V. I. *Recueil du Turkestan comprenant des livres et articles sur l'Asie Centrale en générale et la province du Turkestan en particulier: Composé sous les auspices du Gouverneur Générale du Turkestan Konstantin Petrovich fon-Kaufman.* Tome 1–150. St. Petersburg, 1878.

Moser, Henri. *A travers l'Asie Centrale.* Paris: Librairie Plon, 1885.

Mustafin, V. "Nikolai Ivanovich Grodekov (1880–1913 gg.). Vospominaniia-zametki." *Istoricheskii Viestnik,* no. 10 (1915): 141–66.

Nalivkin, V. P. *Tuzemtsy ran'she i teper'.* Tashkent, 1913.

*Obzor Syr-Dar'inskoi Oblasti za 1890 god.* Tashkent: Tipografiia brat'ev G. i O. Portsevykh, 1892.

*Obzor Syr-Dar'inskoi Oblast za 1912 god.* Tashkent: Tip-litografiia V. M. Il'ina, 1914.

Ostroumov, N. P. *Konstantin Petrovich fon-Kaufman. Ustroitel' Turkestanskogo Kraia. Lichnaia Vospominaniia N. Ostroumova (1877–1881).* Tashkent: G. Kaminskii, 1899.

———. *Sarty. Ethnograficheskie Materialy (Obshchii Ocherk).* 3rd. ed. Tashkent, 1908.

"O Turkestanskom fotograficheskom al'bome." *Izvestiia Imperatorskago Geograficheskago Obshchestva* 10, no. 3 (1874): 94–97.

P. K. "Russkoe znamia v Srednei Azii." *Istoricheskii Viestnik,* no. 4 (1899): 96–97.

Palen, K. K. *Otchet po revizii Turkestanskogo kraia, proizvedennoi po vysochaishchemu poveleniiu Senatorom Gofmeisterom Grafom K. K. Palenom.* 19 vols. St. Petersburg, 1910.

Pashino, P. I. *Turkestanskii Krai v 1866 godu. Putevye zametki P. I. Pashino.* St. Petersburg, 1866.

*Pobeda Oktiabr'skoi Revoliutsii v Uzbekistane. Sbornik Dokumentov.* 2 vols. Tashkent: Izdatel'stvo Akademii Nauk UzSSR, 1963–72.

Poltoratskii, V. A. "Vospominaniia V. A. Poltoratskago." *Istoricheskii Viestnik* 16, no. 4 (1875): 85–109.

Popov, I. I. *Minuvshee i perezhitoe: vospominaniia za 50 let: Sibir i emigratsiia.* Leningrad: Kolos, 1924.

*Revoliutsiia 1905–1907 gg. v Uzbekistane. Dokumenty i Materialy.* Tashkent: Uzbekistan, 1984.

*Revoliutsiia i natsional'nyi vopros. Dokumenty i materialy po istorii natsional'nogo voprosa v Rossii i SSSR v XX veke.* 3 vols. Moscow: Izdatel'stvo Kommunisticheskoi akademii, 1930.

*Rezoliutsiia i postanovleniia s"ezdov Kommunisticheskoi partii Turkestana (1918–1924 gg.).* Tashkent: Izdatel'stvo "Uzbekistan," 1968.

Rozenbakh, N. A. fon. "Zapiski N. A. fon-Rozenbakha." *Russkaia Starina,* no. 4 (1916): 100–114; no. 5 (1916): 172–241.

Rudyi, A. "Iul'skoe Vosstanie v Tashkente." *Istoricheskii Viestnik,* no. 6 (1909): 891–900.

*Russkii Turkestan: Sbornik izdanno po povodu politekhnicheskoi vystavki.* 3 vols. Moscow: Universitetskoi tipografii, 1872.

Rysqulov, Turar. *Revoliutsiia i korennoe naselenie turkestana.* Tashkent: Uzbekskoe Gosudarstvennoe Izdatel'stvo, 1925.

Safarov, G. *Kolonial'naia Revoliutsiia. Opyt Turkestana.* Moscow: Gosudarstvennoe Izdatel'stvo, 1921.

Salikov, D. "Osipovskii Miatezh v Tashkente (18–22 ianvaria 1919 goda) (Vospominaniia)." *Istorik Marksist* 92, no. 4 (1941): 59–72.

Saltykov-Shchedrin, M. E. "Chto takoe 'Tashkenttsy'?" *Otechestvennye Zapiski,* no. 5 (Oct. 1869): 187–207.

———. *Gospoda Tashkenttsy: Kartina nravov'.* St. Petersburg: Tipografiia V. V. Pratts', 1873.

*Sbornik materialov dlia statistiki Syr-Dar'inskoi oblasti.* Tashkent, 1891–1907.

Schuyler, Eugene. *Turkistan: Notes of a Journey in Russian Turkistan, Khokand, Bukhara, and Kuldja.* 2 vols. New York: Scribner, Armstrong, 1877.

Shlitter, E. "V Turkestane." *Voennyi Sbornik,* no. 2 (1902): 187–216; no. 3 (1902): 196–224.

Shvarts, A. "Meditsinskaia pomosh' tuzemnomu naseleniiu gor. Tashkenta." *Sredniaia Aziia,* no. 8 (1911): 127–42.

"Smes'" [Nekrolog K. P. fon-Kaufmana]." *Istoricheskii Viestnik,* no. 2 (1882): 700–702.

Terent'ev, M. A. *Istoriia zavoevaniia Srednei Azii.* 3 vols. St. Petersburg: Tipo-litografiia V. V. Komarova, 1906.

———. "Turkestan i Turkestantsy." *Viestnik Evropy* 5, no. 9 (1875): 65–112; no. 10 (1875): 500–529; no. 11 (1875): 142–72.

Tol'bukhov, E. "Ustroitel' Turkestanskago Kraia." *Istoricheskii Viestnik,* no. 11 (1913): 891–909.

Trainin, I. "Postanovka natsional'nogo voprosa." *Vlast' sovetov*, no. 5 (1923): 48–62.

Uvarova, P. "Poezdka v Tashkent i Samarkand." *Russkaia Mysl'* 11 (1891): 1–19.

"Vosstanie 1916 g. v Srednei Azii." *Krasnyi Arkhiv* 34 (1929): 39–94.

*Vosstanie 1916 g. v Kirgizstane. Dokumenty i Materialy.* Moscow: Sotsial'no-Ekonomicheskoe Izdatel'stvo, 1937.

*Vosstanie 1916 goda v Srednei Azii i Kazakhstane. Sbornik Dokumentov.* Moscow: Izdatel'stvo Akademii Nauk SSSR, 1960.

Wolff, Joseph. *Narrative of a Mission to Bokhara in the Years 1843–1845 to Ascertain the Fate of Captain Stoddard and Colonel Connolly.* London: J. W. Parker, 1846.

*Zhivopisnaia Rossiia. Otechestvo nashe v ego zemel'nom, istoricheskom, ekonomicheskom, o bytovam znachenii, pod obshchei redaktsii P. P. Semonova . Tom XX: Russkaia Srednaia Aziia.* St. Petersburg, 1885.

## Secondary Sources

Abu-Lughod, Janet L. "The Islamic City—Historic Myth, Islamic Essence, and Contemporary Relevance." *International Journal of Middle East Studies* 19, no. 1 (1987): 155–76.

Adas, Michael. *Machines as the Measure of Man: Science, Technology, and the Ideologies of Western Dominance.* Ithaca, N.Y.: Cornell University Press, 1989.

Alatas, Syed Hussein. *The Myth of the Lazy Native: A Study of the Malays, Filipinos, and Javanese from the Sixteenth Century.* London: P. Cass, 1977.

Alekseenkov, P. "Natsional'naia Politika Vremennogo Pravitel'stva v Turkestane v 1917 g." *Proletarskaia Revoliutsiia* 78 (1928): 104–32.

Ali, Maulana Muhammad. *The Religion of Islam: A Comprehensive Discussion of the Sources, Principles, and Practices of Islam.* New Delhi: S. Chand, 1968.

Allworth, Edward A. *The Modern Uzbeks: From the Fourteenth Century to the Present, A Cultural History.* Stanford, Calif.: Hoover Institution, 1990.

———, ed. *Central Asia: 130 Years of Russian Dominance.* Durham, N.C.: Duke University Press, 1998.

———, ed. *The Tatars of the Crimea: Return to the Homeland.* 2nd ed. Durham, N.C.: Duke University Press, 1998.

Alsayyad, Nezar. *Forms of Dominance: On the Architecture and Urbanism of the Colonial Enterprise.* Aldershot, U.K.: Avebury Press, 1991.

Anderson, Warwick. "Where Is the Postcolonial History of Medicine?" *Bulletin of the History of Medicine*, no. 72 (1998): 522–30.

Anwar Khan, Mohammad. *England, Russia, and Central Asia: A Study In Diplomacy, 1857–1879.* Peshawar, Pakistan: University Book Agency, 1969.

Applewhite, Harriet, and Darlene Levy, eds. *Women and Politics in the Age of Democratic Revolution.* Ann Arbor: University of Michigan Press, 1990.

Arnold, David. *Colonizing the Body: State Medicine and Epidemic Disease in Nineteenth-Century India.* Berkeley: University of California Press, 1993.

———. "European Orphans and Vagrants in India in the Nineteenth Century." *Journal of Imperial and Commonwealth History* 7, no. 2 (1979): 104–27.

———. "White Colonization and Labour in 19th Century India." *Journal of Imperial and Commonwealth History* 9, no. 2 (1983): 133–58.

Azadaev, F. *Tashkent vo vtoroi polovine XIX veka: Ocherki Sotsial'no-Ekonomicheskoi i Politicheskoi Istorii.* Tashkent: Izdatel'stvo Akademii Nauk Uzbekskoi SSR, 1959.

Bacon, Elizabeth E. *Central Asians under Russian Rule: A Study in Culture Change.* Ithaca, N.Y.: Cornell University Press, 1966.

Baldauf, Ingeborg. "Some Thoughts on the Making of the Uzbek Nation." *Cahiers du monde russe et soviétique* 23, no. 1 (1991): 79–96.

Balzer, Harley D., ed. *Russia's Missing Middle Class: The Professions in Russian History.* Armonk, N.Y.: M. E. Sharpe, 1996.

Baratov, A. "Oktiabr' i Grazhdanskaia Voina v Srednei Azii." *Istoriia Proletariata SSSR*, no. 1 (1934): 144–55.

Barrett, Thomas M. "The Remaking of the Lion of Dagestan: Shamil in Captivity." *Russian Review* 53 (July 1994): 353–66.

Bartlett, Rosamund, and Linda Edmondson. "Collapse and Creation: Issues of Identity and the Russian Fin de Siecle." In *Constructing Russian Culture in the Age of Revolution, 1881–1940*, ed. Catriona Kelly and David Shepherd. Oxford: Oxford University Press, 1998.

Bartol'd, V. V. *Sochineniia.* 9 vols. in 10. Moscow: Izdatel'stvo Vostochnoi Literatury, 1963–77.

Bassin, Mark. *Imperial Visions: Nationalist Imagination and Geographical Expansion in the Russian Far East, 1840–1865.* Cambridge: Cambridge University Press, 1999.

———. "Russia between Europe and Asia: The Ideological Construction of Geographical Space." *Slavic Review* 50, no. 1 (1991): 1–17.

Bauman, Zygmont. *Modernity and Ambivalence.* Cambridge, U.K.: Polity Press, 1991.

Becker, Seymour. "Russia between East and West: The Intelligentsia, Russian National Identity, and the Asian Borderlands." *Central Asian Survey* 10, no. 4 (1991): 47–64.

Belk, Fred Richard. *The Great Trek of the Russian Mennonites to Central Asia 1880–1884.* Scottsdale, Pa.: Herald Press, 1976.

Bell, Catherine. *Ritual Theory, Ritual Practice.* Oxford: Oxford University Press, 1992.

Bennigsen, Alexandre, and Chantal Quelquejay. *Les mouvements nationaux chez les musulmans de Russie: Le "Sultangalievisme" au Tatarstan.* Paris: Mouton, 1960.

Bennigsen, Alexandre, and S. Enders Wimbush. *Muslim National Communism in the Soviet Union.* Chicago: University of Chicago Press, 1979.

Bensidoun, Sylvain. "'A propos d'une centenaire': Le cholera et les émeutes de 1892 dans l'empire de Russie." *Revue Historique* 287, no. 2 (1992): 379–85.

Bhabha, Homi. *The Location of Culture.* London: Routledge, 1994.

Bianca, Stefano. *Urban Form in the Arab World: Past and Present.* London: Thames and Hudson, 2000.

Bohstedt, John. "The Myth of the Feminine Food Riot: Women as Proto-Citizens in English Community Politics, 1790–1810." In *Women and Politics in the Age of Democratic Revolution*, ed. Harriet Applewhite and Darlene Levy. Ann Arbor: University of Michigan Press, 1990.

Bolotov, S. "Iz istorii Osipovskogo miatezha v Turkestane." *Proletarskaia Revoliutsiia* 53, no. 6. 1926: 110–37.

Bradley, Joseph. *Muzhik and Muscovite: Urbanization in Late Imperial Russia.* Berkeley: University of California Press, 1985.

Brower, Daniel R. *The Russian City between Tradition and Modernity, 1850–1900.* Berkeley: University of California Press, 1990.

———. *Turkestan and the Fate of the Russian Empire.* London: RoutledgeCurzon, 2003.

Brower, Daniel R., and Edward J. Lazzerini, eds. *Russia's Orient: Imperial Borderlands and Peoples, 1700–1917.* Bloomington: Indiana University Press, 1997.

Brumfield, William Craft. *A History of Russian Architecture.* Cambridge: Cambridge University Press, 1993.

Bulatov, M. C. "Urda i Krepost' 1865 g. v Tashkente." *Stroitel'stvo i Arkhitektura Uzbekistana,* no. 6 (1969): 32–4.

Buriakov, Iu. F. *Po ulitsam Tashkenta.* Tashkent: Izdatel'stvo "Uzbekistan," 1971.

Burov, N. A. "Istoricheskaia spravka o vremeni osnovaniia Tashkentskoi Publichnoi (Nyne Sredne-Aziatskoi Gosudarstvennoi) Biblioteki." In *V. V. Bartol'du. Turkestanskie druz'ia ucheniki i pochiteteli.* Tashkent, 1927.

Burton, Antoinette. *At the Heart of Empire: Indians and the Colonial Encounter in Late-Victorian Britain.* Berkeley: University of California Press, 1998.

Bushmin, A. S. *Satira Saltykova-Shchedrina.* Moscow: Izdatel'stvo Akademii Nauk SSSR, 1959.

Buttino, Marco. "Study of the Economic Crisis and Depopulation in Turkestan, 1917–1920." *Central Asian Survey* 9, no. 4 (1990): 59–74.

———. "Turkestan 1917: La révolution des russes." *Cahiers du monde russe et soviétique* 32, no. 1 (1991): 61–78.

———, ed. *In a Collapsing Empire: Underdevelopment, Ethnic Conflicts, and Nationalisms in the Soviet Union.* Milan: Feltrinelli Editore, 1993.

Carrère d'Encausse, Hélène. "Civil War and New Governments." In *Central Asia: 130 Years of Russian Dominance,* ed. Edward A. Allworth. Durham, N.C.: Duke University Press, 1998.

———. "Encounter." In *Central Asia: 130 Years of Russian Dominance,* ed. Edward Allworth. Durham, Duke University Press, 1998.

———. *The Great Challenge: Nationalities and the Bolshevik State, 1917–1930.* Trans. Nancy Festinger. New York: Holmes and Meier, 1972.

———. *L'empire éclaté: la revolte des nations en U.R.S.S.* Paris: Flammarion, 1978.

Cavanaugh, Cassandra Marie. "Backwardness and Biology: Medicine and Power in Russian and Soviet Central Asia, 1868–1934." Ph.D. diss., Columbia University, 2001.

Chabrov, N. G. "Russkie arkhitektory dorevoliutsionnogo Turkestana (1865–1916gg.)." In *Arkhitekturnoe Nasledie Uzbekistana.* Tashkent: Izdatel'stvo Akademii Nauk Uzbekskoi SSR, 1960.

Chekovich, O. D. "Gorodskie samoupravlenie v Tashkente XVIII v." In *Istoriia i kul'tura narodov Srednei Azii.* Moscow: Izdatel'stvo "Nauka," 1976.

Chokayev, Mustafa. "Turkestan and the Soviet Regime." *Journal of the Royal Central Asian Society* 18 (1931): 403–20.

Clancy-Smith, Julia, and Frances Gouda, eds. *Domesticating the Empire: Race, Gender, and Family Life in French and Dutch Colonialism.* Charlottesville: University Press of Virginia, 1998.

Clowes, Edith, Samuel D. Kassow, and James L. West, eds. *Between Tsar and People: Educated Society and the Quest for a Public Identity in Imperial Russia.* Princeton, N.J.: Princeton University Press, 1991.

Cohn, Bernard S. *Colonialism and Its Forms of Knowledge: The British in India.* Princeton, N.J.: Princeton University Press, 1996.

———. "Representing Authority in Victorian India." In *The Invention of Tradition,* ed. Eric Hobsbawm and Terence Ranger. Cambridge: Cambridge University Press, 1983.

Conklin, Alice J. "Colonialism and Human Rights: A Contradiction in Terms?" *American Historical Review* 103, no. 2 (1998): 419–42.

———. *A Mission to Civilize: The Republican Idea of Empire in France and West Africa, 1895–1930.* Stanford, Calif.: Stanford University Press, 1997.

Conner, Patrick. *Oriental Architecture in the West.* London: Thames and Hudson, 1979.

Cooper, Frederick, and Ann Laura Stoler, eds. *Tensions of Empire: Colonial Cultures in a Bourgeois World.* Berkeley: University of California Press, 1997.

Demidov, A. P. *Ekonomicheskii Ocherk khlopkovodstva, khlopkotorgovli i khlopkovoi promyshlennosti Turkestana.* Moscow, 1922.

Edelman, Robert J. *Gentry Politics on the Eve of the Russian Revolution: The Nationalist Party, 1907–1917.* New Brunswick, N.J.: Rutgers University Press, 1980.

Edwards, Penny. "Womanizing Indochina: Fiction, Nation, and Cohabitation in Colonial Cambodia, 1890–1930." In *Domesticating the Empire: Race, Gender, and Family Life in French and Dutch Colonialism,* ed. Julia Clancy-Smith and Frances Gouda. Charlottesville: University Press of Virginia, 1998.

Ehrenberg, John. *Civil Society: The Critical History of an Idea.* New York: New York University Press, 1999.

Eklof, Ben, John Bushnell, and Larissa Zakharova, eds. *Russia's Great Reforms, 1855–1881.* Bloomington: Indiana University Press, 1994.

Eley, Geoff, and Ronald Grigor Suny, eds. *Becoming National: A Reader.* New York: Oxford University Press, 1996.

Engel, Barbara Alpern. "Not by Bread Alone: Subsistence Riots in Russia during World War I." *Journal of Modern History* 69 (Dec. 1997): 696–721.

Engelstein, Laura. "Holy Russia in Modern Times: An Essay on Orthodoxy and Cultural Change." *Past and Present,* no. 173 (Nov. 2001): 129–56.

———. *The Keys to Happiness: Sex and the Search for Modernity in Fin-de-siecle Russia.* Ithaca, N.Y.: Cornell University Press, 1992.

———. *Moscow 1905: Working-Class Organization and Political Conflict.* Stanford, Calif.: Stanford University Press, 1982.

*Entsiklopedicheskii slovar' Russkogo bibliograficheskago instituta Granat.* Moscow, 1912.

Evans, Hubert. "Indian Revolutionary Organizations in Central Asia." *Central Asian Review* 16, no. 4 (1968): 322–27.

Evans, Richard J. *Death in Hamburg: Society and Politics in the Cholera Years 1830–1910.* Oxford: Clarendon Press, 1987.

———. "Epidemics and Revolutions: Cholera in Nineteenth-Century Europe." *Past and Present,* no. 120 (Aug. 1988): 123–46.

Faibushevitch, B. M. "Nauchnye Trudy Russkikh Vrachei v Turkestane v XIX veke." *Sovetskoe Zdravookhranenie*, no. 12 (1962): 58–63.

Figes, Orlando, and Boris Kolonitskii. *Interpreting the Russian Revolution: The Languages and Symbols of 1917*. New Haven, Conn.: Yale University Press, 1999.

Flier, Michael, and Daniel Rowland, eds. *Medieval Russian Culture*. Vol. 2. California Slavic Studies 19. Berkeley: University of California Press, 1994.

Frank, Stephen P. "Confronting the Domestic Other: Rural Popular Culture and Its Enemies in Fin-de-Siecle Russia." In *Cultures in Flux: Lower-class Values, Practices, and Resistance in Late Imperial Russia*, ed. Stephen P. Frank and Mark D. Steinberg. Princeton, N.J.: Princeton University Press, 1994.

Frank, Stephen P., and Mark D. Steinberg, eds. *Cultures in Flux: Lower-Class Values, Practices, and Resistance in Late Imperial Russia*. Princeton, N.J.: Princeton University Press, 1994.

Frankel, Edith Rogovin, Jonathan Frankel, and Baruch Knei-Paz, eds. *Revolution in Russia: Reassessments of 1917*. Cambridge: Cambridge University Press, 1992.

Freeze, Gregory. "The Sosloviia (Estate) Paradigm and Russian Social History." *American Historical Review* 91, no. 1 (1986): 11–36.

Frieden, Nancy. *Russian Physicians in an Era of Reform and Revolution, 1856–1905*. Princeton, N.J.: Princeton University Press, 1981.

Frierson, Cathy A. *Peasant Icons: Representations of Rural People in Late Nineteenth-Century Russia*. New York: Oxford University Press, 1993.

Galuzo, P. G. *Turkestan-Koloniia. (Ocherk istorii Turkestana ot zavoevaniia russkimi do revoliutsii 1917 goda)*. Moscow: Izdatel'stvo kommunisticheskago universiteta trudiashchikhsia Vostoka, 1929.

Gatrell, Peter. *A Whole Empire Walking: Refugees in Russia during World War I*. Bloomington: Indiana University Press, 1999.

Geraci, Robert. *Window on the East: National and Imperial Identities in Late Tsarist Russia*. Ithaca, N.Y.: Cornell University Press, 2001.

Geyer, Dietrich. *Russian Imperialism: The Interaction of Domestic and Foreign Policy 1860–1914*. Trans. Bruce Little. New York: Berg, 1987.

Gillard, David. *The Struggle for Asia, 1828–1914: A Study in British and Russian Imperialism*. London: Methuen, 1977.

Gilroy, Paul. *The Black Atlantic: Modernity and Double Consciousness*. Cambridge, Mass.: Harvard University Press, 1993.

Ginzburg, A. I. *Russkoe Naselenie v Turkestane (konets XIX–nachalo XX veka)*. Moscow: Akademii Nauk SSSR, 1992.

Graham, Stephen. *Through Russian Central Asia*. New York: MacMillan, 1916.

Habermas, Jürgen. "The Public Sphere." *New German Critique* 3 (1974): 49–55.

Hobsbawm, Eric, and Terence Ranger, eds. *The Invention of Tradition*. Cambridge: Cambridge University Press, 1983.

Holquist, Peter. *Making War, Forging Revolution: Russia's Continuum of Crisis, 1914–1921*. Cambridge, Mass.: Harvard University Press, 2002.

Hopkirk, Peter. *The Great Game: The Struggle for Empire in Central Asia*. New York: Kodansha, 1992.

Horowitz, Donald L. *The Deadly Ethnic Riot*. Berkeley: University of California Press, 2001.

*Istoriia i kul'tura narodov Srednei Azii.* Moscow: Izdatel'stvo "Nauka," 1976.

*Istoriia Tashkenta s drevneishikh vremen do pobedy fevral'skoi burzhuazno-demokrat-icheskoi revoliutsii.* Tashkent: Izdatel'stvo "Fan," 1988.

*Istoriia Uzbekskoi SSR.* 2 vols. Tashkent: Izdatel'stvo Akademii Nauk UzSSR, 1956.

*Istoriia Uzbekskoi SSR.* 4 vols. Tashkent: Izdatel'stvo "Fan" Uzbekskoi SSR, 1968.

Jahn, Hubertus. *Patriotic Culture in Russia during World War I.* Ithaca, N.Y.: Cornell University Press, 1995.

Joffe, Muriel. "Autocracy, Capitalism, and Empire: The Politics of Irrigation." *Russian Review* 54, no. 3 (1995): 365–88.

Kadyrov, A. A. *Istorii Meditsiny Uzbekistana.* Tashkent: Ibn Siny, 1994.

Kamp, Marianne. "Unveiling Uzbek Women: Liberation, Representation, and Discourse, 1906–1929." Ph.D. diss., University of Chicago, 1998.

Kappeler, Andreas. *The Russian Empire, A Multiethnic History.* Trans. Alfred Clayton. London: Longman, 2001.

Kassow, Samuel D. "The University Statute of 1863: A Reconsideration." In *Russia's Great Reforms, 1855–1881,* ed. Ben Eklof, John Bushnell, and Larissa Zakharova. Bloomington: Indiana University Press, 1994.

Kasymova, A. G. "Turkestanskii Sbornik." *Sovetskaia Bibliografiia* 57, no. 5 (1969): 70–77.

Kelly, Catriona, and David Shepherd, eds. *Constructing Russian Culture in the Age of Revolution, 1881–1940.* Oxford: Oxford University Press, 1998.

Kennedy, Dane. *Islands of White: Settler Society and Culture in Kenya and Southern Rhodesia, 1890–1939.* Durham, N.C.: Duke University Press, 1987.

———. *The Magic Mountains: Hill Stations and the British Raj.* Berkeley: University of California Press, 1996.

Khalfin, N. A. *Politika Rossii v Srednei Azii.* Moscow: Izdatel'stvo Vostochnoi Literatury, 1960.

———. *Prisoedinenie Srednei Azii k Rossii (60–90-e gody XIX v.).* Moscow: Izdatel'stvo "Nauka," 1965.

Khalid, Adeeb. "Nationalizing the Revolution in Central Asia: The Transformation of Jadidism, 1917–1920." In *A State of Nations: Empire and Nation-Making in the Age of Lenin and Stalin,* ed. Ronald Grigor Suny and Terry Martin. Oxford: Oxford University Press, 2001.

———. *The Politics of Muslim Cultural Reform: Jadidism in Central Asia.* Berkeley: University of California Press, 1998.

———. "Representations of Russia in Central Asian Jadid Discourse." In *Russia's Orient: Imperial Borderlands and Peoples, 1700–1917,* ed. Daniel R. Brower and Edward J. Lazzerini. Bloomington: Indiana University Press, 1997.

———. "Russian History and the Debate over Orientalism." *Kritika: Explorations in Russian and Eurasian History* 1, no. 4 (2000): 691–700.

Khodarkovsky, Michael. *Russia's Steppe Frontier: The Making of a Colonial Empire, 1500–1800.* Bloomington: Indiana University Press, 2002.

King, Anthony D. *Colonial Urban Development: Culture, Social Power, and Environment.* London: Routledge and Kegan Paul, 1976.

Koenker, Diane P. "Urbanization and Deurbanization in the Russian Revolution and Civil War." *Journal of Modern History* 57 (Sept. 1985): 424–50.

Koenker, Diane P., William G. Rosenberg, and Ronald G. Suny, eds. *Party, State, and Society in the Russian Civil War: Explorations in Social History.* Bloomington: Indiana University Press, 1989.

Knight, Nathaniel. "Grigor'ev in Orenburg, 1851–1862: Russian Orientalism in the Service of Empire?" *Slavic Review* 59, no. 1 (2000): 74–100.

Kollmann, Nancy Shields. "Pilgrimage, Procession, and Symbolic Space in Sixteenth Century Russian Politics." In *Medieval Russian Culture*, vol. 2, ed. Michael Flier and Daniel Rowland. California Slavic Studies 19. Berkeley: University of California Press, 1994.

Kovalev, P. A. "Zhenskii 'babii' bunt v Tashkente." *Nauchnye Trudy Tashkentskogo gosudarstvennogo universiteta imeni V. I. Lenina* 233 (1964): 11–32.

Kunavina, G. S. *Formirovanie Zheleznodorozhnogo Proletariata v Turkestane (1881–1914 gg.).* Tashkent: Izdatel'stvo "Fan," 1967.

Kuper, Leo. *Race, Class and Power: Ideology and Revolutionary Change in Plural Societies.* Chicago: Aldane Press, 1974.

Layton, Susan. *Russian Literature and Empire: Conquest of the Caucasus from Pushkin to Tolstoy.* Cambridge: Cambridge University Press, 1994.

Lazzerini, Edward J. "Ismail Bey Gasparinskii (Gasparali): The Discourse of Modernism and the Russians." In *The Tatars of the Crimea: Return to the Homeland*, ed. Edward A. Allworth. 2nd ed. Durham, N.C.: Duke University Press, 1998.

———. "Local Accommodation and Resistance to Colonialism in Nineteenth-Century Crimea." In *Russia's Orient: Imperial Borderlands and Peoples, 1700–1917*, ed. Daniel Brower and Edward J. Lazzerini. Bloomington: Indiana University Press, 1997.

Levi, Scott C. *The Indian Diaspora in Central Asia and Its Trade, 1550–1900.* Leiden: E. J. Brill, 2002.

Lewis, Robert A., ed. *Geographic Perspectives on Soviet Central Asia.* London: Routledge, 1992.

Lih, Lars T. *Bread and Authority in Russia, 1914–1921.* Berkeley: University of California Press, 1990.

Liu, Morgan. "Recognizing the Khan: Authority, Space, and Political Imagination among Uzbek Men in the Post-Soviet Osh, Kyrgyzstan." Ph.D. diss., University of Michigan, 2002.

Loomba, Ania. *Colonialism/Postcolonialism.* London: Routledge, 1998.

Lunin, B. V. *Istoriia Obshchestvennykh Nauk v Uzbekistane.* Tashkent: Izdatel'stvo "Fan," 1974.

———. *Nauchnye obshchestva Turkestana i ikh progressivnaia deiatel'nost' (konets XIX–nachalo XX v.).* Tashkent: Izdatel'stvo Akademii Nauk Uzbekskoi SSR, 1962.

MacKenzie, David. "The Conquest and Administration of Turkestan, 1860–85." In *Russian Colonial Expansion to 1917*, ed. Michael Rywkin. New York: Mausell, 1988.

———. "Expansion in Central Asia: St. Petersburg vs. the Turkestan Generals, 1863–1866." *Canadian Slavic Studies* 3, no. 2 (1969): 286–311.

———. "Kaufman of Turkestan: An Assessment of His Administration 1867–1881." *Slavic Review* 26, no. 2 (1967): 265–85.

————. *The Lion of Tashkent: The Career of General M. G. Cherniaev.* Athens: University of Georgia Press, 1974.

MacKenzie, John M. *The Empire of Nature: Hunting, Conservation, and British Imperialism.* Manchester, U.K.: Manchester University Press, 1988.

Makashin, S. A. *Saltykov-Shchedrin Seredina Puti 1860-e–1870-e gody: Biografiia.* Moscow: Khudozhestvennaia Literatura, 1984.

Maksheev, A. I. "Prebyvanie v Vernom' i vstrecha Kaufmana." *Russkaia Starina*, no. 3 (1913): 644–49.

Mallitskii, N. G. "Tashkentskie makhallia i mauza." In *V. V. Bartol'du. Turkestanskie druz'ia ucheniki i pochiteteli.* Tashkent, 1927.

Marks, Steven G. *Road to Power: The Trans-Siberian Railroad and the Colonization of Asian Russia.* Ithaca, N.Y.: Cornell University Press, 1991.

Martin, Virginia. *Law and Custom in the Steppe: The Kazakhs of the Middle Horde and Russian Colonialism in the Nineteenth Century.* London: Curzon Press, 2001.

Mazaeva, L. M., and N. Kh. Usmanova. "K voprosu o prodovol'stvennom polozhenii v Turkestane i merakh sovetskoi vlasti po likvidatsii goloda v gody grazhdanskoi voiny (1917–1920 gg)." *Nauchnye Trudy Tashkentskogo gosudarstvennogo universiteta imeni V. I. Lenina* 441 (1973): 118–32.

McAuley, Mary. "Bread without the Bourgeoisie." In *Party, State, and Society in the Russian Civil War: Explorations in Social History*, ed. Diane P. Koenker, William G. Rosenberg, and Ronald G. Suny. Bloomington: Indiana University Press, 1989.

McClintock, Anne. *Imperial Leather: Race, Gender and Sexuality in the Colonial Contest.* New York: Routledge, 1995.

McGrew, Roderick E. *Encyclopedia of Medical History.* New York: McGraw-Hill, 1985.

McLean, Fitzroy. *A Person from England and Other Travelers to Turkestan.* London: Jonathan Cape, 1958.

McReynolds, Louise. *The News under Russia's Old Regime: The Development of a Mass Circulation Press.* Princeton, N.J.: Princeton University Press, 1991.

Mehta, Uday S. "Liberal Strategies of Exclusion." In *Tensions of Empire*, ed. Frederick Cooper and Ann Laura Stoler. Berkeley: University of California Press, 1997.

Metcalf, Thomas. *An Imperial Vision: Indian Architecture and Britain's Raj.* Berkeley: University of California Press, 1989.

Mintsa, I. I., ed. *Basmachestvo: vozniknovenie, sushchnost, krakh.* Moscow: Izdatel'stvo "Nauka," 1981.

Morris, R. J. *Cholera 1832: The Social Response to an Epidemic.* London: Croon Helm, 1976.

Muminov, I. M., ed. *Iz istorii rasprostraneniia Marksisto-Leninskikh idei v Uzbekistane. Sbornik Materialov.* Tashkent: Izdatel'stvo Akademii Nauk UzSSR, 1962.

Nabiev, R. N. *Tashkentskoe vosstanie 1847 g. i ego sotsial'no-ekonomicheskie predposylki.* Tashkent: Izdatel'stvo "Fan," 1966.

Nelson, C., and L. Grossberg, eds. *Marxism and the Interpretation of Culture.* Basingstoke, U.K.: MacMillan Education, 1988.

Neuberger, Joan. *Hooliganism: Crime, Culture and Power in St. Petersburg, 1900–1914.* Berkeley: University of California Press, 1993.

Neweroff, Alexander (Aleksandr Skobolev). *City of Bread.* Westport: Hyperion, 1973.

Nil'sen, V. A. "Iz istorii zastroiki Tashkenta." *Arkhitektura i Stroitel'stvo Uzbekistana,* no. 9 (1983): 3–7.

Nil'sen, V. A., and A. Ziaev. "Pervye Proekt Planirovok Tashkenta." *Stroitel'stvo i Arkhitektura Uzbekistana,* no. 2 (1981): 33–38.

Northrop, Douglas. *Veiled Empire: Gender and Power in Stalinist Central Asia.* Ithaca, N.Y.: Cornell University Press, 2004.

Nurullin, R. *Bor'ba Kompartii Turkestana za osushchestvlenie politiki "Voennogo Kommunizma."* Tashkent: Izdatel'stvo "Uzbekistan," 1975.

———. "Osushchestvlenie leninskikh printsipov prodovol'stvennoi politiki v Turkestane (1918–1921)," *Obshchestvennye nauki v Uzbekistane,* no. 4 (1968): 14–19.

Owen, Roger, and Bob Sutcliffe. *Studies in the Theory of Imperialism.* London: Longman, 1972.

Owen, Thomas C. "Impediments to a Bourgeois Consciousness in Russia, 1880–1905: The Estate Structure, Ethnic Diversity, and Economic Regionalism." In *Between Tsar and People: Educated Society and the Quest for Public Identity in Late Imperial Russia,* ed. Edith W. Clowes, Samuel D. Kassow, and James L. West. Princeton, N.J.: Princeton University Press, 1991.

———. *Russian Corporate Capitalism from Peter the Great to Perestroika.* New York: Oxford University Press, 1995.

Palen, K. K. *Mission to Turkestan.* Trans. N. J. Couriss. London: Oxford University Press, 1964.

Park, Alexander. *Bolshevism in Turkestan, 1917–1927.* New York: Columbia University Press, 1957.

Perry, Adele. *On the Edge of Empire: Gender, Race, and the Making of British Columbia, 1849–1871.* Toronto: University of Toronto Press, 2001.

Piaskovskii, Anatolii V. *Revoliutsiia 1905–1907 godov v Turkestane.* Moscow: Izdatel'stvo Akademii Nauk SSSR, 1958.

Pierce, Richard A. *Russian Central Asia, 1867–1917: A Study in Colonial Rule.* Berkeley: University of California Press, 1960.

———. "Toward Soviet Power in Tashkent, February–October 1917." *Canadian Slavonic Papers* 17 (1975): 261–69.

Poovey, Mary. *Uneven Developments: The Ideological Work of Gender in Mid-Victorian England.* Chicago: University of Chicago Press, 1998.

Prashad, Vijay. "Native Dirt/Imperial Ordure: The Cholera of 1832 and the Morbid Resolutions of Modernity." *Journal of Historical Sociology* 7, no. 3 (1994): 243–60.

Pratt, Mary Louise. *Imperial Eyes: Travel Writing and Transculturation.* London: Routledge, 1992.

Prochaska, David. *Making Algeria French: Colonialism in Bone, 1870–1920.* Cambridge: Cambridge University Press, 1990.

Pulatov, Guliam, and Guliamkadyr Rashidov. *Tashkent v Pervye Gody Sovetskoi Vlasti* (Noiabr' 1917–1920 gg). Tashkent: Izdatel'stvo "Uzbekistan," 1972.

Rabinow, Paul. *French Modern: Norms and Forms of the Social Environment.* Cambridge, Mass.: MIT Press, 1989.

Rabinowitch, Alexander. "The Petrograd First City Soviet during the Civil War."
    In *Party, State, and Society in the Russian Civil War: Explorations in Social History*,
    ed. Diane P. Koenker, William G. Rosenberg, and Ronald G. Suny. Blooming-
    ton: Indiana University Press, 1989.
Rakhimov, A. "K voprosu o kharaktere prodovol'stvennoi politiki sovetskoi
    vlasti v Turkestane v gody grazhdanskoi voiny (1918–1921 gg.)." *Nauchnye
    Raboty i Soobshcheniia (Akademii nauk Uzbekskoi SSR, Otdel Obshchestvennykh
    nauk)* 2 (1961): 61–73.
———. "Mobilizatsiia prodovol'stvennykh resursov v Turkestane v periode
    voennoi interventsii i grazhdanskoi voiny (1918–21 gg.)." Ph.D. diss., Aka-
    demii Nauk UzSSR, Tashkent, 1962.
Raleigh, Donald J. "Languages of Power: How the Saratov Bolsheviks Imagined
    Their Enemies." *Slavic Review* 57, no. 2 (1998): 320–49.
———. *Revolution on the Volga: 1917 in Saratov*. Ithaca, N.Y.: Cornell University
    Press, 1986.
Rashidov, Guliamkadyr. *Tashkentskii Sovet v Bor'be za Uprochnenie Sovetskoi Vlasti
    (Noiabr' 1917–1918 gg.)*. Tashkent: Gosudarstvennoe Izdatel'stvo Uzbekskoi
    SSR, 1960.
Reichman, Henry. *Railwaymen and Revolution: Russia, 1905*. Berkeley: University
    of California Press, 1987.
Riasanovsky, N. V. "Asia through Russian Eyes." In *Russia and Asia: Essays on
    the Influence of Russia on the Asian Peoples*, ed. W. S. Vucinich. Stanford, Calif.:
    Stanford University Press, 1972.
Richards, Jeffrey, and John MacKenzie. *The Railway Station: A Social History*. New
    York: Oxford University Press, 1986.
Rieber, Alfred J. *Merchants and Entrepreneurs in Imperial Russia*. Chapel Hill: Uni-
    versity of North Carolina Press, 1982.
———, ed. *The Politics of Autocracy: Letters of Alexander II to Prince A. I. Bariatinskii
    1857–1864*. Paris: Mouton, 1966.
Robinson, Ronald. "Non-European Foundations of European Imperialism:
    Sketch for a Theory of Collaboration." In *Studies in the Theory of Imperialism*,
    ed. Roger Owen and Bob Sutcliffe. London: Longman, 1972.
Rogger, Hans. *Russia in the Age of Modernization and Revolution 1881–1917*. Lon-
    don: Longman, 1983.
Rosenberg, Charles E. "Cholera in Nineteenth-Century Europe: A Tool for Social
    and Economic Analysis." *Comparative Studies in Society and History* 8, no. 4
    (1966): 452–63.
Rosenberg, William G., and Diane P. Koenker, "The Limits of Formal Protest:
    Worker Activism and Social Polarization in Petrograd and Moscow, March to
    October, 1917." *American Historical Review* 92, no. 2 (1987): 296–326.
Rozhkova, M. K. *Ekonomicheskie sviazi Rossii so Srednei Aziei (40–60 gody XIX
    veka)*. Moscow: Izdatel'stvo Akademii Nauk SSSR, 1963.
Sahadeo, Jeff. "Epidemic and Empire: Ethnicity, Class, and 'Civilization' in the
    1892 Tashkent Cholera Riot." *Slavic Review* (Official Journal of the American
    Association for the Advancement of Slavic Studies) 64, no. 1 (2005): 117–39.
———. "The Search for the Russian Nation: Notes from the Periphery." *Canadian
    Review of Studies in Nationalism*, 31, nos. 1–2 (2004): 113–26.

————. "Empire of Memories: Conquest and Civilization in Imperial Russian Tashkent." *Canadian Slavonic Papers* 46, nos. 1–2 (2004): 395–417.

Said, Edward W. *Culture and Imperialism.* New York: Vintage, 1994.

————. *Orientalism.* New York: Vintage, 1979.

Salikov, D., and S. Bolotov. "Iz istorii Osipovskogo miatezhe v Turkestane." *Proletarskaia revoliutsiia* 53, no. 6 (1926): 10–37.

Sanders, Jonathan. "Lessons from the Periphery: Saratov, January, 1905." *Slavic Review* 46, no. 2 (1987): 229–44.

Schimmelpennick Van Der Oye, David. *Towards the Rising Sun: Russian Ideologies of Empire and the Path to War with Japan.* De Kalb: Northern Illinois University Press, 2001.

Schorske, Carl E. *Fin-de-siècle Vienna: Politics and Culture.* New York: Knopf, 1979.

Scott, James C. *Weapons of the Weak: Everyday Forms of Peasant Resistance.* New Haven, Conn.: Yale University Press, 1985.

Semeniuta, V. "Golod v Turkestane v 1917–1920 godakh." *Chelovek i Politika* (Dec. 1991): 72–78.

Semmel, Bernard. *The Liberal Ideal and the Demons of Empire.* Baltimore, Md.: Johns Hopkins University Press, 1993.

Siegelbaum, Lewis. *Soviet State and Society between Revolutions, 1918–1929.* Cambridge: Cambridge University Press, 1992.

Siegelbaum, Lewis H., and Ronald Grigor Suny, eds. *Making Workers Soviet: Class, Power, and Identity.* Ithaca, N.Y.: Cornell University Press, 1994.

Singha, Radhkia. "Settle, Mobilize, Verify: Identification Practices in Colonial India." *Studies in History* 16, no. 2 (2000): 153–98.

Sinha, Mrinalini. *Colonial Masculinity: The "Manly Englishman" and the "Effeminate Bengali" in the Late Nineteenth Century.* Manchester, U.K.: Manchester University Press, 1995.

Sinnott, Peter. "The Physical Geography of Soviet Central Asia and the Problem of the Aral Sea." In *Geographic Perspectives on Soviet Central Asia*, ed. Robert A Lewis. London: Routledge, 1992.

Siscoe, Frank G. "Eugene Schuyler, General Kaufman, and Central Asia." *Slavic Review* 27, no. 1 (1968): 119–24.

Skalov, G. "Sotsial'naia priroda basmachestva v Turkestane," *Zhizn' natsional'nostei* 3–4 (1923): 51–62.

Slezkine, Yuri. *Arctic Mirrors: Russia and the Small Peoples of the North.* Ithaca, N.Y.: Cornell University Press, 1994.

Sokol, Edward Dennis. *The Revolt of 1916 in Russian Central Asia.* Baltimore, Md.: Johns Hopkins University Press, 1954.

Sokolov, Iu. A. *Tashkent, Tashkenttsy, i Rossiia.* Tashkent: Izdatel'stvo "Uzbekistan," 1965.

"Soviet Central Asia: The Turkestan Commission, 1919–1920." *Central Asian Review* 12, no. 1 (1964): 5–15.

Spivak, G. C. "Can the Subaltern Speak?" In *Marxism and the Interpretation of Culture*, ed. C. Nelson and L. Grossberg. Basingstoke, U.K.: MacMillan Education, 1988.

Starr, S. Frederick. *Decentralization and Self-Government in Russia, 1830–1870.* Princeton, N.J.: Princeton University Press, 1972.

Steinberg, Mark D. *Moral Communities: The Culture of Class Relations in the Russian Printing Industry.* Berkeley: University of California Press, 1992.

———. "Vanguard Workers and the Morality of Class." In *Making Workers Soviet: Class, Power, and Identity,* ed. Lewis H. Siegelbaum and Ronald Grigor Suny. Ithaca, N.Y.: Cornell University Press, 1994.

Stoler, Ann Laura. "Rethinking Colonial Categories: European Communities and the Boundaries of Rule." *Comparative Studies in Society and History* 31, no. 1 (1989): 134–61.

———. "Sexual Affronts and Racial Frontiers: European Identities and the Cultural Politics of Exclusion in Colonial Southeast Asia." In *Tensions of Empire: Colonial Cultures in a Bourgeois World,* ed. Frederick Cooper and Ann Laura Stoler. Berkeley: University of California Press, 1997.

Strong, John Wentworth. "Russian Relations with Khiva, Bukhara, and Kokand 1800–1858." Ph.D. diss., Harvard University, 1964.

Suny, Ronald Grigor. *The Baku Commune 1917–1918: Class and Nationality in the Russian Revolution.* Princeton, N.J.: Princeton University Press, 1972.

———. "Nationalism and Class in the Russian Revolution: a Comparative Discussion." In *Revolution in Russia: Reassessments of 1917,* ed. Edith Rogovin Frankel, Jonathan Frankel, and Baruch Knei-Paz. Cambridge: Cambridge University Press, 1992.

Suny, Ronald Grigor, and Terry Martin, eds. *A State of Nations: Empire and Nation-Making in the Age of Lenin and Stalin.* Oxford: Oxford University Press, 2001.

Surh, Gerald D. *1905 in St. Petersburg: Labor, Society, and Revolution.* Stanford, Calif.: Stanford University Press, 1989.

Sutcliffe, Anthony. *Towards the Planned City: Germany, Britain, the United States and France, 1780–1914.* New York: St. Martin's Press, 1981.

Suvorov, V. *Istoriko-Ekonomicheskii ocherk razvitiia Turkestana.* Tashkent: Gosizdat Uzbekskaia SSR, 1962.

Taylor, Charles. *Philosophical Arguments.* Cambridge: Cambridge University Press, 1995.

Thompson, E. P. *The Making of the English Working Class.* London: Penguin, 1963.

Tillett, Lowell. *The Great Friendship: Soviet Historians on the Non-Russian Nationalities.* Chapel Hill: University of North Carolina Press, 1969.

Treadgold, Donald W. *The Great Siberian Migration: Government and Peasant in Resettlement from Emancipation to the First World War.* Princeton, N.J.: Princeton University Press, 1957.

Vaidyanath, R. *The Formation of the Soviet Central Asian Republics.* New Delhi: People's Publishing House, 1967.

Vambery, Arminius. *History of Bokhara.* London: Henry S. King, 1873.

Voronina, V. L. "Deiatel'nost Russkikh gradostroitelei v Turkestane vo vtoroi polovine XIX v." *Arkhitekturnoe Nasledstvo* 25 (1976): 79–85.

Vucinich, W. S. *Russia and Asia: Essays on the Influence of Russia on the Asian Peoples.* Stanford, Calif.: Stanford University Press, 1972.

Weeks, Theodore R. *Nation and State in Imperial Russia: Nationalism and Russification on the Western Frontier.* De Kalb: Northern Illinois University Press, 1996.

Werth, Paul. *At the Margins of Orthodoxy: Mission, Governance, and Confessional Politics in Russia's Volga-Kama Region, 1827–1905*. Ithaca, N.Y.: Cornell University Press, 2002.

Williams, John A., ed. *Islam*. New York: George Braziller, 1961.

Wirtschafter, Elise Kimerling. *Social Identity in Imperial Russia*. De Kalb: Northern Illinois University Press, 1997.

Wolff, David. *To the Harbin Station: The Liberal Alternative in Russian Manchuria, 1898–1914*. Stanford, Calif.: Stanford University Press, 1999.

Wortman, Richard S. "Rule by Sentiment: Alexander II's Journeys through the Russian Empire." *American Historical Review* 95, no. 3 (1990): 745–71.

———. *Scenarios of Power: Myth and Ceremony in Russian Monarchy*. 2 vols. Princeton, N.J.: Princeton University Press, 1995–2000.

Wright, Gwendolyn. *The Politics of Design in French Colonial Urbanism*. Chicago: University of Chicago Press, 1991.

Wynn, Charters. *Workers, Strikes, and Pogroms: The Donbass-Dnepr Bend in Late Imperial Russia, 1870–1905*. Princeton, N.J.: Princeton University Press, 1992.

Yaroshevski, Dov B. "Russian Regionalism in Turkestan." *Slavonic and East European Review* 65, no. 1 (1987): 81–82.

Young, Robert. *Postcolonialism: A Historical Introduction*. New York: Blackwell, 2001.

Zelnik, Reginald. *Labor and Society in Tsarist Russia: The Factory Workers of St. Petersburg, 1855–1870*. Stanford, Calif.: Stanford University Press, 1971.

Zenkovsky, Serge. *Pan-Turkism and Islam in Russia, 1905–1920*. Cambridge, Mass.: Harvard University Press, 1960.

Zykin, V. "Pod Dvoinom Pressom: Vosstanie v Tashkente v 1892 tn. 'Kholernyi Bunt.'" *Uchenye Zapiski Permskogo Gosudarstvennogo Universiteta (otdel Obshchestvennykh Nauk)*, Vyp. 2 (Perm, 1931): 315–52.

# Index

**JEFF SAHADEO** is Assistant Professor of Political Science and European and Russian Studies and Associate Director of the Institute of European and Russian Studies at Carleton University in Ottawa. With Russell Zanca, Sahadeo is co-editor of *Everyday Life in Central Asia* (Indiana University Press, 2007).

LaVergne, TN USA
11 March 2011
219749LV00002B/1/P